Empirical Approaches
to the Psychosocial Aspects
of Disability

Empirical Approaches to the Psychosocial Aspects of Disability

Myron G. Eisenberg, PhD
Robert L. Glueckauf, PhD
Editors

Springer Publishing Company
New York

Springer Publishing Company, Inc.
536 Broadway
New York, NY 10012-3955

91 92 93 94 95 / 5 4 3 2 1

Library of Congress Cataloging-in-Publication Data

Empirical approaches to the psychosocial aspects of disability / edited by
  Myron G. Eisenberg, Robert L. Glueckauf
     p. cm.
    Includes bibliographical references and index.
    ISBN 0-8261-7600-3
    1. Rehabilitation— Psychological aspects. 2. Rehabilitation—
Social aspects. 3. Handicapped—Vocational guidance.
  I. Eisenberg, Myron G. II. Glueckauf, Robert L.
    [DNLM: 1. Handicapped. 2. Mental Disorders—rehabilitation.
3. Rehabilitation, Vocational. WB 320 E55]
RM930.E46 1991
617.1'03—dc20
DNLM/DLC
for Library of Congress   90-10435
                                                     CIP

Printed in the United States of America

Contents

SECTION I
ATTITUDES TOWARD PEOPLE WITH DISABILITIES
Norman L. Berven, Section Editor

SECTION II
ISSUES AFFECTING THE REHABILITATION OF PERSONS WITH PHYSICAL DISABILITIES
Allen W. Heinemann, Section Editor

SECTION III
ISSUES AFFECTING THE REHABILITATION OF PERSONS
WITH PSYCHIATRIC IMPAIRMENTS
Gary R. Bond, Section Editor

SECTION IV
COMMUNITY INTEGRATION:
VOCATIONAL AND INDEPENDENT LIVING REHABILITATION
Nancy M. Crewe, Section Editor

SECTION V
ASSESSING REHABILITATION POTENTIAL
AND EVALUATING CLIENT OUTCOMES
Brian Bolton, Section Editor

Preface

The purpose of this text is to explore some major issues affecting the psychosocial functioning of persons with disabilities. It differs from other books on the topic in two significant ways. First, because many of the issues considered transcend a specific type of disability, an organizational framework was adopted to permit primary categorization of material into the least number of topical areas possible, including attitudes toward persons with disabilities, issues affecting the rehabilitation of persons with physically disabling conditions, issues affecting the rehabilitation of persons with psychiatric impairments, and issues affecting the mainstreaming of persons with disabilities into the able-bodied community. Each section is then subdivided to finely focus discussion on a single issue. Because the effectiveness of interventions ultimately determines the extent to which issues are resolved and goals are met, the text's final section, "Assessing Rehabilitation Potential and Evaluating Client Outcomes," considers the interrelationship existing between the diagnostic assessment of rehabilitation potential and the evaluation of client outcomes.

The second significant difference between *Empirical Approaches to the Psychosocial Aspects of Disability* and other texts is in its use of materials which present issues within the context of empirically based discussion. Typically, books of this nature consider issues via narrative discourse. While certain specific readings found in these texts occasionally allude to or present data to substantiate concepts being advanced, our treatment of the subject matter varies from this traditional approach through presentation of information within a research paradigm. This approach was assumed because rehabilitation psychology is both an art and a science. As a science, its concepts and practices are data based. This fact, while implicitly acknowledged, often is not stressed or reinforced. The text's emphasis on this fact is meant to heighten the reader's awareness of the field's scientific underpinnings.

The rehabilitation counselor systematically attempts to modify targeted aspects of a disabled, handicapped, or impaired person's social or physical surroundings which have been identified as (1) contributing to or maintaining the client's disabled, impaired, or handicapped state, and (2) remediating presenting interpersonal, occupational, or architectural barriers. They are charged with assisting their clients to achieve a more satisfying and functionally effective response to demands of living. The editors hope that this book will encourage its readers to critically examine issues impacting the psychosocial adjustment of persons with disabilities. They also hope the book will promote improved practice techniques by developing within the reader a greater level of comfort accessing and utilizing research-based informational source materials.

The current text provides an overview of research on the psychosocial aspects of disability for the rehabilitation counseling and psychology graduate student. The latter should be encouraged to critically review the underlying theory, methodolgy, and clinical implications of each research article. Classroom presentations and follow-up group discussions can be used to further enrich the student's understanding of the research process and its many challenges. Finally, the instructors of psychosocial aspects of disability courses may want to utilize this volume in conjunction with pertinent theory-focused readings on the subject.

Introduction

The roots of rehabilitation psychology and the foundation for research on the psychosocial aspects of disability can be traced to longstanding concern about the constraints imposed by society on the work and social roles of persons with disabilities. Unfortunately, limited job opportunities, inadequate housing, and lack of transportation persist as handicapping conditions in today's technological society (Wood & Badley, 1980). These shortcomings are currently a source of much legislative debate, as the U.S. Congress contemplates passage of the watershed American With Disabilities Act (Treanor, 1990).

A distinctive feature of research on the psychosocial aspects of disability is its focus on predicting and controlling the consequences of role restriction and role loss. The disadvantaged life circumstances of disabled individuals have shaped the nature and direction of psychosocial research in two major ways: (1) rehabilitation researchers have focus on interpersonal and attitudinal processes closely linked to the role of deprivation experiences of disabled individuals; and (2) program development and evaluation aimed at improving quality of life have emerged as prominent psychosocial research interests. First, stimulated by the early work of Parsons (1958) and Goffman (1961, 1963), rehabilitation researchers have developed an abiding interest in the stigmatizing effects of the so-called "sick role." These authors described the process by which persons are inducted into the ranks of the "sick and disabled." They also emphasized the rituals (e.g., periodic visits to the psychiatric hospital) required of the "disabled" to avoid chastisement for "failing" to perform traditional work and social activities. Much of the impetus for independent living and psychiatric rehabilitation research comes from the deeply held value that, given the choice and appropriate supports, individuals with disabilities can sustain themselves in mainstream work and social roles (see Sections III and IV).

In a related vein, considerable research has been devoted to the negative attitudes and expectations of the public about the role performances of disabled individuals. The somatopsychology school of rehabilitation psychology (e.g., Barker, Wright, Meyerson, & Gonick, 1953) spawned scientific investigation on the devaluing attitudes of the public and their effects on social transactions between disabled and nondisabled persons (see Wright, 1983, for a review). As found in diverse survey and field investigations, nondisabled employers, coworkers, and same-aged peers have demonstrated both avoidant attitudes and behavior when faced with the prospect of close interaction with disabled individuals (see Section I).

The preponderance of research on roles and attitudinal processes in the study of the psychosocial aspects of disability stands in sharp contrast to related disciplines such as health psychology. Research in this area typically has paid greater attention to internal, physiological factors than situational demands. This may reflect the *nonhandicapped* status of the majority of populations studied by health psychologists. For example, one of the fastest growing research domains is the study of reciprocal relationships among behavioral characteristics, physiological responding, and life stressors in coronary-prone individuals (e.g., Matthews, 1989). Although an increased understanding of the interactions between physiological functioning and health-related behavior may benefit persons who are at risk for impairment, it does not address the salient needs of persons with chronic disabilities who are confronted with obstacles to obtaining employment, suitable living arrangements, and managing social prejudice.

A second, defining characteristic of the literature on the psychosocial aspects of disability is its emphasis on program development and evaluation. As reflected by the content of the current text, a substantial proportion of research in rehabilitation psychology has been devoted to implementing and evaluating role intervention strategies to empower disabled consumers.

Programs for independent living (see Sections III and IV) and vocational rehabilitation of physically and mentally disabled individuals have generally focused on the enhancement of the precursors of role attainment: developing skill in job acquisition and social problem-solving abilities. Only in the past decade have investigators (see Bond & Boyer, 1988) assessed the effects of directly and permanently altering the social environment and work roles (i.e., providing permanent job coaches and active community outreach) of chronically handicapped persons instead of training prior to placement. This is an exciting development in the field of psychosocial rehabilitation, one that challenges our basic assumptions about the previous, linear (train-first, work placement-second) ordering of role interventions.

It is important that we recognize the contributions of rehabilitation research in improving the quality of life of persons with disabilities. By all accounts, demands for rehabilitation evaluation and treatment services will continue to expand well into the 1990s (Rubin & Rubin, 1988). This will mean that more of our time and efforts will be directed at solving challenging human dilemmas such as independent living.

In order to effectively meet these objectives, we need to more fully comprehend the cognitive processes (e.g., self-efficacy beliefs) which guide disabled individuals' behavior, the special characteristics of the psychological situation (e.g., the role of equal opportunity legislation), and finally, the individual's typical modes of responding to pertinent outside, social forces. While the five major topical areas included in this book are not considered to be all inclusive, they are seen as representing topics critical to the service provider's understanding of the dynamics of the psychosocial rehabilitation process. The new cadre of rehabilitation psychologists facing the challenges of the 1990s will require not only a mastery of intervention techniques, but also a firm grounding in psychosocial theory and research methods. The purpose of the present text, therefore, is to introduce the reader to several important theoretical and empirical developments in the study of the psychosocial aspects of disability. We also hope to stimulate current and future rehabilitation professionals to utilize psychosocial research in their clinical practice and program evaluation efforts.

MYRON G. EISENBERG
ROBERT L. GLUECKAUF
Editors

REFERENCES

Barker, R. B., Wright, B. A., Meyerson, L., & Gonick, M. R. (1953). *Adjustment to physical handicap and illness: A survey of the social psychology of physique and disability* (2nd ed.). New York: Social Science Research Council.

Bond, G. R., & Boyer, S. L. (1988). Rehabilitation programs and outcomes. In J. A. Ciardiello & M. D. Bell (Eds.), *Vocational rehabilitation of persons with prolonged psychiatric disorders* (pp. 231–263). Baltimore, MD: Johns Hopkins University Press.

Goffman, E. (1961). *Asylums: Essays on the social situation of mental patients and other inmates.* Garden City, NY: Anchor Books.

Goffman, E. (1963). *Stigma: Notes on the management of spoiled identity.* Englewood Cliffs, NJ: Prentice Hall.

Matthews, K. A. (1989). Interactive effects of behavior and reproduction hormones on sex differences in risk for coronary heart disease. *Health Psychology, 8,* 373-387.

Parsons, T. (1958). Definitions of health and illness in the light of American values and social structure. In E. G. Jaco (Ed.), *Patients, physicians, and illness* (pp. 165-187). New York: Free Press.

Rubin, S. E., & Rubin, N. M. (1988). *Contemporary challenges to the rehabilitation counseling profession.* Baltimore, MD: Paul H. Brookes.

Treanor, R. (1990, Winter). Americans With Disabilities Act grinds through the legislative mill. *Spinal Network Extra,* pp. 52–53.

Wood, P. H. N., & Badley, E. M. (1980). *People with disabilities: Toward acquiring information which reflects more sensitively their problems and needs.* New York: World Rehabilitation Fund.

Wright, B. A. (1983). *Physical disability: A psychosocial approach* (2nd ed.). New York: Harper & Row.

Acknowledgments

Chapters 1 and 4 originally appeared in *Rehabilitation Psychology, 28*(2), pp. 79–91 and pp. 105–114, 1983. © 1983 by the Division of Rehabilitation Psychology of the American Psychological Association.

Chapter 2 originally appeared in *Rehabilitation Psychology, 34*(4), pp. 243–257, 1989. © 1989 by the Division of Rehabilitation Psychology of the American Psychological Association.

Chapter 3 originally appeared in *Rehabilitation Psychology, 28*(4), pp. 207–215, 1983. © 1983 by the Division of Rehabilitation Psychology of the American Psychological Association.

Chapter 5 originally appeared in *Rehabilitation Psychology, 29*(2), pp. 77–84, 1984. © 1984 by the Division of Rehabilitation Psychology of the American Psychological Association.

Chapter 6 originally appeared in *Rehabilitation Psychology, 31*(2), pp. 95–102, 1986. © 1986 by the Division of Rehabilitation Psychology of the American Psychological Association.

Chapter 7 originally appeared in *Rehabilitation Psychology, 32*(4), pp. 205–213, 1987. © 1987 by the Division of Rehabilitation Psychology of the American Psychological Association.

Chapter 8 originally appeared in *Rehabilitation Psychology, 28*(3), pp. 177–184, 1983. © 1983 by the Division of Rehabilitation Psychology of the American Psychological Association.

Chapter 9 originally appeared in *Rehabilitation Psychology, 30*(3), pp. 131–143, 1985. © 1985 by the Division of Rehabilitation Psychology of the American Psychological Association.

Chapter 10, 13, and 15 originally appeared in *Rehabilitation Psychology, 33*(1), pp. 5–14, pp. 47–55, and pp. 27–36, 1988. © 1988 by the Division of Rehabilitation Psychology of the American Psychological Association.

Chapter 11 originally appeared in *Rehabilitation Psychology, 27*(2), pp. 67–85, 1982. © 1982 by the Division of Rehabilitation Psychology of the American Psychological Association.

Chapter 12 originally appeared in *Rehabilitation Psychology, 32*(2), pp. 99–112, 1987. © 1987 by the Division of Rehabilitation Psychology of the American Psychological Association.

Chapter 14 originally appeared in *Rehabilitation Psychology, 28*(1), pp. 35–44, 1983. © 1983 by the Division of Rehabilitation Psychology of the American Psychological Association.

Chapter 16 originally appeared in *Rehabilitation Psychology, 34*(2), pp. 117–130, 1989. © 1989 by the Division of Rehabilitation Psychology of the American Psychological Association.

Chapter 17 originally appeared in *Rehabilitation Psychology, 27*(3), pp. 131–145, 1982. © 1982 by the Division of Rehabilitation Psychology of the American Psychological Association.

Chapter 18 originally appeared in *Rehabilitation Psychology, 27*(1), pp. 23–35, 1982. © 1981 by the Division of Rehabilitation Psychology of the American Psychological Association.

Chapter 19 originally appeared in *Rehabilitation Psychology, 29*(1), pp. 21–35, 1984. © 1984 by the Division of Rehabilitation Psychology of the American Psychological Association.

Chapter 20 originally appeared in *Rehabilitation Psychology, 30*(4), pp. 195–208, 1985. © 1985 by the Division of Rehabilitation Psychology of the American Psychological Association.

Chapter 21 originally appeared in *Rehabilitation Psychology, 32*(1), pp. 5–15, 1987. © 1987 by the Division of Rehabilitation Psychology of the American Psychological Association.

Rehabilitation Psychology is published by Springer Publishing Company, 536 Broadway, New York, NY 10012.

Contributors

BOOK EDITORS

Myron G. Eisenberg, PhD, is Chief of the Psychology Service at the Department of Veterans Affairs Medical Center in Hampton, Virginia and is Associate Professor of both Physical Medicine and Rehabilitation and of Psychiatry and Behavioral Sciences at Eastern Virginia Medical School, Norfolk Virginia. He obtained his PhD from Northwestern University and received postdoctoral training at the University of Toronto's Clarke Institute. Dr. Eisenberg has published extensively in the area of rehabilitation, holds editorial board positions on several journals, serves as Editor of *Rehabilitation Psychology,* and is a member of several national task forces charged with investigating various quality-of-life issues of importance to persons with chronic disabling conditions. Dr. Eisenberg has received recognition at the local, regional, and national level for contributions he has made to the rehabilitation of persons with physical impairments. A Fellow and past President of the American Psychological Association's Division of Rehabilitation Psychology, he is actively involved in heightening the public's awareness of the importance of rehabilitation through the promotion of research. In addition, he is interested in the development of standards that will establish a more effective and consistent basis for evaluating the performance of individual rehabilitation service providers.

Robert L. Glueckauf, PhD, is an Assistant Professor in the Department of Psychology at Indiana Univeristy–Purdue University at Indianapolis where he teaches in the masters and doctoral rehabilitation psychology graduate programs. He received his MS and PhD degrees in clinical psychology at Florida State University. He serves as an Executive Board Member and Chairman of the Research Committee of the American Psychological Association's Division of Rehabilitation Psychology and is a Consulting Editor for *Rehabilitation Psychology.* He has authored several articles and chapters in the field of rehabilitation psychology. His current scholarly pursuits focus primarily on the application of family therapy techniques to disability, and on the evaluation of rehabilitation interventions.

EDITORIAL CONSULTANT

Lisa A. Ruble, BS, is a rehabilitation psychology graduate student at Indiana University-Purdue University at Indianapolis. She received her undergraduate degree in biology at Indiana University. She serves as the Student Affiliate to the Research Committee of Division 22 (Rehabilitation Psychology) of the American Psychological Association. Her research interest lies in the area of the psychosocial aspects of autism.

SECTION EDITORS

Norman L. Berven, PhD, Professor and Chairman of the Rehabilitation Psychology Program Area, Department of Rehabilitation Psychology and Special Education, University of Wisconsin-Madison.

Brian Bolton, PhD, Professor at the Arkansas Research and Training Center in Vocational Rehabilitation, University of Arkansas, Fayetteville.

Gary R. Bond, PhD, Director of the doctoral program in Rehabilitation Psychology and Professor, Department of Psychology, Indiana University–Purdue University at Indianapolis.

Nancy M. Crewe, PhD, Coordinator of the Rehabilitation Counselor Education Program, Michigan State University.

Allen W. Heinemann, PhD, Associate Professor in the Department of Rehabilitation Medicine at Northwestern University Medical School, and Director, Rehabilitation Services Evaluation Unit, Rehabilitation Institute of Chicago.

SECTION I
Attitudes Toward People with Disabilities

Norman L. Berven, Section Editor

Introduction

Norman L. Berven

For people with disabilities many of the most significant barriers to living full and productive lives may be found in the environments in which they live. For people with some types of disabilities, barriers to physical accessibility can make it difficult, if not impossible, to move about freely and to participate fully in the mainstream of human activity. However, even more significant are the barriers existing within the social-psychological environment—the attitudes which people with disabilities confront in their day-to-day interpersonal interactions with the general public and with particularly significant individuals, such as family, friends, associates, employers, and rehabilitation professionals. A number of classic texts have focused primarily on interpersonal and social-psychological influences on the behavior of people with disabilities (e.g., Safilios-Rothschild, 1970; Vash, 1981; Wright, 1983), examining person-by-situation interactions and the stimulus value of disability in social and interpersonal encounters.

As discussed by Michener, DeLamater, and Schwartz (1986), an attitude may be defined as a behavioral disposition to respond to an individual or object in a particular way. Attitudes may be conceptualized as having three general components: (a) a cognitive component, which is comprised of beliefs about the individual or object; (b) an evaluative component, varying in terms of favorability; and (c) a behavioral disposition component, leading to behavior toward the individual or object in a manner consistent with the cognitive and evaluative components of the attitude. Concepts drawn from social psychology, which can be helpful in understanding attitudes toward people with disabilities include "stereotypes," the tendency to make assumptions about people and their characteristics on the basis of their group membership; "impression formation," the process by which information is added to impressions already formed about an individual; and "attributions," assumptions made about the causes underlying observed behavior or events.

The topic of attitudes toward people with disabilities has been one of the most popular topics in the rehabilitation literature. For example, an annotated bibliography on attitudes and disability included more than 900 documents published between 1975 and 1981 (Makas, 1981). In addition, one recently published text has been devoted entirely to the topic of attitudes toward people with disabilities

(Yuker, 1988) and another to the measurement of those attitudes (Antonak & Livneh, 1988). In the process of identifying potential selections for the present text, approximately 20% of recent studies published in *Rehabilitation Psychology* were seen as dealing primarily with attitudes toward people with disabilities, and four were selected for inclusion.

The selection by Kleck and DeJong examines the social relationships among children attending a summer camp. Based on sociometric status hierarchies, Kleck and DeJong studied the social status and attractiveness of children with disabilities as viewed by their nondisabled peers, the extent to which their choices of best friends were reciprocated, and their skills In making friends. Contrary to the "spread of stigma" notion, higher-status children expressed greater rather than lesser liking for children with disabilities than did lower-status children, and this unexpected finding was interpreted in terms of theoretical constructs drawn from social psychology. The results of the study show that negative attitudes toward people with disabilities may begin early in childhood, and these negative attitudes can have detrimental effects for the healthy and positive development of children with disabilities. The results also demonstrate that inclusion of children with disabilities in activities with their nondisabled peers does not automatically insure their full participation and integration. Finally, this selection exemplifies methods which can be used to study social relationships and attitudes, both among children and adults.

The selection by Fichten, Robillard, Judd, and Amsel examines attitudes among college students toward people with disabilities. Nondisabled students were found to be uncomfortable with and to hold negative stereotypes toward students with disabilities. Further, students with disabilities were also found to feel uncomfortable with students with disabilities, when those disabilities were different from their own, and they were also found to hold negative stereotypes, even toward people with disabilities similar to their own. No differences were found between nondisabled students and students with disabilities in terms of self-esteem, social anxiety, dating anxiety, or dating behavior. The authors point out the need for programming within the college environment to influence stereotypes and attitudes in order to facilitate the full integration of students with disabilities, which can be applicable in other settings as well.

The selection by Bordieri, Sotolongo, and Wilson examines the role that physical attractiveness plays in the initial impressions formed about people with disabilities. Using a sample of college students, Bordieri et al. found that physical attractiveness of an individual who had sustained a spinal cord injury as a result of an automobile accident was related to more positive predictions for recovery; further, they found that physical attractiveness was related to a greater suspicion that the individual might have been partially at fault in causing the accident resulting in the disability. Attributions regarding fault for the accident and disability were viewed as possibly related to a commonly held "just world" belief in attempting to explain why misfortune occurs. In addition to demonstrating how theory regarding impression formation, attributions, and the manner in which people make sense out of events occurring around them, the study demonstrates how experimental designs, with random assignment, can be used to understand attitudes toward people with disabilities.

Finally, the selection by Threlkeld and DeJong focuses on the important practical issue of influencing attitudes toward people with disabilities. A media presentation was developed, based on social psychology and communications research, which was designed to influence the attitudes of employers toward hiring people with disabilities and the attitudes of rehabilitation counselors toward encouraging people with disabilities to pursue employment in health careers. The study provides a good example of methodology which can be employed in similar research on influencing attitudes. An experimental design, with random assignment, was used, allowing more definitive conclusions regarding the effects of the media presentation. In addition, three different types of measures were used—an attitude measure based on the semantic differential method; a behavioral intention measure; and a measure of actual behavior based on subject willingness to discuss career opportunities with an individual having a disability.

The studies included in this section enhance understanding of attitudes toward people with disabilities. In addition, they provide models for continuing future research. A variety of measures are used, along with a variety of data collection procedures. Further, examples are provided for the application of true experimental designs with random assignment, which can often permit more definitive conclusions about effects and relationships examined, though sometimes at the expense of generalizability to real life situations. Finally, examples are provided regarding the application of theoretical constructs to the formulation of research questions, the conceptualization of research methods, and the interpretation of results.

REFERENCES

Antonak, R. F., & Livneh, H. (1988). *Measurement of attitudes toward people with disabilities: Methods, psychometrics and scales.* Springfield, IL: Thomas.

Makas, E. (1981). *Attitudes & disability: An annotated bibliography. 1975–1981.* Washington, DC: George Washington University, Regional Rehabilitation Research Institute on Attitudinal, Legal, and Leisure Barriers.

Michener, H. A., DeLamater, J. D., & Schwartz, S. H. (1986). *Social psychology.* San Diego: Harcourt Brace Jovanovich.

Safilios-Rothschild, C. (1970). *The sociology and social psychology of disability and rehabilitation.* New York: Random House.

Vash, C. L. (1981). *The psychology of disability.* New York: Springer Publishing Company.

Wright, B. A. (1983). *Physical disability: A psychosocial approach* (2nd ed.). New York: Harper & Row.

Yuker, H. E. (Ed.). (1988). *Attitudes toward persons with disabilities.* New York: Springer Publishing Company.

1

Physical Disability, Physical Attractiveness, and Social Outcomes in Children's Small Groups

Robert E. Kleck and
William DeJong

ABSTRACT: An analysis of the sociometric status of children with obvious physical handicaps in an integrated (approximately 70% black, 20% Puerto Rican, and 10% white) summer camp setting revealed that such individuals are less preferred as friends than are their nondisabled peers. Physical attractiveness was also found to be related to sociometric standing, as well as to the presence or absence of a physical disability. A separate analysis of the relationship between physical attractiveness and social status for children with disabilities alone indicated that these variables are significantly related for this group. While children with obvious physical disabilities are less likely than their nondisabled peers to have their best-friend liking choices reciprocated, there is no evidence to support the expectation that nondisabled children who express relatively high liking for peers with disabilities are of lower social status than those who are less accepting. Significant differences were found between children with obvious physical disabilities and nondisabled children on a knowledge-of-friend-making task, but among the latter group, role-play scores did not differentiate high- from low-status individuals.

A rapidly growing body of research suggests that physical appearance in children is reliably related to a broad range of social outcomes. Young children are capable, for example, of articulating stereotypes regarding their facially attractive peers (Dion, 1973) and exhibit more interpersonal attraction to them than to those who are facially unattractive even after several weeks of intense social interaction (Kleck, Richardson, & Ronald, 1974). Adams (1977), in reviewing much of the attractiveness literature from a "dialectic-interactional" perspective, argues convincingly that the physical attractiveness of a child may have a strong impact on important aspects of that child's social development.

If relatively normal variations in physical attractiveness can affect the social outcomes of children, it is not surprising to discover that physical deviance of a more dramatic sort is important as well. When children are presented with drawings of other similar-age children who are depicted with various kinds of physical disability, they consistently express a preference for the nondisabled child (Richardson, 1970). Studies involving children with physical disablities in classroom settings are consistent with these preference data (e.g., Centers & Centers, 1963; Force, 1956; Gerber, 1977) and have pointed to some of the specific interaction problems that children with obvious physical disabilities encounter (e.g., Molinaro, 1978).

It is important to note that the bulk of the evidence concerning the impact of physical characteristics on social outcomes derives from studies involving little or no interaction. Further, research that has involved interaction between people with disabilities and nondisabled persons has typically examined either the course of short-term dyadic encounters (e.g., Kleck, 1969) or the outcomes experienced by a single child with a disability in a larger social setting such as a classroom.

To overcome these limitations, a research program was initiated in a summer camp setting involving the integration of large numbers of children with physical disabilities with their nondisabled peers. A primary advantage of this setting is that it permits the assessment of social relationships occurring between children with physical disabilities and nondisabled children from the point of inception of these relationships. Moreover, it is a context within which physical disability is not statistically novel. Previous studies in this setting have found that boys with obvious physical disabilities are less sociometrically popular than are their nondisabled peers (Richardson, Ronald, & Kleck, 1974). Further, it has been found that among the nondisabled boys, highly liked peers are more physically attractive than are boys not well liked within their social groups (Kleck et al., 1974).

The study reported here extends the previous research conducted in this setting in a number of ways. First, although the camp includes both male and female children, only male groups were studied previously. As Dion and Berscheid (1974) have demonstrated, the relationship between physical cues and social popularity may be more complex for female than for male children. In addition, Chigier and Chigier (1968) and Richardson (1970) have found consistent sex differences among children in expressed preference for peers math functional versus cosmetic disabilities. Specifically, girls have been found to be relatively less accepting of facially disfigured and obese peers, whereas males are less accepting of those with functional impairments requiring the use of wheelchairs or leg braces. In the present study, the social acceptability of peers with physical disabilities is examined for both male and female groups.

As noted above, the earlier research in this setting found that low sociometric status was associated with both low levels of facial attractiveness and the presence of an obvious physical disability. The independent contributions of these two factors to sociometric standing were not examined. Also, since attractiveness judgments were made on the basis of facial appearance alone, it was not possible to determine whether children's judgments of attractiveness covary with the presence of physical disabilities.

In the present study, full-body photographs are employed in the assessment of physical attractiveness, and it is hypothesized that children will perceive peers with disabilities to be less physically attractive than nondisabled children. In order to partial out the independent contributions of physical attractiveness and physical disability to social status, the relationship of attractiveness to social acceptance is examined separately for the children with physical disabilities. It is expected that, within this group, those perceived to be more physically attractive will be better liked by their peers than those judged to be less attractive.

If the results confirm our expectations that children with obvious disabilities are perceived to be less physically attractive than are their nondisabled peers, this will provide one plausible explanation for the previously observed low sociometric standing of such individuals. There are, of course, several other variables that may explain the low sociometric standing of children with obvious disabilities, and this study focuses on two of them. Because of the social isolation of children with physical disabilities in segregated schools (at least prior to the implementation of federal legislation mandating placement in the least restrictive environment) and the separation from peers often necessitated by their special medical needs, it is reasonable to expect lower levels of social competence to be displayed by such individuals (Richardson, 1968). While a careful measurement of general social competence is not possible within the limits of the present study, friend-making skills are assessed through a role-play procedure previously developed by Gottman, Gonso, and Rasmussen (1975). The hypothesis tested is that children with physical disabilities will reveal less knowledge of how to go about making friends than will their nondisabled peers.

Another factor that may contribute to the low social acceptance of children with obvious disabilities is related to Goffman's (1963) concept of "spread of stigma." By this he means that negative attributions made to stigmatized individuals, among whom the people with physical disabilities comprise one group, tend to generalize from people with disabilities to their close associates. He argues that one factor causing individuals to avoid deviant individuals is the recognition of negative attribution as a potential cost of affiliating with such persons. If correct, this argument would imply that children will actively avoid becoming involved in friendships with their peers with disabilities in order to avoid becoming victims of this halo effect. This is clearly consistent with the previously reported finding that children who are physically disabled have lower social status.

Children with disabilities are not, however, totally without friends, and relatively intense affiliations between nondisabled children and their peers with disabilities do occur in this camp setting. One plausible extension of Goffman's notion, and one that he has in fact made, is to argue that those who do become involved with peers with disabilities will be those who have the least to lose by such affiliations or those who, because of their own low social resources, are unable to attract nondisabled individuals as friends. One of the purposes of this study is to examine the social status of those nondisabled children who express relatively strong preferences for peers with disabilities. It is hypothesized that such individuals will be of lower social status than those children who do not form such friendships.

METHOD

Subjects and Setting

The subjects were 61 girls and 60 boys attending a 3-week summer camp session in upstate New York. The boys ranged in age from 7.75 to 14 years, with an average age of 10.36 years; the girls ranged in age from 7.5 to 13 years, with an average of 10.13 years. Though the camp's admission policy excluded children with severe levels of functional and cognitive impairment, 23% had obvious physical handicaps (e.g., spinal injuries, limb deformities), and an additional 33% had some form of chronic illness or physical condition requiring medical attention (e.g., sickle cell anemia, pulmonary insufficiency). The predominant racial group was black (70%), with fewer numbers of Puerto Rican (20%) and white (10%) children. The ratio of children with disabilities to nondisabled children did not differ as a function of ethnicity.

The children lived at the camp in small, age-graded, same-sex groups of five or six with one adult counselor. They ate and slept together, and many of the activities of the camp were organized around these primary social groups. The 28 children with physical disabilities were distributed throughout the 24 groups and participated as fully as possible in all camp activities. The primary data reported in this paper are derived from individual interviews with each child, both disabled and nondisabled.

In addition, 24 children from neighboring camps, similar to the subjects in this study in regard to socioeconomic background and geographical residence, were employed to obtain physical attractiveness ratings of each camper. These judges were 12 males and 12 females from two sex-segregated camps and had volunteered to participate in a study requiring them to rate the physical attractiveness of children they did not know.

Procedure

Interview Schedule. During the third week of the 3-week camp session, each child was seen individually by one of two male interviewers. It was explained to the child that the interviewer was interested in children's responses to the camp. The first several questions were intended to place the child at ease and included inquiries regarding where the child lived in New York City, previous experience with summer camping, and the activity the child had found most enjoyable at camp. The interviewer then displayed a set of cards that contained the first names (or nicknames, if these were more commonly used) of all members of the child's bunk group. The interviewer first checked to see if these individuals were recognized as members of the child's group, removed the respondent's own name card, and then asked the child to select the card of the person he or she liked best.

This person's card was removed, and the procedure was repeated until only one card remained. The interviewer then noted that one of the things he was interested in was how children go about making friends in a summer camp. Specifically, the interviewer said to the child, "Pretend you have just arrived at camp. You come into your cabin and find another child there your own age whom you want to become friends with. What would you do or say?" The child's response was tape recorded, and the interviewer used one probe (i.e., "Anything else?") when the child appeared to be finished responding.

To close the session, the child was thanked for helping the interviewer and was engaged in further casual conversation concerning camp activities and upcoming recreational events.

Attractiveness Ratings. Full-body color photographs were taken of each child on the first day of camp. The photographs showed each child seated on an armless chair placed in front of a neutral background. Children using wheelchairs were photographed in their own chairs against the same background. All children were asked to assume a neutral facial expression.

The judges were 12 male and 12 female children from neighboring summer camps, and each was interviewed individually by one of two male experimenters. The child sat opposite the experimenter at a small table and was first shown photographs of three children of the child's own sex who were supposedly found by their peers to be physically attractive ("good looking"), neutral ("average looking"), or unattractive ("not good looking"). These photographs were of children who had attended an earlier camp session and whose photographs had resulted in high consensus ratings from a similar group of judges. The experimenter placed the three photographs on the table in front of the child and asked him or her to select the picture of the attractive individual and place it to the right, the unattractive to the left, and the neutral in the middle. The child was told that the experimenter was going to show them several more photographs and that he or she was to look carefully at each and then place it in the appropriate pile. After answering any questions the child had, the experimenter proceeded through the judgment task at the child's own pace, handing the child the next photograph in the stimulus set only after the previous one had been placed face down in *one* of the three piles. The stimulus set consisted of all children in this study who were the same sex as the judge. The order in which the photographs were presented was randomized across judges. When the rating task was finished the interviewer thanked the child for participating.

RESULTS

For several of the analyses that follow, the children were divided into obviously physically disabled and nondisabled groups on the basis of both direct observation and medical records. The former was composed of all individuals who could be easily recognized by their peers as physically different, including children with facial or limb deformities, spinal injury, cerebral palsy, prosthetic and mobility aids, and gait abnormalities. In all, 13 females and 15 males were identified as obviously disabled; 15 of the bunk groups had one such child, 5 groups had two, 1 group had three, and 3 groups had none. There were 20 male and 33 female nondisabled campers distributed throughout the 24 social groups. The remaining 15 females and 25 males suffered some form of chronic impairment, but of a nature that would not lead them to be immediately perceived as physically deviant by their peers. Examples of children in this category include those with low levels of mental retardation, learning disabilities, sickle cell anemia, and pulmonary insufficiency. Again, these children were approximately evenly distributed throughout the social groups. The assignment of children to one of these three categories was done prior to conducting any of the data analyses for which this division is relevant.

Disability and Sociometric Status

Each child was rank-ordered on the liking dimension by all members of his or her social group. A sociometric status hierarchy was computed for each group based on the liking ranks for each child averaged across perceivers. The mean sociometric statuses for children with obvious physical disabilites and nondisabled children are shown separately for males and females in Table 1.1. An overall comparison, ignoring sex, indicates that nondisabled children tend to be better liked within their groups than are children with obvious disabilities, $t = 4.6$, $df = 79$, $p < .001$. A similar relationship holds when the female groups are considered by themselves, $t = 2.62$, $df = 44$, $p < .02$, and in the male groups by themselves, $t = 3.99$, $df = 33$, $p < .001$.

Physical Attractiveness and Social Status

A physical attractiveness index was calculated for each child by computing the average score assigned to each photograph by the set of 12 same-sex judges and then converting these to a standard score distribution with a mean of 50 and a

Table 1.1 Mean Sociometric Status of Children with Disabilities and Nondisabled Children

	Disabled			Nondisabled		
	M	*SD*	*n*	*M*	*SD*	*n*
Females	3.54*	1.1	13	2.39	1.4	33
Males	3.81**	1.0	15	2.30	1.3	20
Combined	3.71**	1.0	28	2.36	1.3	53

Note: Sociometric status can vary from 1 to 5, with a score of 1 indicating the most preferred child within a bunk group.
*$p < .02$.
**$p < .001$.

standard deviation of 10. Table 1.2 shows mean attractiveness scores for both the sociometrically most-popular and the least-popular children in the 24 male and female bunk groups. An overall comparison of these means reveals that the most-liked children are rated as more attractive than are those less popular with their peers, $t = 2.44$, $df = 46$, $p < .02$. Separate analyses by sex indicate that this difference is contributed to more strongly by the females, $t = 1.98$, $df = 22$, $p = .05$, than by the males, $t = 1.37$, $df = 22$, $p < .20$. It should be noted that in 18 of the 24 groups the child with the highest average liking score is perceived as more attractive by the judges than is the child with the lowest liking score, binomial exact $p = .01$.

An analysis comparing attractiveness judgments for children with obvious disabilities with those for nondisabled individuals reveals that the former are seen as much less attractive, $t = 3.26$, $df = 79$, $p < .002$. Again, separate analyses of the male and female groups reveal that the latter group makes the larger contribution to the overall effect, female $t = 3.14$, $df = 44$, $p < .005$; male $t = 1.46$, $df = 33$, $p = .15$.

Table 1.2 Physical Attractiveness Ratings (in Standard Scores) for Most- and Least-Liked Children in the Social Groups

	Most Liked			Least Liked		
	Rating	SD	n	Rating	SD	n
Females	54.5*	9.9	12	45.7	11.8	12
Males	53.3**	9.5	12	47.8	9.7	12
Combined	53.9***	9.5	12	46.8	10.6	12

Note: Twelve of the 24 social groups were composed of male campers and 12 of females only. The higher the score the more attractive the child is perceived to be.
    *$p = .05$.
    **$p < .20$.
    ***$p < .02$.

Table 1.3 Reciprocation of Most-Liked Peer Choices for Children with Disabilities and Nondisabilities

	Reciprocated		Not Reciprocated	
	n	%	n	%
Females				
Disabled	4	31	9	69
Nondisabled	15	45	10	55
Males				
Disabled	1	7	14	93
Nondisabled	12	60	8	40
Combined				
Disabled	5	18	23	82
Nondisabled	27	51	26	49

Thus, the results above suggest that low interpersonal liking is associated with both the presence of an obvious physical disability and with low physical attractiveness. These variables, in turn, are themselves strongly associated—that is, children with physical disabilities are perceived as less attractive. It is difficult to evaluate their independent contribution to the status measure, particularly since there was but a single child with a physical disability in most (15 out of 24) of the small social groups. In six groups, however, there were two or more individuals with obvious disabilities; for these groups, a comparison of the attractiveness ratings of the most- and least-popular child with a disability in each group reveals a positive relationship between sociometric status and physical attractiveness, $t = 2.53, df = 10, p < .03$. The mean rating in standard scores for the more popular children with disabilities is 52.5 and for the less popular children with disabilities is 41.1.

Friends of Children with Disabilities

The liking measures completed by each child permit an identification of reciprocated best-friend preferences within each small social group. It was our intent to identify these for both children with disabilities and nondisabled children and then to compare the mutual friends of children with disabilities with those of the nondisabled campers on a number of dimensions. The data in Table 1.3 demonstrate, however, that children with obvious disabilities do not have their top-liking choices reciprocated nearly as frequently as do nondisabled children, $\chi^2 = 8.39, p < .005$, a result that is consistent with the overall lower social status of such children. Comparisons for males and females separately reveal that this overall effect is accounted for primarily by the former, male $\chi^2 = 10.44, p = .001$; female $\chi^2 < 1.0$.

Given the small number of reciprocated best-friend choices for children with disabilities, a meaningful comparison of best mutual friends of children with disabilities and nondisabled children cannot be made. Another approach to the spread-of-stigma issue is to examine the relationship between the social status of those nondisabled campers who find peers with disabilities relatively attractive and those who do not. Of the 24 social groups, 16 contain two or more nondisabled children and at least one child with an obvious disability. The liking sociometric data from these 16 groups reveal that in 5 of them the nondisabled children do not differ in rank-order placement of the child or children with disabilities. In the remaining 11 groups, however, the nondisabled children express differential liking for the children with disabilities. It is possible for those groups, therefore, to compare the social status of nondisabled children who express relatively high liking for peers with disabilites with those who express less positive attitudes. Consistent with the hypothesis articulated earlier in this paper, we would expect the social status of the individual who is relatively accepting of peers with disabilities to be lower than that of the nondisabled child who is less accepting. Just the reverse is true. Higher-status children express greater liking for individuals with obvious disabilities, $t = 3.15, df = 20, p = .005$. The mean sociometric rank-order position of the former group is 1.7, while that of the latter is 3.1 (range = 1–5). Further, it should be noted that this relationship holds in 10 of the 11 groups in which it can be tested, binomial $p < .01$.

Social Skills of Children with Disabilities and Nondisabled Children

Children's responses to the friend-making role play were scored as had been done by Gottman et al. (1975). Explicit statement of greeting was given one point, asking for information two points, extending inclusion three points, and giving information four points. This weighting was used by Gottman and his colleagues because it had been found that children tended to proceed in a fixed sequence in performing this role play, with a category later in the sequence (e.g., giving information) less likely to occur than one early in the sequence (e.g., asking for information). A protocol from one of the children in the present study that received a score of 10 (the highest possible) is the following: "Hello" (greeting); "Is this your first year at camp?" (asking for information); "I'll show you around the camp" (extending inclusion); and "We can go to the swimming pool in the afternoon" (giving information). Three judges, following an extensive discussion of the category scheme, independently scored each role-playing protocol. For those on which there was not perfect agreement among all judges (21 % of the cases), the scoring discrepancies were then resolved through discussion. It should be noted that 16 children (13 %) did not generate scorable protocols, either because they had serious communication problems (e.g., profound deafness or severe speech problems) or because they did not appear to understand the role-playing task.

It was hypothesized that children with obvious disabilities would do less well on the friend-making role play than would the nondisabled campers. This expectation is strongly supported in an overall analysis that ignores gender, $t = 2.99$, $df = 79$, $p < .005$. An analysis for each gender separately indicates that this effect is contributed to primarily by the female groups, female $t = 2.99$, $df = 44$, $p < .005$; male $t = 1.08$, n.s.

It would be plausible to conclude, on the basis of this finding and in conjunction with the previous results of Gottman et al. (1975), that the low social status of the children with obvious disabilities is contributed to, in part, by their lack of social skills—in this case knowledge regarding strategies for making friends. The strength of this argument can be examined, in part, by looking at the relationship between friend-making role-play scores and social status for the nondisabled children alone. There are 19 small social groups that contain two or more nondisabled individuals. If the role-play scores of the best-liked nondisabled child in each group are compared with those of the least liked, there is no significant difference between the two groups, $t = 1.0$, n.s..

DISCUSSION

The results clearly replicate the earlier findings obtained in this setting (Richardson et al., 1974): Boys with obvious physical handicaps are less well liked following slightly over 2 weeks of intense social interaction than are their able-bodied, small-group peers. Furthermore, this relationship is found to characterize liking preferences expressed by female children for their samesex peers.

Consistent with a rapidly growing body of empirical data, the most popular children were found to be more physically attractive than those least popular within their small social groups. With gender included as a variable, this relationship was found to be very strong in the 12 female groups, but did not reach a statistical significance in the male groups. While the results for males do not, therefore, replicate an effect previously obtained in this setting (Kleck et al., 1974), it is important to note that the earlier finding is based on a larger number of groups and on attractiveness judgments obtained from a larger number of judges.

As expected, judgments of attractiveness by peers were found to be strongly associated with the presence or absence of a physical disability condition, particularly for females. There are several variables that could account for this finding, and more than one may be operating here. First, since the photograph showed a full-body shot of the child, the presence of any prosthetic device, such as a wheelchair or leg brace, would be obvious to the judge. If the presence of such devices is in itself aesthetically unpleasing, then children who employ them will be found less attractive by their peers.

Second, it might be argued that posing for a photograph requires some skill and that practice in posing, along with appropriate feedback, facilitates the generation of photographs that place an individual in the best light. It is a reasonable hypothesis that the children with disabilities in our sample had less practice in posing for photographs or were given less feedback on the adequacy of their poses, making them less skillful in accomplishing this task. A careful examination of the photographs, however, does not support this in such factors as facial expression, direction of gaze, or posture between the pictures of nondisabled children and those of children with disabilities.

Finally, it may in fact be the case that a specific physical disability or limitation is associated with a generalized reduction in aesthetic attractiveness. Many factors could conceivably mediate this outcome, including less concern for and attention to one's overall appearance, as well as a lack of the type of feedback from adults and peers that facilitates appropriate monitoring of physical appearance. It has been argued elsewhere (Kleck, 1975) that persons with disabilities typically are not given appropriate training in self-presentation skills as these relate to appearance factors.

While it was the case that children with obvious disabilites were less likely to have their top friendship choices reciprocated than were nondisabled campers, the expectation that those nondisabled children who express relatively greater liking for their peers with disabilities will themselves be of low social status was not confirmed. In retrospect, there are several plausible explanations for this finding. One stems from an exchange or transactional analysis of status relationships within small groups (Homans, 1974). An implication of this approach developed by Hollander (1980) is that high-status members of groups accumulate credits over time that permit them to deviate from group expectations or to engage in behaviors that are not approved of by the group as a whole. Thus, in this context, a group member could affiliate with a low-status member (disabled) with less threat to his or her own status than could a member who had not built up what

Hollander refers to as "idiosyncracy credits." A second explanation rests on the notion that there is a strong norm in this society to be kind to people with disabilities (e.g., Kleck, 1968). Actively choosing a peer with a disability as relatively likable in response to an inquiry from an adult may reflect awareness of social norms to be kind to those less fortunate. It is not unreasonable to expect that socially competent, popular children are more aware of or responsive to such norms than are their less socially successful peers.

Finally, several notes of caution need to be injected regarding generalization of findings from this specific social context to others involving the integration of children with physical disabilities with their nondisabled peers. First, though the intensity of social contact is quite high in this camp setting, our data were collected within the first 3 weeks of that contact. It is possible, therefore, that the physical appearance variables, which were shown to be important with this amount of contact, may become less important with further social interaction. Second, within the present research context a large number and variety of children with physical disabilities are integrated with their nondisabled peers. Generalization to settings involving small numbers of children with disabilities or children who are disabled in ways other than our subjects must be tentative. Third, the majority of the campers in this setting are black, with fewer numbers of Puerto Rican and white children. Since the impact of particular racial mixes on interactions between children with disabilities and nondisabled children has not been compared, we cannot assess the implications of this aspect of the research context on the generalizability of the results. Fourth, the children attending the camp come primarily from lower-class homes and may be either more or less accepting of their peers with physical disabilities than children with other socioeconomic backgrounds. Finally, the reader needs to be reminded that the context is that of a summer camp organized around a set of activities (e.g., arts and crafts, swimming, hiking) intended to provide inner-city children with a "vacation" in the woods. It is reasonable to expect that social contact between children with disabilities and nondisabled children under these conditions may have a somewhat different outcome than contact in a more cognitive, achievement-oriented context such as a classroom. What is clearly needed to help put aside concerns regarding the generalizability of the results reported here are data collected in diverse social contexts where children with disabilities have been integrated with their nondisabled peers.

NOTES

1. The friend-making role-play procedure, as originally used by Gottman et al. (1975), asked the respondents to pretend that the interviewer was a child with whom they wished to become friends. In a pilot investigation of this procedure, it was discovered that a number of children refused or found it difficult to imagine the interviewer in the role of a child. The procedure was therefore modified to focus on an imaginary peer whom the child had just met. This change dramatically facilitated the children's ability to complete the role play without further explanation or coaxing.

2. Data have not been reported separately for the group of children who were identified as having chronic disabilities but whose impairments were not immediately obvious to their bunkmates. There are several reasons for excluding them from the analyses reported here, including (1) lack of information on whether their impairment was known to either peers or counselors, (2) high variability within any one category in regard to the degree and nature of the impairment, and (3) the inability to verify the diagnosis of many of the children in this group. In spite of these problems, it is worth noting that, as a group, these children fall between the obviously disabled and nondisabled groups on perceived level of physical attractiveness, sociometric status, the likelihood of having best-friend choices reciprocated, and scores on the friend-making role-play task.

REFERENCES

Adams, G. R. (1977). Physical attractiveness: Toward a developmental social psychology of beauty. *Human Development, 20,* 217–239.

Centers, L., & Centers, R. (1963). Peer group attitudes toward the amputee child. *Journal of Social Psychology, 61,* 127–132.

Chigier, E., & Chigier, M. (1968). Attitudes to disability of children in the multi-cultural society of Israel. *Journal of Health and Social Behavior, 9,* 310–317.

Dion, K. K. (1973). Young children's stereotyping of facial attractiveness. *Developmental Psychology, 9,* 183–188.

Dion, K. K., & Berscheid, E. (1974). Physical attractiveness and peer perception among children. *Sociometry, 37,* 1–12.

Force, D. G. (1956). Social status of physically handicapped children. *Exceptional Children, 23,* 104–107.

Gerber, P. G. (1977). Awareness of handicapping conditions and sociometric status. *Mental Retardation, 15,* 24–25.

Goffman, E. (1963). *Stigma: Notes on the management of spoiled identity.* Englewood Cliffs, NJ: Prentice-Hall.

Gottman, J., Gonso, J., & Rasmussen, B. (1975). Social interaction, social competence, and friendship in children. *Child Development, 46,* 709–718.

Hollander, E. P. (1980). Leadership and social exchange processes. In K. J. Gergen, M. Greenberg, & R. Willis (Eds.), *Social exchange: Advances in theory and research.* New York: Plenum Press.

Homans, G. C. (1974). *Social behavior in its elementary forms* (rev. ed.). New York: Harcourt Brace Jovanovich.

Kleck, R. E. (1968). Physical stigma and nonverbal cues emitted in face-to-face interaction. *Human Relations, 21,* 19–28.

Kleck, R. E. (1969). Physical stigma and task orientations. *Human Relations, 22,* 53–60.

Kleck, R. E. (1975). Issues in social effectiveness: The case of the mentally retarded. In M. J. Begab & S. A. Richardson (Eds.), *The mentally retarded and society: A social science perspective.* Baltimore: University Park Press.

Kleck, R. E., Richardson, S. A., & Ronald, L. (1974). Physical appearance cues and interpersonal attraction in children. *Child Development, 45,* 305–310.

Molinaro, J. R. (1978). The social fate of children disfigured by burns. *American Journal of Psychiatry, 135,* 979–980.

Richardson, S. A. (1968). The effects of physical disability on the socialization of a child. In D. A. Goslin (Ed.), *Handbook of socialization theory and research.* Chicago: Rand McNally.

Richardson, S. A. (1970). Age and sex differences in values toward physical handicaps. *Journal of Health and Social Behavior, 11*, 207–214.
Richardson, S. A., Ronald, L., & Kleck, R. E. (1974). The social status of handicapped and nonhandicapped boys in a camp setting. *Journal of Special Education, 8*, 143–152.

Acknowledgments: This research was supported in part by Grant MH29446 from the National Institute of Mental Health to Robert E. Kleck. We would like to express our appreciation to James J. Biernat and Robert C. Vaughn who assisted in the collection and analysis of the data and to the children and counselors without whose enthusiastic participation this research would not have been possible. Finally, we owe a special debt of gratitude to the individuals responsible for the administration of the camp. They not only permitted our intrusion into their already hectic lives, but also gave generously of their time and energy to assure the completion of the research.

2

College Students with Physical Disabilities: Myths and Realities

Catherine S. Fichten, Kristen Robillard, Darlene Judd, and Rhonda Amsel

ABSTRACT: This investigation (1) explored affect concerning interaction between nondisabled individuals and people with various disabilities, (2) examined stereotyping by both disabled and nondisabled students, (3) compared aspects of the self-concepts of nondisabled and disabled persons and (4) evaluated nondisabled individuals' beliefs about these. Results show that nondisabled college students were less comfortable with disabled than with nondisabled peers. Students with disabilities, although equally comfortable with nondisabled individuals and with those who have the same disability as they do, were as uncomfortable as nondisabled individuals with peers who have a disability different from their own. Wheelchair user, visually impaired, and nondisabled college students had similar self-esteem, social anxiety, dating anxiety, and dating behavior. When predicting the responses of others, nondisabled students scored both nondisabled and disabled peers lower on most dimensions of self-concept than the actual scores of these groups indicate. Differences were greatest, however, between the self-concepts of people with disabilities and nondisabled individuals' beliefs about these. Furthermore, students with disabilities shared the myths believed by their nondisabled peers.

As the number of individuals with disabilities enrolled in colleges and universities is increasing (Fichten, 1988), it has become increasingly important to facilitate their integration. To do this, a better understanding of the attitudes that nondisabled students and students with different disabilities have about themselves and about each other is needed.

Research on attitudes of nondisabled individuals regarding people who have a physical disability suggests that both sympathy and aversion are commonplace. Numerous studies have shown that nondisabled persons evaluate individuals with disabilities more favorably than their nondisabled counterparts (e.g., Belgrave, 1985; Tagalakis et al.,1988). Data also indicate that attitudes can be polarized in either direction when the performance of the individual with a disability is of consequence to the evaluator or when ambivalent attitudes are legitimized (Carver et al., 1979; Gibbons et al., 1980). Despite this, studies demonstrating the existence of aversion and negative attitudes are fewer than those showing positive attitudes and sympathy (Katz & Glass, 1979).

Notwithstanding the prevalence of positive evaluations of individuals with disabilities, nondisabled people are less comfortable with disabled than with nondisabled peers and will avoid an individual who has a disability if there are socially and personally acceptable reasons for doing so (Fichten, 1986; Snyder et al., 1979). This suggests that the prevalence of positive descriptions of individuals with disabilities may be due to social desirability, sympathy, or self-presentation biases.

To avoid these biases, some researchers have employed a modified response prediction paradigm where participants are asked to report the beliefs of similar others, rather than their own views. Three studies using this instructional set have found that students with disabilities are evaluated more negatively than nondisabled students (Babbitt et al., 1979; Fichten & Amsel, 1986; Robillard & Fichten, 1983).

Students with disabilities are cognizant of the negative attitudes toward people with disabilities held by their nondisabled peers (Babbitt et al., 1979; Schroedal & Schiff, 1972). This would be expected to lead to feelings of inferiority and low self-esteem. Certainly both the symbolic interactionist and the social comparison formulations of the development of self-esteem and self-concept would suggest poorer self-attitudes by disabled than by nondisabled individuals (Rosenberg & Kaplan, 1982b). Although some investigations have found that people with disabilities are less well adjusted than nondisabled individuals (e.g., Crandell & Streeter, 1977; Meighan, 1971),the majority of studies have shown that people with disabilities describe themselves the same way as do their nondisabled peers (e.g., Kriegsman & Hershenson, 1987; Weinberg-Asher, 1976).

One purpose of this article is to explore similarities and differences between the self-concepts of individuals with and without a disability. Such an investigation must compare members of both groups on valid measures of personality and social functioning that are relevant to the age and social situation of individuals in both groups. Another objective is to speculate on the mechanism by which self-esteem develops in people with disabilities. This requires that the self-esteem of people with disabilities be compared with *their beliefs* about how others see them is well as with how others *actually* see people who have disabilities, and that the attitudes of people with disabilities toward others who have a similar disability be explored.

Specifically, this study (1) investigated feelings about interaction between nondisabled individuals and their wheelchair user and visually impaired peers, (2) examined stereotyping of people with disabilities by both disabled and nondisabled students, (3) compared various aspects of the self-concepts of nondisabled and disabled students, and (4) evaluated nondisabled individuals' beliefs about these aspects of self-concept.

METHOD

Subjects

Three groups of volunteer college and university students participated: 17 were wheelchair users, 15 had a visual impairment, and 221 had no physical disability. All were part of a larger investigation (Fichten & Amsel, 1988; Fichten et al., 1987). Students with disabilities were recruited through coordinators of services for students with disabilities (mailings, telephone, and face-to-face contact). Nondisabled students were recruited from psychology and geography courses. The mean age of the 11 male and 6 female wheelchair users was 26 (range, 19-36); they had been disabled for an average of 15 years (range, 6-29). Eleven male and 4 female visually impaired students also participated; their mean age was 23 (range 19-31) and they had their disability for an average of 19 years (range, 5-27). Of the nondisabled students, 87 were males and 134 were females; their mean age was 20 [it is common for college students with a disability to be older than their nondisabled classmates (Fichten & Bourdon, 1986)]. The sample of students with disabilities, although quite small, represented approximately 30% of the disabled student population at the institutions sampled.

Measures

General Information Form. This measure includes questions about gender, age, and absence or presence of a physical disability. Ease with nondisabled students, students who use a wheelchair, and students who have a visual impairment are assessed using 6-point scales (e.g., "In general, how comfortable are you with students who use a wheelchair?" 1, very uncomfortable; 6, very comfortable).

Social Activity Questionnaire (SAQ). This eight-item questionnaire was developed by Glasgow and Arkowitz (1975). It is scored on an item-by-item basis and evaluates dating frequency and self-report of comfort and satisfaction with one's current dating situation. Three items that deal with the number of dates during the past month, dating anxiety, and satisfaction with current dating frequency were used (3-point scales). An additional "dating" item was also included. It read: "I am presently dating" and gave the following as possible answers: "no one," "a physically disabled person," and "an able-bodied person."

Social Avoidance and Distress Scale(SAD). The SAD, a 28-item true-false questionnaire that measures anxiety or distress experienced in a variety of social situations is one of the most widely used measures of general social functioning. The scale has demonstrated good reliability and validity (Arkowitz, 1981). Watson and Friend (1969), the developers of the scale, reported a mean score of 9 (SD = 8), with a median of 7 for college students.

College Student Trail Checklists. This measure lists 10 socially desirable and 10 socially undesirable traits. Included are five socially desirable and five socially undesirable traits commonly attributed to male and female wheelchair user (but not to nondisabled) college students and five socially desirable and five undesirable traits commonly attributed to nondisabled students (but not to wheelchair users).

Subjects select five traits from each list that best describe a stimulus person. Three scores are derived: Positive, Negative, and Total "Handicapped" Stereotyping. Data show that nondisabled students attribute more "handicapped" traits, both desirable and undesirable, to disabled than to nondisabled students and that scores on the measure are logically related to relevant criterion variables (Fichten & Amsel, 1986).

Coopersmith Self-Esteem Inventory (SEI)-Adult Form. Coopersmith's (1981) SEI has been shown to be a valid instrument for the evaluation of self-esteem (Demo, 1985). It lists 25 statements that subjects indicate are "like me" or "unlike me." The scale was slightly modified to permit subjects to complete it in three ways: "me as I see myself" (Real Self), "me as I would like to be" (Ideal Self), and "me as others see me" (Reflected Self).

Procedure

Nondisabled, wheelchair-user, and visually impaired college student subjects completed measures individually. Large print and audiotaped versions were prepared for those visually impaired subjects who needed these, and a volunteer student helped wheelchair users who needed assistance.

Visually impaired participants completed the Background Information Form, SAD, SAQ, and the three versions (Real Self, Ideal Self, Reflected Self) of the Coopersmith SEI. They also completed the College Student Trait Checklists stereotyping measure concerning both nondisabled and visually impaired students.

Wheelchair user subjects were administered the same measures with two exceptions. They completed the College Student Trait Checklists concerning nondisabled and wheelchair user students. Due to the requirements of the larger study in which they were participating, these subjects completed only the Real-Self scale of the SEI.

Nondisabled subjects were randomly assigned to the Own or to the Predicted Response experimental condition. All completed the Background Information Form. Sixty-seven subjects completed the SAD, SAQ, and all three versions of the SEI concerning themselves (Own experimental condition). To evaluate nondisabled students' beliefs about disabled and nondisabled students, the 154 nondisabled subjects in the Predicted Response experimental condition were randomly assigned to one of three hypothetical Stimulus Person conditions; these subjects completed the College Student Trait Checklists concerning nondisabled, visually impaired, or wheelchair user students of the same sex as the respondent. For all other measures, subjects in the Predicted Response condition responded as "typical" college students of their own sex and, from that viewpoint predicted the answers of the hypothetical stimulus person on the SAD, SAQ, and the SEI Real Self scale.

RESULTS

All analysis of variance was performed using the SPSS-X package ANOVA procedure with the regression method option selected to give tests of the partials for all effects.

Ease

Comfort levels of members of the various groups with each other were examined in a two-way mixed design ANOVA comparison [3 Group (Nondisabled/Visually Impaired/Wheelchair User Subjects) X 3 Ease (with Nondisabled/Visually Impaired/Wheelchair User Students)]. Results show significant Group and Ease main effects, $F (2,170) = 4.13$, $p <.05$; $F (2,340) = 3.43$, $p <.05$, respectively, as well as a significant interaction, $F (4,340) = 3.68$, $p < .01$. The means presented in Table 2.1 and post hoc Tukey HSD tests show no significant differences among groups on Ease with Nondisabled Students. On Ease with Visually Impaired Students, visually impaired subjects' scores are significantly higher than those of nondisabled subjects, and on Ease with Wheelchair Users, wheelchair-user subjects' scores are higher than those of nondisabled subjects ($p < .05$ for all comparisons). Within the nondisabled group, results show that subjects were significantly less comfortable with visually impaired than with nondisabled students and that they were least comfortable with wheelchair users ($p < .01$).

To explore comfort scores of disabled students with peers having similar, different, or no disabilities, a two-way mixed design ANOVA comparison was made on the scores of disabled subjects [2 Groups (Visually Impaired/Wheelchair User) x 3 Ease (with Nondisabled/Own Group/Other Disabled Group)]. Results show only a significant interaction, $F (2, 58) = 5.38$, $p < .01$. Two planned comparisons on the interaction show that although Ease with Nondisabled Students scores did not differ significantly from Ease with Own Group scores, subjects in both groups were significantly more at ease with their own group than with the other disabled group, $F (1, 58) = 9.74$, $p < .0 1$.

Table 2.1 Ease with Students Who Have Different Disabilities: Means, Standard Deviations, and Ranges

Participants		Ease with Students Who Are		
		Nondisabled	Visually Impaired	Wheelchair User
Nondisabled	M	5.05	4.46	4.22
	SD	1.14	1.25	1.17
	range	1–6	1–6	1–6
Visually Impaired	M	5.07	5.53	4.67
	SD	1.21	0.83	1.50
	range	2–6	3–6	1–6
Wheelchair User	M	5.29	4.77	5.24
	SD	1.05	1.35	0.97
	range	3–6	2–6	3–6

Maximum score = 6; the higher the score, the more comfortable.

Self-Esteem (Real Self/Ideal Self/Reflected Self)

Possible differences between nondisabled and visually impaired students' Real-Self, Ideal-Self, and Reflected-Self scores were explored in a two-way mixed design ANOVA comparison [2 Groups (Nondisabled/Visually Impaired) x 3 Self-Esteem (Real/Ideal/Reflected)]. Results show only a Self-Esteem main effect, F (2, 92) = 7.94, $p < .00$ 1; all scores differ significantly ($p < .05$) with Ideal Self greater than Reflected Self greater than Real Self. There were no significant differences between the two groups of subjects.

Stereotypes

Nondisabled participants' trait ratings were evaluated in a two-way mixed design ANOVA comparison [3 Stimulus Person (Nondisabled/Visually Impaired/Wheelchair User) x 2 Valence (Positive/Negative Traits)]. Results show a significant Valence main effect, with Negative stereotyping being more frequent than Positive, F (1, 79) = 23.73, $p < .001$ [higher negative than positive "handicapped" stereotyping of all groups is normative for the measure (Fichten & Amsel, 1986)]. The Stimulus Person main effect was also significant, F (2, 79) = 5.67, $p < .01$. Means in Table 2.2 and post hoc Tukey HSD tests show that nondisabled participants attributed more "handicapped" stereotypes to wheelchair user and visually impaired students than to nondisabled students ($p < .05$); stereotyping of wheelchair user and visually impaired students did not differ.

Stereotypes of disabled people held by individuals with the disability in question were compared to those held by nondisabled subjects in two-way mixed design ANOVA comparisons [2 participants (Disabled/Nondisabled) x 2 Valence (Positive/Negative Traits)] made separately on stereotypes of wheelchair user and

Table 2.2 "Handicapped" Stereotyping of Students with Different Disabilities: Means, Standard Deviations, and Ranges

| | | "Handicapped" Stereotypes of: | | | | | |
| | | *Nondisabled Students* | | *Visually Impaired Students* | | *Wheelchair User Students* | |
Participants		*Positive*	*Negative*	*Positive*	*Negative*	*Positive*	*Negative*
Nondisabled	*M*	2.24	2.72	2.64	3.84	2.69	3.91
	SD	1.67	1.49	0.95	1.31	1.09	1.28
	range	0–4	0–5	1–5	0–5	1–4	2–5
Visually	*M*	2.27	3.25	2.39	3.62	N/A	N/A
Impaired	*SD*	1.12	0.92	1.04	0.96	N/A	N/A
	range	0–4	1–4	1–5	2–5	N/A	N/A
Wheelchair	*M*	1.61	3.00	N/A	N/A	2.01	3.27
User	*SD*	1.06	1.18	N/A	N/A	1.23	1.22
	range	0–4	1–5	N/A	N/A	0–4	1–5

Maximum score = 5; the higher the score, the more "handicapped" stereotypes attributed.

of visually impaired students. Results show no significant differences between nondisabled and disabled subjects' scores. Disabled participants' stereotypes of nondisabled students and of members of their own group were also compared. A three-way mixed design NOVA [2 Participants (Visually Impaired/Wheelchair User) x 2 Valence (Positive/Negative Traits) x 2 Stimulus Person (Nondisabled/ Own Group)) shows a significant main effect for Valence, $F(1, 24) = 66.86, p < .001$, again indicating higher Negative than Positive scores. The significant Stimulus Person main effect, $F(1, 24) = 7.00, p < .05$, shows that disabled subjects attributed more "handicapped" stereotypes to their Own Groups than to nondisabled students.

Relationships Among Variables

Pearson product-moment correlations were computed for each group of subjects to ascertain the relationships among measures of personality and to explore how personality variables are related to stereotyping and to comfort with different types of students.

Results in Table 2.3 show that scores on the various measures of personality (i.e., social anxiety, dating anxiety, and self-esteem) are related in the expected direction for all three groups of subjects. Real Self and Reflected Self scores are also strongly and significantly related for both nondisabled and disabled subjects. For subjects with disabilities, scores on the personality variables are also related to Ease with Nondisabled students. In the nondisabled sample, none of the personality variables is consistently related to Ease with students who have a disability. Stereotyping, Age, and Duration of Disability are not consistently related to the personality variables for any of the subject groups.

Own Versus Predicted Responses

Similarities and differences between nondisabled, visually impaired, and wheelchair user subjects' Own scores on the various measures and nondisabled subjects' beliefs about these (Predicted Response) were examined using two-way between-groups ANOVA comparisons [2 Experimental]Condition(Own/Predicted Response)x 3 Scores (Nondisabled/Visually Impaired/Wheelchair User)]. Planned comparisons on the three subject groups' own scores were made to evaluate actual differences among groups. Nondisabled subjects' Predicted Response scores in the three experimental conditions were also compared to evaluate beliefs about nondisabled and disabled students.

Self-esteem. Comparisons on the SEI Real-Self scale indicate only that scores were lower in the Predicted Response condition than in the Own condition, $F(1, 138) = 11.64, p < .001$. There were no significant differences between the various groups' Own scores or between the Predicted Responses of nondisabled subjects in the nondisabled, visually impaired, and wheelchair user experimental conditions.

Social anxiety. This construct was assessed by the SAD scale and by the SAQ item that asks about anxiety with a member of the opposite sex. Means are presented in Table 2.4.

Results of the two-way ANOVA comparisons on SAD scores indicate greater social anxiety in the Predicted Response condition than in the Own condition, F $(1, 187) = F (2,187)=3.06$, $P <.05$, suggesting relatively greater social anxiety in the Predicted Response condition than in the Own experimental condition for students with disabilities; the Tukey HSD test shows that the difference is significant for wheelchair users ($p <.05$). There were no significant differences between the various groups' Own Scores. Results on nondisabled

Table 2.3 Correlations Among Scores for Three Groups of Students: Nondisabled, Visually Impaired, and Wheelchair User

| | | | | | SEI | | | Ease with: | | |
| | | SAQ Dating Anxiety | Age | Duration of Disability | Real Self | Ideal Self | Reflected Self | Nondisabled Students | Wheelchair User Students | Visually Impaired Students |
Measures	Subjects									
	Nondisabled	.38*	-.15	N/A	-.43**	.17	-.43**	-.27	-.28†	-.09
SAD	Visually Impaired	.73**	.04	.35	-.76***	.32	-.59*	-.71**	-.53*	.28
	Wheelchair User	.74***	.29	-.13	-.90***	N/A	N/A	-.46†	-.33	-.50*
Dating	Nondisabled		.15	N/A	-.39*	-.08	-.50**	-.20	-.24	.05
Anxi-	Visually Impaired		-.13	-.14	-.76**	.38	-.70**	-.72**	-.53*	.31
ety	Wheelchair User		.12	.11	-.66**	N/A	N/A	-.20	-.20	-.25
	Nondisabled			N/A	-.11	.02	-.19	-.01	-.08	-.12
Age	Visually Impaired			.46†	.02	-.37	-.09	.12	-.05	-.35
	Wheelchair User			-.06	-.25	N/A	N/A	-.08	-.21	-.20
Duration	Nondisabled				N/A	N/A	N/A	N/A	N/A	N/A
of	Visually Impaired				-.42	-.46	-.34	-.49†	-.32	-.48†
Disability	Wheelchair User				.26	N/A	N/A	-.01	-.20	-.07
SEI	Nondisabled					-.04	-.19	-.01	-.03	-.12
Real	Visually Impaired					-.28	.87***	.88***	.26	-.15
Self	Wheelchair User					N/A	N/A	.58*	.50*	.69**
SEI	Nondisabled						-.14	-.46*	-.36†	-.31†
Ideal	Visually Impaired						-.17	-.19	.26	.59*
Self	Wheelchair User						N/A	N/A	N/A	N/A
SEI	Able-Bodied							.16	.02	.11
Reflected	Visually Impaired							.78**	.12	-.28
Self	Wheelchair User							N/A	N/A	N/A
Ease	Nondisabled								.26***	.34***
with	Visually Impaired								.27	.04
Able-Bodied	Wheelchair User								.66**	.76***
Ease	Nondisabled									.45***
with Wheel-	Visually Impaired									.15
chair User	Wheelchair User									.71***

Pearson product-moment correlation coefficients. The *ns* values for the visually impaired sample range from 13 to 15; *ns* for the wheelchair user sample from 11 to 17; *ns* for the nondisabled sample from 28 to 41 (except for Ease scores, where *ns* range from 142 to 193).

†$p < .10$.
*$p < .05$.
**$p < .01$.
***$p < .001$.

Table 2.4 Social Anxiety and Dating Behavior Scores in the "Own" and Predicted Response Conditions: Means, Standard Deviations, and Ranges

Experimental Condition		Scores		
		Nondisabled	Visually Impaired	Wheelchair User
		SAD: Social Anxiety		
Own	*M*	8.71	8.93	5.53
	SD	5.78	7.68	5.90
	range	1–25	1–26	1–20
Predicted Response	*M*	8.82	11.73	10.71
	SD	5.28	5.69	5.95
	range	2–20	4–26	2–25
		SAQ: Dating Anxiety		
Own	*M*	1.32	1.43	1.41
	SD	.52	.76	.62
	range	1–2	1–3	1–3
Predicted Response	*M*	1.43	1.52	1.79
	SD	.54	.51	.59
	range	1–3	1–2	1–3
		SAQ: Number of Dates During Past Month		
Own	*M*	7.28	2.69	4.92
	SD	8.66	2.90	5.26
	range	0–30	0–10	0–16
Predicted Response	*M*	5.13	2.04	2.16
	SD	6.57	2.18	3.10
	range	0–15	0–10	0–20

The higher the score, the greater the anxiety; maximum score is 28 for the SAD and 3 for the SAQ.

subjects' Predicted Response scores were marginally significant ($p < .10$), with higher scores for disabled than for nondisabled students.

On the SAQ social anxiety item the two-way ANOVA comparison also revealed a significant Experimental Condition main effect, $F (1, 187) = 4.37$, $p < .05$, with greater anxiety in the Predicted Response than in the Own condition. The nonsignificant planned comparison on Own scores suggests that in daring situations participants in three groups experience similar levels of anxiety. The comparisons on Predicted Responses show that nondisabled subjects believe that both visually impaired and wheelchair user students experience more anxiety with a member of the opposite sex than do nondisabled students ($p < .05$).

Dating behavior. Two questions of the SAQ (number of dates during that past month, satisfaction with dating frequency) and the "dating" item which asks about current dating partners pertain to this theme.

The two-way ANOVA between groups comparison on the number of dates during the past month yielded a significant Scores main effect, $F(2, 173) = 6.47$, $p < .01$; Tukey HSD test results show more dates for nondisabled students than for visually impaired students ($p < .05$) when Own and Predicted Responses are combined. The comparison on Own scores revealed no significant differences among the groups. On Predicted Responses, the analysis was significant and shows that nondisabled students were believed to have more dates in the past month than either wheelchair user or visually impaired students ($p < .05$). Means for these analyses are presented in Table 2.4.

Results of the two-way ANOVA comparison on satisfaction with dating frequency revealed a significant Experimental Condition main effect, $F(1,186) = 5.53$, $p < .05$, indicating greater dissafisfaction with current daring frequency in the Predicted Response than in the Own condition. Neither the Own nor the Predicted Response between-groups comparison was significant.

The "dating" question asked whether one is dating a nondisabled person, a disabled person, or no one. To evaluate the relationships between Own and Predicted Response scores, χ^2 tests were made separately on nondisabled, visually impaired, and wheelchair user frequencies. The results were significant only for nondisabled frequencies; subjects in the Predicted Response condition believed that nondisabled students were more likely to be in a dating relationship than was actually the case $\chi^2 (2, n = 100) = 9.45$, $p < .01$; there was no overestimator of the number of visually impaired or wheelchair user students who are currently involved in dating relationships.

On Own scores of the three groups, the χ^2 test was not significant. On Predicted Response scores the significant results, $\chi^2 (4, n = 119) = 21.53$, $p < .001$, are due primarily to nondisabled subjects' overestimates of the frequency of dating a disabled person by disabled students. Parenthetically, whereas 3% of subjects with a disability indicated that they were dating a disabled person, 16% of nondisabled subjects believed that disabled students dated others who have a disability.

DISCUSSION

Nondisabled Students' Beliefs

The results show that the nondisabled students believed that their disabled peers were different from nondisabled students in a variety of negative ways: they believed that students with disabilities were more socially anxious, that they were uneasy about dating, and that they date less frequently (although disabled students were not seen as being dissatisfied with this), that they were more likely to date partners who had a disability, and that they fit a "handicapped" stereotype. It was therefore not surprising to find that nondisabled students were more ill at ease with students who have a disability than with nondisabled peers.

The importance of perceived similarity in influencing attraction and liking has been well documented (Byrne, 1969). Given the importance of socializing, friendship formation, and dating for most college students, the beliefs held by nondisabled individuals may constitute a serious barrier to social interaction.

Beliefs of Students with Disabilities Concerning Others Who Have a Disability

Students who have a disability were found to hold beliefs about others with disabilities that are similar to those of nondisabled students; this is consistent with assertions made by others (e.g., Kemp & Rutter, 1986). For example, students with disabilities stereotyped members of their own disability group in the same way as did nondisabled students. Also, they were just as uncomfortable as were nondisabled students with peers who had a disability different from their own. Stereotyping members of one's own group and discomfort with people who have a disability different from one's own can not only hamper interaction between students who have disabilities but can also prevent the formation of groups that promote the integration and social adjustment of people with disabilities.

Realities Concerning Students with a Disability

How "accurate" are the beliefs shared by nondisabled and disabled students." The results show that nondisabled students and those with disabilities did not differ significantly on any of the measures administered: self-esteem (Real Self, Idea, Self, Reflected Self), social anxiety, dating anxiety, dating frequency, the type of individual dated, and satisfaction with dating frequency. Correlational results also show that the constellations of related personality characteristics for nondisabled and disabled students are the same.

Nor did students with disabilities differ from their nondisabled peers on ease with nondisabled students. Indeed, they were as comfortable with nondisabled students as they were with students who had the same disability as themselves. Consistent with previous findings (Fichten & Amsel, 1986; Fichten & Bourdon, 1986; Fichten et al., 1987), the results indicate that college students with disabilities do not prefer to be with "their own kind."

Of course, self-ratings are not immune from self-enhancing or self-deceptive biases. Also, the sample sizes in the present investigation were small. Nevertheless, the consistency of the nonsignificant results suggests that the problematic nature of interaction between disabled and nondisabled students is not caused primarily by discomfort on the part of students with disabilities.

Implications for the Formation of Self-Concept

Most theories about the development of self-concept and self-esteem are based on interaction with the social world. According to these formulations people with disabilities should have lower self-esteem than nondisabled individuals (Rosenberg, 1979; Rosenberg & Kaplan, 1982b).

The theory of reflected appraisals holds that self-image and self-esteem are formed by adopting the views of others. In the present study both nondisabled and disabled individuals were found to hold negative beliefs about people with disabilities.

In addition, students with disabilities have been shown to be aware of the prejudiced views of others (Babbitt et al., 1979; Schroedal & Schiff, 1972). Yet, the self-images and self-esteem of disabled and nondisabled students were not found to differ.

The social comparison view (Festinger, 1954; Rosenberg & Kaplan, 1982a) holds that self-concept is formed through comparisons with "similar" others. If people with a disability compared themselves to nondisabled individuals, their self-images would be poorer, because the most salient characteristics of those labeled "handicapped" are generally defined in terms of limits, inabilities, and inadequacies (Wright, 1983). If the reference group were to consist of others who have a disability, one would not expect such a difference.

A systematic evaluation of the reference group for college students with physical disabilities is beyond the scope of this investigation. Indeed, there may be multiple reference groups depending on age and on the aspect of the self-concept evaluated. Nevertheless, it is unlikely that individuals with disabilities constituted the reference group for the students in this sample. First, college students with disabilities have many more nondisabled than disabled friends and acquaintances (Fichten & Bourdon, 1986). Second, the self-images of students with congenital and longterm disabilities (who have probably had more exposure and socializing experiences with others who have disabilities in special schools and facilities) did not differ from the self-images of students who have acquired their disability more recently.

Nor can the nature of the present sample (i.e., college students) account for the results. Data from non-college samples that show no or few differences between individuals with and without disabilities (e.g., Cameron et al., 1973; McCann, 1967; Weinberg & Williams, 1978) suggest that this is not the most likely explanation.

Why, then, do people with disabilities have positive self-images? Rejection of the "group identity" (Beail, 1983; Rosenberg, 1979) and reliance on overly favorable feedback from nondisabled individuals (Kleck et al., 1966; Hastorf et al, 1979) are likely possibilities. First, characterizations of specific persons with disabilities and of disabled people in general differ considerably (Ravaud et al., 1987). Second, although the present study did not address the issue of the development of self-esteem and self-concept directly, the results do suggest that negative beliefs about people with disabilities may not be accepted as characteristic of the self. For example, students with a disability were found to hold views about others in their disability group that were similar to beliefs held by nondisabled students. Despite this, they believed that others viewed them as favorably as they saw themselves, even though this may not have been the case. It is, perhaps, not society's *actual* views but their *perceived* views, about *oneself* rather than about "the handicapped," which defines the self-image of people who have a disability.

Methodological Issues

The modified response prediction paradigm used in this investigation attempted to eliminate sympathy, social desirability, and self-presentation biases. It may have induced other biases, however, since predicted responses were consistently more negative than subjects' own scores.

That actors' and observers' perceptions and causal attributions for behavior differ has been well documented, as has the tendency for actors to make self-serving attributions (Fichten, 1984). People have also been shown to make more optimistic evaluations of their own behavior than the situation warrants (Alloy & Ahrens, 1987; Gotlib & Meltzer, 1987; Lewinsohn et al., 1980; Roth et al., 1986; Taylor & Brown, 1988). Such self-enhancing, self-deceptive biases result in overly favorable self-evaluations. Predicting the responses of others, an observer rating procedure not influenced by actors' self-serving biases can result in less favorable evaluations than actor ratings.

In evaluations by nondisabled individuals of people who have disabilities, what, then, is the appropriate comparison group? Is it legitimate to compare self-evaluations of individuals who have a disability with nondisabled individuals' evaluations of them, as much of the literature has done? Because this process compares disabled actors' evaluations with nondisabled observers' ratings, the difference in focus might confound the meaning of the results. Clearly, two types of comparisons are needed: self-ratings by all concerned individuals and observer ratings, made by nondisabled people, of the characteristics of both nondisabled and disabled individuals. In this respect, the "typical similar other" response prediction format appears to be particularly useful in eliminating the effects of sympathy, social desirability, and self-presentation biases (Fichten & Amsel, 1986). The method does not purport to produce ratings more "accurate" than self-evaluations, but, rather, attempts to address the issue of evaluations when social desirability and sympathy effects are likely to distort ratings. Also, although a single individual's beliefs about the views of others do not constitute an accurate assessment of that person's own attitudes or perceptions, such ratings made by many subjects probably do provide an accurate picture of commonly held views.

CONCLUSIONS

The results show that nondisabled students believe numerous myths, in domains important to young adults, about their peers who have a disability. They are also ill at ease with their disabled peers. Students with disabilities share these myths, even when the myths concern others with disabilities similar to their own, and they, too, are uncomfortable with individuals who have a disability if it is different from their own. Although the negative beliefs do not seem to influence the self-concepts of individuals with disabilities, the very existence of these beliefs can seriously hamper integration, whether into institutions of higher education or into society at large.

What is then required is attitude-change programming to dispel such myths. Extended equal status contact, the realization of which is possible at colleges and universities, could prove effective in modifying stereotyped beliefs and in fostering problem-free interaction between nondisabled individuals and their disabled peers (Fichten, 1988). To the extent that the potential for such contact is realized, those with disabilities will be enabled to participate fully and without discrimination in our society.

NOTES

1. The five socially desirable traits commonly attributed to disabled students are: quiet, honest, softhearted, nonegotistical, undemanding. Socially undesirable traits attributed to disabled students are: nervous, unaggressive, insecure, dependent, unhappy. Socially desirable traits attributed to nondisabled students are: sociable, optimistic, humorous, popular, dependable. Undesirable traits attributed to nondisabled students are: demanding, argumentative, overconfident, phony, complaining.

2. Sample instructions for the predicted response conditions for males: "Pretend that you are a 'typical' male student at your college. As a 'typical' student, predict how the average male wheelchair user student at your college would complete the questions that follow about himself. Remember, on these questionnaires you, as a 'typical' male student, must predict the answers of the average male wheelchair user student."

Although the task is seemingly complex, few students had difficulty with the instructions. For those who did have problems, the following explanation was given: "You are a typical student here. OK? Now, how do you think a wheelchair user would answer these questions about himself?"

REFERENCES

Alloy, L. B., & Ahrens, A. H. (1987). Depression and pessimism for the future: Biased use of statistically relevant information in predictions for self versus others. *Journal of Personality and Social Psychology, 52,* 366–378.

Arkowitz, H. (1981). Assessment of social skills. In M. Hersen & A. S. Bellack (Eds.), *Behavioral* assessment (2nd ed.) (pp. 296–327). New York: Pergamon Press.

Babbitt, C. E., Burbach, H. J., & Iutcovich, M. (1979). Physically handicapped college students: An exploratory study of stigma. *Journal of College Student Personnel, 20*(5), 403–407.

Beail, N. (1983). Physical disability: The self and the stereotype. *International Journal of Rehabilitation Research, 6,* 56–57.

Belgrave, F. Z. (1985). Reactions to a black stimulus person under disabling and nondisabling conditions. *Journal of Rehabilitation,* April/May/June, 53–57.

Byme, D. (1969). Attitudes and attraction. In L. Berkowitz (Ed.), *Advances in experimental social psychology* (Vol. 4). (pp. 38–89). New York: Academic Press.

Cameron, P., Titus, D. G., Kostin, J., & Kostin, M. (1973). The life satisfaction of nonnormal persons. *Journal of Consulting and Clinical Psychology, 41* (2), 207–214.

Carver, C. S., Gibbons, F. X., Stephen, W. G., Glass, D. C., & Katz, I. (1979). Ambivalence and evaluative response amplification. *Bulletin of the Psychonomic Society, 13,* 50–523.

Coopersmith, S. (1981). *SEI Self-Esteem Inventories.* Palo Alto, CA: Consulting Psychologists Press.

Crandell, J. M., & Streeter, L. (1977). The social adjustment of blind students in different educational settings. *Education of the visually handicapped,* Spring, 1–7.

Demo, D. H. (1985). The measurement of self-esteem: Refining our methods. *Journal of Personality and Social Psychology, 48,* 1490–1502.

Festinger, L. (1954). A theory of social comparison processes. *Human Relations, 1,* 117–140.

Fichten, C. S. (1984). See it from my point of view: Videotape and attributions in happy and distressed couples. *Journal of Social and Clinical Psychology, 2,* 125–142.

Fichten, C. S. (1986). Self, other and situation-referent automatic thoughts: Interaction between people who have a physical disability and those who do not. *Cognitive Therapy and Research, 10*(5), 571–587.

Fichten, C. S. (1988). Students with physical disabilities in higher education: Attitudes and beliefs that affect integration. In H. E. Yuker (Ed.), *Attitudes toward persons with disabilities* (pp. 171–186). New York: Springer Publishing Company.

Fichten, C. S., & Amsel, R. (1988). Thoughts concerning interaction between college students who have a physical disability and their nondisabled peers. *Rehabilitation Counseling Bulletin, 32,* 22–40.

Fichten, C. S., & Amsel, R. (1986). Trait attributions about physically disabled college students: Circumplex analyses and methodological issues. *Journal of Applied Social Psychology, 16,* 410–427.

Fichten, C. S., & Bourdon, C. V. (1986). Social skill deficit of response inhibition: Interaction between wheelchair user and able-bodied college students. *Journal of College Student Personnel, 27,* 326–333.

Fichten, C. S., Bourdon, C. V., Amsel R., & Fox, L (1987). Validation of the College Interact on Self-Efficacy Questionnaire: Students with and without disabilities. *Journal of College Student Personnel, 28*(5), 449–458.

Gibbons, F. X., Stephen, W. G., Stephenson, B., & Petty, C. R. (1980). Reactions to stigmatized others; Response amplification vs. sympathy. *Journal of Experimental Social Psychology, 16,* 591–605.

Glasgow, R. E., & Arkowitz, H. (1975). The behavior and assessment of male and female social competence in dyadic heterosocial interactions. *Behavior Therapy, 6,* 488–498.

Gotlib, I. H., & Meltzer, S. J. (1987). Depression and the perception of social skill in dyadic interaction. *Cognitive Therapy and Research, 11,* 41–54.

Hastorf, A. H., Northcraft, G. B., & Picciotto, S. R. (1979). Helping the handicapped: How realistic is the performance feedback received by the physically handicapped. *Personality and Social Psychology Bulletin, 5*(3), 373–376.

Katz, I., & Glass, D. C. (1979). An ambivalence-amplification theory of behavior toward the stigmatized. In W. G. Austin & S. Worchel (Eds.), *The social psychology of intergroup relations* (pp. 55–70). Monterey, CA: Brooks Cole.

Kemp, N. J., & Rutter, D. R. (1986). Social interaction in blind people: An experimental analysis. *Human Relations, 39*(3), 195–210.

Kleck, R. E., Ono, H,, & Hastorf, A. H. (1966). The effect of physical deviance upon face-to-face interaction. *Human Relations, 19,* 425–436.

Kriegsman, K. H., & Hershenson, D. B. (1987). A comparison of able-bodied and disabled college students on Erikson's ego stages and Maslow's needs levels. *Journal of College Student Personnel,* January, 48–52.

Lewinsohn, P. M., Mischel, W., Chaplin, W., & Barton, R. (1980). Social competence and depression: The role of illusory self-perceptions. *Journal of Abnormal Psychology, 89,* 203–212.

McCann, V. G. (1967). *Perceptions of self-esteem in persons with chronic physical disabilities.* Unpublished master's thesis, University of Kansas. Available from the Clendening Medical library, University of Kansas Medical Center.

Meighan, T. (1971). *An investigation of the self-concept of blind and visually handicapped adolescents.* New York: American Foundation for the Blind.

Ravaud,J. F., Beaufils, B., & Paicheler, H. (1987). Stereotyping and intergroup percep-
    tions of disabled and nondisabled children: A new perspective. *The Exceptional Child*,
    34(2), 93–106.
Robillard, K. & Fichten, C. S. (1983). Attributions about sexuality and romantic involvement
    of physically disabled college students: An empirical study. *Sexuality and Disability*,
    6, 197–212.
Rosenberg, M. (1979). *Conceiving the self* (pp. 149–174). New York: Basic Books.
Rosenberg, M., & Kaplan, H.B. (1982a). Principles of self-concept formation. In M.
    Rosenberg & H. B. Kaplan (Eds.), *Social psychology of the self-concept* (pp. 173–
    178). Arlington Heights, IL: Harlan Davidson.
Rosenberg, M., & Kaplan, H. B. (1982b). Social identity and social context. In M.
    Rosenberg & H. B. Kaplan (Eds.), *Social psychology of the self-concept* (pp. 209–
    223). Arlington Heights, IL: Harlan Davidson.
Roth, D. L., Snyder, C. R., & Pace, L. M. (1986). Dimensions of favorable self-
    presentation. *Journal of Personality and Social Psychology*, *51*, 867–874.
Schroedal, J. G., & Schiff, W. (1972). Attitudes towards deafness among several deaf and
    hearing populations. *Rehabilitation Psychology*, *19* (2), 59–70.
Snyder, M., Kleck, R. F., Strenta, A., & Mentzer, S. (1979). Avoidance of the handicapped:
    An attributional ambiguity analysis. *Journal of Personality and Social Psychology*,
    37, 2297–2306.
Tagalakis, V., Amsel, R., & Fichten, C. S. (1988). Job interview strategies for people with
    a visible disability. *Journal of Applied Social Psychology*, *18* (6), 520–532.
Taylor, S. E., & Brown, J. D. (1988). Illusion and well-being: A social psychological
    perspective on mental health. *Psychological Bulletin*, *103*, 193–210.
Watson, D., & Friend, R. (1969). Measurement of social-evaluative anxiety. *Journal of
    Consulting and Clinical Psychology*, *33*, 448–457.
Weinberg, N., & Williams, J. (1978). How the physically disabled perceive their
    disabilities. *Journal of Rehabilitation*, *44* (3), 31–33.
Weinberg-Asher, N. (1976). The effect of physical disability on self-perception. *Reha-
    bilitation Counseling Bulletin*, *23*, 15–20.
Wright, B. A. (1983). *Physical disability: A psychosocial approach* (2nd ed.) New York:
    Harper & Row.

Acknowledgments: This research was funded by Fonds F.C.A. R. pour l'aide et
le soutien 'a la recherche. Thanks are due to John Martos and Jim Dubois for their
assistance with various stages of this investigation and to Sam Parkovnik and
Betty Sunerton for their valuable comments on an earlier version of this article.

3
Physical Attractiveness and Attributions for Disability

James E. Bordieri, Mary Sotolongo, and Midge Wilson

ABSTRACT: This study investigated the effect of physical attractiveness on forming impressions of a person with a disability. Eighty undergraduate subjects answered questions about a person who had allegedly become a paraplegic as a result of an automobile accident. The persons who were rated varied in attractiveness and sex. The results demonstrated that subjects made different attributions for the accident and assigned more personal responsibility to the person when portrayed as physically attractive. In contrast, when portrayed as physically attractive the person was perceived to have a better prognosis for recovery than when portrayed as unattractive. These findings are discussed within the context of the "just world" hypothesis (Lerner, Miller, & Holmes, 1976), and suggestions for future research are presented.

Numerous studies have examined the effect of physical attractiveness in person perception. In one of the earliest investigations, Dion, Berscheid, and Walster (1972) asked college students to estimate the personal characteristics of other students on the basis of facial photographs. The stimulus photographs had been judged in a pilot study to be either attractive or unattractive. The authors found that subjects perceived the attractive people to be more interesting, sociable, exciting, kind, sensitive, and modest than the unattractive people were perceived to be. Dion, Berscheid, and Waister concluded that physical attractiveness is associated with many other positive traits in forming impressions of others.

The salience of physical attractiveness in impression formation has been documented in a variety of other empirical studies. For example, Dipboye, Arvey, and Tepstra (1977) reported that physically attractive persons are judged to be more qualified as job applicants than unattractive persons. Similarly, physically attractive individuals are perceived to be more intelligent and more likely to enter college (Clifford & Walster, 1973), to get better grades in school (Rich, 1975), and to be more talented (Landy & Sigall, 1974) than unattractive persons. Sigall and Ostrove (1975) and Efran (1974) have also reported that attractive defendants are judged more leniently and receive lighter sentences than unattractive defendants in jury simulation research.

Extending the physical attractiveness stereotype to the health field, Hansson and Duffield (1976) had college students identify a person diagnosed as epileptic from a "line-up" of people ranging in physical attractiveness. They reported a significant tendency for subjects to attribute epilepsy to physically unattractive people. In a recent study of 289 health professionals, Nordholm (1980) concluded that physically attractive patients are judged to have more socially desirable personality traits, more intelligence, more motivation, and greater likelihood of improvement than physically unattractive patients. Similarly, Cash, Kehr, Polyson, and Freeman (1977) and Jones, Hansson, and Phillips (1978) have reported that more attractive individuals are perceived to need less therapeutic intervention for psychological problems, and that they are less likely to be selected as showing symptoms of psychopathology, respectively.

In summary, there is strong empirical evidence that physically attractive people are viewed as having more positive qualities than less attractive people are seen as having. The present study attempted to explore this "what is beautiful is good" stereotype further within the area of rehabilitation. It was expected that people would extend different prognoses for a person with a disability, based upon his or her physical attractiveness. Specifically, it was predicted that an attractive person would be perceived as having a better prognosis for recovery from the disability than an unattractive person would be.

It was also expected that people would make different attributions concerning the cause of the disability on the basis of the disabled person's physical attractiveness. Specifically, it was predicted that an attractive person would be held less personally responsible for his or her disability than an unattractive person would be.

To test these predictions, the present study was designed to have nondisabled subjects give their impressions of either a physically attractive or an unattractive person who had allegedly become paralyzed in an automobile accident.

METHOD

Subjects

The participants were 40 male and 40 female undergraduates volunteering for extra credit in their introductory psychology courses at an urban midwestern university. None of the subjects had a visible physical disability. No attempt was made to determine any hidden disabilities, or the subjects' degree of social contact with people with disabilities.

Procedure

The subjects were informed that the purpose of the experiment was to determine how people form impressions of someone who has become seriously injured in a recent automobile accident. Subjects were stratified according to gender and randomly assigned to one of four accident person conditions. They viewed one of

Table 3.1 Means for Physical Attractiveness in Pilot Study

Stimulus	Attractive	Unattractive
Female	13.30	4.50
Male	13.00	3.70

the following stimulus slides: an unattractive female, an attractive female, an unattractive male, or an attractive male. The degree of physical attractiveness of these slides had been previously established in a pilot study. Subjects in the pilot study rated the stimulus slides on a 15-point scale, with 15 representing high physical attractiveness. The mean ratings for physical attractiveness are presented in Table 3.1. The slides for males, $t(18) = 8.06, p < .01$, and females, $t(18) = 7.69, p < .01$, did significantly differ along this attractiveness dimension in the pilot study.

While subjects viewed the slide, they listened to a tape recording introducing the person and presenting a brief account of the automobile accident. The person was portrayed as a college student who was involved in an automobile crash while driving home alone at night from a party. The victim sustained a spinal cord injury, leaving him or her paralyzed. There were no witnesses to the accident, and the description was purposely designed to be vague in order to allow a wide range of interpretation concerning the possible cause(s) of the accident and extent of the person's disability. All subjects heard precisely the same description of the person and his or her accident. Only the name (i.e., Diane or David) and gender pronouns varied according to the sex of the person.

After listening to the tape recording and viewing the slide, all subjects completed a questionnaire. The questionnaire was comprised of five key questions (measured on 9-point Likert-type scales) assessing potential causes for the accident and the prognosis for the person's disability. Three questions were designed to measure an individual's level of personal responsibility for his or her accident:

1. How much do you consider the automobile accident to be David's/Diane's fault?
2. Would you say that the reason David/Diane sustained his/her injury was because he/she had been drinking at the party and was under the influence of alcohol at the time of the accident?
3. To what extent was David's/Diane's injury caused by his/her own carelessness?

Two questions dealt with disability prognosis:

4. Do you think David's/Diane's paralysis will be permanent or only temporary?
5. How long will it be before David/Diane recovers from his/her injury and returns to his/her studies at college?

All subjects were completely debriefed upon completion of the questionnaire. The true purpose of the study and the reason for deception were carefully explained. All subjects were then sworn to secrecy and dismissed.

RESULTS

The primary purpose of this study was to examine the effect of physical attractiveness on attributions for the cause and prognosis of a person's disability. The means and standard deviations for physical attractiveness on each questionnaire item are presented in Table 3.2.

Separate 2 x 2 x 2 analyses of variance were performed for each dependent measure. In addition to the physical attractiveness of the person portrayed, the gender of the person portrayed and the gender of the subject served as the independent variables of the design. The following significant main effects and interactions were reported. Fisher's test of Least Significant Difference (LSD), with $p < .05$ as the criterion of significance, was used for all post hoc comparisons involving the interpretation of significant interactions.

Physical Attractiveness

One question served as a manipulation check for the physical attractiveness of the person portrayed. Consistent with the pilot study, a significant main effect for physical attractiveness, $F(1, 72) = 80.82$, $p < .001$, revealed that the persons with disabilities were perceived to differ in attractiveness in the anticipated direction.

Disability Prognosis

The two questions designed to measure the subjects' perceptions of the extent of the person's injury revealed the following results. A significant main effect for physical attractiveness, $F(1, 72) = 5.02$, $p < .05$, was found regarding the permanence of the person's disability. The attractive person's paralysis was perceived as significantly less permanent than the paralysis of the unattractive person.

Table 3.2 Means and Standard Deviations for the Physically Attractive and Unattractive Persons Portrayed on Each Questionnaire Item

	Attractive		Unattractive	
Item	M	SD	M	SD
Physical attractiveness	7.43	1.58	4.05	1.77
Disability prognosis				
Permanence	4.80	1.70	5.63	1.60
Recovery time	4.95	1.41	5.58	1.39
Cause of disability				
Person's fault	6.30	1.47	4.20	1.87
Under influence of alcohol	5.93	1.43	5.25	1.95
Carelessness	6.38	1.13	5.35	1.53

Note: Scores ranged from 1 to 9, the higher scores reflecting greater endorsement of the dependent measure.

Similarly, a significant main effect for physical attractiveness, F (1, 72) 4.05, p <.05, was reported for the length of time needed by the person to recover from the accident and return to college. The subjects indicated that it would take less time for the attractive person to recover from the injury than for the unattractive person. Stated another way, the unattractive person was perceived to have a more permanent disability and to need a longer rehabilitation period than the attractive person.

Causes of the Disability

The three questions exploring potential explanations for the person's automobile accident and consequent disability revealed the following results. A significant main effect, F (1, 72) = 31.14, p <.001, and interaction between physical attractiveness and the gender of the subject, F (1, 72) = 5.23, p <.05, were reported for the degree of personal responsibility on the person's part for his or her accident. This main effect indicates that the subjects considered the accident to be more the fault of the attractive person than of the unattractive person. A post hoc examination of the simple main effects of the interaction revealed that the female subjects perceived the attractive person as significantly more to blame ($M = 6.45$) for the accident than the unattractive person ($M = 3.55$). There was a nonsignificant tendency for the male subjects to view the attractive person as more personally responsible($M = 6.15$) for the accident than the unattractive person ($M = 4.85$).

A nonsignificant main effect for physical attractiveness, F (1, 72) 3.10, p <.10, and significant interaction between physical attractiveness and the gender of the subject, F (1, 72) = 4.75, p <.05, were found to the extent that the person was perceived to be under the influence of alcohol at the time of the accident. The main effect revealed a tendency for the subjects to believe more often that the physically attractive person was under the influence of alcohol more than the unattractive person. A post hoc analysis of the simple main effects for the interaction indicated the female subjects perceived the attractive person to be drinking prior to the accident significantly more often ($M = 6.20$) than they did the unattractive person ($M = 4.70$). No significant differences concerning the potential influence of alcohol were found for the male subjects between the attractive ($M = 5.65$) and unattractive ($M = 5.85$) persons.

A significant main effect for physical attractiveness, F (1, 72) = 11.70, p <.01, and interaction between physical attractiveness and the gender of the person, F (1, 72) = 5.02, p < .05, were obtained for the question measuring the extent that the person's injury was caused by his or her own carelessness. The main effect indicated that the subjects more strongly perceived the injury to be caused by the attractive person's, as compared to the unattractive person's, own carelessness. In the post hoc analysis of the simple main effects of the interaction, the subjects did not significantly differentiate between the attractive ($M = 6.05$) and unattractive ($M = 5.70$) male persons' level of carelessness. The attractive female person, however, was significantly more strongly seen to be careless ($M = 6.70$) than was the unattractive ($M = 5.50$) female person.

DISCUSSION

The results of the present study clearly indicate that a disabled person's level of physical attractiveness did influence how observers made attributions concerning the cause and prognosis of the disability. In terms of causal explanations, the physically attractive persons were held more personally responsible for their injury than were the unattractive persons. They were blamed more, were more strongly perceived to have been careless, and were seen as more likely to have been under the influence of alcohol at the time of the accident than the unattractive persons. These findings support Cash and Begley's (1976) claim that attractive persons are perceived as having greater internal control over their outcomes than unattractive persons. Similarly, these results are consistent with Wilson and Dovidio's (Note 1) assertion that attractive people are perceived as more powerful and more in control of their fates. The findings of the present study do, however, appear to violate common sense, and they directly contradict the well-established "beautiful is good" stereotype. Lerner's (see Lerner, Miller, & Holmes, 1976) "just world" hypothesis, however, offers a theoretical explanation for these counterintuitive results.

Lerner et al. claim that many people maintain a belief in what they label a "just world." They reason that many kinds of human tragedies, such as rape, natural disasters, and in the present study, paralysis from an automobile crash, are very threatening to most people because they are so sudden and unpredictable. The idea that a misfortune or tragedy that another person experiences is a random, uncontrolled event is too threatening for most people, and they reduce this threat by convincing themselves that the person must have done something wrong to deserve his or her negative fate. According to the "just world" hypothesis, tragedies do not just happen randomly. People structure their attributions to make the victim appear as though this person received the fate that he or she deserved.

Applying Lerner et al.'s theory to the present study, one can reason that the attractive person was held more responsible and blamed more for the accident and injury than the unattractive person was because the former offers a greater violation of the "just world" hypothesis. That is, if a tragedy can strike an attractive person (i.e., a person of high social value), it can happen to anyone. In order to reduce this increased threat, the subjects convinced themselves that the attractive person must have done something wrong to cause the accident and injury. Conversely, there was not nearly as great a threat, according to Lerner's reasoning, when an unattractive person was the accident victim. With this decreased threat, there was less motivation to blame the unattractive person for his or her misfortune in order to maintain this notion of a "just world."

The results of the present study also demonstrated that the attractive person's paralysis was perceived as less permanent and that this person would recover from the injury and return to college sooner than the unattractive person. These findings are consistent with the "beautiful is good" stereotype, which assumes that positive outcomes are more likely to be attributed to attractive than unattractive people. They also support the research findings of Nordholm (1980) and Cash et al. (1977).

The "just world" hypothesis also offers an explanation for the findings dealing with the prognosis of the disabled person. Extending Lerner et al.'s reasoning, there appears to be a greater violation of this principle when an attractive person remains disabled. In order to reduce this inconsistency, the subjects concluded that this person would overcome the disability in less time than the unattractive person would. The subjects did not have to make this inference for the unattractive person, because there was less violation of the "just world" reasoning. There was less need to rationalize that the unattractive person's disability would be temporary and that this person would quickly recover.

In summary, the data suggest that disability and unattractiveness are not incompatible qualities in the theories and impressions that people form of others, while disability and attractiveness do seem to be mutually exclusive. On the basis of this exclusivity and "just world" reasoning, people are motivated to believe that the attractive person is more responsible for his or her negative fate, but that this person will recover from the injury and return to a normal life more quickly, as compared to an unattractive person. These conclusions, however, must be generalized with caution, due to the obtained interactions between physical attractiveness and gender on the dependent measures assessing attributions of causality for the person's disability.

The significant interactions between physical attractiveness and the gender of the subject on the dependent measures assessing the person's perceived fault and probability of being under the influence of alcohol demonstrated that the female subjects were more affected by the physical attractiveness manipulation. Similarly, the interaction between physical attractiveness and the gender of the person for the question measuring the person's carelessness seems to indicate that attractiveness is a more salient attribute in forming impressions of women. While these findings are consistent with the commonly held belief that women place more emphasis than men do on the physical appearance of others, interactions between gender and physical attractiveness are not frequently reported or extensively discussed in the literature (cf. Dipboye et al., 1977; Nordholm, 1980).

It can be argued that the reported interactions reflect a methodological limitation of the present study. Perhaps they occurred due to the accident situation that was used. That is, driving home alone at night after a party may be construed as more gender-appropriate behavior for males than for females. Similarly, this behavior might be considered more appropriate for unattractive as compared to attractive persons. As a result, attributions for personal responsibility may be interpreted as reflecting reactions to norm violation, rather than "just world" reasoning. Additional research is needed to explore the replicability of the results in less stereotypically masculine situations, as well as in situations that do not represent violations of the stereotype depicting unattractive people as "loners."

A second methodological limitation of the present study involves the use of only one stimulus slide in each condition. Each subject viewed the slide of either an attractive or unattractive male or female and then made attributions for the causes and prognosis of the victim's disability. A shortcoming of this experimental design is that the variance due to the specific characteristics of the stimulus for each sex cannot be distinguished from the degree of physical attractiveness portrayed in the stimulus. A more sensitive test of the hypotheses would entail the use of an experimental design in which subjects viewed and made attributions for a male and female person in each of the attractive and unattractive conditions. This latter design would allow for a better isolation of variance in the dependent measures due to the gender and physical attractiveness of the disabled person. Obviously, the cover story and scenario surrounding the disabled person in the present study would have to be altered to accommodate such a design. However, in light of the obtained interactions between gender and physical attractiveness, future research might be directed toward exploring more fully how gender-role norms and physical attractiveness mediate attributions for disability.

Obviously, there are other inherent limitations of the present study, since it was conducted with college students and with one specific disability (i.e., spinal cord injury). A logical next step would be to explore this issue of physical attractiveness with subjects from more applied settings (e.g., rehabilitation counselors, vocational evaluators) and with persons from other disability groups, such as chronic disabilities (e.g., mental retardation, cerebral palsy) and hidden disabilities (e.g., mental illness, epilepsy). More importantly, an area of future research would be to examine this potential physical attractiveness bias among disabled people themselves. Based on the results of this study, research questions that might be asked are these: Do disabled persons who are judged as physically attractive by others consider themselves attractive? Do they perceive themselves to be more in control and responsible for their fates than physically unattractive disabled persons do? If so, are these perceptions of control and responsibility related to attributions of causality for the disability and expectations for recovery? Answers to these questions would clearly affect the ways in which we counsel the disabled and would ultimately influence our efforts to rehabilitate them.

NOTE

1. Wilson, M., & Dovidio, J. *Effects of perceived attractiveness and feminist orientation on helping behavior.* Unpublished manuscript, DePaul University, Chicago, 1982.

REFERENCES

Cash, T., & Begley, P. (1976). Internal-external control, achievement orientation, and physical attractiveness of college students. *Psychological Reports, 38*, 1205–1206.

Cash, T., Kehr, J., Polyson, J., & Freeman, V. (1977). The role of physical attractiveness in peer attribution of psychological disturbance. *Journal of Consulting and Clinical Psychology, 45*, 987–993.

Clifford, M., & Walster, E. (1973). The effect of physical attractiveness on teacher expectations. *Sociological Education, 46*, 248–258.

Dion, K., Berscheid, E., & Walster, E. (1972). What is beautiful is good. *Journal of Personality and Social Psychology, 24*, 285–290.

Dipboye, R., Arvey, R., & Tepstra, D. (1977). Sex and physical attractiveness of raters and applicants as determinants of resume evaluations. *Journal of Applied Psychology, 62*, 288–294.

Efran, M. (1974). The effect of physical appearance on the judgment of guilt, interpersonal attraction, and severity of recommended punishment in a simulated jury task. *Journal of Experimental Research in Personality, 8*, 45–54.

Hansson, R., & Duffield, B. (1976). Physical attractiveness and the attribution of epilepsy. *Journal of Social Psychology, 99*, 233–240.

Jones, W., Hansson, R., & Phillips, A. (1978). Physical attractiveness and judgments of psychopathology. *Journal of Social Psychology, 105*, 79–84.

Landy, D., & Sigall, H. (1974). Beauty is talent: Task evaluation as a function of the performer's physical attractiveness. *Journal of Personality and Social Psychology, 29*, 299–304.

Lerner, M., Miller, D., & Holmes, J. (1976). Deserving and the emergence of forms of justice. In L. Berkowitz & E. Walster (Eds.), *Advances in experimental social psychology* (Vol. 9). New York: Academic Press.

Nordholm, L. (1980). Beautiful patients are good patients: Evidence for the physical attractiveness stereotype in first impressions of patients. *Social Science and Medicine, 14A*, 81–83

Rich, J. (1975). Effects of children's physical attractiveness on teacher's evaluations. *Journal of Educational Psychology, 67*, 599–609.

Sigall, H., & Ostrove, N. (1975). Beautiful but dangerous: Effects of offender attractiveness and nature of crime on juridic judgment. *Journal of Personality and Social Psychology, 31*, 410–414.

Acknowledgments: The helpful comments of Mary Comninel on an earlier draft of this report are appreciated. A summary of this research was presented at the meeting of the Illinois Rehabilitation Association, Carbondale, Illinois, May 1982.

4

Hiring People with Disabilities: An Attempt to Influence Behavioral Intentions through a Media Presentation

Robert M. Threlkeld and
William DeJong

ABSTRACT: A slide-tape presentation was developed to influence the stated willingness of health professionals to hire wheelchair-using workers for jobs in hospital settings. Beliefs of these health professionals regarding the consequences of hiring such workers were identified during interviews with a small pilot sample (e.g., workers with disabilities cannot physically perform the work). The presentation focused on these beliefs, marshaling evidence to refute them, and showing wheelchair-using hospital workers competently doing their jobs. The results of the study show that those subjects who saw the slide-tape presentation indicated more favorable behavioral intentions to hire both wheelchair-using workers and workers with double amputations than did subjects who saw no presentation. The groups did not differ in their stated intentions to hire persons with cerebral palsy. A companion study conducted with vocational rehabilitation counselors produced similar results.

The purpose of the present study was to test whether a media presentation could influence attitudes and behavior toward persons with disabilities. In contrast to previous efforts, where the content of the presentations derived only from the intuitions of the individual producers, the slide-tape presentation examined here was shaped largely by both social-psychological and communications research. Furthermore, while many rehabilitation films have been developed, formal evaluation of their impact is a rarity (see Moses, 1979-1980).

A major consideration in producing rehabilitation films is the complex relationship between expressed attitudes and actual behavior. Obviously, the assumption made by most producers has been that changes in attitudes result in changes in behavior. At best, however, psychologists have had only modest success in predicting behavior toward an object from attitudes (Zimbardo, Ebbesen, & Maslach, 1977). Thus, even if a media presentation proves effective in changing expressed attitudes, there is no guarantee that actual behavior will be affected.

Faced with this fact, Triandis (1977) and Fishbein and Ajzen (1975) have argued that *behavioral intentions* (what people say they are going to do), rather than expressed attitudes per se, should be the focus of any attempt to change behavior. Such statements of intention have proven to be highly correlated with actual behavior. In turn, a strong predictor of behavioral intentions is the set of beliefs people hold about the consequences of that behavior—that is, whether they believe that performing the behavior will produce positive or negative outcomes for them. To change behavioral intentions (and behavior), then, it is these beliefs that must be addressed.

The slide-tape presentation tested here was designed to address the beliefs that health professionals have about the negative consequences of hiring wheelchair-using persons for jobs in hospital settings. In the present study, health professionals saw the slide-tape presentation, a comparison presentation, or no presentation and then reported their behavioral intentions to hire wheelchair-using and otherwise disabled persons. A second slide-tape presentation targeted for vocational rehabilitation counselors was also produced. Similar to the one for health professionals, it was designed to enhance counselors' willingness to encourage persons with disabilities to consider jobs in the health field. Study 2 investigated the effectiveness of this second presentation.

STUDY 1: HEALTH PROFESSIONALS

Method

Development of Stimulus Materials. The first step in designing the slide-tape presentation was to specify an attitudinal object, an audience, and a target behavior. The attitudinal object selected was that of persons using a wheelchair. A brief presentation of this type is more likely to have impact when it specifically focuses on beliefs about one kind of disability, rather than beliefs about disabilities in general (English, 1971).

A number of persons with disabilities were interviewed to help define a target behavior. These persons indicated that employers see too narrow a range of jobs as being within the abilities of persons with disabilities and that certain jobs are seen as "disabled jobs, " such as clerical work for wheelchair-using persons. In fact, persons with disabilities can perform many types of jobs, including piloting an aircraft and operating heavy equipment, if some equipment adaptations are made. Thus, the slide-tape presentation was designed to expand the range of jobs for which the target audience would be willing to hire a wheelchair-using person.

A media presentation should be designed for a specific target audience, rather than for the public at large (English, 1971). The target audience was narrowed to hospital employers for three reasons. First, persons with disabilities interviewed for this project stated that hospital employers often had misconceptions about the abilities of persons with disabilities. Second, hospitals employ people in a wide range of jobs. Finally, the hospital setting afforded a convenient way to test large numbers of people at once. Next, supervisory personnel from several northern New England hospitals were asked about their beliefs regarding the consequences of performing the target behavior. Specifically, they were asked what thoughts they might have if a person with a disability applied for a particular job in their hospital. Five common themes emerged: (1) persons with disabilities could not physically perform the work; (2) it would be uncomfortable to supervise and, if necessary, to fire workers with disabilities; (3) patients might be depressed by the presence of workers with disabilities; (4) insurance rates and hospital costs would go up; (5) and the necessary building modifications for accommodating workers with disabilities would be too costly.

The slide-tape presentation, which featured interviews with three wheelchair-using hospital workers, addressed each of these five misconceptions. It showed how people with disabilities do their jobs and the ease with which supervisors and patients interact with them. The 20-minute presentation gave statistics on worker safety and insurance costs and demonstrated how building modifications can often be made simply and inexpensively. The tone of the presentation was both informational and understanding of employers' concerns, rather than moralistic.

As a point of comparison, a second media presentation was chosen for investigation. This 20-minute filmograph (a slide-tape show transferred to film) showed a series of still photographs of wheelchair-using and nondisabled people interacting together in a variety of settings. The soundtrack consisted of generally upbeat music with no narration.

Measurement Instruments.

ATTITUDINAL MEASURE. A widely used method of attitude measurement is the semantic differential technique (Osgood, Suci, & Tannenbaum, 1957). Respondents were asked to fill out rating scales for six entities—a chronic alcoholic, a blind person, a person in a wheelchair, a disabled person, myself, and (for subjects seeing one of the two presentations) the film just seen. Each entity was rated on nine bipolar adjective scales, three each from the factors of evaluation, potency, and activity (Osgood et al., 1957).

BEHAVIORAL INTENTION MEASURE. This instrument (for "Project Match," described below) consisted of 48 questions regarding employment of workers with disabilities in hospital settings. A question format suggested by Triandis (1977) was used—for example, "If you had an opening, would you be willing to hire a person in a wheelchair for the occupation of pharmacist's aide?" Responses were indicated on a 7-point scale, with the two endpoints labeled "definitely yes" and "definitely no." The 43 questions represented all possible combinations of three specific disabilities (person confined to a wheelchair, person with an amputated arm and leg, person with cerebral palsy) and 16 hospital jobs. The jobs and the disabilities were described on the instrument.

The 16 hospital jobs differed from one another along four dimensions: amount of training required; extent of mobility (travel) required; amount of contact with the public; and the physical demands of the job. One job, for example, required high training, low mobility, low public contact, and low physical demands. Six hospital supervisors and administrators were asked to identify jobs that fit each of the 16 job categories; the 16 jobs selected for the instrument were consistently categorized by all six persons. The job chosen for the example above was that of a bookkeeper.

Subjects. The health professionals were 199 nondisabled hospital employees from 10 hospitals in Massachusetts, New Hampshire, and Vermont. Drawn from various medical and administrative departments, all of them had hiring responsibilities, but their experience with workers with disabilites was limited. The participants were 110 females and 89 males, averaging 28.1 years of age and 15.7 years of education.

Procedure. Subjects were tested at their worksites. Representatives at each site selected between 10 and 20 persons and assigned them to one of three groups depending on their schedules. Each of these three groups, in turn, was assigned randomly to one of three experimental conditions: project-designed presentation ($n = 68$); comparison presentation ($n = 68$); and no presentation/control ($n = 63$). (A detailed look at responses of the subjects in the no-presentation group is presented in Threlkeld and DeJong (1982).

At the test site, usually a conference room, subjects were greeted by two experimenters. Experimenter A explained that he and Experimenter B were from the same university and shared an interest in the disability field. He further explained that they were working on separate projects and were traveling together to avoid the need for scheduling two separate sessions. At this point, Experimenter B took over, and Experimenter A left the room.

Experimenter B then described her study as a federally funded project to study the effect of media on the attitudes of health professionals toward people with disabilities. For subjects in the control group, the need for baseline measurements was explained, and no presentation was shown. The other subjects were shown either the project-designed slide-tape presentation or the comparison presentation. All subjects completed the semantic differential scales described above, thinking these were the principal measure of the presentations' impact.

Experimenter B collected her questionnaires and left the room. Experimenter A returned and introduced a second project called "Project Match," which was designed to "provide disabled high school students with information about health careers." (The data gathered on the "Project Match" form were later summarized and sent to guidance workers in Maine for use in vocational counseling for disabled students.) Subjects were told they had been chosen as expert advisors to the project since they understood the limitations imposed by certain disabilities for jobs in the health field. They then filled out the behavioral intention instrument, not knowing it was the principal measure of the presentations' impact. Subjects were also requested to say whether or not they would be willing to be interviewed at a later date by students with disabilities about careers in the health field. Interested subjects indicated how many such meetings (from 1 to 5) they could arrange in the next month.

Six weeks later, randomly selected subjects from each experimental condition at each location ($n = 88$) were sent a postcard asking about their availability to talk with a student with a disability from their local area. All of those contacted had previously indicated an interest in such meetings. It was made clear that the student was only seeking information about hospital careers and was not at this time applying for a job. Response to this request was used as a behavioral measure of the media presentations' impact.

Because subjects were assigned *in groups* to one of the three experimental conditions, and it was not feasible to collect pretest data, the pre-experimental equivalency of those groups cannot be asserted with complete confidence. This design limitation had to be accepted in order for the study to be completed and must be kept in mind as the results are reviewed.

Results

Attitudinal Measures. Subjects who saw either the project-designed or comparison presentations were asked to evaluate the film they had seen using nine semantic differential rating scales. From a factor analysis of those items (varimax rotation), two independent factors emerged: Film Evaluation, consisting of the items worthless-valuable, sharp-dull, weak-strong, and bad-good (coefficient alpha = .875); and Film Potency, consisting of the items rugged-delicate and tough-fragile (coefficient alpha = .584). In both cases, an index was formed by taking the average of the constituent items. The project-designed presentation was clearly more preferred, being rated significantly higher on both the Evaluation and Potency indices, $F(1, 134)$ 31.38, $p < .0001$ and $F(1, 134) = 15.27$, $p < .0001$, respectively.

A factor analysis also showed two factors emerging from the several ratings for a blind person, a person in a wheelchair, and a disabled person. A Disability Evaluation index (coefficient alpha = .905) was formed by taking the average value of the five items that loaded on that factor; a Disability Dynamism index (cf. Osgood et al., 1957) consisting of nine items was also calculated (coefficient alpha = .848). The Disability Dynamism index showed no differences among the three experimental conditions, $F < 1$. The Disability Evaluation index did show meaningful differences in expressed attitudes toward the people with disabilities, $F(2, 196) = 4.16$, $p < .02$. Surprisingly, the group that saw the project-designed presentation had the least positive score on this index: no presentation ($M = 5.25$); comparison presentation ($M = 5.00$); project-designed presentation ($M = 4.79$). A multiple-range test (least significant difference, LSD, procedure) showed the last group to be significantly lower than the no-presentation group, $p < .05$ (Nie, Hull, Jenkins, Steinbrenner, & Brent, 1975).

Behavioral Intention Measures. An overall behavioral intention index was formed by taking the average for each subject across all 48 questions. This index revealed that the group that saw the project-designed presentation indicated the greatest willingness to hire people with disabilities: no presentation ($M = 4.58$); comparison presentation ($M = 4.77$); project-designed presentation ($M = 5.07$), $F(2, 196) = 4.59$, $p < .02$. A multiple-range test showed the project-designed presentation group to be significantly higher than the no-presentation group, p < .05, but not significantly higher than the comparison-presentation group.

Separate indices were also formed for each of the three disability types across all 16 jobs. Results for these are presented in Table 4.1. Both groups that saw presentations had higher behavioral intention scores for the potential employee using a wheelchair than did the no-presentation group, F (2, 196) = 9.68, $p < .0001$. Importantly, the project-designed presentation group was also significantly higher than the comparison-presentation group. Those seeing the project-designed presentation were also more likely than the no presentation group to indicate their willingness to hire the person with a double amputation, but those seeing the comparison presentation were not, $F(2, 196) = 2.66, p < .08$. Finally, no differences between the groups emerged on the behavioral intention scores for the person with cerebral palsy, $F < 1$.

Behavioral Measure. Across the three experimental conditions, 142 subjects (71.4%) indicated that they would meet with one or more high school students with disabilities to discuss health careers; an equally high number in all conditions showed an interest, $\chi^2 < 1$. Those responding favorably to the request were asked to say how many meetings they could arrange in the next month. Overall, subjects volunteered to hold an average of 2.27 meetings; again, **no** differences emerged among the three experimental conditions, $F < 1$.

Finally, a random sample of subjects agreeing to that request received an inquiry 6 weeks later about their availability to see a student with a disability. Overall, 73.9% of the subjects returned a postcard indicating their interest in seeing the student. Again, no differences between conditions emerged, $\chi^2 < 1$.

STUDY 2: VOCATIONAL REHABILITATION COUNSELORS

It is the responsibility of vocational rehabilitation counselors to assist their clients with disabilities in entering or re-entering the labor market. Thus, it is important to test whether the approach for influencing behavioral intentions toward people with disabilities in Study 1 will work for these counselors as well.

Table 4.1 Mean Behavioral Intention Scores for Each Disability (Health Professionals)

| | Condition | | |
Disability	Control Group	Comparison Presentation	Project-Designed Presentation
Wheelchair confinement	4.90$_a$ [a]	5.23$_b$	5.61$_c$
Double amputation	4.70$_a$	4.82$_{ab}$	5.18$_b$
Cerebral palsy	4.13$_a$	4.27$_a$	4.41$_a$

Note: Scores for each of the three disabilities were formed by taking an average across the 16 job questions. A score of 7 = "definitely yes."

[a] Reading across each row, means having different subscripts are significantly different ($p < .05$) by the multiple-range test (LSD procedure).

Method

A slide-tape presentation similar to that used in Study 1 was developed for this study. Interviews with persons with disabilities conducted prior to the study indicated that vocational rehabilitation counselors, like health professionals, may believe that only a narrow range of occupations is within the capabilities of people with disabilities. The script of the presentation for the health professionals was modified slightly to make it appropriate for this new audience. The behavioral intention measure ("Project Match") was also altered for this subject group—for example, "Would you advise a client in a wheel-chair to consider the occupation of pharmacist's aide?" The attitudinal and behavioral measures were unchanged.

Subjects. The subjects were 99 state-employed vocational rehabilitation counselors from Massachusetts, New Hampshire, and Vermont. In each state, the agency training director randomly selected offices to participate and notified them of the study; in each of the nine offices used, all counselors available that day were tested. All subjects had case responsibilities and worked with people presenting a variety of physical disabilities; all had at least 1 year's experience. The participants were 55 females and 44 males, averaging 28.9 years of age and 16.7 years of education.

Procedure. The procedures used in Study 2 were similar to those of Study 1. Again, subjects were assigned as a group to one of the three experimental conditions of the study: project-designed presentation ($n = 39$); comparison presentation ($n = 29$); no presentation/control ($n = 31$). Two experimenters went to the subjects' work sites, presenting themselves as being from similar, but separate projects.

Results

Attitudinal Measures. Ratings of the two presentations were again divided into the two indices of Film Evaluation (coefficient alpha = .835) and Film Potency (coefficient alpha = .457). Unlike the hospital employees, the vocational rehabilitation counselors did not give a significantly more positive evaluation to the project-designed presentation, $F (1, 66) = 1.36$, n.s. No differences in ratings on the Film Potency index emerged, $F < 1$.

As found in Study 1, analysis of the Disability Dynamism index (coefficient alpha =.834) revealed no significant differences among the three experimental conditions, $F (2, 96) = 1.28$, n.s. For these subjects, however, no differences were found for the Disability Evaluation index either (coefficient alpha = .787), $F < 1$.

Behavioral Intention Measures. An overall behavioral intention index was formed by taking the average for each subject across all 48 "Project Match" questions. As in Study 1, the group that saw the project-designed presentation had the highest average behavioral intention score, but the overall analysis of variance only approached significance: no presentation ($M =4.96$); comparison presentation ($M =4.66$); project-designed presentation ($M = 5.12$), $F (2, 96) = 2.67$, $p < .08$.

Separate indices were also formed for each of three disabilities as an average across all 16 jobs. As seen in Table 4.2, behavioral intention scores were significantly higher for the group that saw the project-designed presentation when the potential employee was using a wheelchair, $F(2,96) = 5.00, p < .01$. For the case of the person with a double amputation, the group that saw the project-designed presentation did not differ from the no-presentation group; the group that saw the comparison presentation, however, had a lower average behavioral intention score, $F(2,96) = 2.96, p < .06$. Again, for the person with cerebral palsy there were no differences among the groups.

Behavioral Measures. Overall, 67 subjects (67.7%) expressed a willingness to meet with one or more students with disabilities to discuss the health employment picture. This measure revealed no differences among the three experimental conditions, $\chi^2 < (2) = 1.49$, n.s. Subjects responding favorably to this request volunteered to hold an average of 2.58 meetings; no differences among the three experimental conditions emerged on this measure, $F(2,64) = 1.40$, n.s. Response to the follow-up request 6 weeks later to meet with a specific student with a disability was overwhelmingly positive. Of 42 subjects contacted, 38 (90.5%) consented to the request; there were no differences among the three experimental conditions, $\chi^2 < 1$.

DISCUSSION

The results of Study 1 indicate that the health professionals were more positive in their professed willingness to hire disabled workers when shown the project-designed slide-tape presentation. These results become particularly interesting when they are juxtaposed with those from the attitudinal measures, which showed the group seeing the project-designed presentation to have the least positive expressed attitudes toward people with disabilities. Consistent with much of the attitude-behavior literature, in the present study there appears to be no clear link

Table 4.2 Mean Behavioral Intention Scores for Each Disability (Vocational Rehabilitation Counselors)

	Condition		
Disability	Control Group	Comparison Presentation	Project-Designed Presentation
Wheelchair use	4.86 [a]	469 [a]	5.33 [b]
Double amputation	5.31 [a]	4.75 [b]	5.22 [a]
Cerebral palsy	4.72 [a]	4.56 [a]	4.81 [a]

Note : Scores for each of the three disabilities were formed by taking an average across the 16 job questions. A score of 7 = "definitely yes."

[a] Reading across each row, means having different subscripts are significantly different ($p < .05$) by the multiple-range text (LSD procedure).

between subjects' expressed attitudes toward people with disabilities and their stated intention to consider hiring them.

It was found in Study 1 that the most positive behavioral intentions were expressed for the group featured in both the project-designed and comparison presentations—persons using wheelchairs. Both groups seeing a presentation indicated a greater willingness to hire this disability group than did those who did not see a presentation. Interestingly, generalization of this effect to the person with a double amputation only occurred for the group seeing the project-designed presentation. While no person with a double amputation was seen in the project-designed presentation, certain similarities do exist between an amputee with prostheses and a person in a wheelchair: both are limited in their mobility, both use artificial aids, and both typically have no limitations in their ability to communicate.

Neither group seeing a presentation had higher behavioral intention scores for people with cerebral palsy. One explanation for this may be that cerebral palsy is perceived as qualitatively different from the other two disabling conditions. For example, Threlkeld and DeJong (1982) discovered that health professionals were less likely to indicate a willingness to hire people with cerebral palsy for occupations that require a high degree of training. This was not true of the other two disabilities about which they inquired. Furthermore, unlike wheelchair use or amputation, cerebral palsy sometimes affects a person's ability to communicate clearly. These data should not be taken to mean that behavioral intentions toward people with cerebral palsy cannot be changed. Rather, to be effective, a presentation would have to speak to the misconceptions about the consequences of hiring this particular group (English, 1971).

In Study 2, the vocational rehabilitation counselors appeared to be somewhat less swayed by either the project-designed or comparison presentations than were the health professionals. Behavioral intention scores were significantly higher for those using a wheelchair when the counselors saw the project-designed presentation. But, in contrast to Study 1, higher scores were not shown by these subjects in their ratings for the person with a double amputation.

For those counselors seeing the comparison presentation, there was a consistent tendency, significant for the ratings of the person with a double amputation, to indicate a lower probability of encouraging the people with disabilities to pursue jobs in hospital settings. This apparent "boomerang effect" often occurs when subjects doubt the veracity of the material presented to them in an attitude-change effort (Fishbein & Ajzen, 1975; Zimbardo et al., 1977). The comparison presentation used in these studies showed a joyful and optimistic picture of persons with disabilities and nondisabled persons interacting together. The counselors probably felt that this presentation was unrealistic and therefore reacted negatively to it.

While these results show the usefulness of media presentations that are tailored for specific target behaviors and audiences, their development is time-consuming and costly. Future work in this area should explore whether such alternatives as lectures or workshops would be as effective in addressing potential employers' misconceptions about the consequences of hiring the disabled.

NOTES

1. The project-designed slide-tape show can be rented or purchased by writing to the Disability Information Center, Human Services Development Institute, University of Southern Maine, 246 Deering Avenue, Portland, Maine 04102.

2. A difficulty for research of this type is choosing an appropriate comparison presentation. Unfortunately, the budget for this research program did not permit development of a comparison film that could serve as a rigorous, experimental control for testing the utility of the behavioral intentions/beliefs model applied in the project-designed presentation. The filmograph selected is an award-winning film and is representative of recent rehabilitation films (Moses, 1979–1980).

3. The 16 jobs were file clerk, psychiatric nurse, bookkeeper, homemaker, central supply worker, public health educator, unit clerk, nutrition aide, pharmacy aide, laundry worker, visiting nurse, medical technologist, orderly, physical therapist, equipment repair person, and operating room technician.

4. Pretesting was executed to test the procedure and to probe for subject suspicion about the relatedness of the two experimenters' projects. In separate interviews, the pretest subjects were asked directly if they saw a connection between the media presentation they had viewed and the behavioral intention questionnaire for "Project Match." None saw the "Project Match" questionnaire as a veiled assessment for reactions to the presentation. A similar pretest was conducted for Study 2 with similar results.

5. The Disability Evaluation index consisted of the following items: from ratings for "a blind person," the item bad-good; and from ratings for "a person in a wheelchair" and "a disabled person," the items bad-good and unpleasant-pleasant. The Disability Dynamism index consisted of nine items: from ratings for "a blind person," the items rugged-delicate and tough-fragile; from ratings for "a person in a wheelchair," the same two items plus weak-strong and passive-active; and from ratings for "a disabled person," those same items were included, save passive-active.

REFERENCES

English, R. W. (1971). Combating stigma toward physically disabled persons. *Rehabilitation Research and Practice Reviews, 4*, 19–27.

Fishbein, M., & Ajzen, I. (1975). *Belief, attitude, intention and behavior.* Reading, Mass.: Addison-Wesley.

Moses, J. F. (1979–1980). A retrospective look at rehabilitation audiovisual materials: $120,000,000 later. *Rehabilitation World, 5*, 12–19.

Nie, N., Hull, C., Jenkins, J., Steinbrenner, K., & Brent, D. (1975). *Statistical package for the social sciences.* New York: McGraw-Hill.

Osgood, C., Suci, G., & Tannenbaum, P. (1957). *The measurement of meaning.* Urbana, Ill.: University of Illinois Press.

Threlkeld, R. M., & DeJong, W. (1982). Hiring the disabled in hospital settings: The behavioral intentions of rehabilitation counselors and health professionals. *Rehabilitation Psychology, 27*, 175–184.

Triandis, H. C. (1977). *Interpersonal behavior.* Monterey, CA: Brooks/Cole.
Zimbardo, P. G., Ebbesen, E. B., & Maslach, C. (1977). *Influencing attitudes and changing behavior.* Reading, Mass.: Addison-Wesley.

Acknowledgment: This research was supported by Grant No. 12-P-59142 from the National Institute of Handicapped Research (NIHR) (formerly the Rehabilitation Services Administration). The contents of this article are not necessarily endorsed by NIHR.

SECTION II
Issues Affecting the Rehabilitation of Persons With Physical Disabilities

Allen W. Heinemann, Section Editor

Introduction

Allen W. Heinemann

The psychological, social and vocational aspects of physical disability have long been recognized as important dimensions in rehabilitation. One landmark text by Dembo, Leviton and Wright explored these issues as early as 1956. They introduced the concept of value loss in their exploration of how veterans dealt with amputation. The articles in the following section draw on earlier theoretical and empirical studies and emphasize issues of current interest in rehabilitation. Given the space limitations inherent in a text of this nature, this list is not encyclopedic in terms of theory nor disability-specific issues. However, the pieces are important in extending our understanding of the experience of disability and the ways in which persons deal with consequent losses and limitations. This understanding is important in helping to guide the practice of rehabilitation professionals so as to enhance adaptations made by persons with physical disabilities.

The selection of articles illustrates several theoretical understandings of psychosocial issues that emerge in rehabilitation practice. The social psychological perspective of Beatrice Wright (1960, 1983), a student of Kurt Lewin, is reflected in several of these works. Learning theory-based perspectives also provide foundations for these articles as seen in the work of Albert Bandura (1978). While cited less frequently, psychodynamic models such as those described by George Vaillant (Vaillant & Vaillant, 1981) also inform the empirical studies selected here. The focus on empirical studies was made intentionally so as to emphasize the relationship between theory and practice.

The issues raised in the following articles cut across a variety of conditions (sensory, neurological, orthopedic), time periods (initial, longer-term), and concerns (personal, social). A recurrent issue in rehabilitation is dealing with loss: loss of physical ability and function, loss of psychological value of one's self, and loss of social and vocational roles. Indeed, Wright's model identifies the primary issue faced by persons with physical disabilities as one of dealing with misfortune and loss. She describes the ways in which disability can be accepted as a fact of life, neither denied nor over-emphasized. The relationship between physical and psychological health, and ways of enhancing well-being in both realms, is another concern. Identification as a disabled person versus a person with a disability, and the psychological consequences of this identification have concerned psychologists for some time. Finally, how persons adapt following physical disability in terms of vocational development and participation, and the role of work in persons' lives, is another recurrent issue. These concerns are explored in the articles.

Long-term studies examining the psychological, social or vocational impact of disability are rare given the expense and difficulty in conducting research of this type. Two of the included studies are noteworthy for examining long-term outcomes. These studies help us to understand the effects of disability on individuals' lives through time. The specific impact of disability, apart from maturation, is important to distinguish yet seldom examined.

All of the studies in this section are based on nomothetic, group-focused designs. This reflects the predominant emphasis on logical positivism in psychological research generally and rehabilitation research in particular. One consequence is that theory is tested as if one were using a wide-angle lens; the closer view of psychological processes that could be revealed with rigorous studies of representative cases is not afforded by these studies. In spite of this perspective, the authors present data which provide a way of enhancing rehabilitation practice by providing working hypotheses about the nature of disability in individuals' lives.

Frank Shontz builds upon Dembo, Leviton and Wright's (1956/1975) seminal work on physical disability and misfortune and Wright's (1964) concept of spread in which a single aspect of a person such as disability diminishes other valued aspects of a person. He argues that responses to physical disability and chronic illness are not determined by the condition per se, but rather by the meanings ascribed to the loss by each person. His analogue study illustrates the way in which the loss of one goal can diminish the importance of other goals, and how recovery is related to spread.

Nancy Weinberg and Mary Sterritt (1986) examined the impact of identifying as able-bodied or disabled on the psychological adjustment of adolescents with hearing impairments. The value of identifying with the able-bodied majority has been stressed in terms of enhanced social and vocational opportunities, though the psychological "price" paid in doing so in terms of diminished self-esteem has also been argued. They report that an able-bodied identity was consistently associated with poorer outcomes and that a dual identity was associated with better academic, personal, social and family outcomes.

The controversy regarding the relationship between physical disability, psychopathology and vocational adjustment is longstanding. While it may be intuitively appealing to speculate that severity of physical disability is associated with lower levels of psychological adjustment, empirical studies have produced equivocal results. Daniel Cook (1983) explored these constructs in rehabilitation center clients and found that type and severity of physical disability was not related to adjustment. These findings support the conclusion that while psychological and vocational adjustment may be correlated, they are not causally linked.

James Krause and Nancy Crewe (1987) explore the relationship between physical health, mortality and psychological well-being. They report that persons living 11 years after spinal cord injury were rated as having better psychosocial and vocational adjustment, were more socially active, had a greater tolerance for sitting, and were more likely to be working or attending school than were those who died. Recent medical history and life satisfaction did not distinguish the persons who lived and died. The importance of psychological well-being and how it affects survival supports a unified view of persons that incorporates physiological, psychological and social aspects. Their findings also point to the need for integration of psychological services during rehabilitation.

Finally, Daniel Rohe and Gary Athelstan (1985) address issues related to the stability of vocational interests, the effect of work experience on vocational interests, and the relationship between personal abilities and vocational interests in persons with physical disabilities. The opportunity to study the stability of self-concepts over time, and the effects that may be related to physical disability, are important in clarifying these issues. They examined the vocational interests of men with spinal cord injuries over an average period of nearly 10 years and found that they were as stable as those of their peers without disabilities. The changes that did occur were consistent with those found in nondisabled samples. The study highlights the importance of studying developmental changes in interests, and the value of making both longitudinal and cross-sectional comparisons between persons with and without disabilities.

The reader is invited to consider the issues raised in this series of articles. While they do not provide a complete review of current issues, they build on theories which have heuristic value, are testable, and which invite us to understand how persons come to terms with misfortune and physical disability. As with all well-conducted studies, they provoke further thought about psychological processes and suggest ways in which practice can be enhanced.

REFERENCES

Bandura, A. (1978). The self-system in reciprocal determinism. *American Psychologist, 33*, 344–358.

Dembo, T., Leviton, G. L., & Wright, B. A. (1975). Adjustment to misfortune: A problem of social psychological rehabilitation. *Rehabilitation Psychology, 22*, 1–100. (Originally published in *Artificial Limbs,* 1956, *3*, 4–62).

Vaillant, G. E., & Vaillant, C. O. (1981). Natural history of male psychological health: X. Work as a predictor of positive health. *American Journal of Psychiatry, 138*, 1433–1440.

Wright, B. A. (1960). *Physical disability: A psychological approach.* New York: Harper & Row.

Wright, B. A. (1964). Spread in adjustment to disability. *Bulletin of the Menninger Clinic, 28*, 198–208.

Wright, B. A. (1983). *Physical disability: A psychosocial approach* (2nd ed.). New York: Harper & Row.

5

Spread in Response to Imagined Loss: An Empirical Analogue

Franklin C. Shontz

ABSTRACT: A research model has been developed as an analogue of reactions to loss. This report describes a demonstration of the model that employed 48 college students. Each student identified four important life goals. After rating these for relatedness, the students rated the value or importance of each goal and of everything else in life. They then imagined that their goals became impossible, one at a time, from most to least important. After each imagined loss, they re-rated all other goals. After all goals were imagined lost, they rated everything else in life, both immediately and after the imagined passage of 1 year. The resulting data were consistent with the theory that one loss can adversely affect the values of other goals (*spread,* as defined by B. A. Wright), although containment and compensation or displacement were also found to occur. Spread was found to be bimodally distributed and negatively related to later recovery. Future research with the procedure is suggested, including systematic manipulation of conditions and the study of sex differences.

Grief and mourning have been reported in reaction to loss of sexual functioning (Orfirer, 1970; Romm, 1970), sensory loss (Altshuler, 1970), losses of external organs, disfigurement, and chronic illnesses in general (Blacher, 1970; Schoenberg, Carr, Kutscher, & Goldberg, 1974; Schoenberg, Carr, Peretz, & Kutscher, 1970). In the field of rehabilitation, many have assumed that the onset of physical disability is always followed by grief. Recent evidence indicates that such may not be the case, at least in spinal cord injury (Trieschmann, 1980). Reactions to illness and disability are not responses to physical conditions, but to the meanings of those conditions to the individual. When illness or disability do not threaten personal integrity, grief or mourning does not occur (Shontz, 1975, 1980).

Dembo, Leviton, and Wright (1956/1975) used the term "misfortune" or value loss" to refer to alterations in body structure or functions that threaten psychological integrity. Their ideas apply to any form of misfortune, however. Beatrice Wright (1960) stressed the social-psychological basis of reactions to misfortune and delineated the types of value changes that characterize reactions to and recovery from loss. Two of these are of particular importance to the project described in this report. The first is *spread,* the tendency for loss of a particular part or function to lessen the value or worth of other attributes of the person (Wright, 1964). The second is *containment,* which limits the experience of loss to functions that are directly affected (Wright, 1967).

The subject matter of these concepts precludes studying them by direct experimentation. Nevertheless, it is possible to examine their operation in a limited way through the use of an empirical analogue, a research model or simulation of life conditions (Shontz, 1965). To be useful, an analogue must produce results that parallel "real life" and are consistent with expectations derived from theory.

This report describes a research model that appears to be a successful analogue of reactions to losses of the type experienced by many persons with physical disabilities. The design of this model incorporates procedures used in several pilot studies, and it takes advantage of several important lessons that were learned from their conduct.

Pilot studies suggested that imagined loss of an important life goal decreases the rated values of other goals and of everything else in life. However, this outcome was not universal. About 25% of the persons studied exhibited what seemed to be a compensatory tendency. For them, ratings of the value of everything else in life increased immediately after imagined loss of major goals. A significant negative relationship appeared between amount of spread and level of recovery in the value of everything else in life. The present study attempted to produce these findings under more carefully designed conditions. Qualitative analysis of pilot study data suggested that the degree of relatedness among several goals affects reactions to loss of any one of them. Ratings of relatedness among goals were therefore included in the present study.

METHOD

Subjects

Subjects were students in my college-level course on psychological reactions to illness and disability. The 48 respondents were 36 women (age range, 18-47; median, 21) and 12 men (age range, 19-30; median, 21). Most had interests or experience in a health profession, but no readings or lectures on the concept of spread had been provided during the first week of class, when I collected data.

Procedure

Data collection took place in five stages, all administered at a single session. At Stage 1, subjects were told that this was a study of life goals. They were asked to write down, on a half-sheet of paper provided, the four most important goals they had set for themselves in life. They then assigned the letters A, B, C, and D to the listed goals, in the order of their importance (A = "most important").

At Stage 2, subjects used a special booklet containing 16 pages, each with a single rating scale, 150 mm long, marked at each end and at the center with a vertical line 5 mm long. Appropriate endpoint labels were provided. In all procedures, raw data were the number of millimeters from the left endpoint of the scale to the mark made by the subject. On the first six pages, subjects placed one mark on each line to rate the relatedness of each goal to every other, from "Totally unrelated (Independent)" to "Completely related (Inseparable)." Pages were turned after each rating so that previous marks were not visible. Relatedness was rated for the pairs AB, AC, AD, BC, BD, and CD, in that order.

At Stage 3, subjects used the next five pages to rate the values of their goals. The scale endpoints were "Not at all valuable or important" and "Maximum possible value or importance." Subjects first rated Goal D (the one designated in Stage 1 to be least important), then the combination of Goals C and D, then Goals B, C, and D, then all four goals combined. This procedure was intended to produce the strongest possible awareness of goal values before the loss instruction was administered. Therefore, subjects began by rating the *least* important goal, D, and built up from rating the CD and BCD combinations to rating all four goals together. The last step in Stage 3 was for subjects to rate the value of "everything else in life."

Stage 4 introduced the loss instructions. Subjects were asked to "imagine the effect it would have on your life if your most important goal, the one you marked A, were impossible." After taking time to think about this, they re-rated the goal combination BCD, "remembering that A has become impossible." Next, they imagined the additional loss of Goal B and rated the CD combination. Next, they imagined the loss of C, and rated the remaining goal, D. It should be noted that this procedure required subjects to rate the same combinations of goals that were rated in Stage 3, but in reverse order. Finally, they imagined the loss of D and rated the value of everything else in life (E).

In Stage 4, loss of the most important goal was introduced first to maximize the impact of the instruction. Goals were rated in combinations, because pilot studies had shown that requiring subjects to rate all remaining goals separately, after every imagined loss, allowed the impact of instructions to dissipate. The procedures used in this version of the model minimized the number of ratings and preserved the comparability of data obtained before and after imagined loss.

Stage 5 required only one rating. Subjects imagined that a year had gone by and re-rated how everything else in life would seem at the time. To enhance their awareness of what was being analogized, this page of the booklet was titled "Recovery."

Measures

The concept of spread implies that loss of one goal reduces the value *of other* goals. Therefore, imagined loss of Goal A should reduce the rated value of BCD in Stage 4, as compared to Stage 3. Subsequent loss of Goal B should reduce the rated value of CD, and so on. In this demonstration, spread would be demonstrated if ratings at Stage 4 were lower than ratings at Stage 3. Spread (S) was therefore measured by the differences:

$$S < BCD >= BCD<3>-BCD<4>$$
$$SCD = CD<3>-CD<4>$$

$$SD = D<3>-D<4>$$
$$SF = E<3>-E<4>$$

where subscripts are the stages of the procedure, and E is the rating of everything else in life.

Recovery (R) was defined quantitatively as the degree to which everything else in life gained in value after the imagined passage of a year following loss; that is,

$$R=E<5>-E<4>$$

RESULTS

Initial Values

As a check on whether subjects were following instructions appropriately in Stages 1 and 3, the pattern of ratings they provided at Stage 3 was examined. The expected pattern of initial values was as follows:

ABCD>BCD>CD>D

This expectation was borne out by medians for the entire group, as well as for men and women considered separately (see Table 5.1). Distributions were severely skewed, so Friedman's two-way analysis of variance was used to compare ranks derived from individual cases. It yielded an overall chi-square of 48.896, $df = 4$, $p < .01$. However, differences among ABCD, BCD, and CD accounted for the significance. Thus, while the expected pattern was evident in group data, in individuals it showed most clearly for the first three goals only.

Spread

The analogue required that ratings of remaining goals decrease after the imagined loss of a more important goal. All differences in ratings between Stages 3 and 4 were statistically significant at the .01 level, according to z values, derived from the Wilcoxon matched-pairs, signed-ranks test (see Table 5.2).

Differences in magnitude of spread for various goals or combination; of goals were tested by Friedman's two-way analysis of variance, $\chi^2< = 9.58$, $df = 3$, $p < .05$. The major difference was the increase in spread for Goal D (see Table 5.2). However, it was found that spread occurred much earlier for some people, and tended to persist once it started.

It was also found that ratings of remaining goals were strongly bimodal following imagined loss of a more important goal. That is, some people continued to rate remaining goals highly, while for others, these goals lost most of their value suddenly; there appeared to be no middle ground. Inspection of the data showed that these two types of responses could be readily separated by identifying those whose ratings of a given goal dropped by more than 75 mm (half the length of the response line) from Stage 3 to Stage 4, as engaging in *spread*. The rest were

Table 5.1 Initial Ratings of Life Goals

	D	CD	BCD	ABCD	E
Highest value					
Men	147	146	149	149	146
Women	150	149	150	150	151
Entire group	150	149	150	150	151
75th percentile					
Men	125	130	144	149	132
Women	149	148	149	149	148
Entire group	143	143	149	149	146
Median					
Men	112	117	139	148	107
Women	132	135	138	149	123
Entire group	123	132	138	148	113
25th percentile					
Men	93	111	133	145	85
Women	108	122	125	146	95
Entire group	100	111	129	145	94
Lowest value					
Men	47	65	78	89	39
Women	38	82	69	83	55
Entire group	38	65	69	83	39

Note: D is the least important goal; A is the most important goal; E is "everything else in life." Data in millimeters (see text). Group sizes: men, $n = 12$; women, $n = 36$.

identified as engaging in *containment*. This procedure does not permit distinguishing between containment and simple response set. However, from the examination of initial ratings and other group data, it does not appear that subjects were merely providing identical ratings, irrespective of procedural conditions. All appeared to be taking the task seriously, and it seemed safe to assume that, in this study, lack of change in ratings is as meaningful as change.

The number of persons engaging in spread, as defined above, increased from BCD ($n = 10$) to CD ($n = 18$) to D ($n = 32$), reinforcing the idea that less valued goals are more subject to spread than more valued goals. The number of persons engaging in spread for everything else in life was 19. The overall difference in frequencies was significant, $\chi^2 = 21.343$, $df = 3$, $p < .01$.

Recovery

As compared to its rating in Stage 4, the value of everything else in life showed a significant increase in Stage 5 of 37 mm, to a median of 112 ($z = 2.802$, $p < .01$, Wilcoxon matched-pairs, signed-ranks test). Recovery ratings correlated significantly and negatively with degree of spread from loss of Goal A, Spearman $\rho = -.29$,

Table 5.2 Spread Scores Following Imagined Loss

	BCD	CD	D	E
Highest	142	142	150	149
75th percentile	71	75	114	76
Median	14	16	68	36
25th percentile	0	− 5	4	− 8
Lowest	− 71	− 59	− 71	− 57
z^a	3.52	3.21	4.93	3.91

Note: Negative numbers imply increases in ratings following instruction (i.e., negative spread).

[a] z values derived from Wilcoxon matched-pairs, signed-ranks tests, comparing ratings at Stage 4 with ratings at Stage 3 for all subjects. All values significant at $p < .05$.

$p < .05$. That is, the greater the *spread, the* less the *recovery.* Correlations of recovery with measures of spread for other goals and combinations of goals were not significant.

Increases in the ratings of E between Stage 3 and Stage 4, (i.e., immediately after loss of other goals) occurred in 13 cases, about 27% of the group, virtually the same proportion as in a pilot study. Such increases imply that in some persons loss of valued life goals was immediately followed by enhancement of the value of other aspects of life.

Relations Among Goals

No significant patterning was found among ratings of relatedness among goals. Ratings of relatedness obtained in Stage 2 were not associated with values of goals after loss, amount of spread, or recovery obtained in pages 4 and 5.

Types of Goals

Pilot studies produced a five-category coding scheme for goals. Two categories were used much more frequently than all the rest: "Vocational and Economic," and "Prospective Home and Family." In this study, 46 persons (98%) listed 88 goals of the first type (33% of all goals listed); 37 persons (77%) listed 62 goals of the second type (32% of all goals listed). Other types of goals were "Personal Improvement" (19 persons, or 40%, and 21 goals, or 11%); "Interpersonal Relations" (9 persons, or 19%, and 12 goals, or 6%); and "Geographic," such as desire to travel or live in a particular location (8 persons, or 17%, and 9 goals, or 5%).

DISCUSSION

As it had in pilot studies, the analogue proved successful in achieving its purposes. Types of goals listed were appropriate for the group studied and in accord with those obtained in pilot studies. The expected pattern of initial values appeared in group data and, for the first three goals, in individual data as well. Spread and recovery, as defined for this research, appeared as well. These findings are consistent with Wright's theory that loss of one goal can reduce the value of others.

Two other findings were consistent with pilot work. First, recovery correlated negatively with amount of spread in response to initial loss. This finding implies that the occurrence of spread following loss may inhibit a person's willingness to find compensating sources of gratification, even after a period of time has passed. The second important finding is that it is possible for some persons to place increased value on other things in life immediately following loss. This reaction bears a resemblance to the mechanisms of displacement or compensation, in which psychological energy is shifted to other goals when an initial goal becomes unavailable.

Recovery scores were strongly skewed (indicating that many persons expected not to recover), but not bimodal. Instead, bimodality appeared in spread scores. Spread began immediately in some people after the first loss, and only later in others. Once it began, however, it tended not to abate. The negative correlation between recovery and spread, after the first loss only, suggests that the immediate reaction to loss is critical.

Ratings of relatedness among goals were not particularly productive in this demonstration. However, while the subjects were providing them, they were examining and considering their life goals, and this may have enhanced the effect of the loss analogue in Stage 4.

The group included only 12 males, but some sex differences appeared. Men assigned lower initial values to their two most important life goals than did women. They also rated nearly all goals as being more closely related to each other, and they showed less tendency to engage in spread. Variables associated with gender-role differences may affect the analogue. They should be investigated further because such variables probably also affect reactions to loss, and the analogue may be helpful in explicating them.

Findings from this demonstration should not be overinterpreted. The analogue only simulates life, and it is too soon to begin to speculate about how its outcomes will affect clinical or rehabilitation practices directly. Yet this simulation may have merit, because how people think they might react may affect their reactions should real loss occur. The fact that many subjects in this demonstration were interested in health-related activities may have affected the outcome. On one hand, the group is clearly not representative of the general population. On the other hand, their special interests probably induced them to take this task more seriously than might otherwise be expected.

If it is agreed that this analogue yields data that suggest parallels to "real life" reactions, further research seems warranted. Of particular value would be studies in which conditions are altered to minimize or maximize spread or to facilitate or inhibit recovery. For example, during Stage 3, spread might be inhibited by reminding some subjects at each step that other goals in life are still available. When used in this type of research, the analogue is no longer merely a tool for demonstrating the obvious. It becomes a vehicle for modeling theories and suggesting recommendations for possible use in such settings as hospitals and rehabilitation centers, where clients experience important personal losses. A major purpose of this report is to encourage such undertakings.

REFERENCES

Altshuler, K. Z. (1970). Reaction to and management of sensory loss: Blindness and deafness. In B. Schoenberg, A. C. Carr, D. Peretz, & A. H. Kutscher (Eds.), *Loss and grief: Psychological management in medical practice* (pp. 140–155). New York: Columbia University Press.

Blacher, R. S. (1970). Reactions to chronic illness. In B. Schoenberg, A. C. Carr, D, Peretz, & A. H. Kutscher (Eds.), *Loss and grief: Psychological management in medical practice* (pp. 189–198). New York: Columbia University Press.

Dembo, T., Leviton, G. L., & Wright, B. A. (1975). Adjustment to misfortune: A problem of social psychological rehabilitation. *Rehabilitation Psychology, 22*, 1–100. (Originally published in *Artificial Limbs,* 1956, *3*, 4-62.)

Orfirer, A. P. (1970). Loss of sexual function in the male. In B. Schoenberg, A. C. Carr, D. Peretz, & A. H. Kutscher (Eds.), *Loss and grief: Psychological management in medical practice* (pp. 156–177). New York: Columbia University Press.

Romm, M. E. (1970). Loss of sexual function in the female. In B. Schoenberg, A. C. Carr, D. Peretz, & A. H. Kutscher (Eds.), *Loss and grief: Psychological management in medical practice* (pp. 178–188). New York: Columbia University Press.

Schoenberg, B., Carr, A. C., Kutscher, A. H., & Goldberg, I. (Eds.), (1974). *Anticipatory grief.* New York: Columbia University Press.

Schoenberg, B., Carr, A. C., Peretz, D., & Kutscher, A. H. (Eds.). (1970). *Psychological management in medical practice.* New York: Columbia University Press.

Shontz, F. C. (1965). *Research methods in personality.* New York: Appleton-Century-Crofts.

Shontz, F. C. (1975). *The psychological aspects of physical illness and disability.* New York: Macmillan.

Shontz, F. C. (1980). Theories about the adjustment to having a disability. In W. Cruickshank (Ed.), *Psychology of exceptional children and youth* (4th ed., pp. 3–44). Englewood Cliffs, NJ: Prentice-Hall.

Trieschmann, R. (1980). *Spinal-cord injuries: Psychological, social and vocational adjustment.* New York: Pergamon Press.

Wright, B. A. (1960). *Physical disability: A psychological approach.* New York: Harper & Row.

Wright, B. A. (1964). Spread in adjustment to disability. *Bulletin of the Menninger Clinic, 28*, 198–208.

Wright, B. A. (1967). Issues in overcoming barriers to adjustment in the handicapped. *Rehabilitation Counseling Bulletin, 11*, 53–59.

6

Disability and Identity: A Study of Identity Patterns in Adolescents with Hearing Impairments

Nancy Weinberg and
Mary Sterritt

ABSTRACT: Some children with physical disabilities are encouraged to identify exclusively with nondisabled persons, relinquishing any identity with others who have disabilities. This study was conducted to examine the implications of such a personal identification on adjustment. An instrument measuring identity choice was developed and administered to 111 students at a state school for persons with hearing impairments. Based on questionnaire responses, students were classified into three groups: those with a predominant hearing identity (able-bodied identity), those with a primary deaf identity (disabled identity), and those who identified with both groups (dual identity). Analyses focused on the relationship between the students' identity and indicators of the students' social relations, self-evaluations, academic achievement, and perceived family acceptance of their disability. The data indicated that an able-bodied identity was consistently associated with poorer outcomes and a dual identity with better outcomes.

Many parents of children with physical disabilities would like to have their children develop a primary identification with the able-bodied world (Schowe, 1979). Parents of children with disabilities know that society views people with disabilities as less acceptable, and that people with disabilities have difficulty in establishing satisfying social relationships and obtaining jobs (Wright, 1983). To improve their children's chances of succeeding, parents may encourage their children to appear, and to behave, as able-bodied as possible. To the extent that their children can "pass" as able-bodied, these parents believe that the likelihood of their children's being accepted and succeeding is increased (Ayrault, 1964).

Moreover, setting forth the goal of appearing as able-bodied as possible, parents argue, motivates their children to engage in persistent self-improvement (Ayrault, 1963). Without the goal of being accepted as part of able-bodied society, children might be satisfied with a more awkward gait, or a less pleasant-sounding voice.

Finally, if children with disabilities identify with and succeed in being a part of the able-bodied world, the parents' place in the able-bodied world is less disturbed. If, however, parents have children who are unacceptable to able-bodied society, this reflects negatively on them, for they inevitably share their children's negative social identity (Spradley & Spradley, 1973).

But there may be the potential for some negative consequences when parents encourage their children with disabilities to identify primarily with the able-bodied (Michaux, 1970; Weinberg, 1982; Wright, 1983). For example, to pass as able-bodied, children may be encouraged to eliminate as much as possible the visible effects of their disability, even if this leads to poorer functioning. For example, even though visually impaired children might move more easily with a cane, they may be encouraged not to use one, since the presence of a cane immediately labels them as blind. Similarly, hearing impaired people might be able to communicate more effectively using sign language, but may be encouraged not to use sign language, for it identifies them as deaf. In each case, the effort is to hide the disability or even to deny that it exists. The goal is *not* improved functioning, but instead functioning in the most able-bodied way possible.

In stressing the importance of "passing" as able-bodied, parents may also communicate that being able-bodied is good and being disabled is bad (Ayrault, 1963; Michaux, 1970; Weinberg, 1982; Wright, 1983). Children with disabilities are thus being told, "As you are, you are inferior, and to the extent that you can emulate able-bodied people, this is the extent to which you can overcome your inferiority." Yet achieving full able-bodied status is inherently impossible, so children with disabilities may be condemned always to feel inferior, always to work to cover up their deficiencies, and always to be on guard lest their disabilities show. They can rarely be at ease with who they are.

The primary purpose of the present research was to determine whether an able-bodied identity is associated with more positive or more negative outcomes, as compared with a disabled identity or with a dual identity (in which they identify with both the able-bodied and the disabled world). Persons with hearing impairments, as opposed to people with other disabilities, were selected for study, since identity issues are especially important for people with hearing impairments. More than any other disability group, those with hearing impairments have developed their own separate communities. Thus, the potential for fully identifying with a disability group is greater for them than for any other disability group.

METHOD

Subjects

Participants were 111 high-school students at a state school for people with hearing impairments. Of the sample, 31% were freshmen, 38% sophomores, 20% juniors, and 6% seniors. The number of seniors was limited, because testing was done during free periods, and many seniors were involved in work assignments or were in special classes during these times. The participants ranged in age from 15 to 19 years, with a mean age of 17 years, 2 months. Of the group, 51 were females and 60 were males; 19 of the students were black and the rest were white. Only 9 students lived at home, and the remainder were in residence at the school. The school accepts students from the preschool to the highschool levels. On the average, participants had attended the school for 6 years, 4 months, with a modal attendance time of 5 years.

In terms of their degree of deafness, 1 student had a mild hearing loss, 4 had a moderate loss, 16 had a severe loss, and 87 had a profound hearing loss; information on degree of deafness was not available for the remaining 4 students. The cause of deafness was listed on school records as "other" and "unknown" for 45 students, rubella for 39 students, meningitis for 10 students, and heredity for 13 students; again, data were missing for 4 participants. Eighty-eight students, or over 79% of the sample, had been deaf since birth, and the mean age of onset for those who became deaf at a later age was 21 months.

Only 26 of the students came from families in which other members had hearing losses. Approximately 41% of the parents communicated with their children using mainly oral methods, and approximately 34% used mainly manual methods; information about the method of parent-child communication was not available for about 25% of the sample. The school itself advocated total communication. Of the 21 high-school teachers, 8 were deaf.

Instruments

Deaf Identity Scale. A Deaf Identity Scale was developed specifically for this study. It was composed of three subscales—Hearing Identification, Deaf Identification, and Dual Identification. Each of the subscales included five statements which asked about the individual's desire to associate with, and their assumed similarity with, either deaf, hearing, or both groups. Students responded to each of the 15 statements by indicating whether it was true or false for them. Table 6.1 presents the items on the Deaf Identity Scale.

Scores were computed for each subscale by summing responses to items on that scale. Cronbach's alpha was used to test the internal consistency of each of the subscales. Results indicated reliability estimates of .72 for the Dual Identification subscale, .50 for the Deaf Identification subscale, and .60 for the Hearing Identification subscale.

Social Relationship Satisfaction Scale. An adapted form of the Social Relationship Satisfaction Scale (Asher, Hymel, & Renshaw, 1984; Asher & Wheeler, 1985) was administered to measure the extent to which the respondents felt satisfied with their peer relations. The scale was revised so that the items could be easily read and understood by deaf students. The revised scale consisted of 25 items, 16 asking respondents to rate how well they got along with other students and 9 serving as filler items. Respondents rated each item on a 5-point scale ranging from "always true" to "never true" Table 6.2 lists the 16 scored items in this questionnaire. The reported internal consistency for the Social Relationship Satisfaction Scale is .90 (Asher & Wheeler, 1985).

Evaluation of Self as a Deaf Person Scale. This scale, consisting of four truefalse items, was devised to measure how students felt about being deaf and their evaluation of themselves as deaf persons. The four items were as follows:

1. I'd be a much better person if I could hear.
2. Because I am deaf, I cannot do important things in life.
3. Because I am deaf, I can't help other people.
4. Being deaf upsets me and I can't enjoy myself.

The Cronbach alpha measuring internal consistency was .22 for this scale.

Perceived Family Acceptance Measure. Perceived family acceptance was measured by a single true-false item: "My family would love me more if I could hear."

Procedure

Questionnaires were administered during free class periods. It was explained that the questionnaires were part of a research project being conducted through the University of Illinois-Urbana-Champaign, and that the study focused on the perceptions of deaf adolescents. Students were also told that there were no right or wrong answers. All directions were given in total communication. Practice

Table 6.1 The Deaf Identity Subscale Items

Hearing Identification Subscale
I would rather have hearing friends.
I am more like hearing people than deaf people.
One day I will be able to hear.
When I get married, it will be to a hearing person.
I like people to think I am hearing.

Deaf Identification Subscale
I would rather have only deaf friends.
In the future I hope to have only deaf neighbors.
I'd rather be around deaf people only.
When I work, I hope it is around deaf people only.
When I get married it will be to a deaf person.

Dual Identification Subscale
It's important to have both hearing and deaf friends.
It doesn't matter if I work around deaf or hearing people or both.
It doesn't matter if I marry a deaf or a hearing person.
I would rather have both deaf and hearing friends.
When I have children, I don't care if they are deaf or hearing.

items were provided, and students were encouraged to ask to have any parts of the questionnaire signed or words defined if they had any questions. Eight students requested sign-language interpretation of the written items. The approximate time for completion of the questionnaires was 20 minutes.

RESULTS

Each participant's primary identity was determined by comparing his or her total score on the Deaf Identification, Hearing Identification, and Dual Identification subscales. The subscale on which a participant received the highest score was identified as his or her primary identity. It was found that a majority of the sample (58%) had a dual identification. Next, but lagging quite a bit behind, was a deaf identity (24%), followed by a hearing identification (18%). The next set of analyses examined the relationship of primary identity with academic performance, social relations, personal evaluations, and perceived family attitudes.

Academic Achievement

Academic achievement was measured by the type of program students were placed in by the school. Students achieving well were placed in an academic program, while those achieving at a lower level were placed in a general program. Approximately 64% of the participants were in the academic track and 36% in the general program.

The majority of students with a primary hearing identity were in the general program; only 35.9% of this group were in the academic program. Students with a primary identity as deaf were doing somewhat better academically, with 45.8% of this group in the academic track. Students with a dual identification were, by

Table 6.2 Items on the Social Relationship Satisfaction Scale

---

It's easy for me to make new friends at school.

No one will talk to me in class.

I can work with other students in class.

It's hard for me to make friends at school.

I have many friends in my class.

I feel alone at school.

My friends will help me when I need help.

Other students do not like me.

No one will play with me at school.

I get along with my classmates.

Other students will not let me join their group.

When I need help in school I cannot find any kids to help me.

I don't get along with other kids in school.

I'm lonely at school.

Kids in my class like me.

I don't have any friends in class.

---

far, doing best academically; over 80% of the people with a primary dual identity were in the academic program.

A chi-square analysis was performed comparing the students' primary identity (deaf, dual or hearing) with achievement level (academic or general). This analysis revealed a significant relationship between identity categories and academic placements, with those students having a dual identity showing a greater proportion of academic placements and those with a hearing identity showing a greater proportion of general placements, $\chi^2 = 18.697$, $p < .01$.

Social Adjustment

Next, the relationship between identity and social adjustment was examined. Student scores on the Social Relationship Satisfaction Scale were divided using a median-split procedure, thereby grouping students as having either good or poor peer relations.

It was found that a small percentage (25%) of those with a primary hearing identity viewed themselves as having good peer relationships. In contrast, 33.3% of those with a primary deaf identity, and 57.8% of those with a primary dual identity, considered themselves to have positive peer interactions. A chi-square analysis indicated that having a hearing identity was significantly associated with poorer peer relationships and a dual identity with better relationships, $\chi^2 = 8.891$, $p < 05$.

Evaluation of Self as a Deaf Person

As noted earlier, the Evaluation of Self as a Deaf Person Scale was designed to assess how deaf students felt about themselves as deaf people. Again, a median-split procedure was used on this scale, and students were divided into two groups—those who felt more positively about being deaf, and those who felt more negatively. The pattern of results was similar to the earlier patterns. Whereas only 42.1% of those with a hearing identification had positive evaluations of themselves as deaf persons, 64% of those with a deaf identity, and 82.8% of those with a dual identity, had positive evaluations of themselves. The chi-square analysis indicated that a hearing identity was associated with the poorest self evaluation and a dual identity with the most favorable self-evaluation, $\chi^2 = 12.71$, $p < .01$.

Perceived Family Acceptance

In response to the true-false item, "My family would love me more if I could hear," 51% of the sample responded "false" and 45.9% said "true" It certainly seems disturbing that almost half of the sample felt that their deafness limited the love or acceptance they received.

The extent to which respondents felt accepted varied with their dominant identity. The same pattern emerged on this variable as on the others. Of those with a predominant hearing identity, 85% indicated that their families would love them more if they could hear. Of the students with a deaf identity, 59.3% reported that their families would love them more if they could hear. Finally, greatest family acceptance was reported by students who had a dual identity. Among this group, only 28.1% indicated that their families would love them more if they were able to hear. Perceived family acceptance was very strongly related to identity, $\chi^2 =$ 22.39, p <.001.

Additional Analyses

Additional analyses were conducted to examine the relationship of certain demographic variables (obtained from school records) and identity. Chi-square tests were used to examine the relationship between the students' identity choices and the students' degree of deafness (moderate, severe, or profound), etiology of deafness (genetic, rubella, meningitis, or encephalitis), onset of deafness (infancy or early childhood), and sex (male or female). Also examined using the chi-square was the association of type of identity with the presence or absence of other family members who were deaf, and with the parents' use of oral or manual methods when communicating with their children. Nonsignificant chi-squares were found in all of these analyses.

DISCUSSION

The results of the present study are quite clear. A predominant hearing identity was consistently associated with poorer outcomes in terms of academic placement, social relationships, personal adjustment, and perceived family acceptance. Deaf identities were related to somewhat better outcomes than hearing identities, but dual identities were associated with the best outcomes on all of the measures used.

It is impossible to know whether adopting a dual identity helped to bring about more positive outcomes or whether students experiencing better social, academic, personal, and family interactions were more likely to develop a dual identity. Nonetheless, the data do suggest that it may be ill advised to encourage individuals with hearing impairments to identify primarily with hearing people or deaf people. It would appear that encouraging an identity with both groups is advisable.

Why does an able-bodied identity appear to have such negative impact? It may well be that encouraging an identity primarily with able-bodied peers communicates the idea that a disabled identity is an inferior identity—an identity to be shed in favor of a more valuable able-bodied identity. This communication may lead disabled children to feel less acceptance from their parents, less acceptance of themselves as deaf persons, and less comfort with their deaf peers (Wright, 1983). These negative feelings may, in turn, result in poorer academic performance. In contrast, a dual identity may result in a more positive identity, for it does not expressly reject either the disabled world or the able-bodied world. Instead, the disabled person is encouraged to feel part of both worlds, and therefore is encouraged to pursue a wider range of acceptable behavior and social mobility.

Future research in this area might explore whether these results can be replicated with mainstreamed deaf children and whether similar findings will occur with other types of disabilities. Future research is also needed to improve the measures developed for use in the present study (the Deaf Identity Scale, the Evaluation of Self as a Deaf Person Scale, and the Perceived Family Acceptance measure). The Evaluation of Self as a Deaf Person Scale is particularly problematic, since it consists of only four items, and all of these are worded with a negative bias toward deafness. New items need to be added to this instrument, and a balancing of positive and negative items needs to be established. Furthermore, the one-item Perceived Family Acceptance should be developed into a multi-item scale so that it can measure degrees of perceived family acceptance. However, the consistency of findings across measures in the present study provides encouragement for further inquiry into the potential consequences of social identity for individuals with disabilities.

REFERENCES

Asher, S. R., Hymel, S., & Renshaw, P. D. (1984). Loneliness in children. *Child Development, 55*, 1457-1464.

Asher, S. R., & Wheeler, V. A. (1985). Children's loneliness: A comparison of rejected and neglected children. *Journal of Consulting and Clinical Psychology, 53* , 500–505.

Ayrault, E. W. (1963). *Take one step.* Garden City, NY: Doubleday.

Ayrault, E. W. (1964). *You can raise your handicapped child.* New York: Putnam.

Michaux, L. A. (1970). *The physically handicapped and the community.* Springfield, IL: Charles C. Thomas.

Schowe, B. M. (1979). *Identity crisis in deafness: A humanistic perspective.* Tempe, AZ: The Scholars Press.

Spradley, T. S., & Spradley, J. P. (1978). *Deaf like me.* New York: Random House.

Weinberg, N. (1982). Growing up physically disabled: Factors in the evaluation of disability. *Rehabilitation Counseling Bulletin, 25*, 219-227.

Wright, B. A. (1983). *Physical disability: A psychosocial approach* (2nd ed.). New York: Harper & Row.

7

Prediction of Long-Term Survival of Persons with Spinal Cord Injury: An 11-Year Prospective Study

James S. Krause and
Nancy M. Crewe

ABSTRACT: A significant proportion of deaths among persons with spinal cord injury (SCI) have been attributed to self-neglect and suicide. Research-ers have speculated that poor personal adjustment is linked to preventable death, but data have not been gathered prior to recorded deaths to verify this link. The purpose of the present study was to use the answers on question-naires from a 1974 survey to compare the adjustment of persons who were still alive in 1985 (N =179) with those known to have died by 1985 (N =46). The results showed that survivors were rated as having better psychosocial and vocational adjustment, were more socially active, had a greater tolerance for sitting, and were more likely to be working or attending school. None of the items on the questionnaire that were related to recent medical history or life satisfaction discriminated between the two groups. The findings point to the need for more intensive psychological rehabilitation and for an expansion of counseling to include social skills training.

A spinal cord injury (SCI) occurs suddenly and has an immediate impact on all areas of the individual's physical and emotional functioning. Since World War II, great strides in medical care have enabled people to live for years and even decades with this disability, and researchers have become concerned with identify-ing factors related to the length of survival and causes of death following injury.

In a series of studies (Breithaupt, Jousse, & Wynne-Jones, 1961; Geisler, Jousse, & Wynne-Jones, 1977; Geisler, Jousse, Wynne-Jones, & Breithaupt, 1983; Jousse, Wynne-Jones, & Breithaupt, 1968), researchers at Toronto's Lyndhurst Hospital traced all SCI patients discharged between 1945 and 1980 to determine the relative mortality rate and causes of death. They reported significantly higher death rates among SCI patients than among persons in the general population of similar age and gender. They also noted much higher mortality rates among persons who were older and quadriplegic and had complete injuries.

Significant decreases in mortality were noted for groups with complete paraplegia and quadriplegia from the initial period (1945-58) to the most recent period studied (1973-80). The percentage of deaths from renal complications decreased over the years, while deaths related to suicide and alcohol-related liver damage increased. Evidence from another recent study (Le & Price, 1982) also suggested significantly greater-than-expected mortality rates among SCI patients, but no differences between paraplegics and quadriplegics were identified. The study's authors calculated the duration of survival to be 110.5 months following injury for all deceased subjects. Most deaths were due to cardiovascular dysfunction, not renal complications.

Three decades ago, Seymour (1955) first observed that many deaths following SCI could have been prevented with responsible self-care. Seymour termed these deaths "physiological suicide," suggesting a link among emotional health, self-care, and survival. Evidence from more recent research (Nyquist & Bors, 1967) indicates that at least 67% of all deaths among persons with SCI are related to the injury itself (22% unrelated, 11% undetermined). Suicides accounted for 8.1% of all deaths. Wilcox and Stauffer (1972) found 9 of 50 deaths (18%) in their study to be due to suicide. Drugs and alcohol (four cases) and multiple pressure sores (four cases) accounted for another 16% of the deaths.

Although these studies collectively suggest a link between poor emotional adjustment and high mortality rate following SCI, they are based on retrospective analyses of the causes of death. Poor emotional adjustment is inferred from the cause of death rather than from any objective measures of personality or emotional health.

Price (1973) found evidence of the relationship between personal maladjustment and preventable death in a small number (n = 11) of persons with SCI. She based her conclusions on case histories and cited the scores on the Minnesota Multiphasic Personality Inventory for some persons but not for others. However, she did not have access to the same information on each subject and may have had knowledge of the cause of death before reviewing a case history, which raises the question of unintentional selective bias. Prospective research that generates objective data on personal adjustment before death is needed to establish firmly the link between emotional health and survival suggested by these retrospective studies.

The purpose of the study presented here was to use the responses of 256 persons with SCI to a 1974 survey in order to compare the psychosocial, vocational, and medical adjustment of those persons who survived their injuries with those who had died by 1985. Comparisons of the responses of persons in the survivor group with those who were known to be dead, it was believed, would help identify differential adjustment patterns related to survival. Two main hypotheses were suggested by previous research:

Hypothesis 1: Persons in the survival group will have superior psychosocial and medical adjustment when compared with persons who are known to have died since the 1974 survey. (Previous research did not establish a precedent for a hypothesis on vocational adjustment.)

Hypothesis 2: Medical adjustment will be more central to survival than either psychosocial or vocational adjustment.

In contrast to previous research, the results of the present study were based on identical objective data obtained from all subjects before the determination of their survival status. Bias from selective recall, therefore, was not of concern. Because no data are presented on the cause of death, any differences obtained from comparisons of the survivor group and those who died will apply to all deaths, not just to deaths for which a preventable cause can be identified.

METHOD

Subjects

The Life Situation Questionnaire (LSQ) was developed in 1974 and mailed to 301 persons with SCI. All the subjects had traumatic injuries, had been injured at least two years before, and had participated in the Renal Function Studies program at the University of Minnesota Hospital. Of the initial sample, 256 persons returned questionnaires (85%). Eighty-two percent of the subjects were male, and 54% had cervical lesions. The average age at the time of injury was 25.2 years, and the average age at the time of the survey was 35.1 years; the average duration of the injury was 9.7 years. Most persons were single (51.2%); 37% were married; and 12% were divorced, widowed, or separated. Less than half the subjects (41%) were working, and 22% were attending school. Most persons were living with their spouses (36%), with parents or other relatives (25%), in nursing homes (14%), or alone (12%).

Procedures

In 1985, revised questionnaires were sent to all subjects. Follow-up telephone calls were made to all the subjects who did not return their questionnaires to determine if they were still alive. Attempts were made to call their next of kin or any telephone number listed in the patients' charts. In addition, state death records were checked for the years 1974-85.

Of the original 256 subjects, 179 were known to be alive, 46 were known to be dead, and 31 could not be located. Subjects in the deceased group had lived an average of 16.9 years following injury, and the average age at the time of death was 53.4 years. Because many of the subjects had moved to different parts of the country before their death, the results of autopsies and hospital records were not consistently available, which made it impossible to do an accurate analysis of the deaths.

Instruments

The LSQ was designed to elicit mostly objective information regarding a broad range of behaviors relevant to psychological, social, vocational, and medical adjustment. Some items required subjects to rate aspects of their lives (satisfaction, overall adjustment) on a 5- or 10-point scale, while other items required numerical estimates of certain behaviors, such as hours per week spent in various activities. In some cases, numerical frequencies were grouped into four categories (e.g., 1 to 4; 5 to 8; 9 to 12; more than 12) to improve the reliability of responses and to minimize missing data. Other items were open ended and elicited more qualitative information, such as organizational affiliation.

In 1974, three sets of outcome measures were derived from the LSQ. First, three psychologists read the complete questionnaires and rated each individual's psychosocial, vocational, and medical adjustment on a 3-point continuum (good = 1, average = 2, poor = 3). This procedure was used to synthesize all information on the questionnaire, including items that could not easily be combined psychometrically and items that did not apply equally to all subjects (e.g., open-ended questions on such topics as organizational membership and questions on frequency of dating and work hours, since some subjects were married or unemployed). Average interrater agreement across the three adjustment areas was 84%.

Second, indexes of social activity, medical stability, and life satisfaction were generated by combining items with a homogeneous content and format. The social activity index combined three items (frequency of visitors, frequency of social outings, and tolerance for sitting), each of which required the subject to report the frequency of quantitative behaviors that had been grouped into 4-point scales. The medical stability index was generated by combining another set of items, including the frequency of nonroutine visits to physicians, the frequency of hospitalizations, and the number of days the subject had been hospitalized in the past two years. The third index combined six 5-point Likert-type items regarding satisfaction with living arrangements, employment, finances, social life, sex life, and general health.

The final set of outcome measures was individual items, including all items used to generate the activity, medical, and satisfaction indexes. In addition, two items required the subjects to rate their overall adjustment on a 10-point ladder and to predict their adjustment five years into the future. Present work and school status were also used as categorical outcome variables.

Analyses

In the first set of analyses, chi-square and t-test statistics were used to compare the survivor and deceased groups on basic demographic and injury-related variables, such as age, duration of injury, and age at onset of injury. Pearson product moment correlations were then calculated between these variables and the outcome variables. Differences between the groups on metric outcome variables were then assessed using an analysis of covariance (ANACOVA). Age and age at onset were used as covariates on the basis of their correlations with the outcome measures and the large differences between the survivor and deceased groups on these variables. Nonmetric outcome variables were assessed using chi-square.

RESULTS

Demographic Variables

Chi-square comparisons revealed no differences between groups for gender, $\chi^2 <$ $(1, N = 225) = .00$, n.s., or marital status, $\chi^2\, 2\, (4, N = 225) = 6.88$, n.s. Significantly more paraplegics were in the deceased group (63%) than in the survivor group (41%), $\chi^2\, (1, N = 225) = 7.32$, $p < .01$. Survivors were younger ($M = 32$ years) at the time of the 1974 study than were those who died ($M = 48$ years), $t\,(215) = 7.07$, $p < .001$. They were also younger at the time of their injury ($M = 23$ years) than were those in the deceased group ($M = 36$ years), $t\,(215) = 6.56$, $p < .001$. No significant differences were observed between the groups on the duration of SCI (survivor group $M = 9.6$ years, deceased group $M = 11.0$ years), $t\,(223) = 1.14$, n.s.

In addition to discriminating significantly between the groups, both age variables were significantly correlated with several important outcome variables as well as with each other ($+.86$, $p < .001$). Significant correlations were observed between age at onset and ratings of psychosocial adjustment ($+.20$, $p < .01$), vocational adjustment ($+.19$, $p < .01$), the social activity index ($-.37$, $p < .001$), and several individual items. A similar pattern was observed for age at the time of the survey and psychosocial adjustment ($+.15$, $p < .05$), vocational adjustment ($+.18$, $p < .01$), and the social activity index ($-.34$, $p < .001$).

Analysis of Metric Variables

ANACOVA was performed on all metric variables. The effects of the covariates (age and age at onset) were assessed jointly before the main effects were evaluated. The main effects were then adjusted for the covariates.

The presentation of results is hierarchical, with variables containing the most information discussed first and the least important items presented last. Therefore, the judges' ratings are discussed first, followed by the indexes of social activity, medical stability, and life satisfaction. Comparisons using individual items are presented last.

The results of the ANACOVA show significant differences favoring the survivor groups on two of three adjustment areas and in combined ratings (see Table 7.1). Survivors were judged to have superior vocational ($F\,[1,208] = 7.52$,

Table 7.1 Analysis of Covariance Results: Psychologists' Ratings of Adjustment

Rating	Adjusted Means[a]		Covariates		Main Effects	
	Survivors	Deceased	F	df	F	df
Psychosocial	1.64	1.85	4.09	2,208*	3.95	1,208*
Vocational	1.60	1.90	4.57	2,208**	7.52	1,208**
Medical	1.66	1.86	.69	2,208	2.71	1,208
Average overall rating	1.63	1.91	4.05	2,208*	11.64	1,208***

[a] 1 = good; 2 = fair; 3 = poor.
*$p < .05$; **$p < .01$; ***$p < .001$.

$p < .01$) and, to a lesser extent, psychosocial adjustment (F [1,208] = 3.95, $p < .05$) than those in the deceased group. A trend in the same direction was noted for medical adjustment (F [1,208] = 2.71, n.s.), but it failed to reach significance. The combined rating across adjustment areas shows that the judges clearly rated the overall adjustment (F [1,2081 = 11.64, $p < .001$) of the survivors as superior to that of the persons who died since the 1974 survey. The covariates did not significantly affect the ratings of medical adjustment.

Less impressive results were obtained from the ANACOVA with the three indexes generated from combinations of objective items. As can be seen from Table 7.2, only social activity significantly differed between groups, with the difference again favoring the survivors (F[1,203] = 10.37, $p < .001$). The covariates were also significant for social activity (F [2, 203] 18.76, $p < .001$) but not for either medical stability or life satisfaction.

Of the 12 individual items used to generate these indexes, only two were significant. Persons in the survivor group left their homes significantly more than

Table 7.2 Analysis of Covariance Results: Questionnaire Items and Combined Indexes

Combined Indexes	Adjusted Means		Covariates		Main Effects	
	Survivors	Deceased	F	df	F	df
Social activity[a]	9.31	8.07	18.76	2,203***	10.37	1,203***
Medical stability	2.81	2.56	.41	2,198	.69	1,198
Life satisfaction	14.86	15.53	1.24	2,152	.31	1,152
Individual Items						
Visitors[a]	3.09	3.04	1.58	2,212	.08	1,212
Outings[a]	3.05	2.32	16.06	2,210***	15.69	1,210***
Tolerance for sitting[a]	3.20	2.82	14.99	2,207***	4.88	1,207*
Times hospitalized	.66	.81	.17	2,212	1.49	1,212
Days hospitalized	1.09	1.49	.17	2,199	2.73	1,199
Physicians' visits	1.11	1.01	.91	2,211	.31	1,211
Years of education[a]	13.00	12.65	24.37	2,151***	.44	1,151
Satisfaction Ratings						
Living arrangement	1.80	2.12	1.09	2,207	2.66	2,207
Employment	2.84	3.14	3.74	2,163*	.85	1,163
Finances	2.85	2.99	2.80	2,208	.28	1,208
Social life	2.15	2.18	.01	2,205	.02	1,205
Sex life	2.99	3.13	2.15	2,187	.22	1,187
General health	2.35	2.36	1.03	2,209	.00	1,209
Adjustment Ratings						
Present[a]	7.45	7.02	5.83	2,203**	.92	1,203
Future[a]	8.05	8.35	10.86	2,187***	.43	1,187

[a] For these items, a higher score is better.
*$p < .05$; **$p < .01$; ***$p < .001$.

did persons in the deceased group (F [1, 210] = 15.69, p <.001) and had a greater tolerance for sitting (F [1, 207] = 4.88, p <.05). No differences were noted in the frequency of visitors, the number or length of medical treatments, or satisfaction with any of the six life areas. The covariates accounted for a significant portion of the variance in the frequency of social outings (F [2, 210] = 16.06, p < .001), tolerance for sitting (F [2, 207] = 14.99, p <.001), and satisfaction with employment (F [2, 163] = 3.74, p < .05). Finally, none of the comparisons for the other three items (self-rated overall adjustment, predicted future adjustment, and years of education) reached significance, although the covariates were significant in each case.

Vocational and Educational Status

It is not possible to use ANACOVA with categorical outcome variables, such as work and school status. An alternative procedure would involve dichotomizing the deceased and survivor groups on the basis of age and then performing separate chi-square analyses on the older and younger subgroups. Considering the small number of subjects in the deceased sample (N = 46), the only feasible way to form subgroups would be to separate them in a manner that would leave an approximately equal number of subjects in each deceased subgroup. When groups were divided at the mean of the deceased subgroup, only 17 survivors fell into the older category. Age differences, although reduced, were still present. Therefore, a single chi-square analysis was performed on the full sample for each categorical variable.

Significant differences between groups were observed for both work (χ^2 <[1, N = 224] = 5.07, p < .05) and school status (χ^2 < [1, N = 221] = 6.09, p < .05). Only 26% of the deceased subjects were working in 1974, compared with 44% of the survivors. Similarly, 9% of the deceased group were in school in 1974, compared with 26% of the survivors.

DISCUSSION

The results of the present study provide strong empirical support for the existence of a relationship between personal adjustment and survival following SCI. Persons who were more vocationally and socially active were more likely to have survived the 11 years following the initial survey. The most consistent evidence of differences between the survivor and deceased groups came from the judges' ratings of vocational and psychosocial adjustment. In addition, analyses of scales combining objective items also indicated differences in social activity favoring the survivors. These relationships persisted following the statistical control of systematic variations between the groups in age and age at onset of SCI. Differences between groups in work and school status were also present, but these findings are confounded, to an undetermined degree, by concomitant differences in age.

It is surprising that none of the six life-satisfaction items used in the study was significantly related to survival. It is particularly interesting that ratings of satisfaction with social life, sex life, and employment were not lower in the deceased group, because these persons were rated as having poorer psychosocial and vocational adjustment, left their homes less frequently for outings, and had a shorter tolerance for sitting than did the survivors. Perhaps persons in the deceased group had come to accept a less active life-style with a lower quality of life. It follows, then, that activity level per se, rather than a mediating emotional state, enhances survival following SCI.

Contrary to the authors' expectations, no evidence was obtained to suggest that recent medical history was predictive of survival. The judges' ratings, the medical stability index, and individual items related to the frequency and duration of medical treatments within the two years before the survey all failed to differentiate significantly between the survivor group and the deceased group.

Three possible explanations can be offered for these findings. First, many deaths may not follow a general decline in health. Some types of respiratory problems, heart attacks, and other cardiovascular complications are prevalent and would not easily be predicted by recent medical history. Although these deaths are generally not regarded as preventable, it is possible that a sedentary life-style may actually be a contributory factor. There is also a substantial number of suicides following SCIs (Wilcox & Stauffer, 1972). It is more likely that these deaths would be related to personal maladjustment than to medical complications.

A second explanation is that persons with a less active life-style and a poorer overall adjustment may have medical problems but not seek treatment for them. This explanation is especially likely for deaths that have traditionally been viewed as preventable. In such cases, untreated medical complications may coexist with poor psychosocial and vocational adjustment and have an undetected contributory effect on death.

One final explanation for the lack of an observed relationship between medical adjustment and survival is methodological. The questions used to measure medical adjustment (the number of nonroutine visits to physicians, the number of hospitalizations, and the number of days hospitalized in the past two years) may not have measured a broad enough range of behaviors to discriminate between the survivor group and the deceased group. This possibility seems unlikely, given the focused nature of items related to social activity and vocational adjustment that did detect group membership.

Overall, the results of the present study establish a strong link between personal adjustment and survival following an SCI. This link does not appear to be bound to age, duration of injury, or a mediating emotional state of dissatisfaction. These findings suggest a possible contributory relationship between inactivity and certain types of death; such a relationship, however, must await further verification.

Future research should step beyond the scope of this project and attempt to define which specific elements of adjustment are linked to various types of death. Such research would require prospective methodology utilizing an expanded survey of the different adjustment areas, including family relationships and chemical dependence. Personality inventories and other psychometric instruments would be helpful. Furthermore, it would be necessary to obtain consistent data on the causes of death to test the hypothesis of a causal link between personal adjustment and survival.

Traditionally, rehabilitation has been concerned mainly with maximizing general health and physical independence and returning the individual to gainful employment. Counseling has been viewed as secondary to medical treatment and has been focused on helping individuals to accept their injuries and increase their satisfaction with life. Less emphasis has been placed on increasing social skills and sexual functioning. The results of the study presented here suggest that the importance of psychosocial rehabilitation needs to be underscored and that it should be even more closely integrated with medical services. Counseling must go beyond facilitating emotional adjustment to teach the skills that persons with disabilities need to become active participants in life. The psychological services received during rehabilitation may influence survival itself.

REFERENCES

Breithaupt, D. J., Jousse, A. T., & Wynne-Jones, M. (1961). Late cause of death and life expectancy in paraplegia. *Canadian Medical Association Journal, 85*, 73–77.

Geisler, W. O., Jousse, A. T., & Wynne-Jones, M. (1977). Survival in traumatic transverse myelitis. *Paraplegia, 15*, 262–275.

Geisler, W. O., Jousse, A. T., Wynne-Jones, & Breithaupt, D. (1983). Survival in traumatic spinal cord injury. *Paraplegia, 21*, 364–373.

Jousse, A. T., Wynne-Jones, M., & Breithaupt, D. J. (1968). A follow-up study of life expectancy and mortality in traumatic transverse myelitis. *Canadian Medical Association Journal, 98*, 770–772.

Le, C. T., & Price, M. (1982). Survival from spinal cord injury. *Journal of Chronic Diseases, 35*, 487–492.

Nyquist, R. H. & Bors, E. (1967). Mortality and survival in traumatic myelopathy during nineteen years, from 1946 to 1965. *Paraplegia, 5*, 22–48.

Price, M. (1973). Causes of death in 11 of 227 patients with traumatic spinal cord injury over a period of nine years. *Paraplegia, 11*, 217–220.

Seymour, C. (1955). Personality and paralysis: 1. Comparative adjustment of paraplegics and quadriplegics. *Archives of Physical Medicine and Rehabilitation, 36*, 691–694.

Wilcox, N. E., & Stauffer, E. S. (1972). Follow-up of 423 consecutive patients admitted to the Spinal Cord Centre, Rancho Los Amigos Hospital, 1 January to 31 December, 1967. *International Journal of Paraplegia, 10*, 115–122.

Acknowledgment: This study was supported, in part, by Grant FSW-93-84 from the Minnesota Medical Foundation.

8

Disability, Psychopathology, and Vocational Adjustment

Daniel W. Cook

ABSTRACT: Using configural decision rules concerning Mini-Mult scores, 286 rehabilitation center clients were sorted by gender into three groups: adjusted, possibly maladjusted, and probably maladjusted. Type and severity of physical disability was not related to adjustment group membership. Psychological disability was related to psychopathology, although the strength of the relationship was less than expected. There were no significant relationships between male psychological status and center outcome, rehabilitation agency outcome, or vocational adjustment at follow-up. Female psychological status was not related to agency outcome or vocational adjustment at follow-up, but was related to center outcome. Female psychological group membership was a more accurate predictor of center outcome than was either the naturally occurring base rate or the work evaluators' client ratings. Finally, there was no relationship between adjustment group membership and vocational adjustment at follow-up. This finding supports previous research suggesting that psychological and vocational adjustment are coeffects and are not causally linked.

In American culture, working is so important as to influence a person's physical and psychological well-being (Brenner, 1977; Menninger, 1964; Neff, 1977; Vaillant & Vaillant, 1981). In order to seek and maintain employment successfully, a person needs some modicum of psychological adjustment. Unfortunately, a physical disability can have psychological consequences with employment-related ramifications. While rehabilitation experts (McDaniel, 1976; Shontz, 1971; Wright, 1960) assert that there is no evidence linking specific kinds of physical disability to specific types of personality, there remains controversy concerning the relationships between severity of disability and psychopathology, and between psychological and vocational adjustment.

In his extensive review of the literature, Shontz (1971) concluded that there is little support for the theory that severity of disability causes psychological maladjustment. In his review of research on emotional factors and disability, McDaniel (1976) cautiously concluded that severity of disability was a determinant of psychological adjustment. Based on their review, Roessler and Bolton (1978) also argued for a relationship, albeit complex, between severity of disability and degree of psychological impairment. Vocational rehabilitation theorists (Gellman, 1953; Hershenson, 1981; Neff, 1977) do believe that a modicum of psychological adjustment (e.g., adequate self-concept, work personality, attitude, and interpersonal skill) is necessary for vocational adjustment to occur.

To facilitate treatment planning, rehabilitationists have sought methods to establish a disabled person's psychological status quickly. Perhaps the most popular instrument for this purpose has been the Minnesota Multiphasic Personality Inventory (MMPI). For example, Sandness (1968) developed scales from MMPI items said to differentiate between employed and unemployed former rehabilitation clients, and Salomone (1972) suggested that differences he found on *Pt* scale score elevation between motivated and unmotivated rehabilitation clients would be useful in treatment prescreening. Bourestom and Howard (1965) reported that those with spinal cord injuries suffered less emotional discomfort than did persons with rheumatoid arthritis or multiple sclerosis. Most of the research on the MMPI has made use of linear relationships. Few investigators have followed Meehl's (1959; cf. Goldberg, 1968) suggestion to use configural strategies, which utilize profile shape and dispersion as well as scale elevation, as analytic strategies. In fact, Freeman, Calsyn, Sherrard, and Paige (1980) were unable to differentiate between renal dialysis patients who had successful or unsuccessful vocational rehabilitation outcomes using mean MMPI scale scores, but were able to do so using profile decision rules. The purpose of the present study was to use MMPI decision rules to examine the relationship among rehabilitation clients' preservice psychological status, type of disability, severity of disability, and vocational adjustment at follow-up.

METHODS

Sample

The research population consisted of 305 vocational rehabilitation clients receiving preservice work evaluations at a comprehensive rehabilitation center located in the Southwest. The population was 62% male, 73% single; nearly half (46%) had a 12th-grade education or higher; 30% had psychological disabilities, while 70% had physical disabilities. At referral all persons were unemployed, although all but 29 had held at least one job prior to enrollment. Average Beta IQ equalled 97 (range 62–20); average Wide-Range Ability Test (WRAT) reading was at the 9.8 grade equivalent level (range 4.6–10.3); average WRAT arithmetic level was 7.4 (range 2.3–17.1); and average age was 29 (range 16-62).

Procedure

The Mini-Mult (Kincannon, 1968), was used to assess client psychopathology. The Mini-Mult uses 71 MMPI items rephrased to a yes-no structured interview-like format. Extensive research on the Mini-Mult (see the reviews of Faschingbauer

& Newmark, 1978; Stevens & Reilley, 1980) suggests that it has adequate reliability. While there is some question concerning use of the Mini-Mult in individual diagnosis, the general consensus is that it is an acceptable device for screening purposes (Lacks & Powell, 1970; Noce & Whitmyre, 1981).

The research population was reduced by deleting persons (n =19) who had Lie raw scores of 11 or more or F scores of 16 or more. The sample (n = 286) was then divided by gender into adjusted or maladjusted groups, according to the configural decision rules developed by Kleinmuntz (1960). The maladjusted group was subdivided by forming a third group, primarily of persons with T scores of 80 or more on the *D, Pd,* or *Sc* subscales. Thus, the sample was divided by gender into three groups categorized as adjusted, possibly maladjusted, and probably maladjusted.

As a validity check on group formation, two additional analyses were conducted. First, as part of a large research project, all clients and their work evaluators had rated the clients' psychological adjustment following the standard 2-week client evaluation process. Those ratings followed a semantic differential format with nine, seven interval, bipolar adjectives. Mean rating scale scores for males and females were contrasted across the three adjustment groups. Neither the females' own ratings nor the work evaluators' ratings of females differed significantly across groups. Males in the adjusted group had significantly higher self-ratings, $F(2, 166) = 14.04, p < .001$, and significantly higher work evaluators' ratings, $F(2, 168) = 4.28, p < .01$), of their psychological adjustment than did males in either the possibly or probably maladjusted groups.

Second, because the Kleinmuntz decision rules were developed on a college population and might not generalize to persons in rehabilitation, mean scores of the three content scales developed by Bolton (1976a) from a factor analysis of Mini-Mult items completed by vocational rehabilitation clients were contrasted by gender and by adjustment group. These scales purport to measure morale, somatization, and psychotic distortion in rehabilitation populations. Group means were in the expected direction, adjusted < possibly maladjusted < probably maladjusted (Fs ranging from 9.94 to 70.95, $p < .007$ for males and females).

Center and rehabilitation agency records provided demographic and service outcome information about clients. Follow-up information was available (Cook, in press) for 105 of these persons 2 to 4 years after center discharge. Severity of disability was defined by state agency disability determination codes. Comparisons between groups were made using multivariate and univariate procedures and parametric and nonparametric statistics.

RESULTS

There were no significant differences in the proportions of males and females sorted into the adjusted, possibly maladjusted, and probably maladjusted groups (see Table 8.1). Adjusted males had significantly higher and more variable scores on the *Hs* subscale, $t(92.5) = 2.34, p < .02$, and the *D* subscale, $t(97.6) = 2.15, p < .03$; probably maladjusted males had significantly higher and more variable scores on *D, $t(66.8) = 2.95, p < .004$.* Females in the possibly maladjusted group scored significantly higher than did males on the Pa subscale, t (112) $= 3.53$, $p <$ *.001,* and the Pa subscale, t (112) $= 2.36$, $p < .02$. Females in the probably maladjusted group were also higher on *Pa, t* (70) $= 2.16$, $p < .03$.

A multivariate analysis of variance revealed no difference, Wilks' criterion F (14, 290) $= 1.16$, among males in the three groups on Beta IQ, WRAT arithmetic, months worked prior to enrollment, expectations for work, age, or education. Females in the probably maladjusted groups scored significantly higher on Beta IQ (100 vs. 92) than did females in the adjusted group, Wilks' criterion F (14, 178) $= 1.91$, $p < .03$. There were no significant differences among groups of females on any other variables.

There were no significant relationships for males or females between kind of physical disability (sensory, neurological, orthopedic, cardiovascular, or amputation) and adjustment group membership. There were no significant relationships by gender between severity of disability and adjustment group membership. Because of restriction of range (79% of the females and 76% of the males were "severely disabled" according to agency codes), any relationship between severity of disability and adjustment could be attenuated. However, there was no fit between a theoretical distribution, in which the severely disabled would be expected to be twice as likely to be in the probably maladjusted group as in the other two groups, and the actual distribution for females ($\chi^2 = 19.4$, $df = 2$, $p <$ .001) or males ($\chi^2 < = 26.9$, $df = 2$, $p < .001$).

As expected, there were significant relationships between diagnosis of a psychological disability for both females ($\chi^2 = 7.22$, $df = 2$, $p < .03$) and males $\chi^2 = 6.67$, $df = 2$, $p < .04$) and adjustment group membership, although the relationships were not exceedingly strong. For example, 20% of the psychologically disabled females were in the adjusted group, while 30% were in the probably maladjusted group.

Table 8.1 Means and Standard Deviations of Mini-Mult Scale Scores by Gender and Subgroup

	Males			Females		
Scale[a]	Adjusted ($n = 62$)	Possibly Maladjusted ($n = 67$)	Probably Maladjusted ($n = 46$)	Adjusted ($n = 37$)	Possibly Maladjusted ($n = 47$)	Probably Maladjusted ($n = 26$)
L	53.9(6.8)	53.4(7.3)	51.2(6.3)	54.4(7.5)	52.6(6.9)	49.5(7.2)
F	53.7(4.8)	60.2(8.6)	66.8(9.7)	53.6(5.5)	62.4(8.9)	67.7(9.6)
K	51.0(6.5)	50.4(8.1)	49.7(6.0)	53.2(6.8)	50.3(6.5)	47.6(7.6)
1Hs	56.7(12.6)	58.8(10.1)	72.6(13.7)	52.2(6.1)	60.5(10.8)	70.7(10.1)
2D	59.7(10.5)	68.1(10.0)	83.4(12.4)	55.7(7.1)	65.5(9.5)	76.1(8.6)
3Hy	59.4(6.5)	62.3(6.9)	72.2(7.3)	56.8(5.8)	62.2(8.8)	69.8(6.6)
4Pd	60.4(6.8)	69.9(8.6)	78.4(9.9)	62.4(5.4)	71.1(7.2)	81.3(10.2)
6Pa	53.3(7.5)	61.4(8.7)	70.0(12.2)	55.9(7.8)	67.3(8.8)	76.0(9.6)
7Pt	50.3(7.3)	63.6(10.2)	76.6(12.5)	52.4(8.7)	63.2(8.4)	74.0(8.1)
8Sc	56.5(8.0)	71.9(9.2)	86.6(13.2)	54.7(8.2)	70.9(8.4)	85.9(10.6)
9Ma	53.2(7.1)	57.8(8.7)	61.5(8.6)	54.5(8.2)	61.4(7.6)	64.2(9.7)
Age	29.7(12.6)	25.1(8.6)	30.3(11.5)	32.2(12.8)	28.4(10.9)	28.0(10.9)

[a] *Hs, Pd, Pt, Sc,* and *Ma* are K-corrected.

Adjustment group membership was not related to agency closure status (e.g., rehabilitated or not rehabilitated, working or not working). Male psychological status was not related to center outcome, but female psychological status was related to center outcome. Females classified as either adjusted or possibly maladjusted were more likely to complete a center program than were probably maladjusted females ($\chi^2 = 4.68$, $df = 2$, $p < .03$). Psychological classification for females was 61% accurate in predicting completion and 64% correct in predicting dropouts. The base rate for female completers was 56%, for dropouts 44%; the average work evaluator was 59% accurate in predicting both completers and dropouts.

At 2 to 4 years postdischarge, 105 former clients completed a follow-up questionnaire. Previous research (Cook, in press) suggested that the followup sample was representative of the research population. Adjustment group membership and gender were proportionally equal in the follow-up sample and in the research population. At follow-up, only ratings of physical health (aside from disability), mental health, and free-time relationships were significantly related to psychological adjustment ($\chi^2 = 9.15$, $df = 2$, $p < .01$; $\chi^2 = 8.33$, $df = 2$, $p < .02$; and $\chi^2 = 10.50$, $df = 4$, $p < .03$, respectively). Persons in the possibly maladjusted group were less likely to rate either their physical or mental health as fair or poor. Persons in the adjusted group were most likely to spend free time with family rather than themselves or friends. There were no significant relationships between psychological adjustment and help needed in activities of daily living, source of income (self-payments vs. transfer payments), amount of income, employment, work-seeking activities, future expectation for work, reason for not working, satisfaction with family relationships, family help in getting a job, or most important type of future goal.

DISCUSSION

Based on configural profile rules, male and female rehabilitation clients were sorted into three groups: adjusted, possibly maladjusted, and probably maladjusted. Homogenous Mini-Mult content scale analysis suggested that the division into these three groups represented a valid differentiation. Male self-ratings, as well as work evaluators' ratings of male psychological adjustment, were significantly related to adjustment group membership. There were no such relationships for females. That finding may be due to a rating bias according to which females consistently give and receive more favorable ratings than do men (Cook, Kunce, & Getsinger, 1976; English, 1971). Group membership for both males and females was independent of demographic characteristics.

As expected, there was no relationship between type of physical disability and psychopathology. There was more adjustment variation within disability classifications than there was between classifications. Also as expected, there was a significant relationship between diagnosis of psychological disability and psychopathology. Yet only 30% of the males and females whose primary disability was psychological were in the probably maladjusted group. In fact, 20%

of the psychologically disabled females and 19% of the psychologically disabled males were in the adjusted group. About one-fifth of those persons with psychological disabilities either had been misdiagnosed, or had improved their psychological functioning between diagnosis and enrollment at the center, or had "behavioral" problems not related to psychopathology.

Following the Rehabilitation Act of 1973, the State-Federal Vocational Rehabilitation Program was mandated to serve the "most severely" disabled. It is not surprising that over 75% of these clients receiving comprehensive center services were determined to be severely disabled. The lack of relationship between severity of disability and psychological maladjustment supports Shontz' (1971) contention that degree of disability per se is not a causal factor in psychological adjustment.

The only significant relationship between outcome and adjustment group membership was found for females. Adjustment group membership was a more accurate predictor of center outcome than was either the base rate for female program completion or the traditional work evaluation procedures. Most important was the lack of relationship between psychological adjustment and vocational outcome. Other research (Ayer, Thoreson, & Butler, 1966; Flynn & Salomone, 1977; Lowe, 1967) has reported on the lack of relationships between preservice MMPI scores and employment of rehabilitation clients. Using factor-analysis-derived scores from three psychological inventories, one of which was the Mini-Mult, Bolton (1976b) and Kraut and Bolton (1976), also reported no relationship between rehabilitation outcome and preservice psychological status of clients. The most parsimonious explanation is that unmeasured differential client change accounts for the lack of relationship. However, previous research on this sample (Cook & Brookings, 1980) failed to identify any link between kinds of services received and clients' center outcome. Other research specifically addressing prepost psychological change (Bolton, 1979; Cook, 1982) found that psychological status remains stable for about 75% of former rehabilitation clients 3 to 6 years postservice. An alternative explanation is that vocational and psychological adjustment are independent dimensions of rehabilitation outcome (Bolton, 1974, 1978; Cook, Bolton, & Taperek, 1980; Growick, 1979). As such, they may be coeffects and not causally linked at all.

If vocational adjustment and psychological adjustment are codetermined facts of rehabilitation outcome, then there are important implications for rehabilitation practice and research. For example, clinicians might devote considerable time to developing the type of outcome that would be most beneficial to any one client. Also, the rationale of using such treatment regimens as work therapy to enhance psychological well-being might be questioned. Finally, different paradigms—such as Bandura's (1978) "reciprocal determinism," which goes beyond Lewin's popular "person by situation" model, and nonlinear analytical strategies such as nonmetric multidimensional scaling—may be necessary to understand how people adjust to a disability. It is noteworthy that one of the first tests of Bandura's model has been conducted on a disabled population (Devins, Binik, Gorman, Dattel, McCloskey, Oscar, & Briggs, 1982).

NOTE

1. Cook, D. W., Bolton, B., & Taperxek, P. *Adjustment to spinal cord injury: A comprehensive follow-up study.* Unpublished manuscript, Arkansas Rehabilitation Research and Training Center, Fayetteville, 1980.

REFERENCES

Ayer, J. M., Thoreson, R. W., & Butler, A. J. (1966). Predicting rehabilitation success with the MMPI and demographic data. *Personnel and Guidance Journal, 44,* 631–637.

Bandura, A. (1978). The self-system in reciprocal determinism. *American Psychologist, 33,* 344–358.

Bolton, B. (1974). A factor analysis of personal adjustment and vocational measures of client change. *Rehabilitation Counseling Bulletin, 18,* 99–104.

Bolton, B. (1976a). Homogeneous subscales for the Mini-Mult. *Journal of Consulting and Clinical Psychology, 44,* 947–954.

Bolton, B. (1976b). A preliminary study of differential personality profiles of rehabilitation clients. *Rehabilitation Counseling Bulletin, 20,* 21–27.

Bolton, B. (1978). Dimension of client change: A replication. *Rehabilitation Counseling Bulletin, 22,* 8–15.

Bolton, B. (1979). Rehabilitation clients' psychological adjustment: A 6-year longitudinal investigation. *Journal of Applied Rehabilitation Counseling, 9,* 133–141.

Bourestom, N. C., & Howard, M. T. (1965). Personality characteristics of three disability groups. *Archives of Physical Medicine and Rehabilitation, 46,* 626–632.

Brenner, M. H. (1977). Personal stability and economic security. *Social Policy, 8,* 2–4.

Cook, D. W. (1982). Dimensions and correlates of postservice adjustment to spinal cord injury. *International Journal of Rehabilitation Research, 5,* 373–375.

Cook, D. W. (in press). Postservice adjustment of former rehabilitation center clients: A longitudinal analysis. *Rehabilitation Literature.*

Cook, D. W., & Brookings, J. B. (1980). The relationship of rehabilitation client vocational appraisal to training outcome and employment. *Journal of Applied Rehabilitation Counseling, 11,* 32–35.

Cook, D. W., Kunce, J. T., & Getsinger, S. H. (1976). Perceptions of the disabled and counseling effectiveness. *Rehabilitation Counseling Bulletin, 19,* 470–475.

Devins, G. M., Binik, Y. M., Gorman, P., Dattel, M., McCloskey, B., Oscar, G., & Briggs, J. (1982). Perceived self-efficacy, outcome expectancies, and negative mood states in end-stage renal disease. *Journal of Abnormal Behavior, 91,* 241–244.

English, R. W. (1971). Correlates of stigma towards physically disabled persons. *Rehabilitation Research and Practice Review, 2,* 1–17.

Faschingbauer, T. R., & Newman, C. S. (1978). *Shortforms of the MMPI.* Lexington, Mass.: Lexington Books.

Flynn, R. J., & Salomone, P. R. (1977). Performance of the MMPI in predicting rehabilitation outcome: A discriminant-analysis, double cross-validation assessment. *Rehabilitation Literature, 38,* 13–15.

Freeman, C. W., Calsyn, D. A., Sherrard, D. J., & Paige, A. B. (1980). Psychological assessment of renal dialysis patients using standard psychometric techniques. *Journal of Consulting and Clinical Psychology, 48,* 537–539.

Gellman, W. (1953). Components of vocational adjustment. *Personnel and Guidance Journal, 31,* 536-539.

Goldberg, L. R. (1968). Simple models or simple processes? Some research on clinical judgments. *American Psychologist, 23,* 483–496.

Growick, B. S. (1979). Another look at the relationship between vocational and nonvocational client change. *Rehabilitation Counseling Bulletin, 23*, 136–139.

Hershenson, D. B. (1981). Work adjustment, disability, and the three R's of vocational rehabilitation: A conceptual model. *Rehabilitation Counseling Bulletin, 25*, 91–97.

Kincannon, J. C. (1968). Prediction of the standard MMPI scale scores from 71 items: The Mini Mult. *Journal of Consulting and Clinical Psychology, 32*, 319–325.

Kleinmuntz, B. (1960). Identification of maladjusted college students. *Journal of Counseling Psychology, 7*, 209–211.

Kraut, C., & Bolton, B. (1976). Client-reported psychological status and rehabilitation success. *Rehabilitation Counseling Bulletin, 19*, 500–503.

Lacks, P. B., & Powell, B. J. (1970). The Mini-Mult as a personal screening technique: A preliminary report. *Psychological Reports, 27*, 909–910.

Lowe, M. C. (1967). Prediction of posthospital work adjustment by the use of psychological tests. *Journal of Counseling Psychology, 14*, 248–252.

McDaniel, J. W. (1976). *Physical disability antihuman behavior* (2nd ed.). New York: Pergamon Press.

Meehl, P. E. (1959). A comparison of clinicians with five statistical methods of identifying psychotic MMPI profiles. *Journal of Counseling Psychology, 6*, 102–109.

Menninger, W. C. (1964). The meaning of work in Western society. In H. Borrow (Ed.), *Man in a world at work.* Boston: Houghton Mifflin.

Neff, W. S. (1977). *Work and human behavior* (2nd ed.). Chicago: Aldine.

Noce, S. F., & Whitmyre, J. W. (1981). Comparison of the MMPI and Mini-Mult with both psychiatric inpatients and screening nursing students. *Journal of Personality Assessment, 45*, 147–150.

Roessfer, R., & Bolton, B. (1978). *Psychosocial adjustment to disability.* Baltimore: University Park Press.

Salomone, P. R. (1972). Client motivation and rehabilitation counseling outcome. *Rehabilitation Counseling Bulletin, 16*, 11–20.

Sandness, D. G. (1968). The Minnesota Multiphasic Personality Inventory as a predictor in vocational rehabilitation. *Rehabilitation Counseling Bulletin, 12*, 111–113.

Shontz, F. C. (1971). Physical disability and personality. In W. S. Neff (Ed.), *Rehabilitation Psychology.* Washington, D.C.: American Psychological Association.

Stevens, M. R., & Reilley, R. R. (1980). MMPI short forms: A literature review. *Journal of Personality Assessment, 44*, 368–376.

Vaillant, G. E., & Vaillant, C. O. (1981). Natural history of male psychological health: X. Work as a predictor of positive health. *American Journal of Psychiatry, 138*, 1433–1440.

Wright, B. A. (1960). *Physical disability: A psychological approach.* New York: Harper & Row.

Acknowledgement: This research was supported in part by a research and training center grant (G008003045) from the National Institute of Handicapped Research, Office of Special Education and Rehabilitative Services, Department of Education, Washington, D.C.

9

Change in Vocational Interests After Spinal Cord Injury

Daniel E. Rohe and
Gary T. Athelstan

ABSTRACT: Change in vocational interests of 117 males with spinal cord injury (SCI) was studied using the Strong-Campbell interest inventory (SCII). The subjects' mean age at injury was 23.3 years; they were studied an average of 9.4 years after injury. Subjects completed two versions of the SCII, one with standardized instructions and one with instructions to recall interests from an earlier, preinjury age. Strong Vocational Interest Blanks taken prior to injury were located for 14 experimental subjects. These provided direct evidence concerning stability of interests and suggested that the larger group was relatively accurate in the recall of preinjury interests. A control group of 130 males, matched on age, also completed the SCII twice. The control group was used to assess the presence of any variance uniquely associated with the "recall" method. Results showed (1) that the interests of SCI males were as stable as those of their nondisabled peers; (2) that changes that did occur were consistent with those found in nondisabled samples; and (3) that the previously untried recall method is potentially useful in future research.

Little is known about the relationship between abilities and vocational interests or about the effects on interests of changes in abilities. This study addressed these issues by examining changes in interests after onset of spinal cord injury (SCI), a major physical disability. Since SCI involves drastic changes in physical capabilities, participation in some preinjury activities is no longer possible. Consequently, new avenues for satisfying some interests may have to be found, and the possibilities for satisfying some interests may be severely restricted. Thus, it seems reasonable to expect that the reduced capacity to act upon interests might be accompanied by some change in the composition or intensity of the interests themselves.

Knowledge of change in interests after disability could have both practical and theoretical value. For example, it may contribute to a better understanding of the process of adjustment to disability and to improved personal and vocational counseling for the disabled. The newly disabled individual is confronted with major, stressful change in the physical, social, psychological, and vocational aspects of life. Counselors must discover how best to aid the individual in making the necessary adjustments. In a separate study involving men with recent SCI, we (Rohe & Athelstan, 1982) found that many subjects had measured interests that seemed incompatible with the limitations imposed by their disability. Counselors would thus find it very helpful to know about the possibility of subsequent change in their clients' interests.

The theoretical implications of change in interests after disability involve three areas of research: (1) the stability of interests, (2) the effect of experience on interest development, and (3) the relationship between abilities and interests. Comprehensive reviews of the literature on stability of interests have been done by Strong (1943, 1955), Darley and Hagenah (1955), King (1956), Joselyn (1968/1969), and Campbell (1971). All indicated impressive stability of interests over time. Test-retest studies have confirmed this stability, both in scores for a single individual over time (Strong, 1951) and in mean scores for groups of individuals (Johannson & Campbell, 1971). Correlations have ranged from .90 for test-retest intervals of 2 weeks to not less than the low .60s for intervals over 20 years (Campbell, 1971, p. 82). The available evidence clearly indicates that age at first testing and time between testings are the primary determinants of interest stability (Strong, 1951). We were unable to locate any studies of the stability of interests after disability.

Literature on the development of interests has focused on genetic determinants (Nichols, 1966; Roberts & Johannson, 1974; Vandenberg & Stafford, 1967), familial influences (Grotevant, 1976; Heilburn, 1969; Hewer, 1965; Werts, 1968; Zytowski, 1970), and experiential learning (Ewens, 1956; Morrison, 1971/1972; Stewart, 1957). Most theories of vocational choice emphasize the developmental nature of interests. They suggest that interests are learned and result from experience, and that occupational choice is a process originating in early childhood behavior. Moreover, Super (1953), Roe (1957), and Holland (1959) seem to agree that interests synthesize an individual's values, needs, and motivations, and reflect the self-concept. Thus, examining the stability of interests in adults after onset of disability might provide insight into stability of the self-concept after injury.

Although the present study was concerned with physical capability, the literature on the relationship between interests and mental abilities seems relevant. In general, authors have concluded there are only low positive correlations between interests and school grades (Hewer, 1954; Strong, 1943) and aptitude test scores (Johnson, 1965; Miller, 1961). The data suggest that abilities and interests are relatively independent, with correlations accounting for only 5-10% of the variance. We could find no studies relating interests and physical capabilities.

Opportunities to obtain actual pre- and postinjury measures of interests are understandably very rare. Consequently, the only way we could make a substantial number of such comparisons was to approximate the preinjury interests of a sample of disabled subjects. We did this by having them complete an interest inventory once according to standardized instructions, and on another occasion when asked to recall their interests from before their injury. Although we could find no studies that used identical methodology, Thorndike (1935) asked subjects to rate their degree of liking for activities from previous age spans. Three studies asked subjects to respond to an interest inventory using an experience or ability set (Dressel & Matteson, 1952; McCall & Moore, 1965; Steinmetz, 1932). Other authors (Kelso & Bordin, 1948; Longstaff, 1948; Stephenson, 1962) have investigated the ability of subjects to change their scores when asked to fake in a specified direction. These studies illustrate successful use of altered instructions with standardized interest inventories and previous use of a recall methodology.

METHOD

Subjects

In order to maximize our chances of finding any effect on interests due to changes in abilities, we wanted to study a sample whose disability characteristics suggested maximum impact on their capabilities. Accordingly, our subjects were selected to meet the following criteria: the disability (1) necessitated a wheelchair for mobility; (2) occurred suddenly, rather than gradually; and (3) was of at least 2 years' duration. Also, we sought to minimize variance due to sex and age by studying only men who were disabled at or after age 18.

The names of 188 potential subjects with SCI were obtained from three sources: (1) former patients of the University of Minnesota's Department of Physical Medicine and Rehabilitation; (2) residents and ex-residents of Courage Center, a rehabilitation facility; and (3) local members of the National Spinal Cord Injury Foundation. All were contacted by mail or telephone and invited to participate in the study; 117, or 62%, consented. Of these subjects, 82 were quadriplegic, having paralysis of all four limbs; 35 were paraplegic, or paralyzed from the waist down. As incentives to participate, subjects were offered a summary of the study's results, a copy of their own interest inventory results, and $4.00.

A control group of 130 men, matched on age, was selected to determine whether any method effect resulted from the interest recall technique. The control group had to be male, 25 to 40 years old, and willing to take the Strong-Campbell Interest Inventory (SCII) twice. Except for subgroups of 20 lawyers and 16 teachers, the majority were attending either engineering or psychology college evening classes. The only inducement offered control subjects was a copy of their SCII results.

Materials

The experimental group's materials included (1) a 10-item Spinal Cord Injury Questionnaire (SCIQ); (2) the SCII, Form T325; and (3) a second SCII, with the standard instructions replaced by the following:

> This inventory is being used to measure the interests that you had during the time period just before your spinal cord injury occurred. The following pages list many

jobs, activities, school subjects, and so forth. You are asked to recall your preinjury interests and show your liking or disliking for each item based on how *you think* you would have responded if the inventory was given to you at that time. Remember, each time you are asked if you are interested, you should be *thinking, " Was I interested at that time?"* This is not a test of your preinjury abilities; it is an inventory of your preinjury interests.

All subsequent test instructions were identical to those in the standard SCII test booklet, except that all verbs were altered to the Past tense in keeping with the initial recall instruction. All test items were left unchanged.

The control group's materials included the SCII and an altered form requesting them to recall their interests from 10 years ago. The 10-year period matched the average duration of the experimental subjects' disability.

Procedure

Experimental subjects were assigned randomly to one of two groups. Group 1 first completed the SCII recalling preinjury interests. They subsequently took the SCII with standard instructions. Group 2 first completed the SCII with standard instructions, followed by the altered form. This counterbalanced design was used to lessen any effect the order of presentation might have on results. This same procedure was used with the control group.

Many Minnesota high school students routinely take interest inventories in a statewide testing program. This created an opportunity to examine some inventories actually completed prior to injury. After a careful search of high school records, Strong Vocational Interest Blank (SVIB) answer sheets were located for 14 experimental subjects.

Analysis of the 14 preinjury SVIBs was problematic in that 3 were the 1938 form; 9, the 1966 form; and 2, the 1974 form. The 1938 form of the SVIB has 202 items in common with the 1974 SCII; the 1966 form shares 254 items. Item responses for those items common to the 1938 and 1974 forms were used to generate new SCII profiles. The 9 subjects having the 1966 form were combined for analysis with the 2 subjects having the 1974 form. SCII profiles were generated for each test condition for the combined group of 11 based on the reduced set of 254 common items. Thus, for these 11 subjects, we obtained SCII profiles reflecting (1) actual preinjury (P-I) interests, (2) recalled (R) interests, and (3) present-day (P-D) interests. The 3 subjects originally tested on the 1938 form were considered separately since they shared only 202 items with the other test-retest subjects. Since one Basic Interest Scale, Domestic Arts, had only one item common to the three SVIB forms, it was not considered in these analyses.

Data Analysis

Item responses, scaled scores, and profiles were used to compare P-I with P-D interests. For most experimental subjects, their preinjury interests could be assessed only through recall, so the pre- and postinjury comparisons used R interests in place of P-I. Finally, to determine whether R interests were a valid substitute for P-I interests, R and P-I were compared for those subjects who had both.

In making item response comparisons, "one-category shifts" are generally defined as changes in response between testings of "like" to "indifferent," "dislike" to "indifferent," or the reverse. "Two-category shifts" are defined as changes from "like" to "dislike" or the reverse. Strong (1943) found that "approximately 60 percent of the responses of high school and college students are identical, 35 percent are 1-category changes, and 5 percent are 2-category changes" (p. 659). For convenience, category shift data are customarily reported as percentages in the 0-1-2 order. Thus, Strong's findings would be displayed as "60-35-5."

Item analyses examined both category shifts and percentage response differences in comparing R to P-D interests. Chi-square analysis indicated that a 12% difference in item responses was significant at the .05 level, and a 15% difference at the .01 level.

After item analyses, similar comparisons were made on standard scores for the 6 General Occupational Themes, the 23 Basic Interest Scales, and the 67 male-normed Occupational Scales. As noted in the SCII manual (Campbell, 1977), 3-point mean differences on the Themes and Basic Interest Scales and 5-point mean differences on the Occupational Scales are considered the minimum differences worth noting. These criteria were utilized in examining the scaled score differences.

Finally, Pearson product-moment correlation coefficients, based on the 67 male-normed Occupational Scales, were computed between R and P-D interests for all subjects. Individual coefficients were averaged to produce mean correlation coefficients for the experimental groups of 3, 11, and 117, and the control group of 130.

Tilton's (1937) "percent overlap" was computed in conjunction with all t-tests. This statistic, which ranges from 0% to 100%, gives the percentage of scores in one distribution that is matched by scores in another distribution. It provides a relatively, "concrete" indication of the size of the difference between two distributions.

RESULTS

Findings are presented in three parts, beginning with the subjects for whom preinjury SVIBs could be located. These are called the "test-retest subjects." Because of the discrepancy in the number of items, the 3 1938 SVIBs were not grouped with the others in all analyses. However, all of the findings for those 3 subjects were consistent with those for the other test-retest subjects, so this discussion combines the results for all 14. After the results for test-retest subjects, findings for the entire group of 1 17 experimental subjects are reported, followed by the controls. Detailed findings not reported here may be found in Rohe's (1980/ 1981) dissertation, which is the basis for this report.

Test-Retest Subjects

The combined group of 14 test-retest subjects' mean age at P-I testing was 17.4. Mean age at injury was 20.8 years, and the average interval between injury and P-D testing was 8.0 years. The mean number of years of education completed at time of P-D testing was 13.9 years.

The median correlations between the three test comparisons of P-I versus R, P-I versus P-D, and R versus P-D were .79, .62, and .81, respectively (see Table 9.1). The mean item category shifts were 63-29-8, 58-31-11, and 67-25-8, respectively.

Examination of the General Occupational Themes, the Basic Interest and Occupational Scales, the special scales, and the item response percentages showed almost exactly the changes expected to result from aging, as found by Campbell (1971) (see Table 9.2). These consisted mainly of increased "like" and decreased "dislike" responses, and higher scores on scales reflecting social and artistic interests. Interestingly, the Adventure Scale remained constant, rather than declining, contrary to Campbell's findings. This was the only finding that distinguished any of the experimental subjects from nondisabled samples, possibly indicating a more enduring interest in adventure among SCI males. Finally, the Athletics Scale failed to decrease, even though most subjects had drastically reduced opportunities to participate in athletics.

Comparison of the mean P-I to the mean P-D profile indicated clearly that the interests of these SCI subjects were as stable as those of their nondisabled peers. As shown in Table 9.1, the test-retest group's median test-retest correlation on the Occupational Scales was .62. This correlation is essentially identical to the median correlation of .64 found on a nondisabled sample first tested at age 17 to 18 and retested 6 to 10 years later (Campbell, 1971, p. 82). It also compares favorably with the .69 mean correlation obtained in Power's (1954) study.

The P-I versus R comparison is useful in estimating recall accuracy for the entire experimental group. There was a slight tendency to over-recall interests associated with the Realistic, Artistic, and Social Themes (i.e., to remember more

Table 9.1 Correlations Between P-I and P-D Interests, P-I and R Interests, and R and P-D Interests for 14 Test-Retest Subjects Having an SVIB Before Injury

	r between P-I and P-D Interests[a]	Years between P-I and P-D Testing	r between P-I and R Interests[a]	Years between P-I Testing and Injury Onset	r between R and P-D Interests[a]	Years between P-D Testing and Injury Onset
M	.59	11.31	.64	3.35	.76	7.96
Median	.62	11.46	.79	2.83	.81	7.63

[a] Mean Pearson correlation coefficients were computed on the two sets of 67 male-normed Occupational Scales.

Table 9.2 Comparison of Mean Scores of Test-Retest Subjects' (n = 11) P-I Interests with P-D Interests on the Themes, Special Scales, Basic Interest Scales, and Male-Normed Occupational Scales

Scale Title	P-I Interests		P-D Interests		Mean Difference	t	Percent Overlap
	Mean	SD	Mean	SD			
Scales on Which P-D Interest Mean Scores Were Higher Than P-I Interest Mean Scores							
Social Theme	36.68	9.23	45.30	11.59	8.62	4.98**	68
Nature	41.35	8.34	51.75	7.98	10.40	4.61**	53
Teaching	35.23	6.96	45.29	9.42	10.06	4.73**	54
Art	44.37	10.48	51.98	9.12	7.61	3.34*	70
Social Worker	3.82	10.05	15.25	17.36	11.44	3.83*	68
Minister	6.36	12.58	17.13	14.32	10.76	4.19*	69
School Superintendent	9.08	8.04	19.28	11.24	10.20	4.25*	60
Speech Pathologist	19.06	10.05	29.22	13.23	10.15	4.01*	67
English Teacher	18.27	9.94	26.97	12.11	8.70	4.11*	70
Guidance Counselor	12.80	8.50	20.89	10.84	8.09	3.57*	68
Recreation Leader	13.34	9.99	20.69	12.28	7.35	3.98*	74
Lawyer	13.73	7.75	20.55	10.76	6.81	3.30*	71
Chiropractor	23.20	11.34	29.41	9.49	6.21	3.61*	77
Scales on Which P-D Interest Mean Scores Were Lower Than P-I Interest Mean Scores							
Introversion-Extroversion	65.43	13.31	56.14	12.21	− 9.29	4.14*	72
Skilled Crafts	42.77	7.94	32.88	14.61	− 9.89	3.48*	66
Farmer	40.92	14.20	31.16	16.05	− 9.75	3.60*	75
Banker	23.30	6.03	16.30	8.39	− 7.00	3.55*	63

Note: Criterion for inclusion in table was a t score with $p ≥ .01$.
*$p < .01$.
**$p < .001$.

interests in those areas than they actually had), and to underrecall interests associated with the Conventional Theme. None of the recall inaccuracies, however, was statistically significant.

These data suggest a couple of important conclusions. First, test-retest subjects were able to recall their P-I interests rather accurately. This is indicated by the correlation of .79 between P-I and R interests and the category shift data (63-29-8) that demonstrate substantial item response stability. Thus, the recall technique appears to be a reasonable way of approximating preinjury interests. Second, the stability of interests in this sample compares very favorably with that found in retests of nondisabled subjects over comparable time periods. Similar results were obtained with the larger sample of experimental subjects, but these findings seem especially significant, since they involved actual retests after injury.

The 117 Experimental Subjects

The median correlations between R and P-D interest profiles for all 117 experimental subjects and the 14 test-retest subjects were .86 and .81, respectively. This finding and the nearly identical item response category shift data, 65-29-6 and 61-32-7, respectively, suggest that the test-retest subjects were similar to the entire group of 117 experimental subjects in recall accuracy.

For the experimental group of 117 SCI males, the mean age at injury was 23.3 years (range, 16-58 years), the mean age at time of P-D testing was 32.2 years (range, 20-72 years), and the mean number of years of education was 13.7 (range 8-20 years). The average time between injury and R testing was 9.4 years.

Table 9.3 Comparison of Mean Scores of Experimental Groups' (*n* = 117) P-D Interests with R Interests on the Themes, Special Scales, Basic Interest Scales, and Male-Normed Occupational Scales

Scale Title	R Interests		P-D Interests		Mean Difference	*t*	Percent Overlap
	Mean	*SD*	Mean	*SD*			
Scales on Which P-D Interest Mean Scores Were Higher Than R Interest Mean Scores							
Social Theme	42.42	10.22	45.86	11.43	3.44	4.26	87
Conventional Theme	44.54	9.61	47.87	9.85	3.32	5.14	87
Artistic Theme	41.82	9.72	44.82	11.01	2.95	4.27	89
Academic Orientation	27.81	13.51	33.68	14.62	5.87	5.90	84
Teaching	40.14	10.05	44.59	11.35	4.49	5.35	83
Public Speaking	42.77	8.63	46.87	10.56	4.11	5.88	83
Social Service	42.88	9.32	46.85	11.01	3.97	4.78	85
Writing	38.61	10.05	42.55	10.86	3.94	5.64	85
Business Managment	44.59	10.01	48.49	10.98	3.90	5.48	85
Law Politics	43.14	9.35	46.87	10.22	3.73	5.06	85
Art	42.50	10.03	45.93	10.86	3.42	4.78	87
Social Worker	8.98	14.22	17.10	16.63	8.12	6.31	79
Speech Pathologist	18.43	12.76	25.81	15.01	7.38	6.83	79
Librarian	11.15	11.24	17.33	12.79	6.17	6.64	80
Priest	16.01	12.42	22.07	13.62	6.06	6.46	81
Psychologist	17.51	10.26	23.18	12.67	5.67	6.43	81
Minister	11.12	13.32	16.71	15.28	5.59	7.78	84
School Superintendent	17.50	13.30	23.03	15.13	5.53	5.64	84
Public Administrator	21.46	11.61	26.94	14.16	5.49	6.27	83
Credit Manager	20.76	13.09	25.75	14.73	5.00	5.18	86
Lawyer	17.95	11.01	22.93	12.50	4.98	5.76	83
Scales on Which P-D Interest Mean Scores Were Lower Than R Interest Mean Scores							
Introversion-Extroversion	60.41	12.15	56.03	13.69	− 4.38	5.08	87
Adventure	58.90	9.36	54.96	8.64	− 3.93	5.30	83
Agriculture	57.66	7.69	54.69	9.77	− 2.97	4.18	87
Farmer	40.71	13.54	33.77	15.29	− 6.94	6.90	81
Skilled Crafts	43.21	13.96	37.01	15.28	− 6.20	6.02	82
Highway Patrol Officer	38.82	13.39	33.11	14.97	− 5.71	5.78	84
Merchant Marine Officer	49.81	10.09	44.89	11.38	− 4.92	6.54	82

Note: Criterion for inclusion in table was a *t* score with a $p \le .001$.

The overall findings suggested stable interests when R results were compared with P-D results (see Table 9.3). The median correlation between R and P-D interests was .86, and the range was - .24 to .99. The greatest changes were on the Social, Conventional, and Artistic Themes, all of which showed statistically significant increases. In addition, subjects recalled (1) having fewer academically oriented interests; (2) being more introverted; (3) liking fewer, and disliking more, occupations; and (4) liking fewer, and disliking more, school subjects, than at present.

The Basic Interest Scales and the Occupational Scales followed the trends suggested by the Themes. Most of the Basic Interest Scales increased, while those associated with the Realistic Theme generally declined on the P-D profile. The Basic Interest Scales showing the greatest declines were Adventure and Agriculture. The decline in the Adventure Scale among these subjects did not seem consistent with its stability among test-retest subjects. However, this difference appeared to be due to recall rather then actual change in interests. The test-retest subjects recalled greater interests in agriculture and adventure than they actually had before injury, but the Agriculture and Adventure Scales remained constant from P-I to P-D testings. Thus it was presumed that inaccurate recall was occurring with the entire experimental group. If this is true of SCI men generally, the Adventure Scale would not decline over time among SCI men as it does in nondisabled samples.

Occupations in the Realistic Theme showed P-D interests lower than R interests, with the greatest declines occurring on Farmer, Skilled Crafts, Highway Patrol Officer, and Merchant Marine Officer. Scales showing the greatest R to P-D increases were Social Worker, Speech Pathologist, Librarian, Priest, and Psychologist.

Responses to 84 of 325 items (26%) changed at a statistically significant level between R and P-D testings, predominantly in the direction of decreased disliking. In addition, a number of items showed increased liking. These included the occupations of City Planner, Psychologist, Vocational Counselor, Advertising Executive, City or State Employee, and Social Worker, and activities involving social-interpersonal skills, such as meeting, directing, interviewing, teaching, and helping others. These changes may be accounted for by the increased contact that SCI people have with several of these occupations and activities after their injury.

Subjects showed decreased disliking for reading, school subjects, ballet dancers, physically sick people, and religious people. There was increased liking for prominent business leaders and activities where groups of people congregate. In general, increased positive endorsement was given to activities that are more sedentary, mental, less physically active, and safer. Those items describing "your characteristics" indicated that subjects perceived themselves as becoming more deliberate, reflective, and patient after injury.

As with the test-retest subjects, many of these changes are quite similar to those found by Campbell (1971, p. 76) and can be accounted for on the basis of age or student status.

The Control Group

The main purpose of the control group was to discover any effect that the interest recall method might have on the findings. Since interest inventory responses are influenced by age and student status, any changes in the control group's profiles not attributable to these two variables might be considered a method effect.

The mean age of the control group was 31.1 years (range, 21-59 years). Since the experimental group's mean age was 32.2 years, age matching was considered successful. The control group had a mean of 16.4 years of education.

In general, the changes seen in the controls were very similar to those occurring among experimental subjects. The experimental and control groups were identical on median test-retest correlation and mean percentage of category shifts (.86 and 64-30-6, respectively) between R and P-D test conditions. The Themes that showed the greatest change from R to P-D testings among the controls were the Artistic, Investigative, and Social. The Artistic and Social Themes also increased in the experimental group. The increased Investigative Theme score, not seen in the experimental group, can be accounted for most plausibly by the distinctive vocational composition of the control group. As compared with the experimentals, they had more education; they were mainly engineers, lawyers and teachers; and most were in college classes at the time of testing.

All of the control group's changes in the Basic Interest Scales, except an increased score on the Domestic Arts Scale, also occurred in the experimental group and could be accounted for on the basis of age. In addition, the Occupational Scales tended to be slightly higher on P-D as compared to R testing, in keeping with Campbell's findings (1971, p. 76).

The control group demonstrated statistically significant change in 15% (49 of 325 items) of their item responses, predominantly due to either increased liking or decreased disliking. In general, they showed increased liking for (1) sedentary and safe activities; (2) traditionally feminine activities such as cooking and sewing; and (3) activities that involve social interaction, particularly in a business environment.

None of these findings suggested a method effect. Rather, most changes in scores were very similar to those of the experimental group and could be attributed to age or student status.

DISCUSSION

Contrary to our expectations, major change in physical abilities does not appear to produce change in measured interests; rather, the interests that are present before injury remain. Changes that do occur are similar to those found in nondisabled samples and appear to be a function mainly of age.

These findings are important to an understanding of several aspects of adjustment to severe physical disability. Conventional wisdom and anecdotal reports in the rehabilitation literature have long held that personality change and psychological disorganization follow the onset of disability. However, this study confirms earlier findings (e.g., Taylor, 1967) suggesting that SCI males do not experience significant psychological disorganization after injury. Rather, continuity with previous behavior is the norm.

Stability of interests after injury may help explain the extremely low rates of employment of SCI men. Trieschmann (1980, p. 117) reviewed the literature and found studies reporting between 13% and 48% of persons with SCI returning to competitive employment. Although much attention has been given to vocational rehabilitation services for this group, employment rates remain very low. Financial, attitudinal, architectural, and transportational barriers are clearly important. However, lack of change in interests would maintain the disparity between interests and physical capabilities that we found earlier (Rohe & Athelstan, 1982); thus lack of change may contribute to difficulties in vocational rehabilitation.

Several additional findings seem noteworthy. First, the SCI men showed no significant shift away from interests that might be considered physically impossible. There was no decrease in liking for amusements of an athletic nature, nor did the Athletics Scale decline. Second, SCI subjects showed significantly more changes in item response percentages from R to P-D testing than the control group (26% vs. 15%), mainly due to decreased disliking for many items. Such a changed response pattern suggests that SCI men may become less judgmental and rigid about what does *not* interest them. Thus, they may be more open to new experiences and interests.

It is possible that sustaining a severe physical disability may create a situation favorable to change in interests. College enrollment is frequently used by state vocational rehabilitation agencies as a retraining option for SCI males. As previously mentioned, artistic interests showed significant gains among student samples and among our SCI subjects. If physical disability had not occurred, it is uncertain how many of these men would have continued their education and whether these artistic interests would have increased.

Finally, a distinctive characteristic of the SCI group was the failure of the Adventure Scale to decline with age. Interests associated with physical risk taking may be a more enduring characteristic of SCI males than of the general population.

These findings also have implications for rehabilitation practice with the physically disabled. Our data suggest (1) that the SCII is psychometrically reliable when used with the physically disabled; (2) that severe physical disability does not produce change in interests; and (3) that interests will continue for those activities that are no longer physically possible. Rehabilitation counselors should assess interests, assume that they are unlikely to change greatly, and help devise strategies for acting on interests that are present but no longer physically possible. Helping clients satisfy their interests might require greater attention to adapting and modifying the environment to permit involvement in a greater range of activities; it might also call for ingenuity in the development of "psychologically equivalent" activities that are less demanding physically but that satisfy similar interests.

Finally, these results have implications for three areas of interest measurement research and theory. Previous research on the stability of interests indicates that interests change little after age 18 in the population. The present data confirm previous findings and extend their applicability to SCI males. If stability of interests is the norm for persons with one of the most severely limiting physical disabilities, it would appear reasonable to expect the same for those with less severe impairments. Further research, however, is needed to confirm this speculation.

These data are also consistent with previous findings regarding the effect of experience on the development of interests. Although some of our SCI subjects apparently developed some new interests after injury, established interest patterns remained consistent for most subjects. Overall, interest profiles changed very little.

The results of this study also support previous research suggesting that interests and abilities are relatively independent of each other. Although the present study considered physical rather than mental abilities, it appears that physical capabilities and interests are also relatively independent.

REFERENCES

Campbell, D. P. (1971). *Handbook for the Strong Vocational Interest Blank.* Stanford, CA:Stanford University Press.

Campbell, D. P. (1977). *Manual for the SVIB-SCII* (2nd ed.). Stanford, CA: Stanford University Press.

Darley, J. G., & Hagenah, T. (1955). *Vocational interest measurement: Theory and practice.* Minneapolis: University of Minnesota Press.

Dressel, P. L., & Matteson, R. W. (1952). The relationship between experience and interest as measured by the Kuder Preference Record. *Educational and Psychological Measurement, 12,* 109–116.

Ewens, W. P. (1956). Experience patterns as related to vocational preference. *Educational and Psychological Measurement, 16,* 223–231.

Grotevant, H. D. (1976). Family similarities in interests and orientation. *Merrill-Palmer Quarterly, 22,* 61–72.

Heilburn, A. B., Jr. (1969). Parental identification and the patterning of vocational interests in college males and females. *Journal of Counseling Psychology, 16,* 342–347.

Hewer, V. H. (1954). Vocational interest-achievement ability interrelationships at the college level (Doctoral dissertation, University of Minnesota, 1954). *Dissertation Abstracts, 14,* 1257. (University Microfilms No. A54–1846).

Hewer, V. H. (1965). Vocational interests of college freshmen and their social origins. *Journal of Applied Psychology, 49,* 407–411.

Holland, J. L. (1959). A theory of vocational choice. *Journal of Counseling Psychology, 6,* 35-45.

Johannson, C. B., & Campbell, D. P. (1971). Stability of the strong vocational interest blank for men. *Journal of Applied Psychology, 55,* 34–36.

Johnson, R. W. (1965). Are SVIB interests correlated with differential academic achievement? *Journal of Applied Psychology, 49,* 302–309.

Joselyn, E. G. (1969). The relationship of selected variables to the stability of measured vocational interests of high school students (Doctoral dissertation, University of Minnesota, 1968). *Dissertation Abstracts, 29,* 2526A. (University Microfilms No. 69–1515).

Kelso, D. F., & Bordin, E. S. (1948). The ability to manipulate occupational stereotype inherent in the Strong Vocational Interest Test. *American Psychologist, 3,* 352–353. (Abstract)

King, L. A. (1956). Factors associated with the stability of vocational interests of general college freshmen (Doctoral dissertation, University of Minnesota, 1956). *Dissertation Abstracts, 16,* 1840. (University Microfilms No. 56–2922).

Longstaff, H. P. (1948). Fakability of Strong Interest Blank and the Kuder Preference Record. *Journal of Applied Psychology*, *32*, 360–369.

McCall, J. N., & Moore, G. D. (1965). Do interest inventories measure estimated abilities? *Personnel and Guidance Journal*, *43*, 1034–1037.

Miller, C. H. (1961). *Foundations of guidance.* New York: Harper.

Morrison, J. W. (1972). An investigation of relationships between the experiences of high school students and changes in their vocational interest profiles (Doctoral dissertation, University of Connecticut, 1971). *Dissertation Abstracts International*, *33*, 270A. (University Microfilms No. 72–32, 158, 272).

Nichols, R. C. (1966). The resemblance of twins in personality and interests. *National Merit Scholarship Corporation Research Reports* (Vol. 2, No. 8).

Powers, M. K. (1954). A longitudinal study of vocational interests during the depression years (Doctoral dissertation, University of Minnesota, 1954). *Dissertation Abstracts*, *14*, 997. (University Microfilms No. A54–1467).

Roberts, C. A., & Johannson, C. B. (1974). The inheritance of cognitive interest styles among twins. *Journal of Vocational Behavior*, *4*, 237–243.

Roe, A. (1957). Early determinants of vocational choice. *Journal of Counseling Psychology*, *4*, 212–217.

Rohe, D. E. (1981). Change in vocational interests after disability (Doctoral dissertation, University of Minnesota, 1980). *Dissertation Abstracts International*, *42*, 7853. (University, Microfilms No. 81–095, 02).

Rohe, D. E., & Athelstan, G. T. (1982). Vocational interests of persons with spinal cord injury. *Journal of Counseling Psychology*, *29*, 283–291.

Steinmetz, H. C. (1932). Measuring ability to fake occupational interest. *Journal of Applied Psychology*, *16*, 123–130.

Stephenson, R. R. (1962). Faking "chance" on the SVIB. *Journal of Applied Psychology*, *46*, 252–256.

Stewart, L. H. (1957). Does knowledge of performance on an aptitude test change scores or the Kuder? *Journal of Counseling Psychology*, *4*, 161–164.

Strong, E. K., Jr. (1943). *Vocational interests of men and women.* Stanford, CA: Stanford University Press.

Strong, E. K., Jr. (1951). Permanence of interest scores over 22 years. *Journal of Applied Psychology*, *35*, 89–91.

Strong, E. K., Jr. (1955). *Vocational interests 18 years after college.* Minneapolis: University of Minnesota Press.

Super, D. E. (1953). A theory of vocational development. *American Psychologist, 8*, 185–190.

Taylor, G. P., Jr. (1967). Predicted versus actual response to spinal cord injury: A psychological study (Doctoral dissertation, University of Minnesota, 1967). *Dissertation Abstracts International*, *28*, 1214B. (University Microfilms No. 67–10445).

Thorndike, E. L. (1935). The interests of adults. *Journal of Educational Psychology, 26*, 401–410.

Tilton, J. W. (1937). The measurement of overlapping. *Journal of Educational Psychology*, *28*, 656–662.

Trieschmann, R. B. (1980). *Spinal cord injuries: Psychological, social and vocational adjustment.* New York: Pergamon Press.

Vandenberg, S. G., & Stafford, R. E. (1967). Hereditary influences on vocational preferences as shown by scores of twins on the Minnesota Vocational Interest Inventory. *Journal of Applied Psychology*, *51*, 17–19.

Werts, C. E. (1968). Paternal influence on career choice. *Journal of Counseling Psychology*, *15*, 48–52.

Zytowski, D. G. (1970). *The influence of psychological factors upon vocational development.* Boston: Houghton Mifflin.

SECTION III
Issues Affecting the Rehabilitation of Persons with Psychiatric Impairments

Gary R. Bond, Section Editor

Introduction

Gary R. Bond

Persons with mental disability constitute the single largest disability group eligible for rehabilitation (NIHR, 1979). Although the estimates vary as a function of operational definitions and methodologies, surveys suggest a range of 800,000 to 1,500,000 adult Americans with severe psychiatric disability living outside of institutions (Goldman & Manderscheid, 1989). Persons with severe mental illness share the same life goals as all of us do: to live in a community where one is accepted, to have a home, to be productive, to have satisfying recreational activities, to have friends, and so forth. The obstacles persons with severe mental illness face in meeting these basic human needs are extraordinary. Psychiatric rehabilitation, however, has not been fully recognized as a subspecialty of rehabilitation, either in practice or within the professional literature.

Why is there such a lack of attention to a high-frequency disability? There are many historical reasons why rehabilitation of persons with severe mental illness has been "no one's business." Because community mental health centers were not originally mandated to provide rehabilitation, they have generally not done so throughout the deinstitutionalization era. Nor has the rehabilitation system been forthcoming in providing services for individuals with psychiatric disabilities, partly because its success rate with them has been so disappointing (NIHR, 1979). In the past, the "rehabilitation process," consisting of the sequence of assessment, training, and placement, has excluded many persons with psychiatric disabilities, either explicitly by determining them to be "unemployable," or implicitly through the discouraging lengthy preparation process (Bond & Dincin, 1986). Only recently have there been adaptations to the conventional rehabilitation procedures more suitable for individuals with severe disabilities (Wehman & Moon, 1988).

Related to the inadequacies in the service delivery systems has been the fact that during the last three decades university training programs in psychiatry, psychology, and social work have done little to prepare professionals to help persons with psychiatric disabilities deal with practical life problems (Lefley & Cutler, 1988). Although clinical psychology programs, for example, train students intensively in psychotherapy and psychometric assessment, these competencies have limited utility with this population. Similarly, few rehabilitation counseling programs have incorporated psychiatric rehabilitation into their training (Weinberger & Greenwald, 1982).

Another contributing factor to the lack of attention is the way rehabilitation psychologists have conceptualized their specialty. Whether psychiatric disability should be included as an area of rehabilitation at all has been a matter of debate (Eisenberg, 1988). There is growing recognition that psychology *as a field* has defined its role too narrowly with regard to treatment and rehabilitation of persons with serious mental disorders (Lefley & Cutler, 1988). This myopia is illustrated by the antiquated view of treatment of serious mental illness portrayed in psychology textbooks (Halter, Bond, & De Graaf-Kaser, 1989). For example, recent introductory psychology textbooks discuss lobotomy in as much detail as all forms of community treatment for the mentally ill combined. Moreover, abnormal and introductory texts rarely mention such important developments as the Fountain House clubhouse approach (Beard, Propst, & Malamud, 1982) or the community support program (Turner & TenHoor, 1978). Mainstream psychology has not incorporated the remarkable developments in psychiatric rehabilitation over the last two decades.

It is, therefore, not surprising that psychiatric rehabilitation is underrepresented in the rehabilitation literature. Like other rehabilitation journals, *Rehabilitation Psychology* has given it only modest attention. Of the 184 articles appearing in the journal since 1982, 15 (8%) have dealt with psychiatric rehabilitation. An encouraging note is that the journal recognized the growing importance of this topic with a special issue devoted to it in 1988.

The four articles chosen for inclusion in this monograph reflect the diverse foci of psychiatric rehabilitation. Rogers, Anthony, and Jansen provide a description of the domain of psychiatric rehabilitation and a demographic profile of the target population. They conclude with an optimistic note about the field's emerging data base.

To understand the psychosocial impact of serious mental illness, we also must examine environmental factors. Ryan, Bell, and Metcalf demonstrate the application of a methodology for studying the social climate of a treatment environment. They have provided a rare glimpse of systems change documented by a quantitative process analysis. Their study showed that introducing a new program philosophy as an adjunct did not effect change in the treatment environment; instead, substantive change occurred only when the staff went beyond verbal endorsement of rehabilitation values by introducing fundamental policy changes. These changes included patient governance in the residential unit and the development of paid community employment positions.

Bond and Friedmeyer's finding about the power of staff ratings of current work behavior for predicting future employment appears at first glance to do little more than to confirm common sense. Unfortunately, "common sense" also tells us that psychiatric symptoms and relapses suggest poor employment potential, that clinicians can judge when someone is work-ready, and that prior work history is the best predictor of future employment. Bond and Friedmeyer's study, and the larger project from which it was taken (Bond & Dincin, 1986), challenge some of these widely held assumptions. One possible implication of this report is that every person deserves an opportunity for community employment, regardless of prior psychiatric history. This conclusion resonates with a deeply felt value within the clubhouse tradition (Beard et al., 1982).

Blanch, Carling, and Ridgway trace the mushrooming of state-funded transitional residential programs over the last decade. They believe that this policy is fundamentally flawed, because consumers *have not been consulted in formulating this policy.* Their concept of "supported housing" is based on helping consumers to live successfully in permanent housing of their own choosing. In supported housing, rehabilitation planning is focused in large part on defining the kinds of supports needed. As with the parallel concept of supported employment, a key question becomes that of finding creative solutions, starting with the consumer's perspective, rather than fitting clients into existing programs. The supported housing model has prompted a paradigm shift in thinking about rehabilitation services. Its ultimate policy impact remains to be seen.

Rogers et al. note the shift in the locus of treatment from inpatient to community settings between 1955 and the present. It is not accidental that the three remaining articles in this section, based on the temporal sequence in which they were published, reflect three stages of community integration: Ryan, Bell, and Metcalf's 1982 study describes an attempt to introduce rehabilitation principles in an inpatient setting. Bond and Friedmeyer's 1987 study was conducted in a community setting emphasizing transitionalism, in which clients are expected to move from prevocational activities to transitional employment, and subsequently to competitive employment. Blanch, Carling, and Ridgway's 1988 article proposes that consumers *begin* in normal settings, with professionals identifying the supports necessary for them to survive. The shift in the *locus of rehabilitation* reflects a current working hypothesis among some researchers about where the impact of interventions is likely to be greatest (Stein, 1988; Wehman & Moon, 1988).

Another theme suggested by this group of articles is the role of expectations in psychosocial adjustment. Ryan et al. found that inpatients were capable of greater autonomy than the hospital staff had traditionally assumed. In a related vein, staff ratings in the Bond and Friedmeyer study were apparently affected by the setting in which clients were observed, presumably because of shifting staff and client expectations in different environments. Finally, the implications of the Blanch et al. article are that consumer and mental health professional expectations for housing are seriously out of synchrony. All three articles suggest the value of positive expectations, or what Dincin (1975, p. 132) has labeled "dynamic hopefulness," in helping persons with serious mental illness reach their full potential.

Inclusion of a section on psychiatric disability in a collection of readings on psychosocial aspects of disability fills an important gap in the rehabilitation literature. Less than a decade ago, Weinberger and Greenwald (1982) noted the absence of a well-organized relevant information base on psychiatric rehabilitation. Recently, however, texts by Black (1988), Ciardiello and Bell (1987), Farkas and Anthony (1989), Liberman (1988; in press), and Stroul (1986) have suggested the maturation of psychiatric rehabilitation to the point that it is becoming a coherent subdiscipline. Research on the long-term course of schizophrenia (Harding, Zubin, & Strauss, 1987), positive and negative symptoms (Andreasen,

1982), expressed emotion and family management (Falloon, 1985), psychoeducation and social skills training (Hogarty et al., 1986), and assertive community treatment (Stein & Test, 1980) are a few of the current active research initiatives lending vitality to the field. The research studies reported in *Rehabilitation Psychology* are also suggestive of the growing conceptual and methodological sophistication and diversity of interests among psychiatric rehabilitation researchers.

REFERENCES

Andreasen, N. (1982). Negative symptoms in schizophrenia: Definition and reliability. *Archives of General Psychiatry, 39*, 784–788.

Beard, J. H., Propst, R. N., & Malamud, T. J. (1982). The Fountain House model of rehabilitation. *Psychosocial Rehabilitation Journal, 5* (1), 47–53.

Black, B. J. (1988). *Work and mental illness: Transitions to employment.* Baltimore: Johns Hopkins University Press.

Bond, G. R., & Dincin, J. (1986). Accelerating entry into transitional employment in a psychosocial rehabilitation agency. *Rehabilitation Psychology, 31*, 143–155.

Ciardiello, J. A., & Bell, M. D. (Eds.). (1988). *Vocational rehabilitation for persons with prolonged mental illness.* Baltimore: Johns Hopkins University Press.

Dincin, J. (1975). Psychiatric rehabilitation. *Schizophrenia Bulletin, 1*, 131–148.

Eisenberg, M. G. (1988). Introduction to special issue: Rehabilitation psychology and persons with psychiatric disabilities: Are they mutually exclusive? *Rehabilitation Psychology, 33*, 3–4.

Farkas, M., & Anthony, W. A. (Eds.). (1989). *Psychiatric rehabilitation programs: Putting theory into practice.* Baltimore: Johns Hopkins University Press.

Falloon, I. R. H. (1985). *Family management in schizophrenia.* Baltimore: Johns Hopkins University Press.

Goldman, H. H., & Manderscheid, R. W. (1989). Chronic mental disorder in the United States. In K. E. Davis, R. Harris, R. Farmer, J. Reeves, & F. Segal (Eds.), *Strengthening the scientific base of social work education for services to the long-term seriously mentally ill* (pp. 1–29). Richmond, VA: Virginia Commonwealth University.

Halter, C. A., Bond, G. R., & De Graaf-Kaser, R. (1989). *Coverage of community treatment in psychology textbooks.* Unpublished manuscript.

Harding, C. M., Zubin, J., & Strauss, J. S. (1987). Chronicity in schizophrenia: Fact, partial fact, or artifact? *Hospital and Community Psychiatry, 38*, 477–483.

Hogarty, G. E., Anderson, C. M., Reiss, D. J., Kornblith, S. J., Greenwald, D. P., Javan, C. D., & Madonia, M. J. (1986). Family psychoeducation, social skills training, and maintenance chemotherapy in the aftercare treatment of schizophrenia. *Archives of General Psychiatry, 43*, 633–642.

Lefley, H., & Cutler, D. (1988). Training professionals to work with the chronically mentally ill. *Community Mental Health Journal, 24*, 253–257.

Liberman, R. P. (1988). *Psychiatric rehabilitation of chronic mental patients.* Washington: American Psychiatric Association Press.

Liberman, R. P. (in press). *Handbook of psychiatric rehabilitation.* New York: Pergamon Press.

National Institute of Handicapped Research (NIHR) (1979). Postemployment services aid mentally disabled clients. *Rehab Brief, 2* (6), 1–4.

Stein, L. I. (1988). "It's the focus, not the locus." Hocus-Pocus! *Hospital and Community Psychiatry, 39*, 1029.

Stein, L. I., & Test, M. A. (1980). Alternative to mental hospital treatment, I: Conceptual model, treatment program and clinical evaluation. *Archives of General Psychiatry, 37*, 392–397 .

Stroul, B. A. (1986). *Models of community support services: Approaches to helping persons with long-term mental illness.* Boston: Center for Psychiatric Rehabilitation, Boston University.

Turner, J. C., & TenHoor, W. J. (1978). The NIMH Community Support Program: Pilot approach to a needed social reform. *Schizophrenia Bulletin, 4,* 319–348.

Wehman, P., & Moon, M. S. (1988). *Vocational rehabilitation and supported employment.* Baltimore: Paul H. Brookes.

Weinberger, J., & Greenwald, M. (1982). Training and curricula in psychiatric rehabilitation: A survey of core accredited programs. *Rehabilitation Counseling Bulletin, 26,* 287–290.

10

Psychiatric Rehabilitation as the Preferred Response to the Needs of Individuals with Severe Psychiatric Disability

E. Sally Rogers, William Anthony and Mary A. Jansen

ABSTRACT: Persons who are defined as severely psychiatrically disabled comprise a population in the United States of approximately two million people. They consume enormous health care resources. Traditional psychiatric interventions have not been successful in improving their rehabilitation outcomes. Research suggests that interventions based on a rehabilitation model show promise as a way to reduce a person's psychiatric disability. Psychiatric rehabilitation interventions are based on strategies to increase a person's skills and supports in order to reduce his or her disability and handicap.

The emergence of psychiatric rehabilitation during the past decade coincides, in great part, with the emergence of psychopharmacological interventions and with the deinstitutionalization movement. Since the 1950s state mental institutions have been radically depopulated, resulting in greater numbers of individuals with severe psychiatric disability in the community. Coincidentally, legislation and changes in treatment philosophies have fostered the growth of community-based treatment. Thus, individuals with severe psychiatric disability are no longer cloistered in distant institutions, but more often are attempting to integrate into the mainstream of American life.

The dramatic shifts in the locus of treatment for persons with severe psychiatric disability are evident in data published by the National Institute of Mental Health that show significant decreases in inpatient care and concomitant increases in community treatment of individuals with psychiatric disability. For example, in 1955, 77% of patient care episodes occurred in inpatient settings and 23 % in outpatient settings. In contrast, in 1981, 27% of patient care episodes occurred in inpatient settings and 73% in outpatient settings (Redick, Witkin, Bethel, &

Manderscheid, 1985c). Total expenditures for all mental health services (excluding mental health services to veterans) rose from $2.84 billion in 1969 to $10.69 billion in 1981, an increase of 48% when adjusted for inflation (Redick, Witkin, Bethel, & Manderscheid, 1985b). Similarly, from 1955 to 1981 outpatient care increased sixfold, from 379,000 episodes to over 2.3 million episodes (Redick, Witkin, Bethel, & Manderscheid, 1985a). Thus, not only is the proportion of inpatient to outpatient care shifting, but the volume of mental health treatment and dollars spent for that treatment have burgeoned. These data make clear the magnitude of the need for rehabilitation services to individuals with severe psychiatric disability.

DEFINING SEVERE PSYCHIATRIC DISABILITY

Defining severe psychiatric disability is complex—until recently the criterion of institutionalization was sufficient. With the advent of deinstitutionalization, however (and in some states, active programs to divert individuals from psychiatric institutions), a psychiatric hospitalization can no longer be used as the sole criterion.

Several definitions of severe psychiatric disability exist. According to Goldman, Gattozzi, and Taube (1981), delimiting individuals with chronic mental illness involves three factors: diagnosis, disability level, and duration of disability. They define chronic mental illness in the following way:

> The chronically mentally ill population encompasses persons who suffer certain mental or emotional disorders (organic brain syndrome, schizophrenia, recurrent depressive and manic-depressive disorders, and paranoid and other psychoses, plus other disorders that may become chronic) that erode or prevent the development of their functional capacities in relation to three or more primary aspects of daily life—personal hygiene and self-care, self-direction, interpersonal relationships, social transactions, learning, and recreation—and that erode or prevent the development of their economic self-sufficiency. (p. 23)

The Social Security Administration, on the other hand, defines chronic disability as that which has lasted or which can be expected to last for a continuous period of not less than 12 months and which prevents the individual from engaging in any "substantial gainful activity."

The Community Support Program, a division of the National Institute of Mental Health that was developed to serve persons with severe psychiatric disability, has defined severe psychiatric disability in relation to the type of treatment an individual has received and how impaired he or she is in several categories of role functioning (e.g., employment, social interaction, basic living skills, and so forth) (Stroul, 1984).

Estimates of the numbers of individuals with severe mental illness who reside in institutional settings and in the community vary. According to Goldman et al. (1981), the numbers of individuals with chronic mental illness range from 1.7 million to 2.4 million, including 900,000 who are institutionalized. Research conducted by the Urban Institute (1975) indicates that there are between 350,000 and 800,000 individuals with severe emotional disorders living in the community.

DEMOGRAPHIC CHARACTERISTICS OF PERSONS WITH SEVERE PSYCHIATRIC DISABILITY

The largest data base describing individuals with severe psychiatric disability is available from the Community Support Program (CSP) of the National Institute of Mental Health. Results of surveys in 1984 indicate that 93,214 individuals with "chronic and serious mental illness" were being served nationwide by the Community Support Program (Mulkern & Manderscheid, 1986). Analyses of a sample of CSP clients (N = 1053) revealed that slightly more CSP clients were male than female (51 % vs. 49%). The mean age of CSP clients was 44 years (median = 41.3 years; SD = 15.3). The preponderance of clients was white (82%) and the remainder was black (11%), Hispanic (6%), or other (1%). Results of the survey regarding marital status are consistent with other studies that suggest that individuals with severe psychiatric disability tend never to have been married (53%); only 14% reported being married at the time of the survey. In addition, this population tends to have a lower mean level of education than the general population; only 53% of the sample had completed high school, versus 71% of the general population (Mulkern & Manderscheid, 1986).

Interestingly, these data suggest that the majority of CSP clients resided in private homes or apartments (57%), and another 26% lived in group or transitional homes, foster care, cooperative apartments, or board and care homes. Only 9% of CSP clients were living in unsupported boarding houses or hotels, and another 1% either had no regular residence or were incarcerated.

In terms of diagnosis, the largest majority of CSP clients were diagnosed as having schizophrenia (59%), followed by depressive and affective disorders (24%), organic brain syndrome (4%), other psychoses (2%), and nonpsychotic mental disorders (6%). Social maladjustment, substance abuse, mental retardation, and others account for the remaining 5%. Ninety-one percent of the clients had been hospitalized at least once for psychiatric treatment, 87% had been prescribed psychotropic medications, and the average lifetime total number of months hospitalized was 45.6.

Only 16% of this group of clients had earnings as a source of income; the majority received Social Security Supplemental Income (44%), Social Security Disability (20%), or Social Security retirement (11%). Regardless of the source of income, the median monthly income was $350.

Results of these CSP surveys may not be representative of all persons with severe psychiatric disability. Other researchers examining different samples have found, for example, that between 52% and 92% of individuals with severe psychiatric disability are high school graduates, and that between 15% and 60% have attended college (Dion & Anthony, 1987). Similarly, other studies suggest different proportions of clients living in different types of residential settings. For example, a survey of the National Alliance for the Mentally Ill members (a self-help group for those who have a disabled family member) found that only 30% of the disabled family members lived at home (Zipple & Spaniol, 1984).

Studies suggest that no more than 20% to 30% of individuals with psychiatric disability are competitively employed (Anthony, 1979; Dion & Anthony, 1987; Walker & McCourt, 1965). According to Dion and Anthony (1987), if only individuals with severe psychiatric disability are considered, the full-time competitive employment rate drops to below 15%. These conclusions are consistent with other authors (Farkas, Rogers, & Thurer, 1987; Spivack, Siegel, Sklaver, Deuschle, & Garrett, 1982; Zipple & Spaniol, 1984), who report rates of 0% to 15% for competitive employment among individuals with severe psychiatric disability. The CSP surveys described earlier reported that only about 8% of the clients surveyed were employed competitively, either full or part time. Another 17% were in transitional employment or other job training programs, sheltered workshops, volunteer positions, or other work activity.

TWO EMERGING GROUPS OF INDIVIDUALS WITH SEVERE PSYCHIATRIC DISABILITY

Describing individuals with psychiatric disability in terms of group statistics—or averages—can be misleading at best and stigmatizing at worst. However, two groups of individuals with psychiatric disability are being described regularly in the literature and have become sources of public policy debate. First are individuals with psychiatric disability who are also homeless. Farr, Koegel, and Burnam (1986), in one comprehensive study of homelessness, found a disproportionately high number of individuals with severe psychiatric disability among the homeless population. For example, 13.7% of this sample had a diagnosis of schizophrenia, 35 times higher than the comparison group of inner city males who were not homeless. A total of 26.2% of their sample were described as having a "chronic and severe mental illness" (schizophrenia, major and recent affective disorders, or cognitive impairment; see Farr et al., 1986, for specific criteria).

The second group of interest is young adults with severe psychiatric disability (ages 18-35). According to some researchers, the shift in locus of treatment from the hospital to the community has resulted in a new generation of individuals with severe psychiatric disability who have vastly different characteristics than those who are older and once-institutionalized (Pepper & Ryglewicz, 1984; Woy, Goldstrum, & Manderscheid, 1981). Woy et al. (1981) argue that this group of individuals have more severe social disruption and fewer social supports, are highly dependent upon their parents well into adulthood, are transient, and have higher rates of criminal activity than other individuals with psychiatric disability. While research suggests that the most frequent diagnosis among young individuals with severe psychiatric disability is schizophrenia, personality disorders and affective disorders are also frequently diagnosed (Bachrach, 1984). Impulsivity, "frequent failures of judgement and an inability to learn from experience" (Woy et al., 1981, p. 3) are other characteristics used to describe young individuals with severe psychiatric disability. Several authors have argued that this group of individuals shows a pattern of inappropriate, intermittent, and erratic demand for mental health services (Bachrach, 1984; Pepper, Ryglewicz, & Kirshner, 1982; Robbins, Stern, & Robbins, 1978; Test, Knoedier, Allness, & Burke, 1985).

ATTEMPTS TO IMPACT CLIENT REHABILITATION OUTCOME

Historically, efforts to rehabilitate individuals with severe psychiatric disability have been discouraging. For example, in 1979, the National Institute of Disability Research and Rehabilitation concluded that, of all clients served by the vocational rehabilitation system, individuals with psychiatric disability had the least probability of success.

In their first research reviews of the efficacy of services to individuals with severe psychiatric disability (Anthony, Buell, Sharratt, & Althoff, 1972; Anthony, Cohen, & Vitalo, 1978), Anthony and his colleagues concluded that traditional inpatient hospitalization interventions (e.g., individual therapy, group therapy, work and drug therapy) do not differentially affect recidivism or posthospital employment. Only multiple, innovative approaches appear to be comprehensive and potent enough to positively affect outcome. Braun et al. (1981) later examined experimental alternatives to hospitalization (such as day hospital treatment, group home placement, family crisis therapy, "total community care," vocational training) and concluded that such alternatives appeared to have resulted in outcomes equivalent to, or only *occasionally* superior to, the hospital alternatives received by control subjects. Dellario and Anthony (1981) drew similar conclusions, stating that, in those studies that are directly comparable, the "clear-cut superiority" of hospitalization versus community alternatives has not been definitively established.

This lack of definitive superiority of nonhospital alternatives is discouraging for those who expected that deinstitutionalization and community-based care would improve rehabilitation outcomes. Other studies have drawn similar conclusions (Dickey, Gudeman, Hillman, Donatelle, & Grinspoon, 1981; Presly, Grubb, & Semple, 1982). Bond and Boyer (1988), in a critical review of vocational programs for individuals who are psychiatrically disabled, drew similar conclusions. Of 19 adequately controlled studies, only four resulted in significantly better vocational outcomes for the subjects receiving experimental alternatives (such as psychosocial rehabilitation, job counseling, transitional employment, and so forth); 13 studies reported no differences between experimental and control groups; and two studies found marginally significant differences.

Harding, Brooks, Ashikaga, Strauss, and Breier (1987) describe one of the few studies of individuals with severe psychiatric disability in which more encouraging vocational outcomes were found. A 20-to-25-year followup of once-institutionalized individuals with severe psychiatric disability revealed that 26% of the cohort were competitively employed; 27% were elderly or retired; 33% were unemployed; and the remaining 14% were not working for other reasons.

THE PSYCHIATRIC REHABILITATION APPROACH AS THE PREFERRED RESPONSE TO THE NEEDS OF INDIVIDUALS WITH SEVERE PSYCHIATRIC DISABILITY

Many persons with severe psychiatric disability are functioning poorly. While traditional treatment may ameliorate many of their psychiatric symptoms, their rehabilitation outcomes, such as degree of living independence and social and vocational functioning, have not been positively affected. What we have is a group of individuals who may be "less sick" but not "more well."

The psychiatric rehabilitation approach is designed to help persons with severe psychiatric disability improve their functioning (Anthony, 1979). The psychiatric rehabilitation approach is based on a rehabilitation model, the same model of impairment-disability-handicap that underlies the field of physical rehabilitation (Frey, 1984).

The rehabilitation model and its underlying philosophy were initially explicated by leaders in physical medicine and rehabilitation and can be logically extended to serve as a conceptual base for psychiatric rehabilitation (Anthony, 1982). While there are obvious and vast differences between a severe psychiatric disability and a severe physical disability, there is enough similarity to draw this analogy. For example, both severely physically disabled persons and severely psychiatrically disabled persons exhibit handicaps in role performance; need a wide range of services, frequently for a long period of time; and may not experience a total recovery from their disabilities.

There are a number of advantages in using the physical rehabilitation model as a conceptual model for psychiatric rehabilitation. A physical disability is considered less stigmatizing than a psychiatric disability. Furthermore, the rehabilitation of physically disabled persons appears more credible and understandable to the layperson.

Table 10.1 illustrates the rehabilitation model. The basic rehabilitation concepts of impairment, disability, and handicap have been described somewhat differently over the years. However, the integrative work of Wood (1980) and Frey (1984) has brought conceptual clarity to these terms. As depicted in Table 10.1, the impairment of structure or function can lead to a decreased ability to perform certain skills and activities, which in turn can limit the person's fulfillment of certain roles.

Historically, mental health treatment has developed interventions at the impairment stage. Somatic and psychological treatment efforts have been directed at alleviating the signs and symptoms of pathology. Leitner and Drasgow (1972), in analyzing the differences between treatment and rehabilitation, point out that, in general, treatment is directed toward minimizing sickness and rehabilitation toward maximizing health. Eliminating or suppressing impairments does not lead automatically to more functional behaviors. Likewise, a decrease in disability does not automatically lead to reductions in impairment.

The clinical practice of psychiatric rehabilitation, like its counterpart in physical rehabilitation, is comprised of two intervention strategies: (1) client skill

Table 10.1 The Rehabilitation Model

Term:	*Impairment*	*Disability*	*Handicap*
Definition:	Any loss or abnormality of psychological, physiological, or anatomical structure or function.	Any restriction or lack (resulting from an impairment) of ability to perform an activity in the manner or within the range considered normal for a human being.	A disadvantage for a given individual (resulting from an impairment or disability) that limits or prevents the fulfillment of a role that is normal (depending on age, sex, social and cultural factors)
Intervention:	Treatment	Clinical rehabilitation	Societal rehabilitation

development and (2) support development. Psychiatric rehabilitation practice should be guided by the basic philosophy of rehabilitation, that is, disabled persons need *skills and environmental supports* to fulfill the role demands of various living, learning, and working environments. The assumption of clinical rehabilitation is that by changing the skills and the supports in their immediate environment, persons with psychiatric disability will be better able to function in roles of their choice. In other words, interventions designed to lessen a disability also lessen the handicap.

Skill and support development are the quintessential rehabilitation interventions in both physical and psychiatric rehabilitation. For example, a physical rehabilitation team might help a paraplegic learn new skills (i.e., how to make a wheelchair-to-chair transfer) or help make the environment more supportive (i.e., equip the chair with hand controls) so that the person can function in the role of worker. Thus, the rehabilitation intervention decreases the person's disability in order to overcome the person's vocational handicap.

In addition to clinical rehabilitation interventions, persons with psychiatric disability can be helped to overcome their handicaps through societal rehabilitation interventions (Anthony, 1972). Societal rehabilitation is designed to change the system in which psychiatrically disabled persons must function. Unlike clinical rehabilitation, the focus is on system changes that can help many persons with psychiatric disability overcome their handicaps. Examples of system interventions are the Targeted Job Tax Credit legislation, changes in the length of the trial work period in the Social Security Disability program, the development of a European-type quota system for the employment of disabled workers, and so forth. The importance of these system interventions is the compelling evidence that the ability to overcome a handicap may be more a function of an accommodating and nondiscriminating social and economic system than it is the person's impairment and disability. A person who suffers severe psychiatric problems is often in need of both clinical and societal rehabilitation.

RESEARCH ON THE PSYCHIATRIC
REHABILITATION APPROACH

Dion and Anthony (1987) reviewed experimental and quasi-experimental research studies that used a skill development or support development intervention or both and that examined the impact on client disability and handicap. They concluded from this review of over 30 studies that psychiatric rehabilitation interventions have a positive effect on the rehabilitation outcome of persons who are psychiatrically disabled. A decade earlier Anthony and Margules (1974) conducted a similar review and tentatively suggested that persons who are severely psychiatrically disabled can learn skills in spite of their symptomatology, and that skill and support interventions have a positive impact on rehabilitation outcome. From 1974 until the present time, additional data and more sophisticated research designs point to the same conclusion.

The early research studies, typically quasi-experimental, provided a conceptual and empirical base for the more recent experimental studies. Much of this earlier research can be viewed as exploratory in nature, testing out the applicability of skill and support development interventions. As Dion and Anthony (1987) concluded:

> Given the present state of our knowledge, large-scale experimental studies of psychiatric rehabilitation are not only needed, they are increasingly feasible. Currently, a number of rehabilitation-oriented interventions can be described at a level of detail which permits their implementation to be observed and monitored reliably. Several examples of psychiatric rehabilitation interventions that are capable of monitoring and replicating are those developed by Anthony and his associates (Anthony, 1979), Fountain House (Beard, Propst, & Malamud, 1982), Paul (Paul & Lentz, 1977), and Azrin (Azrin & Philip, 1979). In summary, the research reviewed on the development and evaluation of innovative rehabilitation programs has illustrated that the stage is set for experimental studies of replicable, measurable psychiatric rehabilitation interventions. (pp. 198-199)

The field of psychiatric rehabilitation is prepared and poised for the additional experimental studies that must be done. Psychiatric rehabilitation is a field that is grounded in an emerging data base, anchored in the model and the philosophy common to all of rehabilitation, and targeted toward persons who are severely psychiatrically disabled and clearly in need of improved rehabilitation outcomes.

REFERENCES

Anthony, W. A. (1972). Societal rehabilitation: Changing society's attitudes toward the physically, and mentally disabled. *Rehabilitation Psychology, 19*, 117–126.

Anthony, W. A. (1979). *Principles of psychiatric rehabilitation.* Baltimore: University Park Press.

Anthony, W. A. (1982). Explaining "psychiatric rehabilitation" by an analogy to "physical rehabilitation." *Psychosocial Rehabilitation Journal, 5*, 61–65.

Anthony, W. A., Buell, G. J., Sharratt, S., & Althoff, M. E. (1972). Efficacy of psychiatric rehabilitation. *Psychological Bulletin, 78*, 447–456.

Anthony, W. A., Cohen, M. R., & Vitalo, R. (1978). The measurement of rehabilitation outcome. *Schizophrenia Bulletin, 4*, 365–383.

Anthony, W. A., & Margules, A. (1974). Toward improving the efficacy of psychiatric rehabilitation: A skills training approach. *Rehabilitation Psychology, 21*, 101–105.

Azrin, N. H., & Philip, R. A. (1979). The job club method for the job handicapped. A comparative outcome study. *Rehabilitation Counseling Bulletin, 23*, 144–155.

Bachrach, L. (1984). The concept of young adult chronic psychiatric patients: Questions from a research perspective. *Hospital & Community Psychiatry, 35*, 573–580.

Beard, J. H., Propst, R. N., & Malamud, T. J. (1982). The Fountain House model of psychiatric rehabilitation. *Psychosocial Rehabilitation Journal, 5*, 47–59.

Bond, G. R., & Boyer, S. L. (1988). Rehabilitation programs and outcomes. In J. A. Ciardiello and M. D. Bell (Eds.), *Vocational rehabilitation Of persons with prolonged mental illness*. Baltimore: Johns Hopkins University Press.

Braun, P., Kochansky, G., Shapiro, R., Greenberg, S., Gudeman, J. E., Johnson, S., & Shore, M. F. (1981). Overview: Deinstitutionalization of psychiatric patients. *American Journal of Psychiatry, 131*, 736–749.

Dellario, D., & Anthony, W. A. (1981). On the relative effectiveness of institutional and alternative placement for the psychiatrically disabled. *Journal of Social Issues, 37*, 21–33.

Dickey, B., Gudeman, J. S., Hillman, S., Donatelle, A. E., & Grinspoon, H. (1981). A followup of deinstitutionalized chronic patients four years after discharge. *Hospital & Community Psychiatry, 32*, 326–329.

Dion, G. L.. & Anthony, W. A. (1987). A review of psychiatric rehabilitation research. *Rehabilitation Counseling Bulletin, 30*, 177–203.

Farkas, M., Rogers, E. S., & Thurer, S. (1987). Rehabilitation outcome of long term hospital patients left behind by deinstitutionalization. *Hospital & Community Psychiatry, 38*, 264–270.

Farr, R. K., Koegel, P., & Burnam, A. (1986). *A study of homelessness and mental illness in the Skid Row area of Los Angeles*. Los Angeles: Los Angeles Department of Mental Health.

Frey, D. (1984). Functional assessment in the 80's: A conceptual enigma, a technical challenge. In A. Halpern & M. Fuhrer (Eds.), *Functional assessment in rehabilitation* (pp. 11-43). New York: Paul H. Brookes.

Goldman, H. H., Gattozzi, A. A., & Taube, C. A. (1981). Defining and counting the chronically ill. *Hospital & Community Psychiatry, 32*, 21–27.

Harding, C. M., Brooks, G., Ashikaga, T., Strauss, J. S., & Breier, A. (1987). The Vermont longitudinal study of persons with severe mental illness, 1: Methodology, study sample, and overall status 32 years later. *American Journal of Psychiatry, 144*, 718–726.

Leitner, L., & Drasgow, J. (1972, July/August). Battling recidivism. *Journal of Rehabilitation*, 29-31.

Mulkern, V. M., & Manderscheid, R. W. (1986). *Community support program client follow-up study: Executive summary*. Cambridge, MA: Human Services Research Institute.

Paul, G. L., & Lentz, R. (1977). *Psychosocial treatment of chronic mental patients*. Cambridge, MA: Harvard University Press.

Pepper, B., & Ryglewicz, H. (1984). Treating the young adult chronic patient: An update. In B. Pepper & H. Ryglewicz (Eds.), *Advances in treating the young adult chronic patient, New directions in mental health services* (Vol. 21, pp. 5–16). San Francisco: Jossey Bass.

Pepper, B., Ryglewicz, H., & Kirshner, M. C. (1982). The uninstitutionalized generation: A new breed of psychiatric patients. In B. Pepper and H. Ryglewicz (Eds.), *The young adult chronic patient, New directions in mental health services* (Vol. 14, pp. 3–14). San Francisco: Jossey-Bass.

Presly, A. S., Grubb, A. B., & Semple, D. (1982). Predictors of successful rehabilitation in long-stay patients. *Acta Psychiatrica Scandinavica, 66*, 83–88.

Redick, R. W., Witkin, M. J., Bethel, H. E., & Manderscheid, R. W. (1985a). *Changes in inpatient, outpatient & partial care services in mental health organizations, U.S.*,

1970–80 (Statistical Note No. 168). Rockville, MD: National Institute of Mental Health, Division of Biometry and Epidemiology, Survey and Reports Branch.

Redick, R. W., Witkin, M. J., Bethel, H. E., & Manderscheid, R. W. (1985b). *Expenditures by mental health organizations, U.S.*, 1969–81 (Statistical Note No. 170). Rockville, MD: National Institute of Mental Health, Division of Biometry and Epidemiology, Survey and Reports Branch.

Redick, R. W., Witkin, M. J., Bethel, H. E., & Manderscheid, R. W. (1985c). *Trends in patient care episodes in mental health organizations, U. S., 1970–81* (Statistical Note No. 171). Rockville, MD: National Institute of Mental Health, Division of Biometry and Epidemiology, Survey and Reports Branch.

Robbins, E., Stern, M., & Robbins, L. (1978). Unwelcome patients: Where can they find asylum? *Hospital & Community Psychiatry, 29*, 44–46.

Spivack, G., Siegel, J., Sklaver, D., Deuschle, L., & Garrett, L. (1982). The long term patient in the community: Life style patterns and treatment implications. *Hospital & Community Psychiatry, 33*, 291-295.

Stroul, B. (1984). *Toward community support systems for the mentally disabled: The NIMH Community Support Program.* Boston: Boston University, Center for Psychiatric Rehabilitation.

Test, M. A., Knoedier, W. H., Allness, D. J., & Burke, S. S. (1985). Characteristics of young adults with schizophrenic disorders treated in the community. *Hospital & Community Psychiatry, 36*, 853–858.

Urban Institute. (1975). *Report of the comprehensive service needs study.* Washington, DC: Department of Health, Education, and Welfare.

Walker, R., & McCourt, J. (1965). Employment experience among 200 schizophrenic patients in hospital and after discharge. *American Journal of Psychiatry, 122*, 316-319.

Wood, P. H. N. (1980). Appreciating the consequences of disease—The classification of impairments, disability and handicaps. *The WHO Chronicle, 34*, 376–380.

Woy, J. R., Goldstrum, I. D., & Manderscheid, R. W. (1981). *The young chronic mental patient: Report of a national survey.* Unpublished manuscript, National Institute of Mental Health, Washington, DC.

Zipple, A., & Spaniol, L. (1984). *Current research on families that include a person with a severe mental illness: A review of the findings.* Unpublished manuscript, Boston University, Center for Psychiatric Rehabilitation, Boston.

11

The Development of a Rehabilitation Psychology Program for Persons with Schizophrenia: Changes in the Treatment Environment

Edward R. Ryan, Morris D. Bell,
and John C. Metcalf
Veterans Administration Medical Center, West Haven,
Connecticut and Yale University

ABSTRACT: This article reports the changes that occurred over a 4-year period at a therapeutic community for persons with schizophrenia when a rehabilitation psychology program was added to the traditional inpatient treatment and eventually replaced it. Data collected using the Community Oriented Programs Environment Scale (COPES) revealed several significant and desirable changes in the quality of the perceived treatment environment, including increases in practical orientation and autonomy subscales. The article describes the specific interventions that account for improvement in the rehabilitation potential of the treatment environment. Conceptual differences between the traditional inpatient psychiatric model and the rehabilitation psychology model are outlined. Value differences between these two models are presented as an explanation for the failure of rehabilitation services offered adjunctively with traditional psychiatric services. The treatment environment changed only when rehabilitation became a central part of the treatment philosophy. The fundamental differences between these two treatment approaches are related to reports of improved outcome from programs using psychosocial models of treatment.

It is widely recognized that traditional forms of psychiatric inpatient treatment for persons with schizophrenia have led to very poor outcomes. Anthony, Buell, Sharratt, and Althoff (1972) found the recidivism base rate for all programs for schizophrenics to be 30% to 40% at 6 months, 40% to 50% at 1 year, and 65% to 75% at 3 to 5 years. Bachrach (1976) found similar results in her review of the literature, and Taube (1974) reported that more than 72% of psychiatric institutional admissions were actually readmissions. Anthony, Cohen, and Vitalo (1978) recently updated their own review of recidivism rates and found virtually no changes except that, when the follow-up was extended to 5 to 10 years, only 25% to 30% of the patients had never been readmitted. They also reported that only 10% to 30% of the former patients were employed full time regardless of the follow-up period. These authors concluded that traditional inpatient psychiatric treatments of all kinds (e.g., chemotherapy, group therapy, individual therapy) do not differentially affect psychosocial and vocational outcomes.

The present authors, working as clinicians and researchers in a long-term inpatient psychiatric program for persons with schizophrenia, had found that outcomes from this program were similar in terms of recidivism and unemployment to the studies reported above. It became apparent that such traditional insight-oriented programs failed to recognize the distinction between reducing symptoms and *preventing* future breakdown and recidivism. Mechanic (1968) points out that the limitation of treatment to the reduction of symptoms is an inadequate model for the maintenance of either physical or emotional health. Yet inpatient psychiatric treatments are usually limited to symptom reduction. Even those treatments that also endeavor to understand the development of psychiatric problems do not generally provide preventive rehabilitation that might sustain emotional health and thus prevent the need for rehospitalization.

In addition, there is growing theoretical evidence to support the view that psychosocial elements are critical factors in rehospitalization. For example, Fontana, Dowds, Marcus, and Rakusin (1976) found that former psychiatric patients may seek readmission as a last-ditch attempt to cope with life stresses and other social factors. Other investigators have concluded that life stresses and the failure of social supports play a significant and direct role in the development of symptoms and rehospitalization (Marsella & Snyder, 1981; Mosher & Keith, 1980). Social competence has been found repeatedly to be the best single predictor of posthospital adjustment (Zigler & Phillips, 1961a, 1961b), and more recent work has shown that such specific current life stresses as high expressed emotionality (hostility) toward the patient by his or her family (Birley & Brown, 1970) or rejection of the family by the patient (Vaughn & Leff, 1976, 1981) directly affect recidivism. Other investigators have reported that social supports can mediate stressors, thus reducing their impact (Andrews, Tennant, Hewson, & Valliant, 1978; Dean & Linn, 1977).

In line with this reasoning, a few programs have been designed to assist the psychiatric patient in preparing for the stresses of community living. Some have been limited to teaching specific social skills following cognitive and behavioral training models (Goldstein, Sprafkin, & Gershaw, 1976; Guthrie, Goldstein, & Hunter, 1973; Hersen & Bellack, 1976; Monti, Curran, Corriveau, & Delancy, Note 1). While they have demonstrated their effectiveness in terms of social skills acquisition, they have not yet demonstrated their impact on recidivism (for a review and critique of social skills training, see Wallace, Nelson, Liberman, Aitchison, Lukoff, Elder, & Ferris, 1980). Reports of more comprehensive social rehabilitation programs have indicated better-than-baseline recidivism rates.

Jacobs and Trick (1974) referred to their program as an "inpatient teaching laboratory" and reported a recidivism rate of 21% at 1-year follow-up. Furthermore, 74% of the patients had returned to their homes or job responsibilities. Becker and Bayer (1975) report a recidivism rate of 12% for patients contacted over a 3-month to 5-year follow-up period following discharge from a program emphasizing social skills training, token economy, and milieu therapy. Paul and Lentz (1977) report the success of a social-learning approach as compared to milieu therapy for chronic inmates of a state psychiatric hospital, although their criteria of success are limited to self-care and community tenure. An evaluation of another program with better-than-baseline results concluded that assistance during transition prolongs community tenure, that intervention in housing, finances, and medication were especially important, and that treatment follow-up increased community tenure during the first 6 months after discharge (Kociemba, Cotten, & Frank, 1979). Other approaches that have reported better-than-baseline outcomes include the use of transitional facilities (e.g., half-way houses and day treatment centers) as reported by Rog and Raush (1975) and the use of community volunteers as "enablers" (Weinman, 1975).

The literature described above suggests that a program of psychological services for the preventive rehabilitation of persons with schizophrenia that directly addresses the needs for social supports, social skills training, and vocational rehabilitation leads to better outcomes. In response to this evidence, the authors developed a program of social and vocational rehabilitation as an adjunct to the traditional forms of psychiatric therapy already in use on their treatment unit. They hoped that these additions, phased into the traditional program beginning January 1978, would better prepare veterans for successful adjustment to their communities following discharge. In June 1980, a rehabilitation psychology program fully replaced this revised traditional psychiatric treatment, and the unit became solely devoted to preparing psychiatric patients for return to the community. The impact of these changes on the treatment environment was recorded using the Community Oriented Programs Environment Scale (COPES) (Moos, 1974a). This measure of the treatment environment was administered at 4-month intervals over a 4-year period, beginning prior to the introduction of any rehabilitation program on the unit and continuing through the period during which the unit became a purely rehabilitation psychology program.

METHOD

Setting

The study spanned a 4-year period (February 1977-February 1981) of change on a treatment unit located on the top floor of a general medical/surgical teaching hospital at a Veterans Administration (V.A.) medical center.

The insight-oriented program, which was established in 1973, proceeded unchanged until 1978. The ward chief was a psychoanalyst, and the principal treatment modality was psychoanalytically oriented psychotherapy. While milieu therapy, group therapy, family therapy, and chemotherapy were employed, the major emphasis was on self-exploration and insight. All management decisions were based on supporting and promoting the psychotherapeutic work. Patients were expected to have long lengths of stay because it was believed by the staff that only prolonged exposure to treatment could bring about any meaningful and long-lasting change.

In 1978, several major changes occurred on the unit that resulted in its being renamed the Therapeutic Residential Treatment Center (TRTC). The unit was designated as a V.A. regional center for the treatment of schizophrenia. The rights and obligations of patients and staff were established in a formal, written constitution. A much greater emphasis was placed on the therapeutic community and the work of patient self-help groups, and most importantly, a work program and rehabilitation services program was created.

In June 1980, the TRTC was replaced by the Veterans Resource Program (VRP). The VRP is solely devoted to the preventive rehabilitation of psychiatric patients. In keeping with the preventive rehabilitation philosophy, the residents at the VRP are referred to as veterans, not patients. The 6-month program has three principal aspects—vocational, social, and community living—that define the aims of the program. The veteran's progress is based on a mutual contract that spells out what the veteran is trying to accomplish and what the program can provide to help attain these goals.

For vocational development, a thorough evaluation, including history taking, psychological testing, and counseling is done. Then the veteran is placed in the hospital-operated, paid-work program or in part-time placement with industry. The state or V.A. division of vocational rehabilitation, working with the staff, may sponsor the veteran in a prevocational assessment. Following these preparatory experiences, the veteran learns job-seeking skills and works with a counselor toward job placement. The veteran usually begins a job, training, or schooling while still a resident at the VRP, where he or she can be supported through the critical initial period of work adjustment.

Since persons diagnosed as schizophrenic have often become socially isolated, increasing the social support network as a buffer against daily stress is considered a very significant part of rehabilitation. Individual therapy helps the veteran to develop a more viable sense of personal meaning and significance in the world, to understand current life experience in its social context, to face conflicts that have interfered with personal growth, and to confirm the courage to overcome anxieties despite disability. Family therapy focuses on whatever adaptive assistance families can provide and also aids the veteran in separating from families that are assessed as likely to increase stress for the veteran. The veteran learns more than 30 social skills in structured workshops following the procedure of Goldstein, Sprafkin, and Gershaw (1976) and others and is encouraged to generalize the learning by identifying interests and joining community groups and social clubs. Structured learning modules on such topics as leisure planning, time management, civics and citizenship, health and hygiene, sex education, financial management, and assertiveness training are also available.

To prepare for independent community living, the veteran's previous history of living situations is evaluated, and strengths and deficits in basic living skills are assessed. The veteran receives training in social skills (e.g., shopping, housekeeping, cooking), makes out a detailed financial statement and budget, and begins the search for adequate housing. The veteran receives assistance in finding roommates (sometimes other veterans) and applying to a half-way house, a supervised apartment, or an independent living arrangement. Veterans using medication attend training modules in which they learn about the medications they use. Veterans are also taught to administer their own medication while still at the VRP. Out-patient therapy and follow-up also may be arranged.

The VRP is a residential program, and all those participating in the program have previously spent several months or years on the psychiatric units of the hospital. In order to prepare the veteran for an adjustment outside the hospital, the VRP faces the challenge of creating a social environment that reduces the patient role and increases autonomy even while the veteran is physically subject to the stimulus cues of the hospital environment. To accomplish this goal, the VRP has developed a veterans' self-governing body, The Veterans Alliance. There are no staff on duty from 8:00 P.M. to 8 A.M. and no staff on weekends. The veterans are responsible for their own conduct and quality of life during those times. The staff consults and monitors, but it is the veterans themselves who have created a social environment that meets the requirements of the hospital for safety and cleanliness and that affords them considerable autonomy and responsibility. As a result, the veteran gains experience in independent living skills, in coping with difficult situations, and in exercising authority over his or her life and the lives of others while still living at the VRP.

Subjects

Subjects were patients and staff members of the treatment unit between February 1977 and February 1981. The patients on the unit were veterans admitted to the program with a variety of diagnoses-80% were diagnosed as schizophrenic, 15% had affective psychoses, and 5% were from other diagnostic categories (infantile personality, borderline personality, etc.). As a group, the patients were largely males (mean % male across administrations: 90%) in their twenties (mean age: 25.8). Staff members participating in the study included administrative and clinical personnel (psychologists, social workers, occupational therapists, psychiatrists, social rehabilitation specialists, psychology graduate students and residents in training, and nursing personnel). The number of patient and staff members participating in each administration of the COPES questionnaire varied due to fluctuations in patient population and staffing patterns. The number of patients participating in each of the 13 questionnaire administrations ranged from a low of 13 to a high of 26 with a mean of 19.5. The number of staff ranged from 14 to 27 with a mean of 19.4.

Instrument

The COPES (Moos, 1974a) was selected for administration to the unit members as a measure of the perceived atmosphere of the treatment environment. It is a

100-item, true-false instrument designed to measure the social climate of community-oriented programs. Each item is a statement about the structural or interpersonal relationships within treatment programs (e.g., "This program emphasizes training for new types of jobs" or "Members seldom help each other"). Moos (1974b) has derived 10 subscales from the 100-item scale: involvement, support, spontaneity, autonomy, practical orientation, personal problem orientation, anger and aggression, order and organization, program clarity, and staff control.

Procedure

The COPES was administered a total of 13 times to the entire community of patients and staff at 4-month intervals between February 1977 and February 1981. Each administration of the COPES was presented at the end of a regularly scheduled staff patient community meeting.

Design and Analyses

The design of the study is essentially a time-series design in which the independent variable, treatment program, evolves over a period of time. This design approach permits the monitoring of change in the perceived treatment environment through periodically repeated measurement of patients and staff using the COPES. The analysis of these data is complicated, however, by partial statistical dependencies among the administrations for both the patients and staff. Members of both groups entered and left the program throughout the 4-year period during which the COPES was administered. The number of administrations completed by any single patient or staff member ranged from 1 to 13. Since the same members did not participate in all 13 administrations of the measures, analysis of the data as a repeated measures design was deemed inappropriate, and the data have been analyzed within a standard analysis of variance (ANOVA) design. Partial correlations across administrations have had the likely effect of deflating the error variance, and consequently, the results of the various ANOVAs presented here should be treated conservatively. For the purposes of our discussion, the alpha for rejection of the null hypothesis is .01 for ANOVA and linear trend analyses.

RESULTS

The principal question addressed in this article is whether the veterans' and staff members' perceptions of the treatment environment changed as the treatment program changed. In order to answer this question, separate ANOVAs were conducted on staff and veteran scores on each of the 10 subscales of the COPES. Additionally, analyses of the linear trend component across the 13 COPES administrations were computed.

Summaries of the ANOVAs and linear trend analyses are presented in Table 11.1. These results indicate that changes in the environmental perceptions of the staff and the veterans were most conspicuous for the involvement, autonomy, and practical orientation subscales, on each of which both staff and veterans showed highly significant linear trends. Mean scores for each group across the 13 administrations on these three subscales are presented graphically in Figures 11.1, 11.2, and 11.3, respectively. Staff perceptions of support and spontaneity also showed significant linear trends over the period, but not so for those of the veterans. Neither staff's nor veterans' linear analyses showed significant change

Table 11.1 Analysis of Variance and Linear Trend Analyses of COPES Subscales, Administrations 1-13 for Staff and Veterans

Subscale	Analysis of Variance			Linear Trend Analysis		
	df	MS	F	df	MS	F
Staff						
Involvement	12,198	20.65	3.85***	1,198	144.57	27.01***
Support	12,198	9.47	2.54**	1,198	43.55	11.67***
Spontaneity	12,199	8.49	1.94*	1,199	29.57	6.73**
Autonomy	12,199	14.03	6.19***	1,199	127.18	56.15***
Practical orientation	12,191	36.24	5.30***	1,191	361.41	52.91***
Personal problem orientation	12,202	7.09	2.14*	1,202	12.11	3.64
Anger and aggression	12,201	2.78	1.00	1,201	.57	.21
Order and organization	12,198	7.37	1.64	1,198	27.98	6.23*
Program clarity	12,203	7.94	1.34	1,203	22.37	3.78
Staff control	12,196	5.18	1.56	1,196	8.87	2.69
Veterans						
Involvement	12,210	10.61	1.86*	1,210	69.39	12.21***
Support	12,210	8.91	2.01*	1,210	2.14	.48
Spontaneity	12,209	3.21	.83	1,209	8.09	2.11
Autonomy	12,215	8.52	3.39***	1,215	46.06	18.34***
Practical orientation	12,208	7.84	2.55**	1,208	64.68	21.05***
Personal problem orientation	12,215	6.13	1.43	1,215	0.00	0.00
Anger and aggression	12,212	6.18	1.78	1,212	6.41	1.85
Order and organization	12,217	8.60	1.87*	1,217	.84	.18
Program clarity	12,208	3.65	.85	1,208	2.25	.52
Staff control	12,206	6.89	2.30**	1,206	4.45	1.49

*p < .05.
**p < .01.
***p < .001.

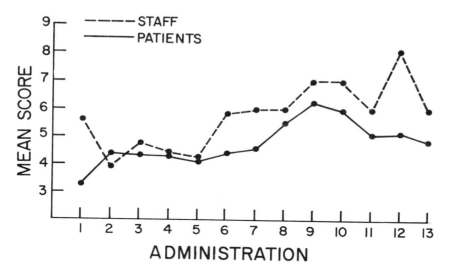

Figure 11.1 Mean involvement subscale scores for staff and veterans, COPES administrations 1-13, February 1977-February 1981.

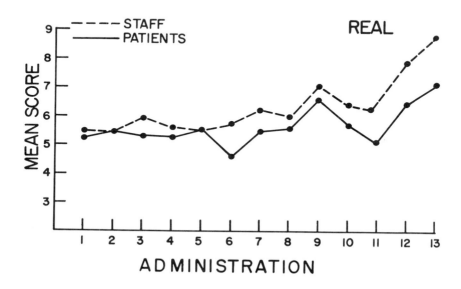

Figure 11.2 Mean autonomy subscale scores for staff and veterans, COPES administrations 1-13, February 1977-February 1981.

in those subscales (order and organization, program clarity, and staff control) reflecting the systems maintenance dimension of the program environment.

Mean scores on all 10 COPES subscales for veterans and staff for administrations 1, 7, and 13 are presented in Table 11.2. These administrations were selected as illustrative of the three phases of the treatment environment discussed below. Administrations 1, 7, and 13 were each made in February, at 2-year intervals. Further, these administrations were conducted when each of the three respective treatment models was in fully realized operation. Post hoc range comparisons of the three sets of means for veterans and staff amplify the linear trend analyses presented in Table 11.1. The range tests indicate that both veteran and staff means for autonomy and practical orientation were rated as higher on the 13th administration, while those from the 1st or 7th administrations were not significantly different from each other. in addition, staff saw the environment of the unit as offering more support since the inception of the VRP, and veterans saw the staff as less controlling. Multivariate ANOVAs (MANOVAS) were computed for the set of 10 COPES subscales on administrations 1, 7, and 13 for both veterans and staff. Each of these MANOVAs revealed significant differences among the administrations (veterans: $\chi^2 = 34.8$, $df = 20$, $p = .021$; staff: $\chi^2 = 67.4$, $df = 20$, $p < .001$).

Finally, standard scores were computed based on norms provided by Moos (1974a) for staff and patients. Profiles of the standard scores for the veterans on the 10 COPES subscales for administrations 1, 7, and 13 are presented in Figure 11.4. Similar standard score profiles for staff are presented in Figure 11.5.

Table 11.2 Mean COPES Subscale Scores for Administrations 1, 7, and 13,[a] Staff and Veterans

Subscales	Staff Administrations			Veterans Administrations		
	1	7	13	1	7	13
Involvement	5.6	5.1	6.0	3.3	4.6	4.9
Support	6.4	6.9	8.7	5.4	5.4	6.6
Spontonaneity	4.9	6.9	6.2	5.0	5.4	5.3
Autonomy	5.5	6.2	8.8	5.2	5.5	7.2
Practical orientation	4.7	5.2	9.6	5.7	6.2	7.6
Personal problem orientation	7.1	8.2	6.0	6.8	6.9	5.6
Anger and aggression	8.1	9.0	8.8	6.9	7.9	6.9
Order and organization	4.1	4.1	4.8	5.4	5.1	5.1
Program clarity	6.3	6.4	7.2	5.7	5.4	6.6
Staff control	4.4	4.4	2.9	7.3	6.4	4.9

Note: Underlined means are homogeneous subsets which do not differ by $p < .05$, Student-Newman-Keuls procedure.

[a] Administrations 1, 7, and 13 were conducted in February 1977, 1979, and 1981, respectively.

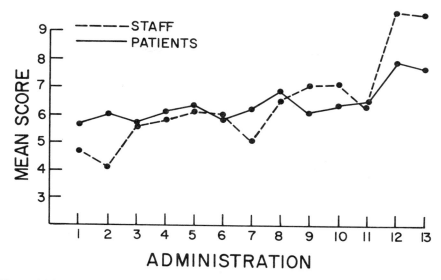

Figure 11.3 Mean practical orientation subscale scores for staff and veterans, COPES administrations 1-13, February 1977-February 1981.

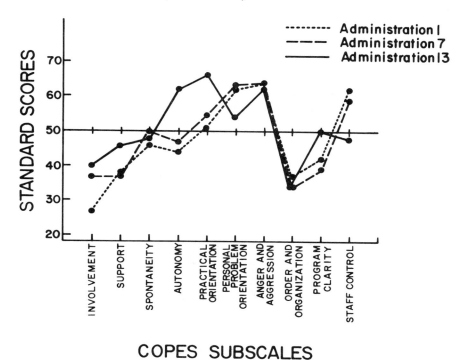

Figure 11.4 Standard score profiles for staff and veterans, COPES administrations 1 (February 1977), 7 (February 1979), and 13 (February 1981).

DISCUSSION

Changes in the Treatment Environment

Results of the linear trend analyses indicate that there were several significant changes in the perceived treatment environment over the 4-year period of the study. The staff demonstrated significant changes on 5 of the 10 subscales, and the data for veterans supported those changes on 3 of the subscales. Since involvement, autonomy, and practical orientation showed changes for both veterans and staff, graphs of those subscales are presented for discussion. The involvement subscale (Figure 11.1) shows a gradual increase beginning after the development of the TRTC. This program, with its emphasis on the therapeutic community, the development of a constitution, and the introduction of the work program, placed a great deal of emphasis on involvement within the boundaries of the unit. The figure also shows a slight decline in involvement over the last several observations. It was during this period that plans to end the TRTC program were announced and the VRP was introduced. Since the VRP places greater

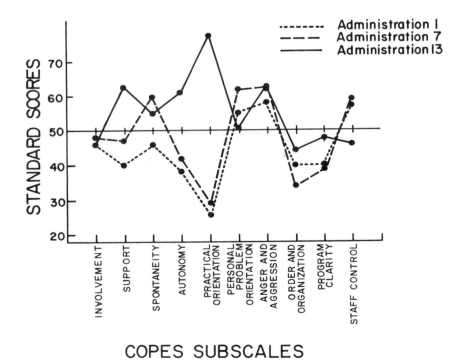

Figure 11.5 Standard score profiles for staff, COPES administrations 1 (February 1977), 7 (February 1979), and 13 (February 1981).

emphasis on activities off the unit and in the veteran's own community, the involvement subscale has remained at a somewhat lower level.

The autonomy subscale (Figure 11.2) had remained unchanged during the insight-oriented program and the TRTC. No meaningful change occurred until the VRP began. The figure shows a dramatic upward turn for veterans and staff at that point. This trend became even more pronounced as the VRP continued to develop.

The practical orientation subscale (Figure 11.3) is probably the most important subscale for illustrating the shift in the treatment dimension across time. The first administrations represent the insight-oriented program before the introduction of the work program. The staff regarded the program as very low on this dimension, while the veterans gave it a somewhat higher rating. With the beginning of the work program, the staff's perception of practical orientation jumped to the same level as that of the veterans, but the veterans' perceptions did not change at that time. Slowly, over the next 3 years, the level of practical orientation increased slightly as the work program and the adjunctive rehabilitation psychology program became more sophisticated. For example, the vocational resource program was introduced, in which the veterans were presented to state and V.A. vocational counselors who worked with the staff on vocational planning. It is not until the VRP was operative however, that practical orientation made its most dramatic increase. Although the staff's perception is considerably higher than the veterans' perception of practical orientation, both groups showed a strong increase, which was sustained through the last administration.

Comparison of the Insight-Oriented, TRTC, and VRP Treatment Environments

Table 11.2 illustrates the similarities of the insight-oriented program and the TRTC, and their differences from the VRP. While the first two programs do not differ on any subscale using post hoc comparisons of means, the VRP shows dramatic differences on the treatment dimension subscales of autonomy and practical orientation as well as on some of the other subscales.

The significant increase in the perception of autonomy since the inception of the VRP reflects the social expectations of the treatment environment, which supports the goal of preparing the veteran for making the best independent adjustment possible in his or her chosen community. It is interesting to note that the autonomy subscale continued to rise after the introduction of the VRP (see Figure 11.2). This appears to have been the direct result of two important changes in the VRP: the veterans began self-administration of their medications, and the staff hours were limited to 8:00 A.M. to 8:00 P.M. with no staff on weekends. Prior to the change, there had been two opinions on the impact of these two interventions. While the staff on the whole believed that limiting staff hours would increase autonomy and responsibility, many experienced clinicians were apprehensive that these changes would leave the veterans feeling unsupported and abandoned, that they would experience the withdrawal of the evening and night nurses as a deprivation, and that the unit would become chaotic and disorganized as a result of this frustration. There was also concern expressed by the hospital administration that the unit might be vandalized and become dirty and unsafe. The COPES data demonstrated that there were no decreases in perceived support or in perceived order and organization, and, as hoped, there was a considerable increase in perceived autonomy. The changes in the autonomy subscale, along with the significant decrease in the veterans' perception of staff control, reflect the program expectation that veterans give up their sick role behaviors and take responsibility for their own lives.

The difference on the practical orientation subscale between the VRP and the earlier programs indicates that the aims of rehabilitation have become central to the treatment on the unit. Despite the addition of a rehabilitation psychology program to the TRTC, the goals of rehabilitation never become fully incorporated into the perceived treatment environment. The dramatic increase in practical orientation signifies that the treatment environment supported the rehabilitation psychology program, and this change has distinguished this treatment environment from the ones that came earlier.

Treatment Environment Profile of the VRP

As illustrated in Figures 11.4 and 11.5, the VRP is distinctly different from the TRTC and the insight-oriented programs that preceded it. The standard score profiles provide information on how the VRP also differs from the normative population of the COPES. The norms are based on an assessment of a broad range of programs providing alternatives to hospitalization, including rehabilitation workshops, partial hospitalization programs, half-way houses, day hospitals, foster homes, and patient self-help units (Moos, 1974b). While most of these programs would not be located within a general medical-surgical hospital, the aims of these programs are generally consistent with those of the VRP. This similarity of purpose makes comparisons meaningful.

The veterans' standard score profile for the VRP is distinguished by the following: high autonomy, practical orientation, and anger and aggression; above-average personal problem orientation; average spontaneity, support, program clarity, and staff control; below-average involvement; and low order and organization.

Moos (1974b) divides treatment environments into three broad dimensions: relationship, treatment, and maintenance. The *treatment dimension* (composed of autonomy, practical orientation, personal problem orientation, and anger and aggression subscales) shows the highest standard scores, suggesting that the VRP is perceived as offering a great amount of direct treatment. The high practical orientation may reflect the VRP goal of adjustment and the wide range of training experiences in work, social skills, and community living provided. The next highest scale is autonomy. This scale has risen dramatically, perhaps because of the change in staffing hours and self-administration of medication, and is quite high even when compared to normative programs, which generally are not offered in the hospital. These data suggest that persons in a program designed like the

VRP experience more autonomy than they would be likely to experience were they out of the hospital in a half-way house or other rehabilitation program. The anger and aggression subscale reflects the staff's acceptance of the appropriate expression of angry feelings, and this interest in feelings was not sacrificed by the VRP. In line with the value the staff places on the expression of anger as therapeutic, personal problem orientation revealed fairly high expectations for the expression of feelings and the understanding of life experiences and development. These findings may be evidence that the VRP has moved closer to an integration of practical and personal problem orientations. That the personal problem orientation score has declined from the earlier programs may signify the greater emphasis the VRP places on the future than upon the past; that it has not decreased further may indicate the concern at the VRP for understanding the phenomenological world of the veteran as he or she goes through rehabilitation.

The relationship dimension (involvement, support, spontaneity), shows that the program is perceived as having only moderate expectations for veterans to be involved in this program and to support each other. A possible reason for this finding is that the focus of the program is adjustment outside the hospital, and so staff encourages veterans to focus their energies on activities that are occurring in their own communities. Most veterans are spending at least part of their day in work or training, and many attend outside social activities during the evening.

The maintenance dimension (order and organization, program clarity, staff control) reveals that the VRP is not perceived as stressing orderliness and tidiness, but that the veterans do understand the purposes of the program, what they are expected to accomplish, and approximately when they will be considered ready to leave the program. The moderate level of perceived staff control is in keeping with the high autonomy scale, but suggests that the veterans may continue to perceive the staff as still being in charge. These findings are in line with the staff's determination that the veterans should have control of their rules for living together, and that staff should be in charge of the assistance they provide. This policy is a shift from the traditional program in which staff took total control of the veterans' personal freedom (e.g., locking the ward door, physical restraints, patient privilege system) but often appeared to have only vaguely defined goals and little clarity about the relationship of the treatment interventions to specific goals.

Comparison of Treatment Models

The treatment environment did not change until the full rehabilitation psychology program was in operation. The attempt to add rehabilitation psychology as an ancillary service to the dominant traditional psychiatric treatment did not alter the perceived treatment environment. While the rehabilitation psychology program was quite active during the years of the TRTC, it could not get the treatment environment to support its aims. The reason for this resistance may lie in the significant differences between the treatment models of traditional insight-oriented treatment and rehabilitation psychology. Table 11.3 provides a comparative list of the differences between these two approaches.

Table 11.3 Comparison of Traditional Insight-Oriented Hospital Treatment and Rehabilitation Psychology Approaches

	Traditional Insight-Oriented Hospital Treatment	Rehabilitation Psychology
Source of the problem	Mental illness; distorted development	Lack of social skills and social support network; hospitalization itself
Staff perception of patient needs	Insight and control	Social and vocational readjustment
Treatment alliance	Traditional staff and patient roles	Written contract directed toward specific goals
Mode	Psychotherapy, chemotherapy, and socialization	Limited, task-oriented action; instruction; working; managing fear and anxiety through support and exposure to challenging experience
Locus of behavioral control	External containment: ward restrictions, restraints used to control acting out and to allow psychotic disorganization to be lived through while being protected externally	Self-control: autonomy encouraged and regression discouraged; ego strength bolstered by focusing on adaptive capacity
Locus of therapeutic work	Internal: in the patient's mind and brain	Behavioral: present- and future-oriented
Presumed agency of change	Synthetic function of ego, supported by medication and behavior management	Cognitions, attitudes, and behaviors; change through action
Criteria for judgment of change	Qualitative: self-expressions of change, staff's judgment	Quantitative: How has behavior changed? Can it be measured?
Goal	Symptomatic relief and insight	Behavioral change through practice and successive specific skills; increased self-confidence, increased social supports

The insight-oriented approach creates a treatment alliance based upon staff and patient roles that prevent effective rehabilitation. Traditional hospital psychiatry begins with containment of a mentally sick patient who is not only in great personal distress but is causing others distress as well. This initial role taking is maintained throughout the treatment, and the psychoanalytic understanding of behavior is sometimes used to support these roles: The patient is seen as having a distorted development that the treatment is going to uncover and correct. While the patient is expected to obtain insight by joining his or her observing ego with that of the therapist in exploring the meaning of past experience, the patient is simultaneously treated as someone who requires careful supervision and parental control. Since the real therapy is thought to occur only in the therapist's office and its success is dependent upon internal changes in the patient, the behavior and actions of the patient on the unit do not have any defined goals. While the patient quickly understands that his or her personal freedom depends in part on his or her ward behavior, the patient is not guided by a sense of purpose. Since a great deal of attention is given to those patients who are the most disruptive and disturbed, there is a powerful regressive force at work on such a unit, encouraging patients to act childishly and to be drawn into parent-child interactions with the staff. As immaturity is encouraged in the spirit of a regressive transference, the patient's yearnings for lost gratifications may very well get the better of him or her (or whatever fragile ability he or she may have to stay organized might give way), so that the patient may bring upon himself or herself ward restriction, security room, or physical restraints. Unfortunately, this not only provides the patient with a good deal of attention, it has the added reinforcement of providing an avoidance and distraction from the really frightening tasks of taking on adult responsibilities and returning to the community.

Rehabilitation is a process of confronting limitations and the fears that such confrontation inevitably brings. The patient must be supported, taught, and encouraged to meet the demands of adult independent life tasks—especially when the patient experiences himself or herself as disabled. Someone who is recovering from a psychotic experience may be demoralized and fearful that encountering stress may cause another frightening relapse. This is not unlike the psychological condition of any person following a traumatic illness or injury who faces a long period of readjustment. In a traditional psychiatric program, these common fears are themselves misinterpreted by both the patient and the staff as a sign of relapse. The patient who considers making a plan for leaving the hospital begins to feel panicky and, because the patient becomes anxious and depressed, thinks that he or she must not have recovered from his or her psychiatric problem. The staff, in responding to the patient's distress, reacts in ways they would act with any new patient coming onto the unit who was depressed or anxious. They might increase medication, arrange more therapy sessions, restrict the person to the unit, and thus discourage the patient from proceeding with his or her plans. In this context, it is very difficult for a rehabilitation psychology program to be effective. The rehabilitation of the patient is regarded as secondary to the concerns for the patient's psychiatric symptoms and his or her development of insight into their meaning.

It may not be psychoanalytic concepts themselves that are responsible for the incompatibility of an effective rehabilitation psychology program and the insight-oriented approach, but rather the way they are applied within traditional treatment roles in an inpatient psychiatric treatment unit. Indeed, a psychoanalytic under-standing of the psychosocial development and deficits of this population has played a conceptual role in the VRP and seems to enhance the rehabilitation work by providing the staff with a framework for understanding the personality of the veteran and their own reactions to him or her. Such phenomena as splitting, projection, hallucinations, and delusions are difficult to observe or be a part of without some way of understanding what occurs. The rehabilitation psychology approach, however, with its emphasis on ego strengthening through changes in cognitions, attitudes, and behaviors, and its concrete assistance in providing important social resources, may well be the preferred way of treating the psychological condition of the person with schizophrenia precisely because of the development described by psychoanalytic theory.

These differences between a rehabilitation approach and traditional psychiatric care may explain why psychosocial treatments reported in the literature have led to better outcomes. Traditional inpatient psychiatric care bases its treatment approach on the role of the mentally sick patient who requires insight and containment. This role requirement can unwittingly discourage the patient from making efforts toward adjustment outside the hospital by creating a great deal of environmental press toward self-exploration with little press toward practical problem solving and personal autonomy. The rehabilitation psychology approach, by contrast, creates an environmental press toward facing the difficult challenges of adult life tasks, toward recognizing strengths as well as weaknesses, and toward taking responsibility for one's own feelings, choices, and actions. Studies relating outcome to specific aspects of perceived treatment environments (Ellsworth, Maroney, Klett, Gorden, & Gunn, 1971; Moos, Shelton, & Petty, 1973) have shown that programs that emphasize autonomy, practical orientation, and the functional expression of feelings within structured environments appear to be most effective in promoting long-term community tenure. The results reported in this study indicate that these are precisely the characteristics that were most improved when the VRP was introduced and that may, therefore, lead to better outcomes for the veterans it serves. Studies are underway to measure the outcome of veterans from the VRP and to compare these results with those of traditional programs.

NOTE

1. Monti, P. M., Curran, J. P., Corriveau, P. P., & Delancy, A. L. Effects of social skills training groups and sensitivity training groups with psychiatric patients. Unpublished manuscript, 1980.

REFERENCES

Andrews, G., Tennant, C., Hewson, D., & Valliant, G. (1979. Life event stress, social support, coping style, and risk of psychological impairment. *Journal of Nervous and Mental Disease, 166*, 307–316.

Anthony, W. A., Buell, G. J., Sharratt, S., & Althoff, M. E. (1972). The efficacy of psychiatric rehabili*tation. Psychological Bulletin, 78*, 447-456.

Anthony, W. A., Cohen, M. R., & Vitalo, R. (1978). The measurement of rehabilitation outcome. *Schizophrenia Bulletin, 4*, 365-383.

Bachrach, L. L. (1976). A note on some recent studies of released mental hospital patients to the community. *American Journal of Psychiatry, 133*, 73-75.

Becker, P., & Bayer, C. (1975). Preparing chronic patients for community placement: A four stage treatment program. *Hospital and Community Psychiatry, 26,* 448-450.

Birley, J. L., & Brown, G. (1970). Crises and life changes preceding the onset or relapse of acute schizophrenia. *British Journal of Psychiatry, 116,* 327-333.

Dean, A., & Linn, N. (1977). The stress-buffering role of social supports. *Journal of Nervous and Mental Disease, 165,* 403-417.

Ellsworth, R., Maroney, R., Klett, W., Gorden, H., & Gunn, R. (1971). Milieu characteristic; of successful psychiatric treatment programs. *American Journal of Orthopsychiatry, 41,* 427-441.

Fontana, A. F., Dowds, B. N., Marcus, J. L., & Rakusin, J. M. (1976). Coping with interpersonal conflicts through live events and hospitalization. *Journal of Nervous and Mental Disease, 162,* 88-98.

Goldstein, A. P., Sprafkin, R. P., & Gershaw, N. J. (1976). *Skill training for community living: Applied structured learning therapy.* New York: Pergamon.

Guthrie, M. E., Goldstein, A. P., & Hunter, G. E. (1973). The use of modeling and role playing to increase social interaction among asocial psychiatric patients. *Journal of Consulting and Clinical Psychology, 40,* 408-415.

Hersen, M., & Bellack, A. S. (1976). Social skills training for chronic psychiatric patients: Rationale, research findings, and future directions. *Comprehensive Psychiatry, 17,* 559-580.

Jacobs, M. K., and Trick, O. L. (1974). Successful psychiatric rehabilitation using an inpatient teaching laboratory. *American Journal of Psychiatry, 70,* 337-342.

Kociemba, A. B., Cotten, P. G., & Frank, M. A. (1979). Predictors of community tenure of discharged state hospital patients. *American Journal of Psychiatry, 136,* 1556-1561.

Marsella, A. J., & Snyder, K. K. (1981). Stress, social supports, and schizophrenic disorders: Toward an interactional model. *Schizophrenic Bulletin, 7,* 152-163.

Mechanic, D. (1968). *Medical sociology.* New York: Free Press.

Moos, R. H. (1974a). *Community Oriented Programs Environment Scale.* Palo Alto, Calif.: Consulting Psychologist Press.

Moos, R. H. (1974b). *Evaluation of treatment environments: A social ecological approach.* New York: Wiley-Interscience.

Moos, R. H., Shelton, R., & Petty, C. (1973). Perceived ward climate and treatment outcome. *Journal of Abnormal Psychology, 82,* 291-298.

Moos, R. H. (1975). Toward a taxonomy of inpatient treatment environments. *Journal of Abnormal Psychology, 84,* 181-188.

Mosher, L. R., & Keith, S. J. (1980). Psychosocial treatment: Individual, group, family, and community approaches. *Schizophrenia Bulletin, 6,* 10-41.

Paul, G. L., & Lentz, R. J. (1977). *Psychosocial treatment of chronic mental patients.* Cambridge, Mass.: Harvard University Press.

Price, R. H., & Rog, D. J., & Rausch, H. L. (1975). The psychiatric halfway house: How is it measuring up? *Community Mental Health Journal, 11,* 155-162.

Taube, C. A. (1974). Readmission to inpatient services of state and county mental hospitals in 1972. *Statistical Note* 110. Bethesda, Md.: National Institute of Mental Health, Division of Biometry, Survey and Reports Branch.

Vaughn, C. E., & Leff, J. P. (1976). The influence of family and social factors on the course of psychiatric illness: A comparison of schizophrenic and depressed neurotic patients. *British Journal of Psychiatry, 129,* 125-137.

Vaughn, C. E., & Leff, J. P. (1981). Patterns of emotional response in relatives of schizophrenia patients. *Schizophrenia Bulletin, 7,* 43-44.

Wallace, J. C., Nelson, C. J., Liberman, R. P., Aitchison, R. A., Lukoff, D., Elder, J. P., & Ferris, C. (1980). A review and critique of social skills training with schizophrenic patients. *Schizophrenia Bulletin, 6,* 42-63.

Weinman, B. (1975, Fall). Chronics make it in the community. *Innovations,* 32-33.

Zigler, E., & Phillips, L. (1961a). Social effectiveness and symptomatic behaviors. *Journal of Abnormal and Social Psychology, 61*, 231-238.
Zigler, E., & Phillips, L. (1961b). Social competence and outcome in pschiatric disorder. *Journal of Abnormal and Social Psychology, 63*, 264-271.

Acknowledgments: The authors wish to thank Dr. Ruth Grant and Ms. Debra Letai for their assistance in collecting the data presented herein. The research was supported by a grant from the Veterans Administration.

12

Predictive Validity of Situational Assessment at a Psychiatric Rehabilitation Center

Gary R. Bond and Mark H. Friedmeyer

ABSTRACT: Situational assessment was used to predict employment outcomes for 77 individuals attending a community psychiatric rehabilitation program. The assessment form was a 22-item checklist comprised of four dimensions: work readiness, work attitudes, interpersonal relations, and work quality. Ratings were made in two work settings: prevocational work crews and transitional employment. Situational assessment predicted outcome better than did work history. Staff ratings were significantly higher for members working in transitional employment, although ratings made in both settings were predictive of later employment outcomes. It was concluded that situational assessment may be a method better suited for screening out members who have poor work potential than selecting members who will definitely succeed.

Estimating vocational potential is a fundamental issue in rehabilitation, both practically and scientifically. From a practical standpoint, determination of employability is critical for funding decisions by the Social Security Administration (SSA) and by state vocational rehabilitation (VR) services. At the level of the rehabilitation agency, workers must frequently decide when a client is ready to be placed in a community job. The broader scientific question is the identification of factors, including client characteristics and objective assessment procedures, that predict future vocational behavior.

Assessment of vocational potential has proved to be particularly elusive for psychiatric rehabilitation. Much to their detriment, clients who have had psychiatric hospitalizations with diagnoses of schizophrenia or major affective disorder have, until recently, been largely ignored by the VR system, in part because their employment potential is so poor and because predicting employment success is difficult. As described by Anthony and Jansen (1984), SSA regulations have discriminated against persons with psychiatric disabilities by using such criteria as diagnosis, symptomatology, and hospitalization history, none of which have any empirical relationship to employment potential. The single best demographic predictor, suggested by many studies, is prior work history. Even this factor, however, is of limited value, for example, when a client's psychotic episodes postdate the sole period of stable employment. The need for reliable methods for predicting employment is apparent.

Anthony and Jansen (1984) conclude that staff ratings of clients' work adjustment skills are the best clinical predictors of future work performance. Although they have workshop settings in mind, the more general concept is that of situational assessment, defined as a method of vocational evaluation that focuses on general skills and behaviors important to any occupation (Berven, 1984; Neff, 1966). Used informally in many rehabilitation settings, it is appropriate whenever staff have an opportunity to observe client work behavior directly. Situational assessment is perceived as the most useful tool in evaluating future vocational outcomes for clients with psychiatric disabilities, according to a national survey of rehabilitation professionals (Hursh & Dellario, 1984).

Most research on the psychometric properties of situational assessment has been methodologically unsophisticated. A comprehensive review by Van Allen and Loeber (1972) located seven studies of psychiatric work rating scales in which reliability and validity issues were considered. Four reported predictive validity data, although only two of these used vocational outcome criteria. Their review focuses on the dimensions of the rating scales, in which the authors group the items into the categories of work personality, work competency, social competency, and psychiatric symptoms. A review by Watts (1978) concludes that ratings of social relationships, response to supervision, and enthusiasm were predictive of return to work, but task competence was not. Anthony and Jansen (1984) suggest three work skill categories: getting along, doing the job, and being dependable. Of these, they hypothesize that the interpersonal dimension (getting along) is the most important. There is good consensus among reviewers about the critical dimensions, although as yet there is no single, widely used, standardized form.

The situational approach is particularly compatible with psychosocial rehabilitation (PSR), a pragmatic approach to helping persons with severe mental illness achieve optimal community adjustment (Beard, Propst, & Malamud, 1982; Dincin, 1975). Once accepted into a PSR program, members (as clients are called) are given a chance to progress toward competitive employment without regard to employment or rehospitalization history. They often receive no formal vocational evaluation, in contrast to traditional rehabilitation practice. Members usually are placed initially in prevocational work crews, which are unpaid work experiences conducted at the PSR agency. The tasks performed are not simulated but involve meaningful jobs. The staff attempt to convey to members that their contributions are needed as much as in paid employment. Staff workers evaluate members' appropriateness for the next stage, which uses transitional employment program (TEP) positions. TEP differs from the prevocational training in several respects. TEP provides a paid work experience in the community in which members come into daily contact with regular employees. They are paid directly by the community employer and are expected to function as regular employees. Situational assessments are also conducted in TEP.

Because TEP more closely approximates competitive employment, it might be hypothesized that TEP ratings would be more predictive of future employment. On the other hand, prevocational crews offer more extensive contact between staff and members. Ethridge (1968) has shown that a single form can be used in different sites without affecting the validity of the ratings. The direction for development of scales is logically toward more nomothetic scales, rather than scales that ask about specific skills required in a given setting, because the goal of PSR is teaching good work habits, not specific skills *per se.* Yet despite the widespread informal use of rating scales, little work has been done in determining if this nomothetic approach is feasible.

Surprisingly, with the exception of one early study by Gellman (1957), there are no published validity studies of situational assessment with individuals having psychiatric disabilities served in community settings. The earlier hospital-based studies are of limited value. With deinstitutionalization, the major focus of rehabilitation is now in the community.

This study, therefore, had several purposes. The overriding goal was to determine the predictive validity of a situational assessment procedure in a community rehabilitation program, especially as compared with the predictive validity of work history. A second question was whether the setting in which the ratings are made influences their predictability. Finally, other psychometric properties, such as reliability and subscale differences, were examined.

METHOD

Subjects

The sample consisted of 84 members attending a PSR program. All had received staff ratings of work performance in either a prevocational crew ($N = 40$) or TEP ($N = 44$) between three and eight months after admission. The subjects were drawn from a larger controlled evaluation study in which 131 members were randomly assigned initially to either a "gradual" prevocational condition or an "accelerated" TEP condition and followed for 15 months (Bond & Dincin, 1986). There were 47 subjects from the original study excluded in the current report. In this excluded sample, nine had not received any situational assessments, 28 had no ratings during the stipulated time frame, and 11 had forms that were incomplete; most had terminated within a few months after admission and/or had poor attendance. The study sample did not differ from the excluded sample on any demographic variable examined, except that the study sample averaged significantly more years of education.

Vocational outcomes at 15 months were available for 77 of the 84 subjects. The study sample had significantly better outcomes than the excluded sample. This difference was not surprising, in that the excluded sample consisted primarily of early terminators, who already had been found in the original study to have poorer outcomes.

The sample had a mean age of 24.5 and a mean of 13.1 years of education; 70% were male. Subjects had a mean of 3.2 prior psychiatric hospitalizations. The diagnoses received at last hospitalization were as follows: schizophrenia, 49%; major affective disorder, 46%; other, 5%. At admission 60% were receiving government assistance, 33% were supported by parents, and 5% stated they were self-supporting. Further sampling details are given by Bond and Dincin (1986).

Training Sites and Raters

The study was conducted at Thresholds, a private PSR agency described elsewhere (Bond, Dincin, Setze, & Witheridge, 1984; Dincin, 1975). The prevocational component consists of morning work crews assigned to food preparation, clerical, and janitorial chores conducted on the agency premises. Members are expected to meet community standards with regard to punctuality, appropriate dress, taking instructions, and so forth. Each of the three work crews is supervised by a crew leader.

TEP includes group placements, in which two or more members work at a community job site under the supervision of a job coach. Group placement sites include warehouses, libraries, hotels, and concession stands. Individual placements are TEP positions for more advanced members, who work without direct supervision from PSR staff; in this case the employer gives regular feedback to the PSR placement worker on the member's job performance.

In this study, the members rated on prevocational crew included 15 on kitchen crew, 17 on clerical crew, and 8 on janitorial crew. Of the TEP members rated, 42 were on group and 2 on individual placement.

Ratings are made by crew leaders, job coaches, and placement workers, each of whom make monthly ratings on between 10 and 25 members. Staff workers have at least bachelor's degrees (typically in psychology, social work, or a similar area) and a range of prior work experiences in mental health and industry; most have not had specialty training in rehabilitation. Changes in staff assignments occur frequently as a result of promotions, lateral transfers, and resignations. Ratings from 18 different workers were used in the current study.

Situational Assessment Form

The Thresholds Monthly Work Evaluation Form (TMWEF) was developed by the Thresholds staff as a standard form for use with all prevocational crews and TEP positions. Its primary use is to provide continuous, systematic feedback to members on their progress. Prior to this study, each of the crews and TEP positions used its own evaluation form. Although the contents of these forms overlapped, they had idiosyncracies and specific questions tailored to the job site. For the cross-site evaluation study, the form was standardized, based on the principle that generic work skills and attitudes could be assessed in a variety of work settings. The form, however, could not be too specific in its wording and still retain its value as a generic instrument.

As shown in Table 12.1, the TMWEF is comprised of four dimensions: work readiness (e.g., good attendance, grooming, control of inappropriate behavior), work attitudes (e.g., initiative, acceptance of responsibility), interpersonal relations

Table 12.1 Thresholds Monthly Evaluation Rating Form

Work Readiness
  Attendance
  Personal grooming/appearance
  Punctuality
  Controls inappropriate behaviors
Work Attitudes
  Initiative
  Accepts responsibility
  Persistence with task, tolerance
  General disposition
  Flexibility and adaptability to change
  Reasonable speed in task completion
  Willingness to accept disagreeable tasks
Interpersonal Relations
  Cooperation and rapport with co-workers
  Cooperation and rapport with supervisor
  Willingness to help others voluntarily
  Asks others for help appropriately
  Ability to accept criticism
Work Quality and Performance
  Follows and retains directions
  Accuracy
  Efficiency/thoroughness
  Productivity
  Able to work without close supervision
  Acknowledges errors and corrects them

(e.g., cooperation with supervisor and peers), and work quality and performance (e.g., accuracy, productivity). Item ratings are made on a five-point scale ranging from unsatisfactory (1) to outstanding (5). A category for insufficient information is also included.

For each subject, a rating form was selected that had been completed three to eight months after admission. A variable timeframe, rather than a fixed period of time, was necessary, because a form was not completed on every member every month (due to poor attendance, member reassignments, and other factors). Ratings made at least three months following admission were used, on the assumption that assessments made earlier might be less valid because staff workers would have had less familiarity with members. The eighth month was chosen as the latest point, since the outcome measures were based on the six-month period between nine and 15 months. As part of the design of the original evaluation study, members had been randomly assigned after the first month either to continue in their prevocational crew assignment or to go immediately on a TEP placement. For each member, a rating form, consistent with this assignment, was selected from the work site. The only exceptions were seven subjects who were either assigned to crew and assessed on TEP (because of rapid progress) or assigned to TEP and assessed on crew (because of serious problems on TEP).

When a member had more than one rating form that met all criteria, one form was randomly selected. Ratings used in the study were completed an average of five months after admission.

Within each subscale, item scores were summed. The alpha coefficient for homogeneity of the total scale, based on the sum of the means on the four subscales, was .86. Alpha coefficients for homogeneity of items were also calculated for each subscale; they ranged from .74 to .93. Items coded as insufficient information, which comprised less than 2% of the responses, were recoded as the modal response for that subscale. The range of possible values for the total scale was from 22 to 110. The actual scores ranged from 45 to 108, with a mean of 68.3, median of 67.5, and standard deviation of 12.2.

Despite the heterogeneity of work sites and the fact that staff received little specific training in completing the TMWEF, test-retest reliability proved to be satisfactory. Ratings on two successive months were obtained for 30 members. In each case the same staff worker made ratings on both occasions. The reliability coefficient for the total scale was .76 ($p < .001$), with reliability for the subscales ranging from .64 for work quality to .78 for work readiness.

Work History Variables

Three variables assessing work history were obtained from the member during an interview conducted within two weeks after admission: months employed, months unemployed, and work experience. Months unemployed was defined as the aggregated total of time in paid employment prior to admission. The mean for the sample was 36.3, ranging from 0 to 152 months. Months unemployed was measured between the termination from the last job held to the date of admission. Among those who had ever been employed, the mean was 16.9 and the range was from 1 to 67 months. For data analysis purposes, the 15 members who had never worked were assigned a value of 70 for this variable. Work experience was a dichotomous variable based on a criterion of continuous employment. Members who had worked one year continuously in competitive employment were classified as work-experienced (48% of sample); otherwise, they were classified as work inexperienced (52%).

Outcome Measures

Subjects were interviewed 15 months after admission. Computerized agency records of employment, based on weekly caseworker reports, and other program evaluation data (such as post-termination interviews conducted with all members) were consulted as cross-checks on the accuracy of member reports.

Three outcome measures were obtained at 15 months: number of weeks worked, total earnings from employment, and employment status. Weeks worked and total earnings were based on the preceding six-month period. In tabulating weeks worked, any week in which a member worked six hours or more was included. (Those in competitive employment ranged from 20 to 40 hours of employment per week; individual placement was typically 20 hours, and group placement ranged from six to 20 hours.) Most of the wages were at or slightly above the minimum wage. Employment status was determined from the member's status during the week in which the follow-up interview was due and was a categorical variable consisting of five criterion groups: competitively employed, individual TEP placement, group TEP placement, prevocational crew, and unemployed. The prevocational crew category included six members who were in other vocational training programs, and the unemployed category included one member in a sheltered workshop.

RESULTS

Correlations of Situational Assessment with Outcome

As shown in Table 12.2, the correlations between the ratings of weeks worked and earnings were all significant. The correlations between work history variables and outcome, although all in the expected direction, were significantly smaller in magnitude, using Fisher's r-to-z transformation.

To examine differences in 15-month employment status, a series of one-way analyses of variance was conducted, using the five categories of employment as the criterion groups. Post-hoc comparisons were examined, using the Student-Newman-Keuls procedure with an alpha level of .05. In all cases the homogeneity of variance assumption was met (using Cochran's C), so pooled variance estimates were used.

All four subscales showed significant differences between the five criterion groups, as shown in Table 12.3. The total scale provided the best overall results, discriminating the competitive employment subgroup from the prevocational and unemployed subgroups and the individual TEP subgroup from the unemployed

Table 12.2 Correlations of Situational Assessment with Vocational Outcome

	Outcome Variable	
Predictor Variable	Total Weeks Worked	Total Earnings
Situational Assessment		
Work Readiness	.35**	.32**
Work Attitudes	.53***	.51***
Interpersonal Relations	.45***	.52***
Work Quality	.48***	.48***
Total Scale	.54***	.54***
Work History		
Months Employed	.19*	.17
Months Unemployed	−.15	−.20*
Work Experience	.20*	.13

*$p < .05$.
**$p < .01$.
***$p < .001$.

subgroup. Neither of the work history variables examined showed significant differences between groups.

From a practitioner's standpoint, the pertinent question is whether a specific score can be interpreted in relation to future employment success. To this end, a median split was used to define a dichotomous assessment rating. The above-median group worked a mean of 14.8 weeks, compared with 4.9 weeks for the below-median group, $t(75) = 5.26, p < .001$. The mean earnings of $1081 for the above-median group was also significantly higher than the $251 of the below-median group, $t(75) = 4.87, p < .001$ (t-test with separate variance estimates for unequal variances). Cross-tabulating the dichotomized rating variable with employment status yielded significant differences, as shown in Table 12.4. Altogether, 84% of the 31 members in paid employment scored above the median, while 67% of the 46 who were not employed scored below the median. By contrast, work experience was not associated with employment status.

Comparisons Between Sites

Between-site differences were examined in assessment ratings and outcomes. The seven subjects who were not assessed at the site to which they were assigned were eliminated from these analyses because they were atypical, either regressing after assignment to TEP or progressing more rapidly than expected to TEP after initial prevocational assignment. The two samples were demographically similar, except that there was a significantly higher percentage of males on TEP (82%) than on prevocational crews (55%), $\chi^2<$ (with Yates' correction) $= 5.2, p < .05$. The mean rating for the total scale was 71.0 for TEP and 65.7 for the prevocational crews, $t(75) = 2.00, p < .05$. Among the subscales, the TEP ratings were significantly higher for work quality, $t(75) = 2.12, p < .05$. At the 15-month follow up, nine of 37 members assigned to TEP were competitively employed, compared with two of 33 assigned to prevocational crew. For weeks worked, the mean for the TEP, condition (13.4) was significantly higher than for the prevocational crew, (6.8), $t(68) = 3.01$, $p < .01$; for total earnings, the mean for the TEP condition ($933) was also significantly higher than for the prevocational condition ($492), $t(67) = 2.10, p < .05$.

Within-site predictive validity was also examined, following the same analytic procedures as for the total sample. Only the results for the total scale are reported. Within-site correlations for weeks worked and total earnings were similar to those reported in Table 12.2, and all were significant. Differences in employment status were found for the prevocational crews, $F(4,30) = 5.7, p < .01$, but not for TEP. Within each site, the median split analysis yielded significant differences on weeks worked and on earnings. The median split analysis on employment status yielded significant differences for the prevocational crews, $\chi^2<$ (4) $= 15.1, p < .01$, but not for TEP, $\chi^2<$ (4) $= 8.0, p < .10$.

DISCUSSION

As in prior research, this study found that staff ratings of work adjustment are predictive of future employment for clients with psychiatric disabilities. This

Table 12.3 15-Month Employment Status and 8-Month Situational Assessment

Predictor Variable	Competitive Employment (N = 11)	Individual TEP (N = 8)	Group TEP (N = 12)	Prevocational Crew (N = 27)	Unemployed (N = 19)	Total (N = 77)	F-value
Situational Assessment							
Work Readiness	14.0^a	13.7	13.1	12.0	11.0^b	12.4	3.1*
Work Attitudes	26.1^a	24.3	22.9	20.7^b	20.9^b	22.2	4.5**
Interpersonal Relations	17.9^a	16.2	15.7	14.3^b	13.8^b	15.1	4.7**
Work Quality	21.8^a	21.8^a	19.8	18.5	17.7^b	19.3	3.7**
Total Scale	79.9^a	75.9^{a,b}	71.5	65.5^b	63.4^c	69.1	5.6***
Work History							
Months Employed	54.2	45.9	48.3	31.9	25.8	37.6	1.4
Months Unemployed	17.1	17.1	30.4	25.7	36.0	26.9	1.4

*p < .05.

**p < .01.

***p < .001.

[a,b,c]: Reading across each row, means having different superscripts are significatly different by the Student-Newman-Keuls test.

Table 12.4 Prediction of 15-Month Employment Status for Situational Assessment and Work Experience

Predictor Variable	Competitive Employment	Individual TEP	Group TEP	Prevocational Crew	Unemployed	Total	Chi-square value
Situational Assessment							22.5***
Above Median	10 (91%)	8 (100%)	8 (67%)	10 (37%)	5 (26%)	41 (53%)	
Below Median	1 (9%)	0 (0%)	4 (33%)	17 (63%)	14 (74%)	36 (47%)	
Work Experience							6.1
One Year or More	6 (55%)	5 (63%)	8 (67%)	13 (48%)	5 (26%)	37 (48%)	
Less Than One Year	5 (45%)	3 (38%)	4 (33%)	14 (52%)	14 (74%)	40 (52%)	

***$p < .001$.

study extends the results to a community setting and, by using multiple outcome measures, offers strong empirical support for this widely used procedure.

Surprisingly, work history was, by comparison, only weakly correlated with outcome. One possible explanation is that as members become increasingly involved in PSR, history and background factors may diminish in importance, while current work performance becomes more influential in deciding future employment. If this interpretation is correct, it would be consistent with the PSR philosophy of giving members a chance to work in paid employment, without regard to their prior record (Beard et al., 1982). However, methodological limitations must also be considered. One issue is whether more refined measures of work history might not have greater predictive power. The self-selection process is a second issue. The sample was not representative in the sense that clients who attend PSR programs are probably more motivated to work and, further, that those who continue attending are more motivated than those who terminate early.

From a practical standpoint, many questions remain unanswered. How early could such ratings be made and still retain substantial predictive validity? Soloff and Bolton (1969) found that situational assessment had considerably greater predictive validity when based on a 13-week period as compared to a four-week period. The average latency of five months used in the current study is not practical for many purposes, although for rehabilitation workers who are gauging members' readiness for the next stage of employment, this timeframe is not unrealistic.

Close examination of the findings suggests caution in extrapolating to the prediction of individual performance. Although over four-fifths of the members who achieved paid employment scored above the median on the rating scale, the converse was not true: a much smaller majority of those above the median were vocationally successful. Thus it may be that the situational approach is more useful for identifying members who are definitely not vocationally ready than for selecting those who will ultimately succeed (Watts, 1978). Examination of open-ended comments on the rating forms suggests why this might be so. Members receiving lower ratings typically had comments reflecting major behavioral deficits: "should work on coming to crew and staying despite her mood swings" ... "must control acting out behavior (banging things, etc.)" ... "should work on tasks without unnecessary wandering from the work area."

The ratings made in the prevocational crews were no less valid than those in TEP. One traditional function of prevocational training has been evaluation of work potential in an environment where the costs of failing are much less than in paid work, and this study supports the viability of this approach.

Even though they had been drawn from a randomly assigned sample and were therefore, at admission, presumably comparable in work potential to members assigned to TEP, members in prevocational training had lower ratings as well as poorer employment outcomes. It may be speculated that this was partly because less was expected of them. An indication that members on crew were less motivated was the frequent reference to poor attendance on their rating forms. The fact that members were not paid for their work on crew may also have contributed to lower levels of performance. Other research has found that external incentives are an important factor in work productivity (Wing & Freudenberg, 1961). The role of expectancy on vocational outcomes merits further study, to determine the potency of a "Rosenthal effect" (Rosenthal & Jacobsen, 1968).

A major limitation in the study was the fact that staff workers completing the ratings were also involved in determining whether members would be promoted into higher-level vocational placements, thereby confounding the prediction process and the decision process. This was less (of a problem for the members evaluated on TEP, because as part of the research design they were expected to remain on TEP regardless of staff evaluations of their rehabilitation progress. The fact that the TEP ratings were predictive of outcomes argues against the rival explanation that the employment outcomes were simply self-fulfilling prophesies. Most members (85%) had at least one placement opportunity to prove themselves. Finally, in terms of ecological validity, the use of raters who also make placement decisions closely replicates actual practice. Nonetheless, a more rigorous design for answering the prediction question would have independent raters.

The subscales of this rating approach did not yield major differences. They were moderately correlated with each other, and each was approximately equal in predictive power. In particular, work quality predicted outcomes as well as interpersonal relationships, unlike some prior research. It is probable that these findings were a result of a halo effect, whereby ratings were largely determined by the raters' global evaluations and not by members' performance in specific areas. Traditional remedies for this problem include behaviorally anchored scales, training of raters, and feedback to raters based on reliability studies. All of these should be considered in future scale development, recognizing the trade-offs involved, for example, in training time for staff.

To conclude, simple ratings of work behavior in a rehabilitation setting are excellent predictors of future paid employment. Such ratings can be reliably made, and they are statistically independent of client characteristics related to psychiatric and vocational history. Because rehabilitation decisions so often depend on judgments of employability, and because many traditional indicators have such limited prognostic value, situational assessment methods should be refined for more general systematic use and incorporated into formal decision processes.

REFERENCES

Anthony, W. A., & Jansen, M. A. (1984). Predicting the vocational capacity of the chronically mentally ill: Research and implications. *American Psychologist, 39*, 537-544.

Beard, J. H., Propst, R. N., & Malamud, T.J. (1982). The Fountain House model of rehabilitation. *Psychosocial Rehabilitation Journal, 5*, 47-53.

Berven, N. L. (1984). Assessment practices in rehabilitation counseling. *Journal of Applied Rehabilitation Counseling, 15*, 9-14, 47.

Bond, G. R., Dincin, J., Setze, P. J., & Witheridge, T. J. (1984). The effectiveness of psychiatric rehabilitation: A summary of research at thresholds. *Psychosocial Rehabilitation Journal, 7*, 6-22.

Bond, G. R., & Dincin, J. (1986). Accelerating entry into transitional employment in a psychosocial rehabilitation agency. *Rehabilitation Psychology, 31*, 143–155.

Dincin, J. (1975). Psychiatric rehabilitation. *Schizophrenia Bulletin, 1*, 131–148.

Ethridge, D. A. (1968). Prevocational assessment of rehabilitation potential of psychiatric patients. *American Journal of Occupational Therapy, 22*, 161–167.

Gellman, W. (1957). Vocational evaluation of the emotionally handicapped. *Journal of Rehabilitation, 23*, 9–11, 32.

Hursh, N. C., & Dellario, D. J. (1984, August). *Situational assessment: Identifying vocational potential of psychiatrically disabled individuals.* Paper presented at the annual meeting of the American Psychological Association, Toronto, Canada.

Neff, W. S. (1966). Problems of work evaluation. *Personnel and Guidance Journal, 44*, 682–688.

Rosenthal, R., & Jacobsen, L. (1968). *Pygmalion in the classroom: Teachers' expectations and pupils' intellectual development.* New York: Holt, Rinehart & Winston.

Soloff A., & Bolton, B. F. (1969). The validity of the CJVS Scale of Employability for older clients in a vocational adjustment workshop. *Educational and Psychological Measurement, 29*, 993–998.

Van Allen, R., & Loeber, R. (1972). Work assessment of psychiatric patients: A critical review of published scales. *Canadian Journal of Behavioral Science, 4*, 101–117.

Watts, F. N. (1978). A study of work behavior in a psychiatric rehabilitation unit. *British Journal of Social and Clinical Psychology, 17*, 85–92.

Watts, F. N. (1983). Employment. In F. N. Watts & D. H. Bennett (Eds,), *Theory and practice of psychiatric rehabilitation* (pp. 215–240). New York: John Wiley.

Wing, J. K., & Freudenberg, R. K. (1961). The response of severely ill chronic schizophrenic patients to social stimulation. *American Journal of Psychiatry, 118*, 311–322.

Acknowledgments: Portions of this research were supported by a grant from the Field Foundation and by Grant No. 8103 from the Illinois Department of Mental Health and Developmental Disabilities. The data were collected when Gary Bond was employed at Thresholds. Thanks to Harry Bender, Karen Daiter, Toni Pristo, Evelyn Segal, Paul Setze, and Barry Sherman, who assisted in the collection of the data, and to the staff and members at Thresholds, all of whom were essential to this study. Special thanks to Jerry Dincin, executive director of Thresholds, who strongly supports empirical evaluation of psychosocial rehabilitation. Finally our thanks to Karli Lindig, who made suggestions on earlier drafts.

13

Normal Housing with Specialized Supports: A Psychiatric Rehabilitation Approach to Living in the Community

Andrea K. Blanch, Paul J. Carling and Priscilla Ridgway

ABSTRACT: This article presents a conceptual and historical overview of residential services for individuals with psychiatric disability and challenges the appropriateness and effectiveness of the "continuum of services" model. The authors propose that the goal of residential services should be to assist all people with psychiatric disabilities to choose, get, and keep normal housing and that rehabilitation technology is currently available to accomplish this goal. Data are presented that indicate that despite high costs, most state mental health systems are continuing to make large scale investments in facility-based residential programs.

A living situation that feels like home is often a primary source of stability and security in our lives. Nest-building is a powerful instinct; most people in the world today spend a great deal of time selecting their dwelling space, customizing and decorating, and establishing rules for relating to neighbors. Unfortunately, mental health professionals have generally overlooked the importance of these factors for people with psychiatric disabilities. Only recently have we begun to recognize that until people's housing needs are met, other treatment or rehabilitation interventions are seriously jeopardized (Carling & Ridgway, 1987).

The history of mental health services shows a persistent disregard for the need of persons with psychiatric disability to choose housing alternatives consistent with their personal desires or goals. For almost 200 years (from the late 1700s to the mid-1900s), institutionalization was the dominant social response to people with deviant behavior. The assumption underlying institutional services (whether they were called "asylums," "state hospitals," or "mental health institutes") was that people with *acute* mental illness would be treated, cured, and sent home, and that people with *chronic* mental illness would receive custodial services, probably forever. In neither case was it the responsibility of mental health professionals to worry about where or how a client was to find normal, stable housing.

In the 1950s and early 1960s, with the advent of deinstitutionalization, there was a widespread growth of community-based custodial care environments, including nursing homes and board-and-care and foster care settings (Carling, 1981, 1984b; Kohen & Paul, 1976; Segal & Aviram, 1978), as well as very large residential facilities. Policymakers of the time defined "community-based" as anything other than state hospitals, including institutions of up to 200 to 300 beds, which apparently seemed small in contrast to existing state hospitals of 10,000 to 12,000 beds (Blanch, 1986).

Some assistance was required for people to make the transition from state hospitals to these new settings, and by the 1970s a whole "residential continuum" had developed. Some of the elements of a typical residential continuum are as follows (from Carling & Ridgway, 1987):

- *Quarterway houses* offering preparation for community living, often in a facility on hospital grounds (American Psychiatric Association Task Force on Community Residential Services, 1982).
- *Halfway houses* with emphasis on the group milieu and on skills development (Cannon, 1975; Cometa, Morrison, & Zishoren, 1979; Piasecki, Leary, & Rutman, 1976; Rog & Rausch, 1975).
- *Three-Quarterway houses* with less intensive staffing than halfway houses (American Psychiatric Association Task Force on Community Residential Services, 1982; Campbell, 1981).
- *Family foster care,* in which alternative families are used as a transitional support as people leave the hospital (Carling, 1984a).
- *Group homes,* which are intensive treatment-oriented transitional residences (American Psychiatric Association Task Force on Community Residential Services, 1982).
- *Apartment programs,* which may involve live-in staff, staff living nearby, or visiting staff; models include "supervised apartments," "semi-supervised apartments," "cluster apartments," "cooperative apartments," "semi-independent living," and "independent living" (Carling, 1978; Goldmeier, 1975; Goldmeier, Mannino, & Shore, 1978; Goldmeier, Shore, & Mannino, 1977).

There are many flaws in a transitional model, which moves people through numerous preparatory settings without a specific end goal. Some of the most serious problems include a lack of individualized programming, repeated dislocation, progress being "rewarded" by forced transitions, access to housing contingent upon participation in treatment, and at the end of the continuum, either homelessness or a return to family, boarding home, or hospital (Carling & Ridgway, 1987). Moreover, there is surprisingly little evidence that transitional residential programs are effective in helping clients achieve stable housing (Carling, Randolph, Blanch, & Ridgway, 1987; Rog & Rausch, 1975).

In short, our public policy on residential services for the past 30 years has been to provide generally undesirable chronic care environments coupled with transitional programs that may lead nowhere. The social consequences of this policy— including increased family burden and the inappropriate use of general hospital settings—has led to a number of more recent program developments, including the following (Carling & Ridgway, 1987):

- *Crisis alternative models,* including family care, crisis residences, special apartment settings, or intensive on-site outreach to any setting in which a person in crisis resides (Polak, 1978; Stein & Test, 1980; Test, 1976, 1981).
- *Shelters for homeless persons,* which provide overnight lodging for individuals and, in some cases, families (Bachrach, 1984; Leaf & Cohen, 1982).
- *Services related to natural families,* which assist families through education and training in coping with mentally ill relatives. Respite options have also been developed for the individual or the family (Hatfield, Fierstein, & Johnson, 1982; Levine, 1984).
- *Mental health-housing partnerships,* collaborative efforts between public housing and mental health agencies to meet housing needs (Randolph, Laux, & Carling, 1987).

Many of these new programs have been excellent responses to very real needs. None, however, addresses the basic flaw in our public policy to date, the failure to help people with psychiatric disabilities identify and meet their individual housing needs and goals.

SUPPORTING PEOPLE IN NORMAL HOUSING

There are a number of reasons why people with psychiatric disabilities have difficulty finding and keeping normal housing (normal housing is that which is available on the open housing market and not necessarily affiliated with mental health programs or systems). As with all disabilities, many of these barriers exist in the environment rather than the individual. One of the most critical problems is the lack of affordable housing. Most people with psychiatric disabilities are poor; if they were not poor to begin with, they quickly become so due to the high cost of psychiatric treatment and high unemployment. In many parts of the country it has become virtually impossible for people on public assistance to compete in the rental housing market, and, except under unusual circumstances, home ownership is out of the question (Randolph, Laux, & Carling, 1987). Moreover, people with psychiatric disabilities face extraordinary discrimination due to widespread public and professional misconceptions and continual misrepresentation by the media (Calicchia, 1981; Kalish & Chang, 1973; Rabkin, 1981). The best way for a person with a psychiatric disability to find a place to live is clearly to avoid being labeled mentally ill, which has usually meant sacrificing all services and supports.

The psychiatric disability itself may also interfere with a person's capacity to find and be successful in a suitable living situation (Bachrach, 1982, 1984;

Budson, 1981; Carpenter & Bourestan, 1976). Both acute symptoms and chronic erosion of self-confidence can affect one's ability to set realistic goals or to learn necessary skills. Moreover, our service system has not been designed to provide integrated supports over long periods of time, or to help people develop their own nonprofessional support networks. This is a critical omission: long-term follow-up studies of persons with severe psychiatric disabilities show that although success in the community is quite feasible, it depends on the development of ongoing supports (Ciompi, 1980; Englehardt, Rosen, Feldman, Englehardt, & Cohen, 1982; Harding, Brooks, Ashikaga, Strauss, & Breier, 1987).

THE REHABILITATION PROCESS APPLIED TO HOUSING GOALS

Psychiatric rehabilitation has been described as a "choose-get-keep" process that targets environmental modifications and client growth and change (Anthony, 1979). With reference to housing, rehabilitation is assistance in the process of choosing, getting, and keeping a decent place to live. Unfortunately, residential rehabilitation efforts to date have given people few real choices and have prepared people almost endlessly for housing situations that often have not materialized. In this regard, traditional residential rehabilitation efforts in most community programs have been quite like vocational rehabilitation efforts in sheltered workshops. Supporting people in normal housing, like supported employment programs, essentially reverses the traditional "train and place" model: The rehabilitation sequence emphasizes *first* securing a desirable living situation, *then* developing the skills and supports necessary to live there. In addition, considerable attention is paid to establishing flexible, ongoing support to ensure long-term success.

CHOOSING A LIVING ENVIRONMENT

People choose their living arrangements for highly idiosyncratic reasons, such as a desirable school district, nice neighbors, or the right number of rooms and windows. Making such a choice can be a difficult process that involves understanding one's own needs, exploring options in detail, anticipating consequences, and prioritizing preferences. For persons with psychiatric disability—many of whom have had their freedom of choice taken away in the past—even believing that choices are possible may be a major step.

Unfortunately, mental health professionals working with people who are psychiatrically disabled have not paid much attention to the idiosyncratic factors that enter into choosing a living environment. Nor have clients been offered many *real* options: choosing between the state hospital and an available bed in a group home can hardly be considered a choice. Yet for people who feel powerless, reestablishing a sense of mastery and control may well be the single most important step toward recovery.

Who makes the final decision about housing is critical because evidence suggests a substantial discrepancy between what clients want and what staff think they need (Dimsdale, Klerman, & Shershow, 1979). At the present time, most residential services place people into prepackaged programs rather than offering real housing options. Until we abandon this model and help people to find living arrangements they truly want to be in, increasing numbers of clients will simply choose not to participate in our services (Bachrach, 1982, 1984; Lamb, 1982).

ACQUIRING A LIVING ENVIRONMENT

Our efforts to help clients acquire a living environment have most often been limited to mental health programs. The possibility of using normal housing situations has been generally unexamined, despite the fact that a high percentage (often 40% or more) of people with a known long-term psychiatric disability live in private homes or apartments (Tessler & Goldman, 1982). In one unpublished study, mental health staff estimated that 65% of their clients needed a structured, transitional group home placement, while 90% of those clients wanted an apartment. Furthermore, most of these clients made very realistic projections about the specialized supports they would need in order to live in community housing (Daniels & Carling, 1986). With the exception of a few innovative residential and case management programs, neither mental health nor rehabilitation professionals have had experience in helping clients access normal housing. In contrast, in the area of vocational services an extensive technology has developed for helping clients get jobs in normal settings (Rusch, 1986). Many of the techniques currently used by "job developers"—for example, techniques for approaching employers, "marketing" clients, negotiating special arrangements, and devising incentives for employers—could easily be adapted for use with landlords, bankers, and housing developers. Successful employment practices emphasizing creative adaptations of normal employment settings also suggest a number of potential housing strategies, such as a housing clearinghouse or a matching service for home-sharing arrangements. Few innovative solutions of this nature have been attempted.

MAINTAINING A LIVING ENVIRONMENT

For people with psychiatric disabilities, learning the skills necessary to succeed in a given environment is often less difficult than performing them consistently over time (Isbister & Donaldson, 1987). Similarly, the "daily living skills" taught in most preparatory programs are often less relevant to success than interpersonal skills such as interacting with a difficult landlord or neighbors. The critical success factors in most living situations include: (1) an accurate assessment of the demands of the specific environment and (2) creating the capacity for ongoing monitoring and support. Again, important lessons can be learned from the field of supported employment: "job coaches" assisting clients in normal employment settings have an extensive technology for assessing the demands of a particular interpersonal environment, teaching and programming site-specific skills, and using coworkers, family, and friends for ongoing feedback and support (Danley &

Mellon, 1987). Similar techniques could be used to help clients maintain normal housing.

Coordination with other services, especially crisis services, is another essential factor in maintaining a living environment over time. All of us experience periods of stress; for a person with a psychiatric disability, in-home crisis support may make the difference between short-term difficulties and permanent loss of housing. Developing the capacity to provide support when and only when it is needed—even after long periods of relative independence from the service system—is one of the key challenges facing mental health providers today.

WHERE ARE WE NOW?

In addition to the obvious benefits for clients and their families, the use of normal housing with supports has many advantages for mental health administrators and state system managers. It eliminates the landlord role, licensing problems, and zoning battles. It makes access to generic services easier and builds on the strengths and resources of local communities rather than imposing a program model developed elsewhere. It allows experimentation with program structure and staffing, can accommodate changing priorities, and does not require large capital investment. It may be initially more costly, but (theoretically at least) costs should decrease over time, along with the need for intensive interventions.

Despite all the advantages, only a few mental health programs or systems have moved in this direction. Community residential programs are currently a large and rapidly expanding sector of mental health services, and most of the growth appears to be in group home and apartment programs. Preliminary data from the first national survey of community residential services (currently being conducted by the authors and associates) indicate a surprising number of residential programs and facilities in operation across the country—well over 3,000. The amount of money invested in residential programs is also surprising. A survey of states, Washington, D.C., and the Virgin Islands conducted in 1986 found a total of $367 million being spent annually on residential services by the 46 states reporting budget data, and almost all states reported having specific funding mechanisms for residential services (Ridgway, 1986). The same survey revealed that 52% of all states have a residential continuum, array of services, or level of care specified in written policy, 71% have or are developing residential program standards, and 54% license residential programs. Moreover, 30% of all states are currently developing group homes or halfway houses. Clearly, many states are continuing to make a large-scale investment in facility-based residential programs. This pattern may be changing somewhat, in that the survey revealed that the highest priority services are independent living or housing supports and case management (37% of states) and semi-independent living (29%).

It does appear that most state mental health agencies still consider transitional residential facilities to be the current state-of-the-art. A survey conducted in 1986 that asked all states and territories to nominate "exemplary" residential programs identified very few programs that support clients in normal housing. Of 272 programs identified as "exemplary," almost half (47%) were group homes, over a quarter were staffed or supported apartment programs (27%), and 14% were crisis, respite, or long-term care facilities such as nursing homes or board-and-care homes. Only 7% of all "exemplary programs" provided support to clients in what could be considered normal housing (Zipple, Randolph, Rowan, Ridgway, & Carling, in preparation).

One of the greatest barriers to supporting people in normal housing is the belief among mental health providers that most clients are too disabled to succeed in normal housing. In addition, there are many organizational issues involved in moving to a non-facility-based housing system. Our conclusions, based on survey data and an in-depth examination of existing residential systems nationwide, are that the logic and the benefits of supporting clients in housing of their own choice (either in place of or as a supplement to existing residential systems) are great. Evaluation studies must be conducted to determine the benefit of such a model for the clients who participate and the viability for mental health and rehabilitation systems.

REFERENCES

American Psychiatric Association Task Force on Community Residential Services. A typography of community residential services (1982). Washington, DC: American Psychiatric Association.

Anthony, W. A. (1979). *The principles of psychiatric rehabilitation.* Amherst, MA: Human Resources Development Press.

Bachrach, L. L. (1982). Young chronic patients: An analytic review of the literature. *Hospital and Community Psychiatry, 33,* 189–197.

Bachrach, L. L. (1984). The homeless mentally ill and mental health services: An analytical review of the literature. In H. R. Lamb (Ed.), *The homeless mentally ill* (pp. 11-53). Washington, DC: American Psychiatric Association.

Blanch, A. K. (1986). Community mental health ideology and administration of state mental health services: Changes in state mental health agencies from 1960–1984. Unpublished doctoral dissertation, University of Vermont, Burlington, VT.

Budson, R. (Ed.). (1981). *New directions for mental health services: Issues in community residential care* (Vol. 11). San Francisco: Jossey-Bass.

Calicchia, J. P. (1981). Deferential perceptions of psychiatrists, psychologists, and social workers toward the ex-mental patient. *Journal of Community Psychology, 9,* 361–366.

Campbell, M. (1981). The three-quarterway house: A step beyond halfway house toward independent living. *Hospital and* Community *Psychiatry, 32,* 500–501.

Cannon, M. S. (1975). *Halfway houses serving the mentally ill and alcoholics, United States,* 1973. National Institute of Mental Health, Survey & Reports Branch, Division of Biometry. Washington, DC: U.S. Government Printing Office.

Carling, P. J. (1978). Residential services in a psychosocial rehabilitation context: The Horizon House model. In J. Goldmeier, E. Mannino, & M. Shore (Eds.), *New directions in mental health care: Cooperative apartments* (pp. 52–64). Adelphi, MD: National Institute of Mental Health, Mental Health Study Center.

Carling, P. J. (1981). Nursing homes and chronic mental patients: A second opinion. *Schizophrenia Bulletin, 7,* 574–579.

Carling, P. J. (1984a). *Developing family foster care programs in mental health: A resource guide.* Burlington, VT: University of Vermont.

Carling, P. J. (1984b). *Housing status and needs of the chronically mentally ill population: A briefing paper.* Rockville, MD: National Institute of Mental Health, Office of State and Community Liaison.

Carling, P. J., Randolph, E L., Blanch, A. K., & Ridgway, P. (1987). *Rehabilitation research review: Housing and community integration for people with psychiatric disabilities.* Washington, DC: DATA Institute.

Carling, P. J., & Ridgway, P. (1987). Overview of a psychiatric rehabilitation approach to housing. In W. Anthony & M. Farkas (Eds.), *Psychiatric rehabilitation: Programs and practices.* Baltimore: Johns Hopkins University Press.

Carpenter, J. O., & Bourestan, N. C. (1976). Performance of psychiatric hospital discharges in strict and tolerant environments. *Community Mental Health Journal, 12,* 45–51.

Ciompi, L. (1980). Catamnestic long-term study on the course of life and aging of schizophrenics. *Schizophrenia Bulletin, 6,* 606–618.

Cometa, M. S., Morrison, J. K., & Zishoren, M. (1979). Halfway to where? A critique of research on psychiatric halfway houses. *Journal of Community Psychology, 7,* 23–27.

Daniels, L. V., & Carling, P. J. (1986). *Community residential rehabilitation services for psychiatrically disabled persons in Kitsap County, Washington.* Unpublished manuscript, Boston University, Center for Psychiatric Rehabilitation, Boston, MA.

Danley, K. S., & Mellon, V. (1987, March). *Training and personnel issues for supported employment programs which serve persons who have a long-term mental illness.* Paper presented at the National Conference on Supported Employment for Persons with Chronic Mental Illness, Washington, DC.

Dimsdale, J. E., Klerman, G., & Shershow, J. C. (1979). Conflict in treatment goals between patients and staff. *Social Psychiatry, 14,* 1–4.

Englehardt, D. M., Rosen, B., Feldman, J., Englehardt, J. Z., & Cohen, P. (1982). A 15-year follow-up of 646 schizophrenic outpatients. *Schizophrenia Bulletin, 8,* 493–503.

Goldmeier, J. (1975). *New directions in aftercare: Cooperative apartment living.* Adelphi, MD: National Institute of Mental Health, Mental Health Study Center.

Goldmeier, J., Mannino, F. V., & Shore, M. E (Eds). (1978). *New directions in mental health care: Cooperative apartments.* Adelphi, MD: National Institute of Mental Health, Mental Health Study Center.

Goldmeier, J., Shore, M. F., & Mannino, F. V. (1977). Cooperative apartments: New programs in community mental health. *Health and Social Work, 2,* 119–140.

Harding, C. M., Brooks, G. W., Ashikaga, T., Strauss, J. S., & Breier, A. (1987). The Vermont longitudinal study of persons with severe mental illness, II: Long-term outcome of subjects who retrospectively met DSM-III criteria for schizophrenia. *American Journal of Psychiatry, 144,* 727-735.

Hatfield, A. B., Fierstein, R., & Johnson, D. (1982). Meeting the needs of families of the psychiatrically disabled. *Psychosocial Rehabilitation Journal, 6,* 27-40.

Isbister, F., & Donaldson, G. (1987, March). *Supported employment for severely psychiatrically disabled individuals: Program development.* Paper presented at the National Conference on Supported Employment for Persons with Chronic Mental Illness, Washington, DC.

Kalish, R. A., & Chang, P. (1973). Two psychological portals of entry for disadvantaged groups. *Rehabilitation Literature, 34* (7), 194-202.

Kohen, W., & Paul, G. L. (1976). Current trends and recommended changes in extended care placement of mental patients: The Illinois system as a case in point. *Schizophrenic Bulletin, 2,* 575–594.

Lamb, H. R. (1982). Young adult chronic patients: The new drifters. *Hospital & Community Psychiatry, 33,* 465–468.

Leaf, A., & Cohen, M. (1982). *Providing services for the homeless: The New York City program.* New York: City of New York, Human Resources Administration.

Levine, I. S. (1984). *Developing community support service programs. A resource manual for family groups.* Boston University Center for Psychiatric Rehabilitation, Boston, and National Alliance for the Mentally Ill, Washington, DC.

Piasecki, J. R., Leary J. L., & Rutman, I.D. (1976). *Halfway houses and long-term community residences for the mentally ill* (DHHS Publication No. ADM 80-1004). Washington, DC: U.S. Government Printing Office.

Polak, P. R. (1978). A comprehensive system of alternatives to psychiatric hospitalization. In L.I. Stein & M. A. Test (Eds.), *Alternatives to mental hospital treatment* (pp. 115–137). New York: Plenum Press.

Rabkin, J. G. (1981). Public attitudes: New research directions. *Hospital & Community Psychiatry, 32,* 157.

Randolph, E, Laux, R., & Carling, P. J. (1987). In search of housing. *Creative approaches to financing integrated housing.* Rockville, MD: National Institute of Mental Health.

Ridgway, P. *(1986). Meeting the supported housing and residential services needs of Americans with psychiatric disabilities: A state by state review.* Boston, MA: Boston University, Center for Psychiatric Rehabilitation.

Rog, D..J., & Rausch, H. L. (1975). The psychiatric halfway house: How is it measuring up? *Community Mental Health Journal, 2* (2), 155–162.

Rusch, F. R. (1986). *Competitive employment issues and strategies.* Baltimore: Paul H. Brookes.

Segal, S. P., & Aviram, U. (1978). *The mentally ill in community based sheltered care and social integration.* New York: Wiley.

Stein, L., & Test, M. (1980). Alternatives to mental hospital treatment: I. Conceptual model, treatment programs, and clinical evaluation. *Archives of General Psychiatry, 37,* 392–397.

Tessler, R. C., & Goldman, H. H. (1982). *The chronically mentally ill: Assessing community support programs.* Cambridge, MA: Ballinger.

Test, M. A. (1976). Use of special living arrangements—A model for decision-making. *Community living arrangements for the mentally ill and disabled: Issues and options for public-policy.* Rockville, MD: National Institute of Mental Health.

Test, M. A. (1981). Effective community treatment of the chronically mentally ill: What is necessary? *Journal of Social Issues, 37,* 71–86.

Zipple, A. M., Randolph, F. L., Rowan, C. A., Ridgway, P., & Carling, P. J. (in preparation). *Community residential programs for people with psychiatric disabilities: A national survey of characteristics, practices, and trends.* Boston, MA: Boston University, Center for Psychiatric Rehabilitation.

SECTION IV
Community Integration: Vocational and Independent Living Rehabilitation

Nancy M. Crewe, Section Editor

Introduction

Nancy M. Crewe

Rehabilitation perspectives have changed dramatically in recent years, especially in psychosocial areas. Consider some of the most significant movements. Independent living has become a priority, recognized as a goal equal in importance to vocational rehabilitation. Deinstitutionalization has reversed a trend that began more than a century ago, resulting in the closure or drastic downsizing of residential facilities. First people with moderate disabilities and eventually many with severe impairments have been discharged into the community. Mainstreaming has led to a thorough reconsideration of the mission of special education and preferred approaches to educating students with disabilities. Most recently, mainstreaming is evolving into the concept of integrative education, an approach that includes the special education teacher as a consultant to the instructor and pupil within the regular classroom.

Even vocational rehabilitation has undergone major shifts. Supported employment provided a new model of service for severely disabled individuals that turned the old model (evaluate, train, and place into employment) upside down. Supported employment begins with placement, and in the context of real, community-based work carries out the functions of assessment and training. Rehabilitation facilities, formerly focused on extended evaluation and work adjustment training in a sheltered environment, have transferred more and more of their activities to business settings.

A common philosophical theme drives all of these innovations: people with disabilities deserve to live and work as part of the mainstream community rather than being segregated into the corners of society. A corollary assumption is that the problems of disability are not inherent in the impairment or in the individual alone but are substantially the result of the limitations imposed by attitudinal and physical barriers within the society. Unquestionably, the driving force that instigated many of these changes was the power of consumers and advocates as participants in policy making and service delivery. Individually and collectively, they now are recognized as partners, not simply beneficiaries, in the rehabilitation enterprise.

Other changes in the vocational and independent living rehabilitation arenas have stemmed from challenges presented by new or greatly enlarged populations of clients. These include individuals with traumatic brain injuries and psychiatric disabilities. In past years fewer people survived serious head injuries, and rehabilitation services for the survivors were virtually nonexistent. The past decade has seen a great increase both in the number of survivors and the development of new treatment programs. Psychiatric rehabilitation began to emerge with the discovery that rehabilitation principles could be effective in meeting the needs of people with mental illness, and that discovery led to the creation of new approaches to service. Traditional programs had stressed psychotherapy and medically oriented treatment, whereas psychiatric rehabilitation included vocational, independent living, and social skills training.

Injured workers are one of the oldest populations targeted by American legislation for vocational rehabilitation, but rehabilitation of this group is also changing. The decade has witnessed a tremendous increase in the number of private providers of rehabilitation services and a growing awareness on the part of business and industry of the cost of disability. Efforts to reduce unnecessary expenses and human suffering spread the development of disability management programs based in corporations. With these innovations many people who formerly would have received only medical services now are being supported with interdisciplinary rehabilitation services.

The articles selected for this section of the text relate to employment and other aspects of community participation. They are intended to sample both the traditional issues of importance to vocational rehabilitation and the newer trends identified above.

Bolton's article, "Psychsocial Factors Affecting the Employment of Former Vocational Rehabilitation Clients," is representative of the best work done within one of the traditional areas of rehabilitation psychology, i.e., research that strives to understand the range of variables within the individual that impacts return to work. Incorporating a two-year follow-up period and more than 200 subjects, the study identifies attitudes and perceptions that relate to better vocational outcomes. For example, clients who perceived the source of their vocational problems to be in the environment rather than intrinsic to themselves tended to persevere with their job searches. Such findings have direct implications for strategies that could be effective in counseling.

"Supported Work: An Innovative Approach to the Vocational Rehabilitation of Persons Who Are Psychiatrically Disabled" describes a program that uses the contemporary strategy of supported employment and demonstrates its effectiveness with a population of clients with severe disabilities. The article not only describes the outcomes for a sample of clients but also describes the components of the program in such a way that readers can compare this model of supported work with others that may be seen in their own communities.

In some rehabilitation circles, cognitive remediation was given the tongue-in-cheek designation, "growth industry of the '80's." Programs have sprung up in every state, utilizing a variety of intuitively appealing approaches to try to address the information-processing deficits of people with head injuries. As Kreutzer, Gordon, and Wehman note in "Cognitive Remediation Following Traumatic Brain Injury," research is still urgently needed to determine what strategies succeed under what circumstances and with what clients. Their article makes an important contribution to understanding this enterprise by presenting a conceptual scheme that classifies models of treatment, specifies their underlying assumptions, and gives examples of remediation strategies. This can provide practitioners with a theoretical rationale for the services they recommend and can also guide researchers toward significant hypotheses for testing.

The remaining article in this section speaks most directly to the philosophical evolution of rehabilitation psychology. Many of the sweeping changes noted above are the outgrowth of new paradigms for understanding the causes and effects of disability. Wolfensberger and Tullman offer a cogent summary of one of the most influential ideas in "A Brief Outline of the Principle of Normalization." A careful reading of this article helps to clarify the philosophical roots and interrelationships of independent living, mainstreaming, and deinstitutionalization. However it warns that desegregation, alone, is not only insufficient, but it may actually be harmful. The principle of normalization offers a means by which devalued members can be effectively and positively integrated into the fabric of society. The principle has implications for the structure of rehabilitation services of all kinds.

14

Psychosocial Factors Affecting the Employment of Former Vocational Rehabilitation Clients

Brian Bolton

ABSTRACT: Questionnaires completed by 211 former vocational rehabilitation (VR) clients 2 years after case closure were analyzed for a clarification of the psychosocial factors that affect vocational adjustment. The major findings of the study were that the primary criteria of vocational adjustment—that is, employment, job satisfaction, and persistence in looking for work—were associated with better self-appraised physical and mental health, greater perceived family support in seeking employment, more optimism about employment prospects, and attribution of the problem source to the environment. These variables suggest useful points for intervention by VR practitioners.

Employment is the primary goal of vocational rehabilitation (VR) services. The best available evidence indicates that two-thirds of former general caseload clients and one-half of former workshop and facility clients are employed at follow-up 2 to 4 years after case closure (Bolton, 1981). Yet, little is known about the psychosocial aspects of the employment problems experienced by handicapped persons (Bolton, 1982; Roessler & Bolton, 1978). Clinically derived knowledge as well as common sense suggests that satisfactory vocational adjustment is determined, at least in part, by supportive elements and favorable attitudes in the life circumstances of former clients.

The general purpose of the present investigation was to contribute to the psychological understanding of the vocational adjustment problems experienced by handicapped persons. Specifically, the objectives were (1) to describe the employment situations of working former VR clients and to document the perceived difficulties of unemployed former VR clients; and (2) to examine the psychosocial, intellectual, and temperamental factors that may influence various facets of employment and unemployment for handicapped persons.

METHOD

The follow-up population consisted of 837 disabled persons referred to the Little Rock district office of the Arkansas Rehabilitative Services between 1975 and 1978. All persons in the population were assigned to a special evaluation unit for "difficult" cases by their counselors. The unit was designed to provide an in-depth assessment of medical, social, vocational, psychological, and psychiatric problems relevant to the provision of VR services (see Bolton & Davis, 1979). Clients referred to the special unit were, in fact, more difficult cases (i.e., greater proportions were severely disabled, multiply handicapped, possessed intellectual and psychiatric disabilities, received public assistance at referral, etc.). Hence, it is fair to conclude that the study population included disabled persons with the more serious employment problems.

A five-page follow-up questionnaire was mailed to each former client in the study population 2 years after case closure. If a response was not received within 1 month, a second copy of the questionnaire was sent. In all, 275 ex-clients could not be located, and 5 were determined to be deceased. Of the 557 persons who received the follow-up questionnaire, 211 responded to either the first (136) or the second mailing (75).

The research sample of 211 respondents constituted 25% of the entire follow-up population and 38% of the subset of the population that was probably contacted. While the response rate was somewhat lower than is typically obtained in rehabilitation follow-up investigations, two points should be noted. First, when the 211 respondents were compared to the entire population of 837 ex-clients on basic demographic characteristics, no differences of appreciable magnitude were discovered. Second, the available evidence for follow-up studies in VR suggests that respondents are not unrepresentative of client populations in ways that would invalidate the generalizability of findings (see Bolton, 1981).

For these reasons, it can be reasonably concluded that the results of this followup study are probably not much different from those that would have been obtained if the entire population had responded to the questionnaire. Of course, this is a matter of judgment and certainly suggests caution in interpreting the findings for the sample of 211 former clients.

A five-page questionnaire accompanied by a brief cover letter requesting the respondents' cooperation comprised the follow-up mailing. The first four pages of the questionnaire contained a mixture of multiple-choice and short-answer items covering employment status and problems, sources of income and financial status and health and psychosocial adjustment. If the former client was employed at the time of follow-up, specific questions about the job were asked (e.g., salary, duties, etc.). For respondents who were not currently employed, questions about difficulties and prospects for employment were provided. Additional items were concerned with health status, family support, public assistance received, and time spent in various types of nonwork activities. The nature of the individual items is detailed in the "Results" section. The fifth page of the questionnaire contained the 20-item short form of the Minnesota Satisfaction Questionnaire (MSQ) and was completed only by employed respondents.

In addition to the follow-up data, demographic information about the 211 respondents had been collected at the time of referral to the Arkansas Rehabilitative Services. The Wechsler Adult Intelligence Scale (WAIS) full-scale IQ was available for 195 respondents, and 120 respondents had completed the Sixteen Personality Factor Questionnaire-Form E (16 PF-E) in conjunction with their preliminary evaluations at the time of application for services.

In summary, the variables examined in this investigation fell into five categories: (1) employment-for example, salary, job satisfaction, looking for work, and the like; (2) employment-related-for example, public assistance being received (if any), employment outlook, family support, and the like; (3) psychosocial-for example, physical and mental health, nonwork activities, and the like; (4) psychometric-that is, WAIS IQ and 16 PF-E profile; and (5) demographic. Variables in the first three categories were obtained from the follow-up questionnaire, while those in the last two categories were assessed at the time of application for rehabilitation services.

RESULTS

The presentation of results consists of several sections corresponding, to classes of variables that (1) describe the characteristics of the research; sample and (2) summarize the relationships among the classes of variables, All analyses were conducted separately for males and females, except for the 16 PF-E. The exception for the 16 PF-E reflects the small magnitude and instability of the correlations obtained; thus, the reported relationships should be interpreted with caution.

Characteristics of the Sample

The research sample was 50% male and 70% white, with a median age of 30 years and an age range from 15 to 61 at the time of referral to the Arkansas Rehabilitative Service. Almost half (45%) were single; 30% were married; and 25% were widowed, divorced, or separated. Slightly more than one-third (37%) had completed 12 grades of school or more. The major disabling conditions were these: orthopedic impairments (34%); mental retardation (15%); emotional disorders (17%); and various medical conditions (30%), such as cardiovascular, circulatory, respiratory, neurological, or other difficulties. Only 15% were primarily self-supporting, with the remainder dependent on family, public assistance, Social Security disability, private insurance, or other sources. The mean WAIS IQ was 87, with a range of 44 to 134. In summary, the research sample can be characterized as extremely heterogeneous on demographic and psychometric variables.

Employment Status at Follow-Up

A total of 86 (41%) of the 211 respondents were employed at followup. Almost all (95%) of the working respondents were employed full-time (35 or more hours per week). The median salary was $150 per week, with a range from $32 to $400.

The vast majority of employed respondents held jobs at the unskilled or semi-skilled level (e.g., plant guard, assembly line worker, farm hand, waitress, janitor, sales clerk, painter, truck driver, etc.). However, some were employed at higher levels (e.g., clerk typist, receptionist, teacher, and licensed practical nurse).

Of the 125 respondents (59%) who were not employed at follow-up, 44% indicated that they had worked at some time during the previous 2 years. A total of 46% of the 125 unemployed respondents said that they were looking for work; 11% did not want or need work, and 6% were in school or some type of training program. Except for those in the last two categories, the unemployed respondents indicated that the following problems were preventing them from obtaining work: disability or medical problem (62%), lack of training or experience (34%), few jobs available in local community (32%), and transportation problems (20%). These former clients estimated their chances of obtaining employment as follows: good (5%), fair (31%), and poor (64%).

Three scores were derived from the MSQ, using the scales developed by the authors of that questionnaire (Tinsley, Warnken, Weiss, Dawis, & Lofquist, 1969): Intrinsic Satisfaction (IS), Extrinsic Satisfaction (ES), and General Satisfaction (GS). The latter scale is simply the sum of IS and ES, which correlated .71 in the current sample of 74 respondents. The average scores for IS (3.5), ES (3.2), and GS (3.4) all fell between the "Satisfied" (3) and "Very Satisfied" (4) anchors on the response continuum, suggesting that the majority of employed ex-clients were reasonably satisfied with their jobs.

Status on Employment-Related and Psychosocial Variables

Some 24% of the individuals in the follow-up sample were receiving some type of public assistance; this assistance was about equally divided among Social Security disability, welfare payments, and other types of financial support. The median amount received was $212 per month, with a range from $57 to $792. In response to a question about encouragement and help from family members in their efforts to find employment, the respondents indicated the following: a great deal (26%), quite a lot (26%), some (17%), and none (31%). When asked to predict what they would most likely be doing 1 year hence, the respondents replied as follows: employed (46%), in school or training (10%), and unemployed (44%). The former clients' judgments concerning their physical and mental health, respectively, were these: excellent (21%/20%), good (27%/25%), fair (34%/39%), and poor (18%/16%).

Because it was reasonable to hypothesize that the nonwork activities of disabled persons should be affected by their employment situations, the respondents were asked to indicate the number of hours per week they engaged in seven activities. The results are shown in Table 14.1.

While there are clear differences in the extent of participation in the various activities (e.g., watching TV and/or listening to the radio was the most popular activity), there is evidence of considerable diversity of preferences. This variability is further supported by the low median correlation among the seven activities (r = .14, with a range from -.09 to .42).

Male-Female Differences

The proportions of males (42%) and females (39%) who were employed were about equal. However, males reported slightly higher weekly salaries ($160 vs. $140, respectively). A larger proportion of unemployed males (54%) than females (38%) were looking for work. But the problems preventing working and optimism about future employment were roughly the same for unemployed male and female respondents. Likewise, employed males and females were about equally satisfied (3.4 vs. 3.3, respectively) with their work situations.

Fewer males (17%) than females (32%) were receiving some form of public assistance. Not unexpectedly, males stated that they received more help and encouragement from family members in their efforts to locate employment (2.7 vs. 2.4, respectively). Males rated their physical health (2.6 vs. 2.3) and mental health (2.6 vs. 2.5) slightly higher than females did. Lastly, females were more likely to engage in hobbies, reading, and religious activities, while males spent more time outdoors, watching TV, visiting friends, and participating in formal social activities.

Correlates of Employment Status

When the 86 currently employed former clients were compared with the 125 unemployed respondents on the various work-related and psychosocial variables, several highly significant relationships were observed. Employed disabled persons reported better physical health ($r = .36, p < .001$), better mental health ($r = .34, p < .001$), greater family support in seeking work ($r = .30, p < .001$), and better prospects for being employed 1 year hence ($r = .43, p < .001$). Employed respondents were less likely to be receiving some form of public assistance ($r = .38, p < .001$).

These correlations were about equal in the male and female subsamples, suggesting a generalized relationship between successful employment and the disabled respondents' self-perceived health and life circumstances. While it is impossible to identify the causal connections in these data, a reasonable hypothesis is that better physical and emotional health and greater family support do increase the disabled person's prospects of employment; yet, at the same time, it

Table 14.1 Hours Spent by Respondents in Seven Nonwork Activities

Type of Activity	None	1–3	4–6	7+
Outdoor	52%	29%	19%	
Hobbies	48%	31%	21%	
TV/radio	3%	17%	28%	52%
Visiting	20%	36%	24%	20%
Social	55%	28%	17%	
Reading	25%	39%	19%	17%
Religious	40%	34%	26%	

is probably also true that holding a job enhances the individual's view of his or her situation. In other words, these relationships most certainly reflect an interactive process between psychosocial adjustment and vocational adjustment.

Surprisingly, employment status was not significantly correlated[with participation in any of the seven nonwork activities. That is, employed disabled persons did not engage in any of the activities any more or any less than did the unemployed respondents. Intelligence was positively correlated with being employed ($r = .24, p < .001$), but this relationship was statistically significant for females only ($r = .32, p < .01$). The only temperamental variable associated with employment was dominance ($r = .20, p < .05$); this isolated finding can be disregarded as a chance-level occurrence.

Correlates of Salary and Job Satisfaction

Few variables were correlated with salary received by employed respondents; this suggests that salary is a relatively independent and unpredictable aspect of employment among disabled workers. In particular, physical health, mental health, family support, optimism, public assistance status, and time spent in the seven nonwork activities were unrelated to salary level. Intelligence was significantly correlated with salary for females only ($r = .40, p < .05$), as was intrinsic job satisfaction ($r = .34, p < .05$). Three temperamental source traits were significantly associated with salary level: outgoingness ($r = .37, p < .02$), venturesomeness ($r = .37, p < .02$), and self-discipline ($r = .35, p < .02$).

A consistent pattern of correlations indicates that job satisfaction is influenced considerably by certain other facets of an employed disabled person's life circumstances. The largest relationship was obtained between job satisfaction and self-perceived mental health ($r = .59, p < .001$). (Because the correlations for IS, ES, and GS are about the same size, only the correlations for GS are reported here.) The second largest correlation was with time spent in religious activities ($r = .39, p < .001$), followed by self-rated physical health ($r = .37, p < .02$). For males only, significant associations were found with time visiting with friends ($r = .43, p < .01$) and time engaging in formal social activities ($r = .37, p < .05$). Job satisfaction was unrelated to intelligence, temperamental characteristics, and family support.

Correlates of Looking for Work

Several variables appear to influence the unemployed disabled person's motivation to continue looking for a job. Former clients who believed that their disabilities or associated medical problems were preventing them from obtaining work were less likely to look for a job ($r = .41, p < .001$). In contrast, ex-clients who attributed their difficulties to lack of training or experience ($r = .42, p < .001$) or to lack of jobs in the community ($r = .56, p < .001$) were more likely to persist in their job searches. The crucial psychological variable underlying this difference would seem to be internal versus external attribution of cause, with those unemployed disabled persons who perceived the source of difficulty to be in the labor market much more likely to continue looking for work.

Consistent with this finding were Positive relationships between looking for work and self-appraised physical health ($r = .38, p < .001$), mental health ($r = .31, p < .001$), encouragement and help from family ($r = .29, p < .005$), and estimated chances of being employed 1 year later ($r = .55, p < .001$). It can be concluded from these correlations that disabled persons who perceive their health to be better and their families to be supportive of their employment goals, and who are optimistic about becoming employed, are more likely to continue looking for work. Temperamental characteristics measured by the 16 PF-E were unrelated to persistence in looking for employment.

Finally, one nonsignificant relationship is especially noteworthy. The correlation between looking for work and receiving some form of public assistance was not statistically significant ($r = .07$, n.s.). Nor was the correlation between amount of public assistance received and looking for work statistically significant ($r = .15$, n.s.). This result contradicts the widely held belief that being a recipient of public assistance uniformly diminishes motivation to look for employment. All of the relationships reported in this section were about equal in magnitude for males and females.

Correlates of Psychosocial Variables

Intelligence was significantly related to former clients' evaluations of their physical and mental health. More intelligent respondents rated their physical health as better ($r = .22, p < .01$), although the relationship was statistically significant for females only ($r = .31, p < .001$). Similarly, more intelligent former clients judged their mental health to be better ($r = .28, p < .001$), and this relationship was of the same magnitude for males and females. Not surprisingly, the more intelligent respondents spent more time reading ($r = .32, p < .001$). Finally, more intelligent females spent more time visiting friends ($r = .25, p < .05$) and less time engaged in religious activities ($r = .23, p < .05$).

Temperamental characteristics measured by the 16 PF-E were not significantly related to perceived family support in looking for work, to estimated chances of being employed 1 year hence, or to public assistance recipient status, with two exceptions: More outgoing respondents perceived their families as less supportive of their employment aspirations ($r = .19, p < .05$) and were more likely to be receiving some form of public assistance ($r = .21, p < .02$). But there were several significant correlations between 16 PF-E traits and self-evaluated physical and mental health and several of the seven nonwork activities. It is important to note that these relationships are truly predictive, since the 16 PF-E was completed more than 2 years before the followup questionnaire was.

Respondents who rated their physical health as better were more emotionally stable ($r = .20, p < .05$), dominant ($r = .20, p < .05$), trusting ($r = .23, p < .02$), imaginative ($r = .19, p < .05$), and relaxed ($r = .23, p < .02$), and were less anxious ($r = .25, p < .01$). Former clients who judged their mental health to be better were more emotionally stable ($r = .19, p < .05$), trusting ($r = .25, p < .01$), conservative ($r = .23, p < .02$), group-dependent ($r = .19, p < .05$, controlled ($r = .22, p < .02$), and relaxed ($r = .23, p < .02$), and less anxious ($r = .23, p < .02$). While the pattern of relationships suggests that self-evaluated physical health and mental health are related to measured temperimental characteristics, the small magnitude of the correlations renders any farther interpretation unwarranted.

Temperamental traits were significantly associated with five of the seven nonwork activities; however, the correlations were of small size. Consequently, only the two activities with four significant temperamental relationships each are summarized here. Respondents who spent more time reading were more venturesome ($r = .23$, $p < .02$), trusting ($r = .19$, $p < .05$), and controlled ($r = .22$, $p < .02$), and less anxious ($r = .19$, $p < .05$). Former clients who spent more time in religious activities were more outgoing ($r = .27$, $p < .01$), venturesome ($r = .22$, $p < .05$), group-dependent ($r = .24$, $p < .02$), and extraverted ($r = .22$, $p < .05$). Again, these relationships do not justify farther comment at this time, except that they are generally consistent with common sense expectations.

Because the respondents' self-appraised physical health and mental health were related to several aspects of their vocational adjustment, a brief discussion of the relationship between these two variables is warranted. While the response distributions were virtually identical (see above), the intercorrelation ($r = .70$, $p < .001$) between physical and mental health indicates that one-half of the variability in each factor is unique. A reasonable interpretation of the common variance is that poor physical health and medical problems can cause depression and emotional difficulties; it is also probable that a positive attitude and hopeful outlook can help handicapped individuals deal with disability-related problems. The latter interpretation of the direction of influence provides a more useful framework for VR practitioners.

CONCLUSIONS

Before listing the major conclusions derived from this investigation, three limitations associated with the research methodology are briefly mentioned. First, the criteria of vocational adjustment used are complex-that is, they are multiply determined. Employment, job satisfaction, looking for work, and the like are influenced by such factors as nature of the handicap, local labor market conditions, and good luck, as well as by the variables measured in the study. Second, the investigation focused for the most part on former *clients' perceptions* of their health, family support, participation in activities, and so on. In other words, health status, family support, time spent watching TV, and the other factors were not independently assessed. But it can be argued that emotional health, family support, and optimism about future employment are essentially *phenomenal* variables-that is, it is the individual's perceptions that are of psychological significance, and not the "objective" aspects of the situation. Thirdly, the study is obviously correlational in design, rendering all interpretations of causal influence tentative; this limitation has been stressed throughout the discussion. The major conclusions are as follows:

1. Although fewer than half (41%) of the respondents were employed at the time of follow-up contact, almost half (440/o) of those unemployed former clients

had worked at some time during the preceding 2 years. These results suggest that considerable employment potential exists, even in a relatively severely handicapped population.

2. Almost one-half (46%) of the unemployed respondents were looking for work, indicating substantial motivation to find suitable employment, despite their awareness of problems and their generally pessimistic appraisal of the prospects of finding employment. In fact, two-thirds (64%) of the unemployed former clients estimated their chances of finding work to be poor.

3. Employed respondents reported better physical health, better mental health, greater family support in seeking work, and greater probability of being employed 1 year later. These findings suggest that better health and greater family support increase the disabled person's prospects of employment.

4. Among employed former clients, greater job satisfaction was associated with better mental and physical health and time spent in religious activities. While the direction of influence here is ambiguous, it can be concluded that satisfaction with employment is not determined entirely by working conditions.

5. Unemployed respondents who believed that their disabilities were preventing employment were less likely to continue looking for a job, while those who attributed their employment problems to lack of training or lack of jobs in the community were more likely to persist in their job searches. These findings suggest that disabled persons who attribute their difficulties to their handicaps are less likely to look for employment.

6. Unemployed former clients who were looking for work also reported better physical and mental health, more encouragement and help from their families, and greater chances of employment 1 year later. These relationships indicate that handicapped persons who perceive their health to be better and their families to be more supportive, and who are more optimistic about future employment, will persist in their job seeking.

7. Vocational adjustment (i.e., employment, job satisfaction, and persistence in job seeking) appears to be essentially independent of nonwork activity patterns, intelligence, and temperamental differences among handicapped persons.

8. In summary, the critical variables affecting the vocational adjustment of handicapped former clients appear to be (a) emotional health status, (b) family support for employment goals, (c) optimism regarding employment prospects, and (d) attribution of the problem source to the environment. These variables suggest potentially useful focal points for the intervention strategies and procedures used by VR practitioners.

REFERENCES

Bolton, B. (1981). Follow-up studies in vocational rehabilitation. In E. Pan, T. E. Backer, & C. L. Vash (Eds.), *Annual review of rehabilitation* (Vol. 2). New York: Springer Publishing Company.

Bolton, B. (1982). (Ed.). *Vocational adjustment of disabled persons.* Baltimore: University Park Press.

Bolton, B., & Davis, S. (1979). Rehabilitation counselors' uses of an experimental RIDAC unit. *Journal of Rehabilitation, 45,* 41–45.

Roessler, R., & Bolton, B. (1978). *Psychosocial adjustment to disability.* Baltimore: University Park Press.

Tinsley, H., Warnken, R., Weiss, D., Dawis, R., & Lofquist, L. (1969). *A follow-up survey of former clients of the Minnesota Division of Vocational Rehabilitation (Minnesota Studies in VR: 26).* Minneapolis: University of Minnesota.

Acknowledgment: This investigation was supported by Research and Training Center Grant G008003045 from the National Institute of Handicapped Research to the Arkansas Rehabilitation Research and Training Center.

15

Supported Work: An Innovative Approach to theVocational Rehabilitation of Persons Who Are Psychiatrically Disabled

**Sharland Trotter, Kenneth Minkoff,
Katherine Harrison, and John Hoops**

ABSTRACT: This paper describes a new model for the vocational rehabilitation of persons with severe psychiatric disability. This model, called *supported work,* helps clients find private-sector jobs and provides high levels of support to both the client and the employer. Preliminary data on a supported work program for individuals with psychiatric disability suggest that this model is effective in returning individuals with severe psychiatric disability to competitive employment. Client and program variables that seem to contribute to successful outcomes are discussed, and directions for further research are suggested.

Work is perhaps the most important integrating institution of any society. The fact that this most basic form of social participation is denied to those with severe psychiatric disability is increasingly viewed as a troublesome failure of deinstitutionalization. Numerous studies of previously hospitalized individuals have, with one exception (Turner, 1977), consistently reported that only 10% to 30% of individuals with psychiatric disability manage to find work in the year following hospital discharge (Anthony, Cohen, & Vitalo, 1978; Minkoff, 1978). Anthony and Liberman (1986) suggest that the true figures are even more grim: only 10% to 15% of formerly hospitalized individuals manage to sustain employment 1 to 5 years after discharge. Clients with severe psychiatric disability show even lower rates of employment (Farkas, Rogers, & Thurer, 1987; Zipple & Spaniol, 1984).

Although their numbers are small, it is clear that some people with severe psychiatric disability are capable of functioning in a work role, given the proper conditions. Efforts to identify those factors that predict successful vocational outcome have resulted in two durable findings. First, no consistent relationship between any specific psychiatric diagnosis or symptom cluster and the potential for work has emerged (Anthony & Jansen, 1984; Douzinas & Carpenter, 1981; Gurel & Lorei, 1972; Strauss & Carpenter, 1972, 1974; Turner, 1977). Secondly, numerous studies have found that vocational potential is a relatively autonomous personality dimension (Simmons, 1965) and an independent outcome variable (Strauss & Carpenter, 1974, 1977), and that successful employment is best predicted by prior work history and by present level of work adjustment skills and social interaction skills (Anthony & Jansen, 1984; Cheadle & Morgan, 1972; Distefano & Pryor, 1970).

For the most part, there are limited resources for implementing a model based on functional, social, and prevocational skills. In Massachusetts, for example, less than 1% of the mental health budget in 1986 was targeted for vocational services. Even where traditional vocational rehabilitation programs exist, however, they have been markedly ineffective for individuals with severe psychiatric disability. Sheltered workshops are a case in point: They do not promote meaningful rehabilitation for the majority of people with psychiatric disabilities, both because the clients are not taught relevant social, emotional, and vocational skills (Ciardello, 1981; Vash, 1977), and because the tasks performed are often regarded as demeaning. For most individuals with severe psychiatric disability, the setting itself increases, rather than diminishes, a sense of stigma, despair, and social isolation (Estroff, 1981). Furthermore, after a comprehensive review of the efficacy of traditional vocational services for persons with psychiatric disabilities, Bond and Boyer (in press) concluded that most programs have had limited success in returning clients to competitive employment.

More recent models, variously called "Workshops without Walls" (Brickley, 1974) or "Transitional Employment Programs" (Beard, Propst, & Malamud, 1982; *Rehab Brief,* 1986) have made significant advances over the workshop approach by placing clients in supervised jobs in private industry to help them develop the skills necessary for competitive employment. However, most of these placements are temporary, and after a few months of working clients may need to change environments and start all over again. This can be an impossible task for some persons with severe psychiatric disability who tolerate change poorly. Temporary job placements, moreover, do not help the client overcome stigma and fear on the part of potentially permanent employers. Stigma remains the single greatest barrier to employment for persons with severe psychiatric disability (Farina & Feiner, 1973; Rabkin, 1972). When employers get to know the client as a person, the problem of stigma is significantly reduced, and employers are more likely to evaluate that individual on the basis of social functioning rather than on his or her psychiatric history (Farina, 1982). Employers also tend to remain loyal to their own employees, even after a relapse (Huffine & Clausen, 1979; Olshansky, Grob, & Malamud, 1958). This suggests the promise of the supported work model (Will, 1984), which is receiving increased attention in the rehabilitation of individuals with psychiatric disability (Anthony & Blanch, in press).

THE ACCESS PROGRAM

Access is a supported work program designed specifically for persons with severe psychiatric disability. It is operated by Transitional Employment Enterprises, Inc. (TEE), a private, nonprofit agency located in Boston. Since 1974, TEE has successfully administered a variety of supported work programs for people who are vocationally disadvantaged. The Access program was created in 1985 through the joint efforts of TEE, the Massachusetts Alliance for the Mentally Ill, the Center for Psychiatric Rehabilitation of Boston University, and the Massachusetts Department of Public Welfare.

The Access program offers an individualized intake process; pre-employment training; placement in a paid internship; comprehensive on-the job training and support; and, within an average of 4 to 6 months, hiring by the host employer. Access is currently staffed by a project director; two "corporate representatives," who develop new jobs and provide on-site support to the clients; a preemployment trainer; a consulting psychiatrist; and a resource developer, whose job it is to bolster the outside social supports each client needs to maintain employment.

Referrals to the Access program come from many sources. Approximately one-third of the referrals are from the Massachusetts Rehabilitation Commission. The remaining two-thirds come from day treatment programs, hospital aftercare programs, halfway houses, private therapists, and from the clients themselves. Program eligibility criteria were established by the program's contract with the Department of Public Welfare and require that the applicant have a severe psychiatric disability, be 21 years of age or older, have been unemployed or underemployed for 3 of the last 4 years, and be engaged in some form of mental health treatment.

Applicants who appear to have the potential to succeed in the supported work program (based upon a screening interview and information regarding mental health status) are scheduled to participate, in groups of about 10, in the preemployment phase of the Access program. The preemployment experience is designed to resemble as closely as possible the world of work. Clients are required to attend classes 3 hours a day, 5 days a week throughout the first 7-week phase of preemployment, during which time they are paid a small stipend of $30 to $40 per week. The brisk, "corporate" environment of the TEE office, along with a regular paycheck, seem to facilitate adjustments to the world of work by creating clear expectations for appropriate dress, grooming, attendance, and punctuality.

The content of preemployment is organized around the triad of choosing, getting, and keeping a job (Anthony, Howell, & Danley, 1984). Its focus is on the exploration of personal and work-related values and on assessing each individual's strengths and deficits in relation to work. Many clients begin for the first time to confront the gap between their (often exaggerated) ideals and their objectively identifiable skills and to develop realistic vocational plans. During this time they also learn to recognize interpersonal deficits and to overcome them through role play, videotape, and continuous feedback from both the staff and their fellow program participants. Making eye contact, engaging in appropriate small talk, and learning to gain better control over psychotic symptoms—these are the typical difficulties clients encounter as they prepare for actual job interviews. These deficits are viewed as skills that can be learned, just as writing a resume can be learned, and not as irremediable aspects of a psychiatric illness.

The single most challenging aspect of preemployment training is learning to present oneself to a stranger in the most favorable light possible, a crucial aspect of interviewing for a job. The combination of long-term unemployment and long-term mental illness means that virtually all clients suffer from low self-esteem and from the sense of shame and insecurity that arises from having a socially stigmatizing disability. The practice interviews during this phase of the program become a process of social relearning: learning about appropriate social distance, learning to present one's strengths and to be reticent about one's problems, and learning to accept objective criticism.

The second phase of preemployment training focuses on preparing clients for outside interviews with prospective employers. Entry into this second phase of training is dependent upon good attendance, participation in the first 7 weeks of the program, and the identification of job choices. About 60 to 70% of each class graduates into the second phase of preemployment training. Participation in the second phase of preemployment ranges, on average, from 1 week to 4 months. Classes are conducted by the resource developer and are aimed at enhancing motivation and peer support and providing information on world-of-work issues.

Throughout both phases of preemployment, the corporate representatives develop jobs commensurate with the interests and abilities of each participant. This is a crucial component of the supported work model. The program's two corporate representatives meet with clients to familiarize themselves with each client's interests and skills. Then, using professional contacts, newspaper ads, and leads from existing employers, the representatives develop job openings that match as closely as possible the needs of program participants. The marketing strategy developed by TEE for privatesector-supported work focuses on scaling TEE's services as an employment agency. Corporate representatives approach companies that have job openings and facilitate the process by which employers can interview and hire skilled, reliable employees. Employers are told matter-of-factly that prospective employees have a history of psychiatric disability but are now stable and ready to work. Employers learn that TEE is responsible for the supervision, support, paperwork, *and pay* of the supported workers for the first 4 to 6 months that they are on the job. The employer, in turn, is billed by TEE for the actual hours that clients work. During its first 2 years of operation, a wide variety of Boston-area employers have worked with the Access program.

Once an Access client is hired for a supported work placement, he or she is visited at least twice a week at the job site by the corporate representative. The representative acts as a supervisor, role model, and liaison between the client and the company and between the client and the Access program. The agreement with the host company is that, if performance is satisfactory, the supported worker will be hired (that is, "rolled over" onto the employer's payroll) as a permanent employee at the end of a 4-to-6-month period. The client's work performance is evaluated first on a weekly and then on a biweekly basis. To facilitate the transition into competitive employment, the corporate representative continues to meet with the program graduate once a week for 4 to 6 weeks after rollover. Maintaining formal but decreased contact after rollover substantially lessens the anxiety many clients experience during this transition. After this 4 to 6 weeks, program graduates are invited to maintain contact with the program through telephone calls, meetings with staff members, and receptions for clients and graduates.

To evaluate the success of the Access Program, two separate studies were undertaken. The first was descriptive in nature, designed to examine the characteristics of the program participants and their success over time. The second was designed to study in depth, but on a small subsample of clients, the psychological and social factors related to vocational success.

DESCRIPTIVE PROGRAM DATA

Method

Program records from the beginning of the Access pilot project in 1985 through June 1987 were reviewed. Sources included referral summaries by each client's mental health treatment provider, written applications to the program, intake summaries completed by Access staff, and outcome data regarding placements and terminations from the program. The program has served 152 people to date, of whom 38 remain in the program. Demographic data suggest that the majority of clients served by Access were diagnosed as having schizophrenia (40%), schizoaffective disorder (16%), depression (12%), bipolar disorder (9%), or other (23%). Clients tend to be white (74%), male (60%), and at least high school graduates (90%). The level of educational attainment among Access clients suggests that the group as a whole was highly educated; 51 % had either attended or graduated from college. Selection processes for program entrance may have favored those with more education because they tended more often to have some previous work history and, therefore, appeared better able to return to work. The generalizability of the program's success should be interpreted with this in mind.

Results

The major variable of interest for this evaluation was the outcome measure of employment. Of the 114 program participants who terminated from Access, 40 individuals (or 35%) completed the program and obtained competitive employment; 74 others left the program either before completing preemployment training or after having failed to obtain permanent employment after initial job placement.

Where the reason for failure to complete the program or to obtain employment was known (65 cases), it was related to the individual's psychiatric illness in 83% of those cases. Just over one third (40%) of the clients left the program due to hospitalizations; 43% left because their symptoms or related issues (such as side effects of medication) were serious enough to prevent their being hired or completing preemployment training. It should be noted, however, that some clients who entered competitive employment did manifest relatively severe symptoms. It is also interesting to note that 10 of the 19 people who terminated from the program without notice or due to hospitalization in 1987 had either stopped or reduced their medication without informing the Access staff.

Follow-up data were gathered on a nonrandom but representative sample of 28 of the 40 people who graduated into competitive employment. Of these 28, 24 remained employed at the time of data collection. The length of employment at follow-up ranged from 1 to 21 months. Of the four who were not employed, one stopped taking medication and was hospitalized; another left the job and is now in a psychosocial rehabilitation program; the third returned to the Access program and entered another supported work placement. The fourth person, after one promotion and two job changes, stopped working and soon after had to be hospitalized. Half the graduates were working in full-time positions, with salaries ranging from $10,000 to $15,000 per year.

These findings raise the question of how the clients who were able to obtain employment differed from those who left the program or did not obtain jobs. A second study, with a sample drawn from this population, specifically examined this question.

SMALL-SAMPLE STUDY

Method

Subjects. A subsample of 34 Access clients was followed intensively during the first year of the program in an attempt to identify those factors most important in obtaining competitive employment. This group was a nonrandom but representative sample of the 87 clients who participated in Access during 1986. Clients who were married or nonwhite were excluded from the study to avoid confounding the variables under study. We eliminated black clients, for example, who might be subject to racial prejudice in the workplace, and married clients who might have supports not available to the majority of Access participants. After these eliminations, there remained a subject pool of 50 people, 3 of whom had left the Boston area and could not be contacted. Thirteen additional individuals declined, for various reasons, to participate in the study.

Instruments

We hypothesized that the return to work would be a stressful transition and that clients most likely to navigate it successfully would be those who had achieved a high degree of stability in their living situations; had not suffered recent or major stresses in their family lives; felt reasonably well supported in their social relationships outside the family; had a stable treatment regimen; and were relatively symptom-free. Two instruments were used to measure these variables. The first was a semistructured interview based on the work of Strauss and his colleagues (Strauss & Carpenter, 1972, 1974, 1977). The interview, developed by Trotter (1987), examined five important environmental contexts: work, family relationships, social relationships outside the family, living situation, and treatment. Within each of these, it focused on four aspects of individual-environment interaction thought to be most relevant to a psychiatric population: structure, self-esteem, stress, and support. A second instrument, the Brief Psychiatric Rating Scale (Overall & Gorham, 1962), was used to measure symptomatology.

Using employment status as the outcome variable, the data were analyzed to see what factors seemed most important in helping individuals make the transition to work.

Results

Our original hypothesis was not confirmed by the data; that is, for those clients in this small-sample study, functioning in other life contexts (family, living situation, and so forth) bore little relationship to success in getting a job. However, another, initially counterintuitive finding emerged: Clients who had earlier onset of psychiatric illness were far more likely to be employed than those who had become ill later in life. Clients whose disabilities were identified in adolescence (age 19 or younger) were almost twice as likely to be employed as those with an adult onset: 59% of the former were employed, compared with 30% of the latter. Of the 34 individuals we followed, 15 were competitively employed at the time of the interview. Of these 15, 10 had an adolescent onset. Looking at the subsample as a whole, of the seven people who had become disabled after the age of 25, only two were competitively employed; at the other extreme, four out of five participants who had become disabled after the age of 16 were employed.

DISCUSSION

Both the descriptive program data and the results of the small-sample study suggest that the supported work program is indeed effective in returning individuals with severe psychiatric disability to competitive work. Although these initial results must be interpreted with caution since they are not based on a controlled study, they are encouraging in light of the widespread belief, even among mental health professionals, that people with severe psychiatric disabilities are simply not able to work. Successful outcome in the Access program was found to be independent of psychiatric diagnosis and severity of manifest symptomatology. This is consistent with the bulk of prior research suggesting that work is a relatively independent dimension of clinical outcome.

These results are also consistent with previous research indicating that no measures of non-work-related functioning can predict with any degree of accuracy who among individuals with severe psychiatric disability will succeed in achieving competitive employment. Our intensive analysis of 34 program participants failed to suggest a connection between stability of non-work-related support systems and vocational outcome, but did indicate a relationship between length of disability and employment.

Anecdotally, two variables that appeared to affect program outcome were clinical stability and level of motivation. It appears that stability of psychiatric disability over time allows for a process of adjustment to take place, during which the individual learns to accept the disability without succumbing to feelings of failure or despair. This is quite congruent with the literature on physical disabilities (Wright, 1983), which emphasizes the importance of accepting the disability and meeting its challenges. Stable adjustment to psychiatric disability over time permits the development of coping strategies, which enable the client to deal with stress without relapsing, thus enhancing a sense of competence and control.

Motivation is notoriously difficult to measure objectively. In our experience with the Access program, however, both the social/financial need to work and the willingness to make sacrifices in order to work (adjusting expectations downward, accepting delayed gratification, modifying dress or hygiene in order to meet the demands of the workplace, and so forth) seem to be indicative of the motivation to return to work. A more rigorous study of the supported work model that examines the effect of these two variables might provide the additional evidence needed to answer the question of who among the severely psychiatrically disabled are most likely to achieve vocational success.

REFERENCES

Anthony, W. A., & Blanch, A. (in press). Supported employment for persons who are psychiatrically disabled. *Psychosocial Rehabilitation Journal.*

Anthony, W. A., Cohen, M. R., & Vitalo, R. (1978). The measurement of rehabilitation outcome. *Schizophrenia Bulletin, 4,* 365–383.

Anthony W. A., Howell, J., & Danley, K. (1984). The vocational rehabilitation of the psychiatrically disabled. In M. Mirabi (Ed.), *The chronically mentally ill: Research and services* (pp. 215–237). Jamaica, NY: SP Medical and Scientific Books.

Anthony, W. A., & Jansen, M. A. (1984). Predicting the vocational capacity of the chronically mentally ill—Research and policy implications. *American Psychologist, 39,* 537–544.

Anthony, W. A., & Liberman, R. P. (1986). The practice of psychiatric rehabilitation: Historical, conceptual, and research base. *Schizophrenia Bulletin, 12,* 542–559.

Beard, J. H., Propst, R. N., & Malamud, T. J. (1982). The Fountain House model of psychiatric rehabilitation. *Psychosocial Rehabilitation Journal, 5,* 47–59.

Bond, G.R., & Boyer, S. L. (in press) The evaluation of vocational programs for the mentally ill: A review. In J. A. Ciardiello & M. D. Bell (Eds.), *Vocational rehabilitation of persons with prolonged mental illness. Baltimore:* John Hopkins University Press.

Brickley, M. (1974). Normalization and behavior modification in the workshop. *Journal of Rehabilitation, 40,* 15–16, *41,* 44–46.

Cheadle, A. J., & Morgan, R. (1972). The measurement of the work performance of psychiatric patients: A reappraisal. *British Journal of Psychiatry, 120,* 437–441.

Ciardiello, J. A. (1981). Job placement success of schizophrenic clients in sheltered workshop programs. *Vocational Evaluation and Work Adjustment Bulletin,* Fall, 125–128.

Distefano, M. K., & Pryor, M. W. (1970). Vocational evaluation and successful placement of psychiatric clients in a vocational rehabilitation program. *American Journal of Occupational Therapy, 24,* 205–207.

Douzinas, N., & Carpenter, M. (1981). Predicting the community performance of vocational rehabilitation clients. *Hospital and Community Psychiatry, 32,* 409–412.

Estroff, S. E. (1981). *Making it crazy: An ethnography of psychiatric patients in an American community.* Berkeley: University of California Press.

Farina, A. (1982). The stigma of mental illness. In A. G. Miller (Ed.), *In the eye of the beholder* (pp. 305–363). New York: Praeger.

Farina, A., & Feiner, R. D. (1973). Employment interviewer reactions to former mental patients. *Journal of Abnormal Psychology, 82,* 268–272.

Farkas, M, Rogers, E. S., & Thurer, S. (1987). Rehabilitation outcome of long-term hospital patients left behind by deinstitutionalization. *Hospital and Community Psychiatry, 38,* 864–870.

Gurel, L. & Lorei, T. W. (1972). Hospital and community ratings of psychopathology as predictors of employment and readmission. *Journal of Consulting and Clinical Psychology, 34,* 286–291.

Huffine, C. L., & Clausen, J. A. (1979). Madness and work: Short and long-term effects of mental illness on occupational careers. *Social Forces, 57,* 1049–1062.

Minkoff, K. (1978). A map of the chronic mental patient. In J. A. Talbott (Ed.), *The chronic mental patient* (pp. 11–37). Washington, DC: American Psychiatric Association.

Olshansky S., Grob, S., & Malamud, M. A. (1958). Employers' attitudes and practices in the hiring of ex-mental patients. *Mental Hygiene, 41,* 391–401.

Overall, J. E., & Gorham, O. R. (1962). The brief psychiatric rating scale. *Psychological Reports, 10,* 799–812.

Rabkin, J. G. (1972). Opinions about mental illness: A review of the literature. *Psychological Bulletin, 77*(3), 153–171.

Rehab Brief. (1986). Community adjustment: Evaluation of the clubhouse model for psychiatric rehabilitation, *9*(2), 1–4. Washington, DC: National Institute of Disability Research and Rehabilitation.

Simmons, O. (1965). *Work, and mental illness—Eight case studies.* New York: Wiley.

Strauss, J. S., & Carpenter, W. (1972). The prediction of outcome in schizophrenia: II. *Archives of General Psychiatry, 27,* 739–746.

Strauss, J. S., & Carpenter, W. (1974). The prediction of outcome in schizophrenia: III. *Archives of General Psychiatry, 31,* 37–42.

Strauss, J. S., & Carpenter, W. (1977). The prediction of outcome in schizophrenia: III, fiveyear outcome and its predictors—A report from the international pilot study of schizophrenia. *Archives of General Psychiatry, 34,* 159–163.

Trotter, S. (1987). *Mental illness and the capacity for work.* Unpublished doctoral dissertation, Harvard University Graduate School of Education, Cambridge, MA.

Turner, K. J. (1977, May-June). Jobs and schizophrenia. *Social Policy,* 32–40.

Vash, C. L. (1977). *Sheltered industrial employment.* Washington, DC: Institute for Research Utilization.

Will, M. (1984). *OSERS programing for the transition of youth with disabilities: Bridges from school to working life.* Paper presented at the 1984 Symposium on Employment for Citizens who are Mentally Retarded, Richmond, VA.

Wright, B. A. (1983). *Physical disability—A psychosocial approach* (2nd ed.). New York: Harper & Row.

Zipple, A., & Spaniol, L. (1984). *Current research on families that include a person with a severe mental illness: A review of the findings.* Unpublished manuscript, Boston University, Center for Psychiatric Rehabilitation, Boston, MA.

16
Cognitive Remediation Following Traumatic Brain Injury

Jeffrey S. Kreutzer, Wayne A. Gordon,
and Paul Wehman

ABSTRACT: Cognitive remediation, a form of rehabilitation, has received increased attention as a means of mitigating the cognitive, psychomotor, and behavioral impairments arising from traumatic brain injury. Because of cognitive impairments, brain injury victims, particularly those with severe injuries, often suffer from long-term unemployment and dependency. Despite the widespread use of cognitive remediation techniques, methodologically sound outcome research regarding efficacy is extremely limited. This article reviews existing cognitive remediation outcome research and needs for additional research, describes a conceptual scheme for remediation strategies, provides a structure for research and program implementation, and discusses recently developed intervention strategies. An emphasis is placed on goals incorporating functional outcomes and direct enhancement of daily living activities.

Improvements in medical care delivery, particularly in the area of emergency medical management, and advances in surgical techniques have contributed to increased survival rates following traumatic brain injury. Unfortunately, the dramatic improvements in survival have not been matched by equally impressive improved outcomes in rehabilitation programs. Thus, for example, Brooks, McKinlay, Symington, Beattie, and Campsie (1987) reported a 70% unemployment rate for persons followed in Glasgow, Scotland, as long as 7 years postinjury. Peck, Fulton, Cohen, Warren, and Antonello (1984) reported similar unemployment rates for a sample of 60 severely injured patients, with a mean of 3.5 years postinjury.

Poor long-term outcomes are also evident on examination of data describing the functional skills and life quality of persons with traumatic brain injury. Jacobs (1988) recently reported the findings of 142 in-depth interviews with victims of head injury and their families. The author concluded: "Most survivors lived with their families, did not work or attend school, and were dependent on others for skills, finances, and services outside the home" (p. 425). Poor dispositions have been attributed to the multiple impairments in cognitive abilities as well as the frequent behavioral and personality disorders that are secondary to traumatic brain injury. Brooks et al. (1987) found that memory, sustained attention, and efficient information processing capabilities were important determinants of employability. Ben-Yishay, Silver, Piasetsky, and Rattok (1987) reported that vocational failures are most often attributable to cognitive impairments (e.g., memory and attentional disorders), poor interpersonal skills, disinhibition, lack of initiative, and poor self-awareness. Clearly, one of the keys to improving vocational outcomes is finding means of improving cognitive function.

Partly in response to the needs of persons with traumatic brain injury, attention has begun to be focused on a heterogeneous group of interventions *labeled cognitive remediation therapy*. The purpose of this article is to provide a brief review of issues pertinent to understanding cognitive remediation as well as a synopsis of some of the sparse outcome research in the area.

For present purposes, cognitive remediation refers to a set of strategies intended to improve the intellectual, perceptual, psychomotor, and behavioral skills of persons with brain dysfunction. The long-term goal of therapy is to enhance the person's ability to perform the activities of daily living that are needed to function in work, academic, and community living environments. This definition of cognitive remediation differs from the one recently offered by Rimmele and Hester (1987) primarily by not restricting goals to restoring competencies that existed premorbidly. The experience of acquired brain dysfunction often necessitates drastic changes from preinjury goals and life-styles, frequently resulting in the need for the development of new skills (e.g., alternative employment). As Diller and Gordon (1981a) have noted, cognitive remediation therapy should not be confused with cognitive therapy or rehabilitation. *Cognitive therapy* is a type of psychotherapy. *Cognitive rehabilitation* refers to the diversity of interventions intended to improve physical and mental functioning offered by a variety of disciplines, including physical therapy, psychiatry, occupational therapy, neuropsychology, and speech pathology. Cognitive remediation is one of the many types of rehabilitation therapies.

MODELS OF INTERVENTION FOR COGNITIVE IMPAIRMENT

The present-day reader is likely to be confused in attempting to develop a clear schema for understanding and classifying the types of intervention used in cognitive remediation. Cognitive remediation has been used to describe holistic day rehabilitation programs, practice sessions using computer software, driver training programs, use of compensatory strategies for memory improvement, social skills training, and strategies to improve reading skills for patients suffering from visual impairments. This confusion is not surprising considering the results of a survey published by Bracy (1984) indicating the great diversity of disciplines and the variety of settings in which cognitive remediation therapy is provided.

Several models for improving cognitive and psychomotor impairments as well as personality, behavior, and life skills have been proposed. Perhaps the most useful system for categorizing models of intervention has been presented by Gross and Schutz (1986) (see Table 16.1). Within their conceptualization scheme, several treatment models can be combined and incorporated in a hierarchical fashion to yield optimal treatment results. The models are distinguishable on the basis of differences in regard to assumptions pertaining to generalizability, requirements for the client's learning potential, the role of the environment, and levels of intervention. Furthermore, although the role of psychotherapy is not addressed within the overall model, Gross and Schutz argue for the provision of psychotherapy within a comprehensive treatment plan.

OUTCOME RESEARCH

Despite the recent proliferation of programs designed to provide cognitive remediation, there has been little research focused on efficacy with persons having traumatic brain injury. Several years ago, Diller and Gordon (1981a, 1981b) first reviewed the literature describing the efficacy of various approaches to cognitive remediation. Since then, there has been much discussion of the need for efficacy research; however, there have been few methodologically sound investigations.

Most of the sparse research published in the area has focused on victims of cerebrovascular accidents (Gouvier, Webster, & Warren, 1986). The lack of research involving traumatic brain injury populations indicates we still have little empirical basis for treatment selection. Based on their reviews (1981a, 1981b) Diller and Gordon encouraged investigation of treatment efficacy in relation to types of disorders, increased utilization of single-case methodologies in the early development of new therapies, and development of therapies focused on affective and motivational problems. An important issue raised by the authors concerned the notion of ecological validity. The authors stated, "To establish more effective remedial programs, continued work must be done to establish parameters of skill generalization to secure maintenance and integration of remediated skills into daily activities" (p. 832).

Recently, Rimmele and Hester (1987) reviewed the literature on cognitive remediation. The review indicated that little has changed since Diller and Gordon first surveyed the literature. Probably little harm is done in applying programs developed for stroke patients to those with traumatic brain injury. The age differences between the two groups, differential learning ability, and heterogeneity of neuropathology, however, all argue in favor of the need for additional research focused specifically on traumatic brain injury.

GENERALIZATION

A key issue in the study of cognitive remediation is generalization of learning. Diller and Gordon (1981a, 1981b) and Gordon (1987) have described three levels of generalization.

Table 16,1 Treatment Models, Underlying Assumptions, and Examples of Intervention Stretegies

Model	Underlying Assumptions	Examples
Environmental Control Model	Maladjustment stems from loss of previously existing competencies or acquisition of unwanted behaviors; ability to learn is irrelevant. Improvement requires modification of patient's social and physical environment. Goals include improving impression of existing responses, suppression of undesirable behaviors, and development of new adaptive responses. Environment is more malleable than the patient; behavior is best controlled through environmental manipulation.	Worker who has difficulty maintaining attention is moved to a quiet and isolated area. Patient is made aware of inappropriate behaviors at dinner and is immediately prompted with instructions for appropriate behavior.
Stimulus-Response Conditioning Model	Client has learning potential and once behavior stabilizes environmental changes are irrelevant. Complex behaviors consist of discrete elements that can be developed and chained together using standard principles of reinforcement theory. Therapy is based on client–environment interactions Generalization may not necessarily occur.	Patient is reinforced by the employer for maintaining attention for increasingly longer periods of time. Patient is reinforced by family for bringing home greater percentages of needed food items on successive shopping trips.

Skill Training Model	Behavior including important skills can be improved through learning and practice. Training basic skills generalizes, resulting in improved performance on similar and more complex tasks as well as in other environments. Skills are addressed in a hierarchical fashion with basic skills (e.g., attention and impulse control) addressed first. Later, more complex skills (e.g., reasoning and judgment) are addressed.	Patient practices memory training software on a computer and remembers to bring home required food items from grocery store. Client participates in a social skills training group and ability to interact appropriately with family members improves.
Strategy Substitution Model	First step in process requires identification of inefficient strategies by patient. In conjunction with patient, therapist develops alternate, more effective strategies. Client can identify appropriate situations for use of alternate strategies.	Rather than rely on his memory, client writes down food items on a grocery list. Student with a brain injury relies on a word processor with built in spell-check features to avoid errors in assignments.

Level I. This level involves task learning of the most fundamental type. Learning is evident on the basis of improved performance on the training task as the number of training sessions increases. Ideally, learning should also be evident when the patient is presented with an alternate form of training materials. Generalization at Level I is a prerequisite for generalization at other levels.

Level II. This level involves a more complex form of generalization that is demonstrated via improved performance on psychometric tests. Improvements should be demonstrable on tests that focus on elements similar to those of the training task. To a great extent, cognitive remediation outcome studies have focused on Level II generalization. Often, researchers have concluded that training was effective because test performance improved as a consequence of treatment. Nevertheless, statistical differences in test results may not be indicative of treatment effectiveness unless the differences are meaningful and are manifested in improved performance of day-to-day activities.

Level III. This level involves the highest order of generalization that is manifested by the fact that improved performance on training tasks has yielded similar improvements in performance of day-to-day activities. In part, the absence of investigations incorporating Level III generalization as a dependent variable may be a consequence of the inherent difficulties in measuring performance of everyday skills and activities.

The importance of Level III generalization has been espoused by other researchers including Fawber and Wachter (1987) and Hart and Hayden (1986). The former authors recently reviewed the literature pertaining to employment outcomes following head injury and critiqued the traditional vocational rehabilitation model of service delivery. The traditional model typically consists of a sequence of steps including vocational evaluation, job training, and placement. The failure of the model was primarily attributed to incorrect assumptions regarding generalization of skills acquired during the job-training process. Fawber and Wachter reported that generalization from the job-training phase is nearly impossible because virtually all severely injured patients suffer from significant memory and learning impairments. The detrimental effect of memory impairment on employability has also been reported by Ben-Yishay et al. (1987).

Hart and Hayden (1986) have developed several methods of improving treatment success and assuring the ecological validity of cognitive remediation approaches. The authors have described a process by which three aspects of remediation tasks are varied: complexity, autonomy, and stress. In regard to *complexity,* the therapist initially focuses on relatively simple tasks that are likely to exist in the patient's behavioral repertoire before the initiation of treatment. Later, tasks are made more complex by linking series of skills and activities together. *Autonomy* refers to the level of independent activity required for task completion. Initially, the patient may be provided with several cues as well as a structured format for task completion. The cues and structure provided by the therapist are gradually withdrawn as therapy progresses. *Stress* dimensions can be varied by altering potential obstacles to task completion including distractions, opportunities for rest, changes in task demands, and criticism from others regarding performance. In each case, the information processing demands of training tasks are gradually increased as the patient's skills improve. Generalization and the ecological validity of training activities are enhanced by teaching, reinforcing, and modeling in a diversity of naturalistic settings.

COGNITIVE REMEDIATION

Considerations in Research and Practice

Given the limited availability of outcome research, the failure of many remediation programs to address the issue of generalization, and the absence of specific standards of practice as well as accredited education programs for cognitive remediation practitioners, formidable obstacles block the development of effective treatment programs (Kreutzer & Boake, 1987). Diller and Gordon (1981a, 1981b) have described a series of issues that should be addressed by medical and rehabilitation professionals involved in cognitive remediation. These and other issues presented in the following section should be considered by researchers, administrators, and practitioners involved in program design, outcome research, and treatment implementation.

Prioritization of Problems. Persons with head injury rarely have a single problem. Treatments should be prioritized in terms of their importance in overall goal attainment, likelihood of success, and interrelationships between deficits. Treatment should not merely have heuristic value but must be related to functional outcome. The term functional denotes that cognitive remediation has impacted the performance of daily living activities.

Problem Definition. The problem of focus should be carefully defined in functional terms. Information should be collected pertaining to frequency, duration, and a description of environments in which the problem exists. The relationship between the problem of interest and other problems should be examined and specified.

Treatment Description. The nature of treatment should be defined and operationalized in ways that not only provide a record of what was done, but a method for replicating one's approach as well. Information regarding frequency and duration of treatment should be documented. Problems of generalization can be minimized partly by providing treatment in the environment where the problem to be treated is most likely to occur.

Patient Selection. Those with traumatic brain injury represent an extremely heterogeneous group. Information should be provided regarding the types of clients most likely to benefit from treatment and those least likely to benefit. Demographic and neurologic variables denoting client types should include chronicity of injury, age, and severity of injury. Prognostic statements of benefit must be grounded in either practice or theory. What works with one client may or may not work with another. Thus the dynamics of learning and the interface of individual differences requires specificity.

Providers of Treatment. Given the diversity of disciplines providing cognitive remediation services, their varying levels of expertise and training, and the absence of accredited educational programs for service providers, information regarding credentialing and training of cognitive remediation therapists should be specified. Administrators and practitioners must carefully plan mechanisms for ongoing staff education given the relative newness of the field, and the numerous changes and developments in treatment approaches that are likely to occur in a relatively brief period of time.

Duration of Treatment. Wehman, Kreutzer, Wood, Morton, and Sherron (1988b) have advocated for continuing assessment and follow-along within supported employment programs for persons with traumatic brain injury. Follow-along and ongoing assessment help assure the maintenance of treatment gains especially considering the changes inherent in both the patient and his or her environment. Continuing follow-along and assessment are cost effective considering the tremendous expense of many rehabilitation programs. Furthermore, therapists are encouraged to specify the duration of treatment and develop ongoing assessment strategies. Unfortunately, little available research exists that addresses the durability of treatment gains.

Functional Approaches

For many rehabilitation professionals, the ultimate goal of cognitive remediation is to improve the performance of daily living activities. The needs of persons with traumatic brain injury are relatively urgent, and many questions remain regarding the efficacy of various treatment approaches. The discussion that follows will describe a series of relatively new intervention strategies: perceptual training for improved driving performance, supported employment, and compensatory strategies. We have chosen to focus on these strategies to illustrate important aspects of cognitive remediation. These techniques have been developed to address the special needs of the traumatic brain injury population and are intended to yield benefits in daily living activities (Level III generalization). We are not "endorsing" these techniques because further data are needed regarding efficacy and appropriateness. Clinicians are encouraged to make their own decisions regarding potential usefulness based on their own criteria and those previously discussed herein.

Perceptual Training for Improved Driving Performance. Sivak, Olson, Kewman, Won, and Henson (1981) and Sivak, Hill, Henson, Butler, Silber, and Olson (1984) have completed a series of investigations focused on driving skills. In their initial study (1981), the performance of persons with brain injury, spinal cord injury, and (uninjured) controls was compared on a series of perceptual-motor and actual driving tests. Examination of statistical analyses comparing test results led the authors to conclude that persons with brain dysfunction performed relatively poorly on paper-and-pencil perceptual-motor tests and on actual driving tests relative to controls. Furthermore, correlational analyses revealed that, to a great extent, actual driving performance was predictable from paper-and-pencil tests.

The authors' second investigation (1984) used a Skill Training Model (Gross & Schutz, 1986) (see Table 16.1) and involved efficacy assessment of a driver's training program. Eight patients with brain dysfunction were given perceptual-motor and actual driving tests before and after treatment. Treatment consisted of approximately 10 hours of perceptual-motor training. Training consisted of practice on a variety of tasks incorporating visual skills such as scanning, visuoperception, visual discrimination, attention, imagery, and problem solving. On the basis of statistical analyses, Sivak et al. concluded that driving as well as paper-and-pencil test performance improved as a consequence of training. Furthermore, the authors detected a relationship between the extent of improvement on paper-and-pencil tests and the extent of improvement on actual driving tests. Apparently, Level III generalization, as described by Gordon (1987), had occurred. The investigators concluded that although their results had important implications for the training of home and work activities, several questions remain. Reportedly, further research is needed to assess durability of treatment effects, suitability of treatment for various populations, and the most appropriate format for treatment implementation.

Supported Employment. Ideally, cognitive remediation programs are delivered in natural settings such as the patient's home, or work site. As more and more persons with traumatic brain injury are attempting to return to work, supported employment is being used as a model of vocational rehabilitation (Wehman et al., 1988a; Wehman et al., 1988b). Supported employment incorporates a variety of rehabilitation strategies and is characterized by the presence of an employment specialist working directly at the job site. As the job is mastered by the client, the amount of intervention time provided by the employment specialist is gradually diminished. This employment model serves as an excellent vehicle for providing individualized cognitive remediation services.

There are several basic assumptions associated with the model of supported employment (Wehman & Moon, 1988). First, vocational intervention occurs at the work site, not in a therapy room, and is carried out to the fullest extent possible beginning at the point of initial paid employment. Second, intervention is ongoing, permanently available, and provided as long as needed. Third, supported employment programs are reserved only for persons with the severest disabilities, having a demonstrated inability to gain and maintain employment. The severity of the problems that these persons face necessitates significant and long-term intervention. A fourth assumption is that work occurs in a normal, socially integrated environment, where predominantly nonhandicapped coworkers function. Sheltered workshops that serve only persons labeled mentally or physically disabled are not used as placement sites. Salary ranges begin at least at the minimum wage level.

In contrast to traditional vocational rehabilitation programs and other holistic cognitive remediation programs (e.g., Ben-Yishay et al., 1987; Prigatano & Fordyce, 1986), few or no preplacement activities exist. Cognitive remediation, work adjustment, work hardening, and social skills training are best provided at the job site while the person is already employed. Individually designed compensatory strategies based on neuropsychological assessment and analysis are provided in the context of normal work activities. Similarly, substance abuse counseling, psychotherapy, and family counseling are provided as needed following the initial placement.

Within the context of supported employment, cognitive remediation can be most effective for several reasons. First, functional use of cognitive remediation is maximized in natural environments (Leland, Lewis, Hinman, & Carillo, 1988) such as work settings. The employment specialist, with the help of the neuropsychologist, occupational therapist, and rehabilitation engineer, can be highly effective in providing cognitive instruction in the context of work. Specific vocational skills that need to be acquired during the initial stages of employment provide an excellent vehicle for cognitive instruction. Furthermore, supported employment incorporates all four of the intervention models described by Gross and Schutz (1986).

A second reason for applying cognitive remediation at the work site is that the transferability of skills learned in one setting to another is typically very poor for severely head-injured persons (Fawber & Wachter, 1987). Memory deficits, learning impairments, and breakdowns in executive function contribute to a marked inability to generalize. Cognitive training at the job site avoids the need to make assumptions regarding generalization of training as well as the need to make adjustments based on differences between pretraining and posttraining work environments and responsibilities.

A third reason for cognitive intervention during actual employment is to enable the employment specialist to customize training and acknowledge the unique needs of the person. The training program can be based on the person's specific strengths and weaknesses that are framed in the context of the employer's requirements. The employment specialist functions as an on-site training specialist who can adjust reinforcement, remediation, and compensatory strategies to the changing environment and demands of the employer. Intervention strategies are based on direct observation rather than solely on the employer's written reports or the client's self-report, which may be entirely inaccurate.

In conclusion, preliminary data indicate that cognitive remediation strategies have been an important component in the successful implementation of supported employment strategies (Wehman et al., 1988a). The goal of cognitive remediation in the context of supported employment is to teach persons with head injury how to work more efficiently. Techniques such as personalized checklists, sequenced cues, and individualized schedules are routinely used with brain-injured workers to ensure job skill acquisition and maintenance.

Compensatory Techniques to Improve Daily Living. Milton and Wertz (1986) have described a set of techniques labeled compensatory strategies. Many persons with traumatic brain injury have difficulty assuming former responsibilities because of cognitive and psychomotor impairments. These strategies, intended to help the patient compensate for his or her limitations, would be classified by Gross and Schutz (1986) (see Table 16.1) as falling within the Strategy Substitution

Model. Examples include memory notebooks, lists, and schedules. Compensatory strategies may be most appropriate when use of alternative treatment models has yielded no significant benefits, or in cases in which environmental barriers or the patient's cognitive limitations make this approach to goal attainment most efficient. Notably, compensatory strategies used in competitive work environments have contributed to the initial successes of supported employment programs for the traumatically brain injured (Wehman et al., 1988a).

The model for development of compensatory strategies proposed by Milton and Wertz (1986) incorporates several fundamental assumptions. First, the focus of rehabilitation is on the patient's skills and strengths, rather than limitations and weaknesses. Existing skills are developed and adapted in the process of compensation. Second, every effort should be made to incorporate the patient's input in development of strategies to assure maximum usage and utility. Third, efficacy can partly be assured by helping the patient to understand the potential value of the technique. Fourth, clinicians must monitor the use of strategies and their appropriateness because the patient's skills and needs are likely to change over time. Fifth, strategies should be introduced gradually, and preferably one at a time, to avoid overwhelming the patient.

Many compensatory strategies are relatively simple and are used by persons without brain injury to facilitate accomplishment of daily living activities. For example, a patient with severe memory impairment may be taught to write down a list of food items before going grocery shopping to compensate for memory impairment. A working patient who previously had an excellent memory may be taught to use a schedule book to reduce the possibility of missing appointments. A client with impaired arithmetic abilities may be instructed to use a calculator to work more quickly and accurately.

Recently, computers have emerged as an important tool for therapists in the development and implementation of compensatory strategies. For example, Kreutzer and Morton (1988) have described the use of computers by clinicians to develop lists and schedules for patients. Computers have proved to be a useful tool because they can help the clinician work more quickly and are extremely flexible. Checklists and schedules are easily revised based on the client's feedback and experience to ensure maximum utility. Furthermore, patients instructed in the use of word processing software with spell-checking features can often perform more effectively in academic and vocational environments. Parente (1988) has described the use of prosthetic devices incorporating microcomputer technology intended to improve performance of skills dependent on memory functioning. The devices are either intended for cuing or data storage. Examples include electronic calendars that can be programmed to remind the user of special events or deadlines, a telephone that dials a programmed number when the user speaks a name, a pill container that beeps each time the patient is scheduled to take medication, an electronic key finder that helps locate lost keys by beeping, and a transmitter and receiver that work together to locate a lost car in a parking lot by causing the vehicle's horn and lights to flash on and off.

CONCLUSIONS

Despite improved survival rates, the life quality of many survivors of traumatic brain injury remains relatively poor. Residual, cognitive impairments, high unemployment rates, and long-term dependence are commonly reported by investigators. The last decade has seen the development of new rehabilitation technologies and methods that are promising but remain relatively unproved. The needs of the traumatic brain injury population are relatively urgent. Researchers and practicing clinicians are asked to move ahead cautiously and deliberately to improve existing therapies, develop new therapies, and answer the important questions regarding which types of cognitive remediation strategies are most efficacious for each patient subtype. Ultimately, judgments regarding treatment efficacy should be based on improvements in daily living skills.

REFERENCES

Ben-Yishay, Y., Silver, S. M., Piasetsky, E., & Rattok, J. (1987). Relationship between employability and vocational outcome after intensive holistic cognitive rehabilitation. *Journal of Head Trauma Rehabilitation 2*, 35-48.

Bracy, O. (1984). Cognitive rehabilitation survey results. *Cognitive Rehabilitation, 2*, 12-15.

Brooks, N., McKinlay, W., Symington, C., Beattie, A., & Campsie, L. (1987). Return to work within the first seven years after head injury. *Brain Injury, 1*, 5-19.

Diller, L., & Gordon, W. A. (1981a). Interventions for cognitive deficits in brain-injured adults. *Journal of Consulting and Clinical Psychology, 49*, 822-834.

Diller, L., & Gordon, W. A. (1981b). Rehabilitation and clinical neuropsychology. In S. Filskoy & T. Boll (Eds.), *Handbook of clinical neuropsychology* (pp. 702-733). New York: John Wiley.

Fawber, H. L., & Wachter, J. F. (1987). Job placement as a treatment component of the vocational rehabilitation process. *Journal of Head Trauma Rehabilitation, 2*, 27-33.

Gordon, W. A. (1987). Methodological considerations in cognitive remediation. In M. Meier, A. Benton, & L. Diller (Eds.), *Neuropsychological rehabilitation* (pp. 111-131). New York: Guilford Press.

Gouvier, D. W., Webster, J. S., & Warren, M. S. (1986). Treatment of acquired visuoperceptual and hemiattentional disorders. *Archives of Behavioral Medicine, 8*, 15-20.

Gross, Y., & Schutz, L. E. (1986). Intervention models in neuropsychology. In B. Uzell & Y. Gross (Eds.), *Clinical neuropsychology of intervention* (pp. 179-204). Boston: Martinus Nijhoff.

Hart, T., & Hayden, M. E. (1986). The ecological validity of neuropsychological assessment and remediation. In B. Uzell & Y. Gross (Eds.), *Clinical neuropsychology of intervention* (pp. 21-71). Boston: Martinus Nijhoff.

Jacobs, H. E. (1988). The Los Angeles head injury survey: Procedures and initial findings. *Archives of Physical Medicine and Rehabilitation, 69*, 425-431.

Kreutzer, J. S., & Boake, C. (1987). Addressing disciplinary issues in cognitive rehabilitation: Definition, training, and organization. *Brain Injury, 1*, 199-202.

Kreutzer, J. S., & Morton, M. V. (1988). Traumatic brain injury: Supported employment and compensatory strategies for enhancing vocational outcomes. In P. Wehman & S. Moon (Eds.), *Vocational rehabilitation and supported employment*. Baltimore: Paul Brookes Publishing.

Leland, M., Lewis, F., Hinman, S., & Carillo, R. (1988). Functional retraining of traumatically brain injured adults in a transdisciplinary environment. *Rehabilitation Counseling Bulletin, 31*(4), 289–290.

Milton, S., & Wertz, R. T. (1986). Management of persisting communication deficits in patients with traumatic brain injury. In B. Uzell & Y. Gross (Eds.), *Clinical neuropsychology of intervention* (pp. 223–256). Boston: Martinus Nijhoff.

Parente, R. (1988). *Prosthetic memory devices for head injury rehabilitation.* Paper presented at the 12th Annual Postgraduate Course on Rehabilitation of the Brain Injured Adult and Child, Williamsburg, VA.

Peck, E., Fulton, O., Cohen, C., Warren, J. R., & Antonello, J. (1984). *Neuropsychological, physical, and psychological factors affecting long-term vocational outcomes following severe head injury.* Paper presented at the annual meeting of the International Neuropsychological Society, Houston, TX.

Prigatano, G. P., & Fordyce, D. J. (1986). The neuropsychological rehabilitation program at Presbyterian Hospital, Oklahoma City. In G. P. Prigatano & others (Eds.), *Neuropsychological rehabilitation after brain injury* (pp. 96–118). Baltimore: Johns Hopkins University Press.

Rimmele, C. T., & Hester, R. K. (1987). Cognitive rehabilitation after traumatic head injury. *Archives of Clinical Neuropsychology, 2,* 353–384.

Sivak, M., Hill, C., Henson, D., Butler, B., Silber, S., & Olson, P. (1984). Improved driving performance following perceptual training in persons with brain damage. *Archives of Physical Medicine and Rehabilitation, 65,* 163–167.

Sivak, M., Olson, P., Kewman, D., Won, H., & Henson, D. (1981). Driving and perceptual/cognitive skills: Behavioral consequences of brain damage. *Archives of Physical Medicine and Rehabilitation, 62,* 476–483.

Wehman, P., Kreutzer, J., Stonnington, H., Wood, W., Sherron, P., Diambra, J., Fry, R., & Groah, C. (1988a). Supported employment for persons with traumatic brain injury: A preliminary report. *Journal of Head Trauma Rehabilitation, 3,* 82–93.

Wehman, P., Kreutzer, J., Wood W., Morton, M. V., & Sherron, P. (1988b). Supported work for persons with traumatic brain injury: Toward job placement and retention. *Rehabilitation Counseling Bulletin, 31*(4), 298–312.

Wehman, P., & Moon, M. S. (1988). *Vocational rehabilitation and supported employment.* Baltimore: Paul H. Brookes Publishing.

Acknowledgments: This work was partly supported by grants H133B80029 and G0087CO219 from the National Institute on Disability and Rehabilitation Research, United States Department of Education.

17

A Brief Outline of the Principle of Normalization

Wolf Wolfensberger and
Stephen Tullman

ABSTRACT: The normalization principle, though it has wide applicability to human service settings, has not been systematically incorporated into the training of psychologists and other rehabilitation professionals. This article defines the principle of normalization and discusses how it can help prevent, minimize, or reverse the psychological and behavioral manifestations of being viewed as different from the rest of society as a result of a physical, mental, or emotional handicap. Psychologists are becoming increasingly prominent in policy-making positions, and implementation of the normalization principle can have profound effects on the outcome of rehabilitation services in our society.

The principle of normalization first appeared in North America in the late 1960s (Wolfensberger, 1980). Since then, it has evolved into a systematic theory that can be used as a universal guiding principle in the design and conduct of human services, but which is especially powerful when applied to services to people who are devalued by the larger society. Unfortunately, the principle is not well known outside the field of mental retardation, and is not extensively implemented even where it is known, even though it is capable of making a most powerful positive impact on the quality of services, especially those of a habitative nature.

In discussing the normalization principle throughout this article, we use the following simple definition: "Normalization implies, as much as possible, the use of culturally valued means in order to enable, establish, and/or maintain valued social roles for people." Though very brief, this definition has a vast number of implications for human services, ranging from the most global to the most minute. The definition reflects the almost paradigmbreaking assumption that the goal of human services with the most impact is social role enhancement or role defense.

Obviously, this definition reflects the assumption that if a person's social role were a societally valued one, other desirable things would be accorded that person within the resources and norms of his or her society. Indeed, the attributes of the person, which might otherwise be viewed negatively by society, may now be viewed positively. For example, a person who has hallucinations that would render him or her devalued in some cultures might be held in awe and respect in others (certain American Indian tribes or in the Arab world) for being favored by God. Or in the Far East, until recently, a very wealthy person might have his or her hands rendered useless, so that what we would consider a serious functional impairment there would be a sign of the person's high status—so high that all would be made aware that the person would have all necessary functions performed for himself or herself by servants and others.

In order to perceive the crucial function of role enhancement, it is necessary to understand the dynamics of deviancy making. A person can be considered "deviant" or devalued when a significant characteristic (a "difference") is negatively valued by that segment of society that constitutes the majority or holds norm-defining power. While numerous differences do exist among individuals, it must be kept clearly in mind that differentness by itself does not become a deviancy until it becomes sufficiently negatively valuecharged in the minds of observers. Thus deviancy is in the eyes of the beholder, and is also culturally relative.

While different cultures define different types of human manifestation as deviant, in all cultures it is human differences in one or more of three broad categories that may be defined as devalued by a society: (1) congenital or adventitious physical differences associated with disease, age, primary and secondary bodily impairments, and the like; (2) overt and covert behaviors (the latter including religious, political, and other beliefs); and (3) descent, nationality, ethnic group, language, or attributive identity, such as caste.

There are various social roles into which a devalued individual may be cast. These roles are depicted in Table 17.1. The people who fall into one or more of these devalued social role categories add up to an astonishing one-third of our population.

Obviously, how a person is perceived affects how that person will be treated, and has the following implications:

1. Devalued people will be badly treated. Others will usually accord them less esteem and status than nondevalued citizens. Devalued people are apt to be rejected, even persecuted, and treated in ways that tend to diminish their dignity, adjustment, growth, competence, health, wealth, life span, and so on. Generally, societal responses to people who are devalued can be viewed as falling into only a few universal categories, primarily, (a) distancing of the devalued people, either by physical segregation, social distancing and degra-dation, or brutalization and outright destruction (e.g., genocide); (b) efforts at reversal or prevention of deviancy, which may include either attempts to change the deviant person or to change society.

2. The negative treatment accorded devalued persons takes on certain forms that express the way society conceptualizes the roles of a devalued person or group. For example, if a group of children is (unconsciously) viewed as animals, then they may be segregated in a special class that is given an animal name—often even the name of animals that are seen as expressive of the

Table 17.1 Some Societally Devalued Groups and the Common Historical Deviancy Roles into which They Are most apt to be Cast.

People Who Are Devalued Due To:	Common Deviancy Roles								
	Pity	Charity	Menace	Sick	Subhuman	Ridicule	Dread	Child-Like	Holy/Innocent
Mental disorder	X	X	X	X	X	X	X	X	X
Mental retardation	X	X	X	X	X	X		X	X
Old Age	X	X		X	X	X		X	
Alcohol Habituation	X	X	X	X		X			
Poverty	X	X	X		X		X		
Racial minority membership			X		X	X	X	X	
Epilepsy	X	X		X			X		
Drug addiction	X	X	X	X					
Criminal offenses			X	X	X		X		
Physical handicap	X	X				X			
Deafness/hearing impairment	X	X							
Blindness/visual impairment	X	X							
Illiteracy	X	X							
Political Dissidence			X						

devalued children's identity. Thus a class for retarded children may be called "The Turtles". The animal kingdom may serve as an analogue for or source of service measures for that group of people, perhaps in the belief that, unlike other people, the people served will benefit from animals more than they would from interactions with people. This might include training monkeys to serve devalued people, doing research on chimpanzee language to improve the devalued people's language development, the invocation of "pet thera-pies," and so on. Adults may be cast into the role of eternal children by calling them "children," "kids," "boys," and "girls" even when they are elderly; by being encouraged to play children's games and to follow children's school schedules rather than adult work schedules; by children's decorations and clothing styles being used for adults; by funding of services for adults coming from departments charged with serving children; and by names such as "day care center" for day programs for adults.

In the habilitation area it is very common for the sick role and perception to be attributed to clients who certainly are no sicker than most of the population, and who really need a developmental approach, adult education, industrial apprenticeship training, and the like. Instead, they are interpreted as sick by association with medically trained staff; by such names as "hospital" or "clinic" for the places where they live, go to school, and work; and by having every conceivable activity of life interpreted as a form of "therapy" (e.g., "work therapy," "reading therapy," "religion therapy... .. garden therapy," "recreation therapy," "pet therapy," etc.). While inappropri-ate use of the medical model is overtly promoted as being positive and image enhancing, it actually serves the function of differentiating devalued clients from staff and society and imaging clients as diseased, contagious, impaired, incompetent, passive, and so on.

3. How a person is perceived and treated by others will, in turn, strongly determine how that person subsequently behaves. The more consistently a person is perceived as deviant, therefore, the more likely it will be that he or she will conform to that expectation and emit the kinds of behavior that are socially expected, often behaviors that are not valued by society. On the other hand, the more social value is accorded a person, the more he or she will be encouraged to assume roles and behaviors that are appropriate and desirable, the more will be expected of him or her, and the more he or she is apt to achieve.

THE NORMALIZATION PRINCIPLE AS A MEANS OF PREVENTING, MINIMIZING, OR REVERSING SOCIETAL DEVALUATION

The fact that deviancy is culturally defined opens the door for psychologists to effect a two-pronged strategy of enabling devalued persons to attain a more valued membership in society by (1) reducing or preventing the differentness or stigmata that may make a person devalued in the eyes of observers and (2) changing perceptions and values regarding devalued persons so that a given characteristic is no longer seen as devalued.

Social role enhancement is the ultimate goal, but both stigma reduction/prevention and societal attitude changing can be pursued through two major subgoals: (a) the enhancement of the social image of a person or group and (b) the enhancement of the competence of the person or group, including bodily, sensory, intellectual and social performance, and the practice of valued skills and habits.

Image enhancement and competency enhancement are believed to be reciprocally reinforcing, both positively and negatively. A person who is competency impaired is at high risk of being seen and interpreted as being of low value and of suffering from image impairment; a person who is impaired in image and social value is apt to be responded to in ways that reduce his or her competency. Both processes work equally in the reverse direction.

The definition of normalization used here places emphasis on "the use of culturally valued means." Service structures, programs, methods, technologies, and tools are all means toward the normalization goal, and their value in the eyes of society is determined largely by the degree to which these means are used within the larger culture with and for *valued* persons of the same age, sex, and so on. For example, the culturally valued analogue for the schedules of an educational program for handicapped children would be the daily, weekly, and yearly schedules of a school for nonhandicapped children of the same age. Culturally valued analogues for a vocational program for young adults might include apprenticeship, vocational school, night classes in vocational subjects, on-the-job training, and adult education. It would not include "job therapy," make-believe work (valued people who perform fake work are at high risk of getting devalued), or playing games.

The reason culturally valued means are so important is at least fourfold.

1. Images are very transferable phenomena, as the worlds of advertising and public relations know only too well. The value message that is contained in a human service approach is highly apt to become attached to the people served. If delinquent boys are disciplined by means of electric cattle prods, they would be apt to be seen as animal-like. Relatedly, if a program utilizes means that deviate widely from cultural standards and norms, the devalued persons whom the program serves are apt to be seen as different and distinct from other citizens—and *not* in a valued sense. As a result, the stigmata already attached to devalued people will be accentuated rather than minimized. In the end, the means that a service program uses will have a powerful long-term effect on public attitudes toward (devalued) people. If the goal is to increase the level of public acceptance of people who are seen as negatively different, the message sent by what a program does is as important as the changes it tries to achieve in its clients—and sometimes even more so.

2. Clients who are "recipients" of certain services are apt to relate much better to them, both attitudinally and competently, if the means by which these services are delivered are familiar to them and are positively valued.

3. The skills, habits, and relationships that are prerequisites for a meaningful life in open society are difficult to acquire in settings that are culture-alien, that lack familiar cues, reduce opportunity, suggest or impose alien or devalued roles, and so on.
4. The public, including families and staff, are less likely to support and relate positively to a human service program that is unfamiliar, culture-alien, and perceived as "outlandish."

It is possible to schematicize the normalization principle in a number of ways that can help one to understand it better, and that can form a basis for the formulation of a variety of specific implementive measures. One way to schematicize the principle is to classify its implications into different levels of social systems as follows:

1. Actions on the level of the person concerned, usually a client.
2. Actions on the level of the person's relevant *primary* social systems (e.g., family) and *secondary* social systems (e.g., neighborhood, community, service agency).
3. Actions on the level of society as a whole; that is, society's values, language usage, laws, customs, and so on.

Thus combining the second and third levels, all action implications could be represented by the schema in Table 17.2.

A second way to conceptualize the normalization principle is to break it into seven major strategies or strategy-related dynamics called *core themes*. We have found that most people understand the normalization principle best by reviewing these themes, which capture and express most of the goals and processes of the principle. These seven core themes are:

1 .The role and importance of (un)consciousness in human services.
2. The relevance of role expectancy and role circularity to deviancy making and deviancy unmaking.
3. The "conservatism corollary" of normalization, with its implications of positive compensation for people's devalued or at-risk status.
4. The developmental model and personal-competency enhancement.
5. The power of imitation.
6. The dynamics and relevance of social imagery.
7. The importance of societal integration and valued social participation.

Each theme is explained below.

THE SEVEN CORE THEMES OF NORMALIZATION

The Role of (Un)Consciousness in Human Services

It is well known that for a variety of reasons human beings function with a remarkably restricted range of consciousness and, therefore, also with a high degree of unconsciousness. A major portion of perception takes place at or below the consciousness threshold, as is true for memory, motivation, and the like. Largely unconscious dynamics control or at least influence many of our routine acts and habits, such as what and how we eat, what we wear and buy, how we spend our money, where we live, what kind of work we do, whom we select as friends and mates, how we interact with other people, and how we raise our children. Further, there may be even more unconsciousness about complex social behaviors, especially on the large-systems level. It is, therefore, fully to be expected that a phenomenon that is so prevalent in every aspect of human existence would also be prevalent in human services. Service planners, administrators, workers, leaders, trainers, and clients are all trapped in webs of individual and collective unconscious patterns. For instance, most people in human services are unconscious of the real functions of these services, the reality, extent, and dynamics of social devaluation of large numbers of people by large numbers of people, and the nature of the plight of handicapped devalued, oppressed, poor, needy, or wounded people. The dynamic that contributes heavily to this high degree of unconsciousness, and that is so relevant to any effort at deviancy unmaking, is that the ideologies controlling much of what goes on in human services are very negative, in that they enact society's real but destructive intentions, and/or address needs

Table 17.2 Implications of the Two Major Goals of the Normalization Principle on Three Levels of Social Organization

	Major Action Goals	
Levels of Action	Enhancement of Personal Competencies	Enhancement of Social Images
The Individual	Eliciting, shaping, and maintaining useful bodily, mental, and social competencies in persons by means of direct physical and social interactions with them	Presenting, managing, addressing, labeling, and interpreting persons in a manner that creates positive roles for them and that emphasizes their similarities to, rather than their differences from, other (valued) persons
Primary and Secondary Social Systems	Eliciting, shaping, and maintaining useful bodily, mental, and social competencies in persons by adaptive shaping of such primary and secondary social systems as family, classroom, school, work setting, service agency, and neighborhood	Presenting, managing, labeling, and interpreting the primary and secondary social systems that surround a person or that consist of persons at risk so that these systems, as well as the persons in them, are perceived in a valued fashion
Societal Systems	Eliciting, shaping, and maintaining useful bodily, mental, and social competencies in persons by appropriate shaping of such societal systems and structures as entire school systems, laws, and government	Shaping cultural values, attitudes, and stereotypes so as to elicit maximum feasible acceptance of individual differences

other than those of the clients. Unpleasant realities such as these are apt to be denied and repressed into unconsciousness to the degree that they stand in contrast to the higher values and ideals that people profess on the conscious level. Such denial and repression can take place on a systemic (e.g., organizational and societal) level, as well as on a personal/individual one. Thus such entire systems as service agencies, service professions, service sectors (e.g., mental health), or even entire societies can be totally unconscious of some of the most important things they are doing.

Normalization is concerned with the identification of the unconscious, and usually negative, dynamics within human services that contribute to the devaluation and oppression of certain groups of people in a society, and with providing conscious strategies for remediating the devalued social status of such people. Furthermore, such normalization-based service evaluation instruments as Program Analysis of Service Systems (PASS) (Wolfensberger & Glenn, 1978a, 1978b) and especially Program Analysis of Service Systems' Implementation of Normalization Goals (PASSING) (Wolfensberger & Thomas) have been deliberately structured so as to reward consciousness of human service issues on the part of human service personnel.

The Relevance of Role Expectancy and Role Circularity to Deviancy Making and Deviancy Unmaking

The social roles that people impose on each other or adopt are among the most powerful social influence and control methods known. As with unconsciousness, the dynamics of role expectancies and role circularities are ever-present. A person who holds certain expectancies about the behavior or potential for growth and development of another person will create conditions and circumstances that have a high likelihood of eliciting the expected behavior. There are at least five powerful media through which role expectancies can be conveyed. These include the way people structure other people's physical environments; the activities that are offered to, provided for, or demanded of people; the language that is used with and about them; the way people are juxtaposed to each other; and other images and symbolisms. All of these factors are powerful in eliciting from a person who is the object of the role expectancies an inclination or commitment to act in the expected manner. When a person then acts as expected, the expectancies held by the others are reinforced, thus further strengthening both their expectancies and their expressions thereof, and so on, until the expected and the emitted behaviors have become very powerfully ingrained.

In the case of socially devalued people, the role expectancies that are imposed upon them are commonly the negative ones noted in Table 17.1. These role circularities are very effective in that devalued people often live up to them. Role expectancy creation is pervasive in the human services, but most often serves the (usually unconscious) societal function of creating and maintaining a certain percentage of deviant people.

In contrast to these traditional negative practices, normalization implies that contributive, positive social roles should be identified for people at risk, and that such corresponding positive role expectancies as those of pupil, student, worker, teacher, owner, guide, tenant, friend, spouse, and citizen should be extended to them. In order for these role expectancies to be conveyed to people at risk, it is important to promote normatively attractive, comfortable, and challenging service settings; age-appropriate and challenging program activities; age-appropriate and culturally valued personal appearance of clients; image-enhancing matches between the needs of clients, the nature of the program, and staff identities; and status-enhancing labels and forms of address for clients. Indeed, desired benefits, including both competency and image enhancement in virtually all areas of people's identities, will flow forth automatically if people at risk occupy valued social roles, because once a person fills a valued social role, society will tend to bestow upon, or at least make available to, the person a plethora of those things that society values. Society will even tolerate, overlook, or even interpret positively oddities that a valued person may have.

Thus human services for devalued people must do everything within its power to break the negative roles into which its devalued clients have been cast, and to establish such clients in as many positive social roles as possible.

The Conservatism Corollary to the Principle of Normalization

Many people have a few negatively valued characteristics, but these are usually so few or minor that they do not place a person into a deviant role or hinder his or her functioning. Unlike other citizens, however, devalued people exist in a state of heightened vulnerability to further devaluations and negative experiences. Consequently, the more vulnerable a person is to societal devaluation, the greater the impact that reduction/prevention of any such vulnerabilities and/or the balancing off of such vulnerabilities by positively valued manifestations or compensations has. For example, if a retarded man has a speech impediment, acts near-sightedly, has an odd hair style, and a few odd mannerisms, these realities will interact more multiplicatively than additively in eliciting negative reactions from most people. If the person also limps and wears shabby, ill-fitting clothes, then even a casual passer-by who had never seen him before would probably conclude on sight that there is something very wrong with this person, perhaps evoking ideas of "deinstitutionalized mentalpatient," "village idiot," or "streetperson." Thus people are stereotyped on sight—and often correctly so.

A devalued person is also put at heightened risk of devaluation and rejection as a result of the number of stigmatized persons with whom he or she is grouped. Six individuals walking about separately in a street crowd would make little impact on an observer if one of those people limped, one had an odd hair style, another had odd clothing, and so on, because people with such small oddities are seen on the street all the time. But when a significant proportion of people in a discrete or compact group have one or more such oddities, then the whole group, including its nonstigmatized members, is apt to be negatively stereotyped. In fact, it takes only one glance out of the corner of one's eye—less than one second—for an observer to conclude that a group of people must be from some nearby group home or institution or that they are street people."

The conservatism corollary of normalization posits, therefore, that the greater the number, severity, and/or variety of deviancies or stigmata of an individual or the greater the number of deviant people there are in a group or setting, the greater the impact of (1) the reduction of one or a few of the individual stigmata, (2) the reduction of the number of deviant people in the group, or (3) the balancing off (compensation) of the stigmata or deviancies by the presence or addition of positively valued manifestations.

A further implication is that people who are cast into a socially devalued status need to experience not only life conditions that are relatively typical, common, and prevalent for nondevalued citizens, but optimally even those conditions that are highly valued by the culture. In other words, what is "normal" for the members of a society may not be what is most normalizing or enhancing for a person who is devalued or at risk of devaluation—and may, in fact, even be nonnormalizing and deviancy making. Thus it is not enough for a human service to be merely neutral in either diminishing or enhancing the status of devalued persons in the eyes of others; it must also seek to affect the most positive status possible to enhance the image of its clients. For example, on occasions where either a suit and tie or a sports jacket and sports shirt are equally appropriate attire, the man at value-risk in society would fare better wearing the suit-and-tie combination.

The Developmental Model and Personal-Competency Enhancement

Often people with physical, mental, or emotional impairments also have functional impairment(s) that render them less competent than nonimpaired persons. Because of such handicaps, such a person may be unable to get or hold a job, relate adaptively or maturely with other people, and so on. Even devalued people who are not handicapped may be severely limited in competence because they have been subjected to low (or outright negative) role expectancies, denied opportunities and experiences that contribute to growth and development, segregated with people who present negative role models, served by human service workers of low competence, and so on.

Normalization requires that the personal competencies of devalued (or at risk) people be enhanced for a variety of reasons, among them the fact that even the appearance of competency in a person tends to elicit other positive feedback from observers, and society will be more accepting of any devalued traits or behaviors of people who otherwise have valued skills and competencies. In addition, a lack of competencies may inhibit devalued persons in many areas of functioning, a crucial one being social interactions, especially with valued persons.

Different normalization themes have different levels of importance for various devalued groups, and personal competency enhancement is particularly relevant to those groups whose social devaluation is related to their low competence: people who are retarded, untrained, physically impaired, socially maladaptive, and the like.

The Power of Imitation

Imitation is one of the most powerful learning mechanisms known. People's personalities, their ways of interacting with others and with their environment, their dress and language habits—just about every aspect of human behavior—is strongly affected by this dynamic.

The models that are available for devalued people to imitate are often negative ones. Devalued people typically are (1) segregated from valued society and models, (2) grouped with other devalued people who very frequently have socially devalued characteristics and exhibit socially devalued behaviors, and (3) often served by less competent human service workers than are valued people. Handicapped children typically have been denied socialization with adaptive, nonhandicapped peers, and have instead been served with each other or with handicapped adults who model handicapped behaviors; mildly impaired persons are often grouped with severely impaired people who emit many more inappropriate behaviors; institution physicians are often unlicensed to practice in open society; and so on.

Normalization requires that the dynamic of imitation be capitalized upon in a positive way so that the role models provided to devalued persons are people who function routinely in an appropriate and valued fashion. Furthermore, normalization implies that one would increase the sense of identification of devalued people with valued models, because people are much more apt to imitate those people with whom they identify.

The Dynamics and Relevance of Social Imagery

The use of unconscious image association is another effective learning and behavioral control mechanism. Historically, devalued people have been attached to and surrounded by symbols and imagery that overwhelmingly represent culturally negatively valued qualities. While these image associations are often made unconsciously, they strongly influence the role expectancies for and the social valuation of the persons so imaged.

Values that are associated with various images transfer to the persons, settings, or objects to which these images are connected and juxtaposed. Especially if the people with whom these images are associated have already been identified or suspected as deviant, these images then tend to elicit in observers the expectation, and even confirmation, that those people are indeed negatively valued, will act deviantly and should be treated differently.

Conversely, if the images associated with societally devalued people were highly valued ones, then at least some of the positive value contained in this imagery would likely transfer to such devalued people, who would then be more apt to be seen in a positive light. The implication of normalization is that, as much as possible, any features of human services that can convey image messages about devalued clients should be positive. The incorporation of the dynamic of image transfer has implications for every aspect of a human service. Such features would include the physical setting in which the service is rendered (location, cleanliness, beauty, what it is near, etc.), the name of the service and its administrative body, the agency logo, the sources of funds, how clients are grouped, what kinds of programming are provided, the appearance projected by clients, what the clients are called, and what the service activities are called.

A human service for devalued clients is more image enhancing if it is located in areas that are highly valued; if it groups its clients with other people who are highly valued and in age configurations that match those of culturally valued analogues. Further, if the staff has an appropriate (positively imaged) identity for the type of service being rendered (e.g., medically imaged staff only in a medical service), and if the activities and schedules for the program are highly valued and consistent with what would be expected for valued people of the same age, clients will be more highly valued. Services should be named consistently with culturally valued analogues and should elicit positive associations in an observer. Funding must come from age-appropriate sources and must avoid pity/charity imagery; the service must support a positive and age-appropriate personal appearance for its clients; and refer to its clients in image-enhancing ways. Many more implications could be spelled out (see Wolfensberger & Thomas, in press, for a detailed presentation of image implications).

The Importance of Societal Integration and Valued Social Participation

Humans have a universal tendency to respond to the presence of an unpleasant person or object by trying to place some distance between themselves and the unpleasant stimulus. Since societally devalued people are experienced by others as unpleasant stimuli, they tend to be rejected and segregated, which has a vast number of negative effects upon those who are segregated. For example, their segregated existence denies them normative, typical experiences that valued members of the culture take for granted, and since they are not exposed to normative growth experiences, their competencies are often diminished. Segregated groups are also negatively imaged as "needing" segregation because the members are so different, so helpless, and so in need of management and services that are profoundly different from those needed by valued people. Especially when handicapped people are segregated together (i.e., congregated) members of the group commonly present negative, inappropriate, and socially devalued behavior models to each other, thus increasing the socially devalued characteristics of the segregated individuals. Similarly, segregation of a societally devalued group has negative effects on society: it tends to reduce the society's level of tolerance for diversity and induces collective unconsciousness of its own practices. Because segregation tends to make people more devalued and more dependent, society pays a high price for it in many complex and deeply hidden ways.

Normalization requires that a devalued person or group has the opportunity to be personally integrated into the valued social life of society. Devalued people would be enabled to live in normative housing within the valued community and with valued people; be educated with their nondevalued peers; work in the same facilities as other people; and be involved in a positive fashion in worship, recreation, shopping, and all the other activities in which members of a society engage.

In order for personally valued social integration to be truly successful in the life of a devalued person, various supports can make significant or decisive contributions. These include the presence of ideological and administrative support, positive imaging of the persons to be integrated, people who can competently transact the integration, sufficient back-up service options in case one level of integrative effort is unsuccessful, supports that will enable the person to remain integrated from childhood on, and a comprehensive continuum of service options.

It must be emphasized that the type of integration implied by normalization theory is very specific: personal social integration and valued social participation. "Physical integration," which merely consists of the physical presence of devalued people in the community, is only *a facilitator* of actual individual valued social participation. Also, social integration is not the same as "mainstreaming" and "deinstitutionalization," which often are not truly integrative.

Interrelationship among Core Themes

While each of the seven themes can be independently sketched, in actual service practice the presence of one theme is often correlated with the presence of one or more of the others. For instance, people's unconscious devaluations are characteristically expressed in the negative images that they attach to devalued persons, and these images often serve to promote devalued role behavior in such people.

Furthermore, the themes of the normalization principle sometimes conflict with each other. For instance, it is not always possible simultaneously to optimize both the image-enhancing and the competency-enhancing features of a service. At present, human service workers have a low awareness of the relative importance of the two, and may resolve conflicts on the basis of incoherent, unconscious, or single criteria. For these reasons, instruments designed to help program personnel become cognizant of such conflicts, such as PASS (Wolfensberger & Glenn, 1978a, 1978b) and PASSING (Wolfensberger and Thomas, in press), have been developed, and may be employed to help weigh the value of conflicting criteria in a given setting.

ADDITIONAL PERSPECTIVES ON THE NORMALIZATION PRINCIPLE

In respect to the goal of normalization, one can say that a person is normalized if he or she has that culturally normative degree of personal autonomy and choice that society extends to its nondevalued members, has access to the valued experiences and resources of open society much as would be the case for a typical citizen, and is free to and capable of choosing and leading a life style that is accessible to at least the majority of other people of the same age. These goals are not attainable for every person, so it is important to keep in mind the qualifying phrase "as much as possible" in the normalization definition. Normalization strategies must take into account the particular individual concerned, the limits of our current know-how, and the individual's own choice of his or her personal goals and means. Low expectations, inappropriate pessimism, stereotyping, and the like, can have a very destructive effect on the person involved. Consequently, an adaptive human management approach is to maintain a healthy skepticism when confronted with the assertion that a specific normative human service measure or interpretation is unattainable or unrealistic.

The normalization principle has sometimes been criticized as imposing cultural uniformity. In truth, it (1) promotes social tolerance and bridge building, (2) opens up an enormous range of valued options that are commonly denied to almost a third of our population, and (3) enables (not coerces) many people who have been devalued and excluded *against their will* to participate more fully. Only a few people or groups can be said to truly and deliberately choose social marginalization and devaluation of their own free will. Even when they say they do, they often do so only reactively in response to *prior* rejection by society. For example, there never existed a self-segregatory movement among elderly people until relatively recently, when aging became a human condition that received strongly patterned rejection and discrimination.

SUMMARY AND IMPLICATIONS

The normalization principle, which has been defined as using culturally valued means to enable devalued individuals to establish and maintain valued social roles, has been discussed in light of implications for human service delivery systems. Psychologists who are program evaluators and policy makers at both the state and federal levels can have an enormous impact on (re)habilitation programs by promoting the incorporation of elements of the normalization principle within those programs under their purview. Simply mainstreaming children with handicaps into regular classrooms, or moving large numbers of people out of institutions without providing the means by which these individuals can become valued members of society, may do more harm than good, especially in the long run. It is crucial, therefore, that true social integration be accomplished, which can only be done by helping devalued individuals become more valued members of society. Incorporation of the normalization principle into training programs for human service workers and into human service delivery systems offers a viable means of accomplishing this goal.

REFERENCES

Wolfensberger, W. (1980). The definition of normalization: Update, problems, disagreements, and misunderstandings. In R. J. Flynn & K. E. Nitsch (Eds.), *Normalization, social integration, and community services.* Baltimore: University Park Press.

Wolfensberger, W., & Glenn, L. (1978a). *PASS (Program analysis of service systems): A method for the quantitative evaluation of human services—Handbook* (3rd ed.). Toronto: National Institute on Mental Retardation.

Wolfensberger, W., & Glenn, L. (1978b). *PASS (Program analysis of service systems): A method for the quantitative evaluation of human services—Field manual* (3rd ed.). Toronto: National Institute on Mental Retardation.

Wolfensberger, W., & Thomas, S. (in press). *PASSING (Program analysis of service systems' implementation of normalization goals)* (2nd. ed.). Toronto: National Institute on Mental Retardation.

SECTION V
Assessing Rehabilitation Potential and Evaluating Client Outcomes

Brian Bolton, Section Editor

Introduction

Brian Bolton

Measurement is indispensable to the development of an empirically based foundation for rehabilitation counseling. Tests and other assessment instruments enable rehabilitation researchers and practitioners to quantify relevant traits and attributes of persons with handicaps. Hence, the concepts and strategies presented in this section may be regarded as essential to the establishment of rehabilitation counseling as a legitimate social science discipline.

Standardized psychosocial and vocational measuring instruments are used for three general purposes in rehabilitation counseling:

1. *Eligibility determination*—to establish a verifiable basis for the rehabilitation counselor's decision about the applicant's eligibility to receive services.
2. *Program planning*—to provide comprehensive information about the client's assets and deficits so that an optimal program of rehabilitation services can be planned.
3. *Outcome evaluation*—to document the specific benefits that accrue to clients as a direct result of the provision of rehabilitation services.

The articles that comprise this section describe four instruments devised for the purpose of measuring various aspects of rehabilitation clients' capabilities and functioning. In addition to the critically important goal of quantification, the four assessment techniques provide frameworks for conceptualizing clients' overt behavior, self-perceptions, or intrapsychic condition. Each instrument can contribute to the three purposes described above—eligibility determination, program planning, and outcome evaluation—although some instruments are more suitable for some applications than others.

Two of the measurement techniques, Rehabilitation Indicators (RIs) and the Preliminary Diagnostic Questionnaire (PDQ), focus on the behavioral capabilities of persons with handicaps, while the other two instruments, the Millon Behavioral Health Inventory (MBHI) and the Human Service Scale (HSS), are concerned with respondent's self-perceptions and internal dynamics. The first two instruments require standardized observations of the examinee; in contrast, the last two are self-report inventories. These vastly different approaches to assessment generate complementary information about rehabilitation clients' status and functioning.

Each of the four instruments can be administered in conjunction with the initial diagnostic assessment of applicants for rehabilitation services. For those applicants who qualify for services, the information acquired may be used in planning the rehabilitation program. The instruments can be administered again at the point of case closure to evaluate improvements (quantified as score changes from pretest to posttest) that result from the provision of services. The measurements can also be repeated at follow-up contact months or years after case closure to evaluate the extent to which improvements in functioning are sustained.

The Millon Behavioral Health Inventory (MBHI) is a 150-item self-report questionnaire that assesses client functioning in four areas—coping style, psychogenic stressors, psychosomatic predispositions, and prognostic indicators. The 20 scales that represent the four areas, used in conjunction with medical and biographical information, may be helpful in suggesting beneficial rehabilitation interventions. Available data indicate that the scales have satisfactory reliability and a variety of evidence supports their construct validity. The MBHI is especially useful in understanding psychosocial problems associated with severe disabilities, such as spinal cord injury, Parkinson's disease, and multiple sclerosis.

Rehabilitation Indicators (RIs) may be used to assess the daily life activities of persons with disabilities. Consisting of skill, status, activity pattern, and environmental indicators, the RIs constitute a large battery from which practitioners can select scales and items for a particular purpose or situation. The RIs provide a flexible approach to the assessment of routine activities and skills that focus on observable behaviors that are described in non-technical language. Reliability and validity have been evaluated for items and scales, and for individuals and groups. The RIs have their greatest potential for assessing activity levels and personal skills in comprehensive rehabilitation facilities and independent living centers.

The Human Service Scale (HSS) is an 80-item self-report inventory based on Maslow's well-known theory of human motivation. The items, which measure the degree of need satisfaction experienced by the respondent, are scored on seven scales that generally parallel Maslow's need categories. The scales (e.g., physiological, emotional security, and economic self-esteem) are arranged in a circular pattern that partially reflects Maslow's postulated order of prepotency. The HSS is especially appropriate for evaluating change because the items refer to client characteristics that are potentially modifiable through rehabilitation services.

The Preliminary Diagnostic Questionnaire (PDQ) assesses four components of employment-relevant functional capabilities: cognitive, physical, motivational, and emotional. The instrument is individually administered by a trained counselor in the office or disabled person's home in about one hour. Reliability and validity data support the intended application of the PDQ, e.g., scores are predictive of earnings of former clients. The PDQ is most useful in establishing a basis for eligibility determination and for planning a program of rehabilitation services with the goal of attaining competitive employment.

Interested readers may consult two comprehensive reference volumes for details about measurement and assessment in rehabilitation. *The Handbook of Measurement and Evaluation in Rehabilitation* (Bolton, 1987) discusses technical issues, overviews standard tests and inventories, and describes applications to rehabilitation clients. A functional classification of 95 tests and inventories useful in assessing persons with handicaps, and detailed reviews of 50 of these instruments are included in *Special Education and Rehabilitation Testing* (Bolton, 1988).

Additional information about the four instruments described in this section can be obtained from the publishers.

Millon Behavioral Health Inventory:
NCS Interpretive Scoring Systems
P.O. Box 1416
Minneapolis, MN 55440

Rehabilitation Indicators:
Research & Training Center
New York University
400 East 34th St.
New York, NY 10016

Human Service Scale:
Rehabilitation Research Institute
University of Wisconsin
432 N. Murray St.
Madison, WI 53706

Preliminary Diagnostic Questionnaire:
PDQ Coordinator
West Virginia Research & Training Center
Dunbar Plaza, Suite E
Dunbar, WV 25064

REFERENCES

Bolton, B. (Ed.) (1987). *Handbook of measurement and evaluation in rehabilitation*. Baltimore, MD: Paul Brookes.
Bolton, B. (Ed.) (1988). *Special education and rehabilitation testing: Current practices and reviews*. Austin, TX: Pro-Ed.

18

A New Psychodiagnostic Tool for Clients in Rehabilitation Settings: The MBHI

**Theodore Millon, Catherine J. Green,
and Robert B. Meagher, Jr.**

ABSTRACT: There are very few psychodiagnostic instruments for assessing the emotional stability, cognitive outlook, and coping style of clients
seen in rehabilitation settings. Established clinical tools have been designed
for psychiatric populations and are only tangentially relevant. Excellent
recent instruments for rehabilitation populations tend to focus on overt
behavioral indices or vocational aptitudes. To supplement these latter
realms of functioning, the Millon Behavioral Health Inventory (MBHI), a
150-item self-report inventory, may be seen to provide measures relevant to
the client's psychological outlook and prognosis. It also appears useful as
a guide for treatment planning and psychological counseling. The rationale,
development, and uses of the MBHI are briefly described, while the focus of
each of the instrument's 20 scales is also outlined.

The client with rehabilitation needs may enter the health care system with a
physical, functional, and/or psychological problem. Although medically stabilized,
at least in regard to life-threatening concerns such as postsurgical complications, the
client is now beginning a long, arduous, and highly individualized recovery process.
Clinical health psychologists (Millon, Green, & Meagher, in press) play a central
role in all phases of this process—from diagnosis, to treatment planning, to direct
work with the client in facilitating recovery.

The responsibilities of this multifaceted role neither require that the psychologist
discard familiar clinical skills or techniques nor transform himself or herself into a
totally new professional. However, they do call for the use of assessment and
treatment tools that are more relevant to rehabilitation populations than those in the
standard clinical armamentarium. The psychologist should seek creatively to
extend previously acquired competencies to fit these new responsibilities. One such
skill, that of psychodiagnostic assessment in rehabilitation settings, is the focus of
this article. Fulfilling the role of psychodiagnostician in this setting may require

considerable ingenuity and flexibility, since the task calls for tools, concepts, and strategies other than those that psychologists are likely to have been trained to employ in conventional mental health settings.

THE ROLE OF ASSESSMENT IN REHABILITATION SETTINGS

Psychological assessment will focus on different rehabilitative issues depending on the stage of the client's disability, treatment focus, and level of adaptation. The question of what is relevant to assessment in these settings must be looked at first. As Shontz (in press) has stated, psychologists must stop being "diagnosticians" and "therapists" who identify, label, and treat psychopathology; rather, they must uncover and utilize information that is relevant to the special concerns and needs of each rehabilitative client. Not only must the client's physical capacities and deficits be accurately gauged, but the initial evaluation must also include an assessment of the client's emotional needs, motivation, and style of coping—especially as they relate to rehabilitation management issues. An adequate psychodiagnostic evaluation seeks data on the client's psychic strengths, as well as his or her perceived social and familial support network. Integrated in a logical and coherent fashion with information on the client's physical and behavioral competencies, these data may then serve as the basis for formulating a comprehensive, yet focused, treatment plan. The essential issue is that of characterizing the psychological make-up of clients in a manner relevant to their physical problems and then recommending the best means available for modifying the impact of identified negative psychological influences. This information is particularly useful not only in advising staff and therapists regarding methods for optimizing client compliance and management, but also in understanding their own reactions to the client's disabilities and behaviors.

Both physicians and clinical health psychologists seek to make precise assessments of the character of physical and nonphysical functions. Psychometric evaluations by psychologists can be separated into two broad categories. The first concerns the identification of physical and behavioral strengths and deficits that will determine the scope of the client's capabilities for rehabilitative progress. These psychometric measures can be utilized to gauge functional and vocational progress as well. The second category of assessment centers on specifying emotional and personality characteristics that foster adjustment or exacerbate the client's functional limitations. These measures are especially relevant in treatment planning because they denote the client's predisposing attitudes and current psychological state. It is interesting that it is increasingly the health psychologist, rather than the psychiatrist, who is given major responsibility for assessment and interpretation of these psychogenic factors, as well as management of their therapeutic implications.

INSTRUMENTS FOR ASSESSING PHYSICAL AND BEHAVIORAL STRENGTHS AND DEFICITS

In recent years, a number of well-designed and appropriately focused assessment tools have been developed that seek to gauge the physical and behavioral capabilities and limitations of physically disabled rehabilitative clients (Bolton & Cook, 1980). Among these is the problem-oriented record, which has had considerable success in identifying patient's physical disabilities and providing objective and standardized profiles for systematically comparing each component of rehabilitative progress (Dinsdale, Mossman, & Gullickson, 1970; Weed, 1969). Unfortunately, no problem-oriented record has as yet been developed that can adequately handle the many psychological and social problems that affect the client's physical and rehabilitative state (Abrams, Neville, & Becker, 1973).

The wide variety of Activity of Daily Living (ADL) scales that have been developed are also worth noting (a useful review has been prepared by Donaldson, Wagner, & Gresham, 1973). Combining what they judged to be the most useful components of earlier rating scales, Donaldson et al. constructed a single, comprehensive "unified ADL evaluation form." These scales seek to assess the client's functional ability to engage in a variety of everyday tasks such as dressing, ambulation, bathing, feeding, toileting, and so on. Oriented toward sequential time comparisons, ADL forms limit their focus to explicit behavioral acts rather than emotions and attitudes that may covary and influence them.

An impressive new series of behavioral and physical measures have been undergoing development over the past several years (Brown, Caplan, & Swirsky, 1978; Brown, Diller, Fordyce, Jacobs, Barry, Gordon, & Mayer, 1977; Brown, Diller, Fordyce, Jacobs, & Gordon, 1980). Termed *rehabilitation indicators* (RIs), they comprise a wide variety of tools used to assess clients with diverse disabilities seen in different settings and undergoing appraisal for a range of purposes. Although these indicators include data from psychosocial, as well as physical spheres, information comes explicitly from behavioral observables, thus excluding subjective reports such as would illuminate the client's self-esteem, motivation, future outlook, and so on. Although designed to be multidimensional in scope, subsuming as it does *status* indicators (e.g., vocational and educational standing), *activity-pattern* indicators (e.g., frequency of social contacts), *skill* indicators (e.g., ability to read, drive, type), and *environmental* indicators (e.g., family finances), the failure of the RI to include the broad realm of subjective, emotional, and personological data limits its assessment utility to the psychodiagnostician. Undoubtedly a major new tool in the psychologist's diagnostic kit, the RIs must nevertheless be supplemented by instruments that are designed explicitly to provide data on intrapsychic dimensions and longstanding personality attitudes and traits.

INSTRUMENTS FOR ASSESSING PSYCHOGENIC ATTITUDES, EMOTIONAL BEHAVIORS, AND COPING BEHAVIORS

Psychodiagnostic tools are an established method for obtaining symptomatological and personality data relevant to client management in mental health settings. However, most of these instruments are not applicable in either their focus or content to clients seen in physical health settings. Using psychiatrically oriented tests in facilities of a primarily medical and rehabilitative nature requires that their concepts be translated constantly to fit new populations and purposes. Stated simply, rehabilitation populations are not psychiatric populations; moreover, viewing clients within the framework of traditional mental health constructs may prove neither valid nor useful. Of course, standard psychodiagnostic tests often provide valuable information, such as the general state of a client's emotional health or the presence of distinctive symptoms (e.g., depression or anxiety). However, even in these spheres, problems arise with these psychiatrically oriented tools because of the unsuitability of their norms, the questionable relevance of their clinical signs, and the consequent difficulty in trusting and using their interpretations.

Standard interpretations of data obtained with a rehabilitation sample on a diagnostic test, developed and designed to assess a psychiatric population, opposes every principle of sound assessment. On examination of the majority of current psychodiagnostic tests in use (for example, the Minnesota Multiphasic Personality Inventory (MMPI), the 16PF, the Symptom Check List-90 (SCL-90), or even the Cornell Medical Index) it soon becomes apparent that they continue to be employed for no major reason other than the lack of more relevant tools. A thorough review of these well-established psychiatrically oriented instruments has been provided by Green (in press). Her careful evaluation gives little reason for confidence in either their relevance or validity for rehabilitation clients.

A first effort to develop a more relevant inventory sought to assess the areas where the needs of the physically ill or disabled client were being met. In contrast to the aforementioned instruments, developed for and oriented to issues relevant to the psychiatric patient, the Human Service Scale (Kravetz, 1974; Reagles & Butler, 1976) is organized to evaluate the problems of the nonpsychiatric medical and rehabilitation client. Following the personality theory of Maslow, the developers constructed seven need categories: Physiological need, Emotional need, Economic Security, Family, Social need, Economic Self-esteem, and Vocational Self-actualization. Relatively brief to administer, it is essentially a screening tool, rather than a clinical diagnostic instrument. Its prime utility appears to be that of assisting the intake worker in deciding which clients may benefit from psychological or social interventions. Although scoring services are available at modest cost (Rehabilitation Research Institute, 1976), there are few data on its interpretive utility. Significant psychometric analyses and validity studies are only in their early stages of development.

SEARCH FOR RELEVANT PERSONOLOGICAL AND PSYCHOGENIC HEALTH DIMENSIONS

One major area of investigation into the development of health dimensions focuses on what may be termed general *coping style*. Investigators in this area believe that the client's enduring interpersonal and personality pattern is central to understanding both the development of a disease and how the patient copes with it (Kahana, 1972; Millon, Green, & Meagher, in press). According to this thesis, enduring psychological tendencies cause individuals to react to stimuli with specific patterns of emotional, cognitive, behavioral, and physiological responses

(Lipowski, 1977; Twaddle, 1972). One model for constructing coping styles was developed by Millon (1969) that outlines distinctive interpersonal patterns of behavior, and enables each individual's habitual behaviors to be organized into distinctive profile patterns of coping.

Other researchers have focused their attention on the impact of specific *psychogenic attitudes* rather than more broadly integrated personality or coping styles. These studies typically concentrate on single influences or dimensions, for example, stress is repeatedly found to relate to the incidence of a variety of diseases. More specifically, studies of "chronic stress," such as self-imposed pressures and a persistent undercurrent of time urgency, have been carried out with particular reference to their impact on heart disease (Friedman & Rosenman, 1974; Gersten, Frii, & Lengner, 1976; Jenkins, 1976; Rahe, 1977). Approaches along the same line of investigation that relate more to current life problems and tensions have also been used (Holmes & Masuda, 1974; Rabkin & Struening, 1976). These studies focus on the incidence of "recent life stress," relative to the appearance of illness or the exacerbation of a preexistent condition.

Another major psychogenic area of study has been termed the helplessness-hopelessness constellation. Evidence for the impact of either a "premorbid pessimistic" attitude or an outlook of "future despair" on physical disease seems well established. This constellation is in no way illness specific, however; there are studies showing its relationship to a wide variety of diseases such as multiple sclerosis, ulcerative colitis, and cancer (Mei-Tal, Meyerowitz, & Engel, 1970; Paull & Hislop, 1974; Schmale, 1972). This depressive pattern has also been researched in relation to postoperative course; a good surgical outcome seems to be correlated with an acceptance of one's health problems and a positive, future-oriented attitude (Boyd, Yeager, & McMillan, 1973).

Another significant psychogenic factor pertains to the role of what we have termed *social alienation*. The level of familial and friendship support, both real and perceived, appears to be a significant moderator of the impact of various life stressors (Cobb, 1976; Rabkin & Struening, 1976). All of these stressors seem to be significantly modulated upward or downward by the preoccupations and fears that clients may express about their physical state. Studies of what may be called psychogenic "somatic anxiety" reflect the general concerns that clients have about their bodies (Lipsitt, 1970; Lucente & Fleek, 1972).

The diverse psychogenic components noted previously evidence strong interrelationships. For example, the loss of a spouse means not only dealing with feelings of despair and depression, but also with the increased stress of social isolation, possible financial hardship, and/or a variety of increased responsibilities—each of which serves as an additional source and compounding of stress.

A third group of researchers have focused their primary attention on establishing various *psychosomatic correlates* of disease. They have studied clients with identical physical ailments, but differentiated by the degree to which psychological factors were central contributors. This realm of investigation is closest to the classical concerns of the psychosomatic clinician. For example, does the client have an ulcer because of psychic stressors or because of some physiological-nutritional dysfunction? Questions such as these are addressed by physicians who direct their therapeutic attention to the prime source of difficulty; for example, should treatment be geared to psychotherapy, medication, surgery, environmental management, or what? Among the major disease syndromes studied in this manner are allergies, gastrointestinal problems, and cardiovascular disorders (Crown & Crown, 1973; Lipowski, 1975; McKegney, Gordon, & Levine, 1970; Pinkerton, 1973).

Still another area addressed by clinicians is the client's response to disability or treatment and how psychological make-up affects the course of the disability or the treatment's efficacy. This search for *prognostic indices is* particularly significant in work with the major life-threatening illnesses and treatment interventions. For example, chronic pain has been extensively investigated with studies of psychological correlates of response to medical or surgical treatment. Other major projects have focused on how clients cope with life-threatening illnesses and whether certain outcomes can be predicted with reference to client styles of coping. Identifying which clients will display problematic reactions to surgery or renal dialysis may enable the clinician to institute measures to counteract them and thereby diminish the likelihood of a poor outcome (Cohen & Lazarus, 1973).

CONSTRUCTION OF THE MILLON BEHAVIORAL HEALTH INVENTORY (MBHI)

It became apparent as our search continued that there was no single best instrument or combination of instruments available to meet the varied needs of clinical health psychology. Faced with these limitations, we set out to develop a new self-report inventory that would be brief, relevant to medical and rehabilitation issues, comprehensive in the dimensions and traits it measured, and, we hoped, valid. The instrument that was developed over a 4-year span of research has been labeled the Millon Behavioral Health Inventory (MBHI) (Millon, Green, & Meagher, 1981). Extensive psychometric data are available in the manual.

Constructed in a manner similar to that of the Millon Clinical Multiaxial Inventory (Millon, 1977), the MBHI was developed through a sequential process, involving theory-based rationale (substantive validity), internal consistency studies (structural validity), and empirical demonstrations of scale discrimination power (external validity).

The theoretical-substantive construction stage addressed the degree to which the items derive their content from an explicit theoretical framework. Over 1,000 initial items were gathered from numerous sources. This item pool was reduced at this stage by several criteria—too complicated, extreme endorsement frequency, desirability bias, and incorrect scale sorting by 3 out of 10 health professionals fully acquainted with the theoretical model and the intent of each scale.

The internal-structural construction stage evaluates the coherence or homogeneity of each of the scales. Only those items surviving the theoretical substantive validation stage were included in these internal-consistency studies. Point-biserial correlations obtained from data on 2,500 persons were calculated between each statement remaining in the pool and each scale. To maximize scale homogeneity, only items that showed their highest correlation with the scale to which they were originally assigned were retained.

The external-criterion construction stage involves only those items that meet the preceding two developmental criteria. The central idea presented is that the final items comprising a scale be selected on the basis of their empirically verified and cross-validated association with a significant and relevant criterion measure. Numerous "criterion" and "comparison" groups were administered the remaining test items. True-false endorsement frequencies between the paired criterion and comparison groups were calculated. Items that statistically differentiated these two groups in the expected direction were judged "externally valid" and, as a result, were included in the final item list. This approach was followed specifically in constructing the empirical scales, which were designed to identify "psychosomatic correlates" and "prognostic indices." Each of these empirically derived scales was then subjected to at least one cross-validational study. Only those that withstood cross-validation were retained in the final group of MBHI scales.

In its final form, the MBHI consists of 150 self-descriptive true-false items. Table 18.1 contains a listing and brief description of the 20 clinical scales and is divided into four major sections. In the first section are 8 scales that comprise the major coping styles; as noted previously, these were derived as normal variants of personality from a theory of personality pathology (Millon, 1969). The degree to which the client characteristically exhibits each of the eight styles is expressed in a profile pattern. The second set of 6 scales reflects different sources of psychogenic stressors selected on the basis of their support in the research literature as significant and salient factors that contribute to the precipitation or exacerbation of physical illnesses (e.g., chronic tension and social alienation). The third set of scales was empirically derived by differentiating clients with the same physical syndrome in terms of whether their illnesses were or were not substantially complicated by social or emotional factors. High scorers on the allergy, gastrointestinal, or cardiovascular scales are those who are most similar to known psychosomatic patients. The fourth set of scales has also been empirically developed. These prognostic indices seek to identify future treatment problems or difficulties that may arise in the course of the client's illness and rehabilitation.

Scoring of the MBHI can be done with templates derived from the manual. In line with modern technology, scoring can be processed by electronic teleprocessing with computer printouts. Clinically synthesized interpretive reports based on both theoretical and actuarial data are available to all medical and psychological professionals (Millon et al., 1981).

SOME PSYCHOMETRIC FEATURES OF THE MBHI RELIABILITY

Reliability of the scales of the MBHI was analyzed in two ways. The Kuder-Richardson formula (KR-20) was used to assess the internal reliability of the scales. The KR-20s ranged from .66 to .90, with a median of .82. Test/retest was employed as another means of evaluating reliability. Eighty-nine patients were retested at intervals from 1 to 8 months, with a mean interval of 4 1/2 months. Scale reliability ranged from .72 to .90, with a median of .83.

Validity

Comparing scales with others that supposedly measure the same trait is one traditional method of establishing validity, assuming that these other scales successfully measure the specific traits. The psychogenic attitude scales exhibit the following approximate correlations with other instruments: for Chronic Tension—Jenkins Activity Survey ($r = .60$) and California Psychological Inventory Tolerance ($r = .40$); for Recent Stress—Social Readjustment Rating Scale ($r = .65$) and Life Events Survey ($r = .70$); for Premorbid Pessimism—MMPI Depression ($r = .60$) and Beck Depression Scale ($r = .60$); for Future Despair-Zung Depression Scale ($r = .55$) and MMPI Psychasthenia ($r = .55$); for Social Alienation—MMPI Social Introversion ($r = .65$) and SCL-90 Interpersonal Sensitivity ($r = .60$); for Somatic Anxiety—MMPI Hypochondriasis ($r = .65$) and MMPI Hysteria ($r = .60$).

In addition, cross-validation samples were used to assess the validity of individual scales. Life-threat reactivity, for example, exhibited a valid positive of 75% and false positive of 12% on a cross-validation sample.

RECENT EFFICACY RESEARCH WITH MEDICAL AND REHABILITATION PATIENTS

A number of research studies subsequent to the test construction phase have been, and are being, carried out. A few are briefly noted.

The effect upon rehabilitation outcome of client styles of coping in a pain management program has been reported by Green, Meagher, and Millon (1980). Using the MBHI, it was possible to predict behaviors such as noncompliance, isolation, hostility toward health personnel, and excessive complaining and emotionality. These data enabled the staff to modify their rehabilitative procedures so as to minimize difficult and enhance compliant behaviors.

Another relevant study evaluated the value of precounseling sessions on presurgical clients anticipating a life-threatening procedure (Levine, 1980). It was found that MBHI-obtained coping style and premorbid pessimism scores were directly related to both the speed and level of recovery.

In a study evaluating the outcome of an outpatient rehabilitation pain treatment program, Rabinowitz (1979) was able to identify coping styles and a specific series of items that were highly predictive of rehabilitative efficacy.

Current projects are under way with the spinal cord injured, those in renal dialysis programs, Parkinson's disease clients, and clients with a variety of other syndromes and chronic disabilities.

Table 18.1 Brief Descriptions of High Scorers on the 20 Clinical Scales of the MBHI

Coping style

Introversive style	Keeps to self, quiet, unemotional, not easily excited, rarely gets socially involved, lacks energy, vague about symptoms, passive about self-care
Inhibited style	Shy, socially ill-at-ease, avoids close relationships, fears rejection, feels lonely, distrustful, is easily hurt, requires sympathetic support
Cooperative style	Soft hearted, sentimental, reluctant to assert self, submissive with others, lacks initiative, eager to take advice, compliant, dependent, devalues self-competence
Sociable style	Charming, emotionally expressive, histrionic, talkative, stimulus seeking, attention seeking, unreliable, capricious in affect, easily bored with routine
Confident style	Self-centered, egocentric, narcissistic, acts self-assured, is exploitive, takes others for granted, expects special treatment, is benignly arrogant
Forceful style	Domineering, abrasive, intimidates others, blunt, aggressive, strong-willed, assumes leadership role, impatient, easily angered
Respectful style	Serious-minded, efficient, rule conscious, proper and correct in behavior, emotionally constrained, self-disciplined, avoids the unpredictable, orderly, socially conforming
Sensitive style	Unpredictable, moody, passively aggressive, negativistic, a complainer, guilt-ridden, anticipates disappointments, displeased with self and others

Psychogenic attitude

Chronic tension	Is under self-imposed pressure, has difficulty relaxing, constantly on the go, impatient
Recent stress	Has experienced significant changes in preceeding year, life routine has been upset by unanticipated tensions and problems
Premorbid pessimism	Is disposed to interpret life as a series of misfortunes, complains about past events and relationships
Future despair	Displays a bleak outlook, anticipates the future as distressing or potentially threatening
Social alienation	Feels isolated, perceives minimal social and family support
Somatic anxiety	Is hypochondriacally concerned with bodily functions, fears pain and illness

Psychosomatic correlate

Allergic inclination	Is empirically similar to clients evidencing a strong psychological component associated with allergies such as dermatitis and asthma
Gastrointestinal susceptibility	Is empirically similar to clients evidencing a strong psychological component associated with gastrointestinal disorders such as ulcers or colitis
Cardiovascular tendency	Is empirically similar to clients evidencing a strong psychological component associated with cardiovascular symptoms such as hypertension or angina

Table 18.1 *(continued)*

Prognostic index

Pain treatment responsivity	Is empirically similar to clients who fail to respond successfully to medical treatment regimens for chronic pain syndromes
Life-threat reactivity	Is empirically similar to clients with chronic or progressive life-threatening illnesses—carcinoma, renal failure, and heart disease—who display a more troubled course than is typical
Emotional vulnerability	Is empirically similar to clients who react with severe disorientation, depression, or psychotic episodes following major surgery or other life-dependent treatment programs

USE OF THE MBHI IN REHABILITATION SETTINGS

Coping with severe restrictions of traumatic origin such as spinal cord injury, amputation, or disfigurement places a heavy challenge on clients. Personality characteristics determine, in part, the shape and course that coping patterns will follow, from denial on the one hand, to making more of the handicap on the other. An important dimension is future planning. Persons who have a positive, clear view of themselves in the future, who know what they wish for themselves (i.e., low scorers on the MBHI's Future Despair Scale), are more likely to be able to be self-sufficient 1 year after injury (Schmale, 1972) than those whose view of the future is vague and amorphous or even negative.

The problems facing clients following cerebral vascular accident (CVA) are complex and strongly determined by locus and extent of damage. Again, however, personality and attitudes play an important role in mediating return to maximal function. Furthermore, risk of future episodes may be mitigated by changes in lifestyle (Prince & Miranda, 1977); for example, a decrease in the restless, anxious drive embodied in the Type A coronary heart disease (CHD) client, may change the probability of recurrence of stroke in the future (Roskies, Spevak, Surkis, Cohen, & Gilman, 1978). The MBHI is not only useful in pointing to the presence and extent of this kind of risk-related behavior problem (Chronic Tension scale), but also in indicating the directions interventions might take.

A third, but by no means final, area in which use is being made of this inventory is that of working with clients who suffer chronic, progressive, degenerative diseases such as Parkinson's disease, multiple sclerosis, and leukemia. There is a strong tendency for the medical community to give up on such clients, since there is so little that can be done. Clients often adopt the hopeless attitude expressed by their medical caretakers. What is overlooked, however, is the remarkable resources clients possess to cope with and make the most of their intact functions (Moos & Tsu, 1977). Certainly many of the symptoms that accompany the physical disorder are either mitigated or worsened by stress adaptations on the part of the client (Brain, 1955). Stress management training is best accomplished with knowledge of the habitual coping styles used by clients—coping styles that can often be identified with reasonable clarity by the MBHI.

SUMMARY

The MBHI is the first general-purpose instrument of a psychodiagnostic nature designed for use in a wide range of medical and rehabilitation settings. Relevant and brief, it may prove to be a practical tool for obtaining information on both coping styles and specific areas of psychological concern. The instrument has been developed for use with both physically ill and normal populations and has been constructed through a sequential validation process. Each of the 20 clinical scales can be evaluated on its own or interpreted in conjunction with other test or biographical data. The MBHI should be seen as another step toward making the psychologist assume the role of medical and rehabilitation psychodiagnostician more effectively.

REFERENCES

Abrams, K. S., Neville, R., & Becker, M. C. (1973). Problem-oriented recording of psychosocial problems. *Archives of Physical Medicine and Rehabilitation, 54*, 316–319.

Bolton, B., & Cook, D. W. (Eds.). (1980). *Rehabilitation client assessment*, Baltimore: University Park Press.

Boyd, I., Yeager, M., & McMillan, M. (1973). Personality styles in the postoperative course. *Psychosomatic Medicine, 35*, 23–40.

Brain, R. (1955). *Disease of the nervous system* (5th ed). London: Oxford University Press.

Brown, M., Caplan, J., & Swirsky, J. (September, 1978). *Rehabilitation indicators: An overview.* Paper presented at the annual meeting of the American Psychological Association, Toronto.

Brown, M., Diller, L., Fordyce, W., Jacobs, D., Barry, J., Gordon, W., & Mayer, J. (September, 1977). *Accountability: Definitions, problems and the response of rehabilitation indicators.* Paper presented at the annual meeting of the National Rehabilitation Association, Washington, D.C..

Brown, M., Diller, L., Fordyce, W., Jacobs, D., & Gordon, W. (1980). Rehabilitation indicators: Their nature and uses for assessment. In B. Bolton & D. W. Cook (Eds.), *Rehabilitation client assessment.* Baltimore: University Park Press.

Cobb, S. (1976). Presidential address—1976: Social support as a moderator of life stress. *Psychosomatic Medicine, 38*, 300–314.

Cohen, F., & Lazarus, R. S. (1973). Active coping processes, coping disposition and recovery from surgery. *Psychosomatic Medicine, 35*, 375–391.

Crown, S., & Crown, J. M. (1973). Personality in early rheumatoid disease. *Journal of Psychosomatic Research, 17*, 189–196.

Dinsdale, S. M., Mossman, P. L., & Gullickson, G. (1970). Problem-oriented medical record in rehabilitation. *Archives of Physical Medicine and Rehabilitation, 51*, 488–492.

Donaldson, S. W., Wagner, C. C., & Gresham, G. E. (1973). A unified ADL evaluation form. *Archives of Physical Medicine and Rehabilitation, 54*, 175–179.

Friedman, M., & Rosenman, R. H. (1974). *Type A behavior and your heart.* New York: Knopf.

Gersten, J. C., Frii, S. R., & Lengner, T. S. (1976). Life dissatisfactions, job dissatisfaction and illness of married men over time. *American Journal of Epidemiology, 103*, 333–341.

Green, C. (in press). Psychological assessment in medical settings. In T. Millon, C. Green, & R. Meagher (Eds.), *Handbook of clinical health psychology.* New York: Plenum.

Green, C., Meagher, R., & Millon, T. (November, 1980). *Patients' social responses in a pain program: Uses of the MBHI.* Paper presented at the annual meeting of the Society of Behavioral Medicine, New York.

Holmes, T. H., & Masuda, M. (1974). Life change and illness susceptibility. In B. S. Dohrenwend & B. P. Dohrenwend (Eds.), *Life events: Their nature and effects.* New York: Wiley.

Jenkins, C. D. (1976). Psychologic and social risk factors for coronary disease. *New England Journal of Medicine, 294,* 987–994.

Kahana, R. J. (1972). Studies in medical psychology: A brief survey. *Psychiatry in Medicine, 3,* 1–22.

Kravetz, S. (1974). *Rehabilitation need and status: Substance, structure antiprocess.* Unpublished doctoral dissertation, University of Wisconsin.

Levine, R. (1980). *The impact of personality style upon emotional distress, morale, and return to work in two groups of coronary bypass surgery patients.* Unpublished master's thesis, University of Miami.

Lipowski, Z. J. (1975). Psychophysiological cardiovascular disorders. In A. M. Freedman, H. I. Kaplan, & B. J. Sadock (Eds.), *Comprehensive textbook of psychiatry* (Vol. 2, 2nd ed.). Baltimore: Williams & Wilkins.

Lipowski, Z. J. (1977). Psychosomatic medicine in the seventies: An overview. *American Journal of Psychiatry, 134*(3), 233–244.

Lipsitt, D. R. (1979). Medical and psychological characteristics of "crocks." *Psychiatry in Medicine, 1,* 15–25.

Lucente, F. E., & Fleek, S. (1972). A study of hospitalization anxiety in 408 medical and surgical patients. *Psychosomatic Medicine, 34,* 304–312.

McKegney, F. P., Gordon, R. O., & Levine, S. M. (1970). A psychosomatic comparison of patients with ulcerative colitis and Crohn's disease. *Psychosomatic Medicine, 32,* 153–166.

Mei-Tal, V., Meyerowitz, S., & Engel, G. L. (1970). The role of psychological process in a somatic disorder: Multiple sclerosis. *Psychosomatic Medicine, 32,* 67–86.

Millon, T. (1969). *Modern psychopathology.* Philadelphia: Saunders.

Millon, T. (1977). *Millon Clinical Multiaxial Inventory Manual.* Minneapolis: National Computer Systems.

Millon, T., Green, C. J., & Meagher, R. B. (1981). *Millon Behavior Health Inventory manual.* Minneapolis: National Computer Systems.

Millon, T., Green, C. J., & Meagher, R. B. (in press). *Handbook of clinical health psychology.* New York: Plenum.

Moos, R. H., & Tsu, V. D. (1977). The crisis of physical illness: An overview. In R. H. Moos (Ed.), *Coping with physical illness.* New York: Plenum.

Pauli, A., & Hislop, I. G. (1974). Etiologic factors in ulcerative colitis: Birth, death and symbolic equivalents. *International Journal of Psychiatry in Medicine, 5,* 57–64.

Pinkerton, P. (1973). Editorial: The enigma of asthma. *Psychosomatic Medicine, 35,* 461–463.

Prince, R., & Miranda, L. (1977). Monitoring life stress to prevent recurrence of coronary heart disease episodes. *Canadian Psychiatric Association Journal, 22,* 161–169.

Rabinowitz, S. (1979). *Psychological, biographical, and medical data as predictors of successful treatment of chronic pain.* Unpublished doctoral dissertation, University of Miami.

Rabkin, J. G., & Struening, E. L. (1976). Life events, stress and illness. *Science, 194,* 1013–1020.

Rahe, R. H. (1977). Epidemiological studies of life change and illness. In Z. J. Lipowski, D. R. Lipsitt, & P. C. Whybrow (Eds.), *Psychosomatic medicine.* New York: Oxford University Press.

Reagles, K. W., & Butler, A. J. (1976). The Human Service Scale: A new measure for evaluation. *Journal of Rehabilitation, 42,* 34–38.

Rehabilitation Research Institute. (1976). *The Human Service Scale.* Madison, WI: Author.

Roskies, E., Spevack, M., Surkis, A., Cohen, C., & Gilman, S. (1978). Changing the coronary-prone (Type A) behavioral pattern in a nonclinical population. *Journal of Behavioral Medicine, 1*(2), 73–79.

Schmale, A. H. (1972). Giving up as a final common pathway to changes in health. In Z. J. Lipowski (Ed.), *Psychosocial aspects of physical illness.* Basel, Switzerland: Karger.

Shontz, F. C. (in press). Adaptation to chronic illness and disability. In T. Millon, J. Green, & R. B. Meagher (Eds.), *Handbook of clinical health psychology.* New York: Plenum.

Twaddle, A. C. (1972). The concepts of the sick role and illness behavior. In Z. J. Lipowski (Ed.), *Psychosocial aspects of physical illness.* Basel, Switzerland: Karger.

Weed, L. L. (1969). *Medical records, medical education and patient care: Problem-oriented record as basic tool.* Cleveland: Case Western Reserve University Press.

19

Rehabilitation Indicators and Program Evaluation

Margaret Brown, Leonard Diller, Wayne A. Gordon, Wilbert E. Fordyce, and Durand F. Jacobs

ABSTRACT: The Rehabilitation Indicators (RI) Project originated as a response by Division 22 (Rehabilitation Psychology) of the American Psychological Association to President Nixon's veto of the initial version of the Rehabilitation Act of 1973. The RIs were intended to provide a multifaceted, flexible means of measuring the impact of rehabilitation services on clients and patients with a wide range of disabling conditions and in a broad array of service settings. The major principles guiding the creation of the RIs are presented, and the four types of RI instruments now developed or in the planning stage are described: Skill Indicators (SKIs), Status Indicators (SIs), Activity Pattern Indicators (APIs), and Environmental Indicators (EIs). RI reliability and validity are discussed, and supportive data are provided. Several field projects in which the RIs were used for purposes of program evaluation are described.

The Rehabilitation Indicators (RI) Project, which has developed a basic methodology that is broadly useful in program evaluation, began as a direct result of actions taken within Division 22 (Rehabilitation Psychology) of the American Psychological Association. This linkage began in 1973 as a result of many factors, but primarily in response to the vetoing by President Nixon of the initial version of the Rehabilitation Act of 1973. In that version, the state-federal program had been broadened to include an independent-living component. This dramatic confrontation, highlighted by the veto and subsequent rewriting of the bill, brought to a head a widely shared concern among psychologists in rehabilitation that the argument in favor of rehabilitation was weakened because of inadequacies in measuring the impact of services on patients and clients. These inadequacies, in turn, undermined the ability of rehabilitation to compete for limited human service funds.

Division 22 appointed a committee to develop a response to these concerns. Committee members included Leonard Diller, Wilbert Fordyce, and Durand

Jacobs. The eventual response took the form of a proposal submitted to the Rehabilitation Services Administration, requesting funds for a project to develop indicators of rehabilitation progress. The RI Project thus began in 1974 with the central idea of developing better ways of documenting rehabilitation outcomes than were then available. The project sought to create a set of tools to better account for the impact of services on patient/client functioning, and was heavily influenced by five underlying assumptions or guiding principles.

First, in order to insure adequate face validity, it was decided that the exclusive focus of the instruments would be observable components of functioning. This ruled out direct measurement of abstract constructs (e.g., motivation) and of broad behavioral traits (e.g., endurance, mobility). Instead, concrete elements of functioning were to be assessed (e.g., driving a car or van). However, it should be noted that measured, concrete functions could be used singly or in clusters as indicators of abstract concepts (e.g., driving, walking, and use of public transportation as indicators of "mobility").

The emphasis on observability led to a second decision: to couch the RI tools in lay language. This ruled out assessment of functioning from the narrow perspective of a single professional group or at an overly atomistic level (e.g., "range of motion of left upper extremity"). Two benefits were foreseen: The avoidance of jargon would promote ease of communication during assessment and feedback of results, and the functions measured would have a direct rather than remote significance and application in the lives of patients/clients (hereafter referred to as *clients* only). Such an approach would, it was felt, maximize the face validity of the instruments for measuring outcomes.

A third decision was to emphasize a holistic or comprehensive approach to assessment, rather than one with a focus on a single impairment group, a single phase of the rehabilitation process, or the "disabled" aspects of an individual's functioning. The RIs were designed to be applicable to virtually any group of people (rehabilitation clients or others); to medical, vocational or other forms of rehabilitation; and to assessment of intact as well as disrupted areas of functioning. The content of the RIs is thus broad, permitting evaluation of a wide array of functioning in the context of the individual's daily life.

A fourth guiding principle was complementary to the first three: The instruments would have to be able to address a variety of specific needs that exist within any particular rehabilitation setting, in order to permit the setting to adapt the tools to fit its own areas of accountability. For example, a setting that wanted to assess broad areas of client functioning (for purposes of initial planning) might also wish to concentrate primarily on vocational outcomes (for purposes of program evaluation). A second setting, on the other hand, might wish to restrict all phases of assessment to the domain of mobility. Flexibility was built into the RIs in several ways. First, as already noted, the potentially broad scope of the tools can be narrowed, within defined limits, to fit needs of different adopters. Second, three (of the planned four) assessment instruments were developed, each depicting functioning from its own perspective.

The RI tools can be used together or separately. Third, data gathering with each of the instruments may be approached in several ways: self-report within an interview, observation by professionals, self-report in a daily diary, and so forth. These methods of data collection were developed to fit situations that may vary along the dimensions of the population served, the amount of time available for data collection, and so on. Fourth, two of the instruments vary in terms of the types and number of aspects of functioning that a user may select for assessment. For example, one of the RI instruments, the Activity Pattern Indicators, documents activities engaged in by a client. The user may choose to assess one or more of the following activity dimensions: frequency of occurrences, duration of occurrences, assistance received during activities, social contact occurring during activities, and location of activities. If the user were interested in mobility, for example, he or she might want to document two dimensions: frequency or duration of activities engaged in (i.e., either constitutes the basic activity measure), plus the location of activities. Finally, the RI data that emerge from assessment can be summarized and used in a variety of ways. Some users (e.g., physical therapists) may want highly detailed data; others (e.g., program evaluators) may wish to aggregate raw data in order to study broader domains of possible client gains.

The fifth assumption underlying the development of the RIs was that optimally useful instruments would be able to serve a clinical as well as a program evaluation role. Thus, the RIs were designed to provide the rehabilitation professional (or team) with a tool to assess client functioning and to pinpoint those areas needing remediation.

THE CONSTITUENT RI INSTRUMENTS

The RI instruments include four separate approaches to functional assessment. Three have been fully developed, and one is still in the planning stages. The impetus for creating a family of instruments was the fact that description of functioning (and RIs are, first and foremost, descriptive tools) can adopt one or more of several perspectives, depending on how the assessor conceptualizes the nature of rehabilitation and on the stage of the client (admission, in process, follow-up) in the rehabilitation process (Brown, Diller, Fordyce, Jacobs, & Gordon, 1980; Brown, Gordon, & Diller, 1983a, 1983b). For example, traditional approaches to functional assessment have typically focused on assessing behavioral abstractions - that is, on relatively enduring properties of the client's functioning, such as his or her "usual performance" or "capacities." This type of assessment attempts to define what the person "can do," and attempts to establish (holding constant both the individual's environment and factors within the individual that influence functioning) how capably the person will perform. In this tradition, with its emphasis on behavioral competencies, the assessor will focus, for example, either on the functioning of parts of the person (e.g., range of arm motion and scanning of the visual field) or on the whole person (e.g., independence in eating or getting along with supervisors at work). Obviously, these are key data elements. They provide a review of the *behavioral tools* the client may employ in daily living. This approach to assessment is fitting whenever the teaching of skills or competencies is seen as a critical means and/ or goal in rehabilitation.

The various RI instruments were influenced not only by this relatively traditional view of rehabilitation, but also by newer environmental and ecological perspectives on the field. These more recent views hold, for example, that a client's ability to eat independently or to punch a time card is less relevant than what he or she actually does do. A client's competence is only one of the aspects that influence how he or she functions in day-to-day life. Consequently, new modes of functional assessment have shifted from behavioral *competency* to behavioral *output*.

Because a focus on the assessment of behavioral output implies the assessor's accountability for what actually occurs in the individual's daily life, those holding a traditional view might object that a rehabilitation setting cannot be accountable for (since it cannot control) what clients choose to do, but only for remediating their competencies. However, from an ecological view, enhancing a client's competencies is only a means to an end. Service providers are seen as accountable for the "end" in the sense of insuring that factors necessary for competencies to become manifest are addressed in the setting's program. Such factors include the following:

- *Insuring that the environment is able to support the competency's emergence.* This includes the team's assessment of the client's environment to insure that barriers, both physical and social, are minimized. This assessment may be implemented at the macro level (e.g., enhancing social supports within the family, insuring access into and mobility within the home and work setting) or at the micro level (e.g., assessing the individual's ability to use the tools necessary to his or her employment).
- *Insuring that the client values the competency being remediated.* This includes determining which competencies are of low relevance in the client's life (e.g., cooking meals, for an individual whose spouse does the cooking) and educating the client about the importance of skills that have changed in salience since the onset of disability (e.g., jobseeking skills). In effect, the client's participation in rehabilitation planning needs to be insured.

Within this newer view, rehabilitation is seen as being concerned with the client's functioning within a given ecological reality, rather than with functioning in the abstract, unrelated to the person's wants, needs, or context. If one adopts this ecological perspective, competency attainment is important to work toward and to assess, but the *raison d'etre* of remediation is to effect changes in the person's daily-life functioning. Hence, measures of behavioral output are essential.

Each of the four instruments within the RI "package" reflects, in its own way, these traditional and nontraditional assumptions. Together, the tools provide complementary information.

Skill Indicators (SKIs)

The SKIs correspond most directly to traditional approaches to functional assessment, which document behavioral tools of the client. The SKIs measure what the client can or cannot do across a broad range of areas of functioning: self-care, mobility, social behavior, communication, vocational activity, homemaking, and so on. The SKI package consists of (1) an extensive, taxonomized list of specific skills; (2) examples of pretested assessment scales and formats that users may adopt; and (3) rules for shaping SKIs to insure fit between the instrument and the setting, as well as cross-setting comparability of data. To adopt SKIs for use, a setting must select from the skill list the skills most relevant to its mandate and program, adopt an assessment scale that reflects the concerns of the setting at the level of detail needed, and adopt an approach to data reduction that will provide as broad or as narrow a profile of functioning as is required to accomplish the purposes of the assessment.

Because users select items from the skill list to create "tailor-made" measures, SKIs exist in a standard format only at the item level, not at the level of broad skill profiles or skill total scores. There is thus no standard amount of time required to administer the SKIs. A user may choose to do an assessment with all of the skills on the standard list or with only a few, and data can be gathered through observation or through report by the client, his or her family, or others who know his or her skills.

Status Indicators (*SIs*)

The RI Project has developed two assessment tools that describe the client's behavioral output (i.e., what he or she does do) at varying levels of detail. The first of these, the SIs, depict the person's place (i.e., status) in his or her sociocultural environment. Aspects such as employment status, access to and use of transportation, income, education, family role status, and living arrangements are viewed as key behavioral facts about a person that can be affected by both impairment and rehabilitation, and can therefore act as indicators of functional problems and gains. The SIs summarize the individual's access to key societal resources—economic, social, and other. As the SIs change, both with onset of disability and with subsequent rehabilitation, they provide global indicators of the impact of disability and progress obtained through efforts at remediation. SIs are administered in 10-20 minutes through interview, through review of available records, or through a client's written self-report.

Activity Pattern Indicators (APIs)

The second type of RIs developed to describe the client's behavioral output, the APIs, measure functioning in terms of typical patterns of time use and participation in activities—how the client functions in the context of home, work, and community. Although the data that emerge from API assessments have, on occasion, been used to track functioning at the level of involvement in *specific* activities (e.g., watching TV, sleeping, etc.), API data are usually analyzed in terms of activity *clusters.* The resulting API profiles document dimensions of a client's daily activities, such as the following:

- *Mobility,* as measured by these and other factors:
  Percentage of time spent out of residence

Diversity of away-from-residence activities
Percentage of time spent in travel

- *Activity level,* as measured by these and other factors:
Diversity of activities engaged in
Percentage of time spent in inactivity (e.g., napping) and in passive recreation (e.g., TV)

- *Independence and community involvement,* as measured by these and other factors:
Amount of time in activities in which assistance was received
Amount of time spent working or in school
Diversity of activities occurring away from residence

- *Social/recreational involvement,* as measured by these and other factors:
Frequency of engaging in active recreation
Percentage of time spent with people

An extensive body of research has shown that these and similar activity dimensions provide powerful indicators of increasing and decreasing levels of disability. (Cf. Alexander, Willems, Halstead, & Spencer, 1979; Brown, 1978, 1982; Calsyn, 1980; Chapin & Brail, 1969; Dow & Juster, 1980; Efth-imiou, Gordon, Sell, & Stratford, 1981; Fordyce, 1978; Gillespie & Johnston, 1967; Gordon, 1982; Gordon, Brown, Lehman, Sherman, Farber, Buccheri, & Lucido, 1979; Gordon & Diller, 1983; Hartung, 1975; Hill & Juster, 1980; Hobart, 1975; Jeffers & Nichols, 1961; O'Neill, Brown, Gordon, Schonhorn, & Greer, 1981; Stuart, 1973; Willems, 1972; and Zehner & Chapin, 1974. See Brown, 1982, for a review of these studies.) Although use of activity measures as predictors of outcome is only now in its initial stages, the early evidence is strong that activity data will be useful in this additional purpose of functional assessment (cf. Norris-Baker, Stephens, Rintala, & Willems, 1981).

In response to a wide variety of constraints on data collection inherent in clients and settings, APIs were developed to permit a diversity of approaches to be used. For example, activities of the person being studied may be documented through the individual's completion of an activity diary or through an interview or questionnaire. If these forms of self-report are not practicable, API data can be obtained through observation by professional staff or by someone residing with the target person. API instruments vary also in the level of detail used to code activities. At the highly detailed end of the continuum, the duration, location, social content, and assistance received would be recorded for each activity. At the other end of the continuum, only frequency of activity would be coded. The amount of time needed to administer APIs varies from format to format; the briefest approach requires approximately 10-20 minutes of a client's time, while the lengthiest demands 40-60 minutes from both a data collector and a suitable informant.

The various API formats each provide data on behavioral output of daily life. However, API users have two other instruments available to augment this picture of client functioning. The Special Events instrument describes the client's participation in low-frequency activities that may be important indicators in rehabilitation programs (e.g., applying for a job, registering to vote) but that are unlikely to be tapped in the standard API assessment. The Delegatable Activities instrument documents the client's pattern of dependence on others in activities that, because they may be delegated totally to another person, may not appear at all in the standard API assessment (which documents what the person does, not what he or she has delegated). Each of these instruments may be administered through an interview or self-administered format and requires 10-20 minutes to complete.

Environmental Indicators (EIs)

The EIs, the fourth set of RI tools, are still in the planning stages. The purpose of the EIs will be to document factors outside the client that are especially relevant to optimal functioning. The EIs are viewed as a necessary means of shifting the focus from the client alone to the client within a context. As is the case with the other RI tools, the EIs will be used to define points of entry into the context of client functioning.

RELIABILITY AND VALIDITY

A full discussion of reliability and validity issues vis-a-vis functional assessment in general and RIs in particular is beyond the scope of this paper (see Diller, Fordyce, Jacobs, Brown, Gordon, Simmens, Orazem, & Barrett, 1983). Attention is limited here to three aspects of the overall question: first, a definition of reliability and validity in the context of functional assessment; second, a brief discussion of the complexities involved in reliability and validity; and, third, a summary of the evidence on the reliability and validity of the RIs when used for program evaluation purposes.

First, *reliability* refers here to the consistency of measures; a reliable item is thus one that is coded in the same way across observers and across points in time (when no change is expected). *Validity* of an item (when the item is used for descriptive purposes) is defined here as the degree to which what is recorded reflects what actually occurred in the client's life at the point of data collection, or, more broadly, what typically occurs.

Second, reliability and validity are a very complex issue to the degree that either or both of the following hold true: (1) The data that emerge from the process of functional assessment are detailed, extensive, and/or flexibly obtained; and (2) the functioning being assessed is relatively changeable over brief time spans. In the former case, a multitude of reliability indexes may be generated (e.g., the reliability of each constituent item, of each cluster of items, and of the overall score). Also, this array of reliability indexes will vary as setting and data-gathering characteristics vary. In the latter case, traditional methods for measuring reliability may become unwieldy. For example, a frequently feasible method for measuring reliability—the test-retest strategy—becomes untenable, leaving the less feasible approach of using an observer to provide the criterion data against which standard assessment data are compared. (Observers are often feasible in recording functioning within institutional or work settings, but may not be tolerated in the client's home.)

A final consideration related to the complexity issue is that reliability and validity can be determined for measures describing *individuals* (e.g., tracking a specific client's skill attainment) or for measures describing *groups* (e.g., evaluating a program based on gains in skill functioning of all clients). Data that have been shown to describe individuals reliably and validly can be aggregated to describe groups. However, the reverse is not necessarily true.

For RIs, as well as for other functional-assessment instruments that are detailed and primarily descriptive in character, the issues just described constitute problems that are not easy to resolve. The RI Project took the following approach to determining the reliability and validity of RIs:

- Whenever possible, both reliability and validity indexes were determined for each level of data aggregation (e.g., individual items and item clusters; individual clients and groups of clients).

- If this preferred approach was not feasible, priority was given to assessing validity instead of reliability (the latter is a major component of the former), at grosser levels of data aggregation (e.g., cluster scores), and for data aggregated across groups.

Applications of this strategy to each of the RI instruments are summarized at this point.

SIs: Reliability and Validity

Because SIs contain a relatively low degree of detail, compared to other RI tools, and because statuses per se tend to be stable and easily reportable, the optimal course described above was feasible. In fact, reliability was a prime concern during the stage of item development; after the initial development of the SI items, each item was pretested and modified until interrecorder and test-retest consistency was obtained in 10 out of 10 respondents sampled. Once this criterion level had been reached, SIs were field-tested on large numbers of respondents in independent-living centers, offices of state vocational rehabilitation agencies, and other sites. The field tests were carried out to discover items with greater difficulty in coding, and led to many refinements and to production of a detailed training manual.

Validity of the SIs was assessed through comparing the data obtained from over 100 client self-reports (both verbal and written, depending on the form used) with data derived from available records and reports of significant others. The validity coefficients were uniformly high; on all items, agreement was 95% or more.

APIs: Reliability and Validity

With APIs, the strategy of giving priority to demonstrating validity at the level of group data was selected because of the difficulties of assessing reliability and validity at the level of individual clients. This followed from the fact that the assumptions associated with test-retest methods do not hold well with the APIs.

For example, in any one week, specific activities will vary somewhat in comparison to those in another week, even though the reporter of activities may be very reliable in recording. Also, obtaining interrecorder data on activities is virtually impossible (since most individuals will not allow one, let alone two, observers into their homes). Because of these difficulties, the RI Project has relied on evidence supplied by others regarding the reliability of activity data for describing *individuals* (see Brown, 1982, for a review of these efforts; see also Bishop, Jeanrenaud, & Lawson, 1975; Bratfisch, 1972; Converse, 1972; Dougherty, 1977; Robinson, 1977; Smith, 1938; Stephens, Norris-Baker, & Willems, 1983; Widmer, 1978). These studies have shown that under certain conditions the reliability of activity cluster and summary scores can be quite high for individuals in institutions (cf. Stephens et al., 1983) and in the community (cf. Robinson, 1977).

Besides relying on the work of others, the RI Project has also implemented its own studies, assessing the validity of its tools largely in describing *groups* of clients. In these studies, the validity of API data for describing aggregates was assessed through comparison of group API data actually obtained to that expected based on theory, prior research, or clinical experience. The results of these studies are too lengthy to report herein (see Diller et al., 1983); however, the following conclusion may be cited:

> [I]n the RI Project's studies, sufficiently consistent corroboration of predicted differences has been found to conclude that, especially for purposes in rehabilitation that focus on using API data to describe groups of clients/patients, APIs provide a valid descriptive tool. However, potential users must keep in mind that validity of data derived from APIs for describing client/patient functioning varies largely as a function of factors that contribute to reliability. Therefore, some of the API approaches (e.g., those requiring a shorter period of recall vs. relatively lengthier recall) are better choices whenever a user needs a more precise estimate of activity to insure validity of the application (Diller et al., 1983, p. 34).

SKIs: Reliability and Validity

As is indicated above in the description of SKIs, the final choice of a specific set of skill items, and the selection of an assessment scale, are left to the individual user. Reliability data, therefore, are not available for a "standard form" of SKIs, since forms will differ from setting to setting. However, one example of reliability data is presented below to illustrate the high level of consistency that is possible for SKI data.

In this example, a trained data collector interviewed 10 members of the resident staff in apartments in which mentally retarded individuals were being placed as part of a deinstitutionalization effort (O'Neill, Gordon, & Brown, 1983). Each staff member was interviewed twice, with an intervening interval of 2 weeks; on each occasion he or she assessed the client's functioning with respect to 269 skills in 18 skill areas. Functioning was assessed on a 3-point scale, from "null" to "adequate," with the latter defined as needing no assistance and performing the skill without prodding whenever it was situationally called for. At the level of skill area scores, the average test-retest correlation was .92, with half of the correlations above .95; only in two areas did the coefficient fall below .80.

What these data show is that under good conditions (relatively high observability of items, a concrete assessment scale, and adequate training of the interviewer), SKIs can provide highly consistent data. Under other conditions and with different combinations of skills, the reliability coefficients would need to be redetermined, particularly when there is a strong basis for expecting that observers or informants may provide less reliable data.

The validity of SKI data has been studied in several demonstration projects. Again, these studies incorporated the strategy of comparing obtained SKI data with those expected on the basis of prior research and clinical experience. For example, the self-reported skill functioning of paraplegic and quadriplegic patients was tracked over three points in time (admission, discharge, and 1 year postonset). Although the results of these studies are detailed and complex (see Diller et al., 1983), the expected gains in skills over time and differences between groups were seen, with few exceptions. This was true at the level of skill areas and at the more detailed level of specific skill items.

In conclusion, reliability and validity studies relevant to each of the presently existing RI instruments are encouraging but not complete. The incompleteness of these studies has two implications: (1) More such investigations are required, and (2) users should employ the RIs only for those purposes intended (these issues are explored in depth in materials prepared by the RI Project for potential users). A third implication is that potential users may need to explore reliability and validity in their own settings prior to full-scale adoption. Such pilot work is particularly important whenever functional assessment data are to be used for key decision-making purposes (e.g., eligibility determination) and on populations in whom self-report may be distorted.

USE OF RIs IN PROGRAM EVALUATION

In this section, brief descriptions are provided of some of the applications of the RI tools for purposes of program evaluation and policy making. These are drawn from the approximately 50 field tests and demonstrations conducted for a variety of purposes, including program evaluation, from 1977 to 1982 (see Diller et al., 1983, for a review of the full roster of studies).

United Cerebral Palsy (UCP) Associations of New York State, Inc.

O'Neill and his colleagues (Brown, 1978; O'Neill et al., 1981) have conducted a series of studies to measure the impact of deinstitutionalization on the daily lives of severely developmentally disabled individuals, some of whom are also physically disabled. In the first study, activity patterns of a relatively well-functioning group were measured at three time periods, once in an institutional setting and twice after placement of clients in a supportive, community-based program. Examination of the impact of community placement on activity patterns over a 2 1/2 -year period indicated that the tempo of daily life increased greatly, as did the variety of activities engaged in, particularly recreational, household, and out-of-residence activities. Increases were registered within 9 months of deinstitutionalization, with the heightened levels being maintained through the final point of follow-up.

In the second study in the series (O'Neill et al., 1983), a severely retarded, multiply handicapped group was followed, in order to document both SKI and API changes associated with community placement. Activity results similar to those found in the first study were seen. It was also seen that client characteristics (e.g., type and level of retardation, type of physical limitations) had little effect on activity patterns. In terms of the 18 skill areas assessed, many increases (and some decreases) in functioning were documented for individual clients; however, across the total group, only in two skill areas were significant changes seen-in improved eating skills, and in skills of setting tables and doing dishes. Skill changes were also seen to be strongly associated with both client characteristics and placement in particular apartments. Thus, the scheduled program of activities appeared to have had a positive but relatively specific impact on the pattern of clients' daily lives, while the program for teaching skills had varied effects, depending much more on who the target individual was and on where he or she was residing.

Besides illustrating how RIs can be useful in evaluating the impact of programs on clients, this example shows that, even with incomplete validity studies, use of APIs is a low-risk venture whenever the effects of a program's intervention (in this case, placement of a client into a community residence with a community-based program of services) are expected to be large or when the opportunity to validate the results is built into the evaluation design.

The information RIs provide to UCP is being used in several ways. First, the written evaluations have been (and will be) used to justify the existence of the community residence program to UCP's funding source. Second, evaluation information has been used by UCP administrators to make decisions about program policy and structure. Finally, members of the direct care staff are using RI information as a source of feedback regarding clients' development; in the future, they may be using RI data for individualized planning.

Electronic Devices Research, Institute of Rehabilitation Medicine, New York

The purpose of this study (Efthimiou et al., 1981) was to evaluate the impact of electronic control units (ECUs) on activity patterns and other variables in a sample of clients with quadriplegia. A cross-sectional study of 20 male clients was completed, comparing the activity patterns (using an early form of the APIs) of 7 persons with quadriplegia using ECUs with 13 who were eligible to receive ECUs but did not use them. A number of psychometric tests were also administered in this study, but only APIs provided clear evidence of differences between the two groups: (1) The ECU users made greater use of a variety of adaptive devices in order to function relatively more independently and with minimal physical assistance; (2) the users were more active (i.e., they took part in more activities, overall, than the nonusers); (3) the nonusers participated more frequently in inactivities (e.g., napping), compared to the users; and (4) the nonusers spent considerably more time in passive recreational activities in their residences. These data demonstrate the utility of RIs for evaluating the impact of environmental modifications on the lives of disabled persons.

Adult Competency Training (ACT) Program, Widener College, Philadelphia

In the ACT program, directed by Jeanne Waxman, severely physically disabled young adults participated in a 6-week residential experience in independent living. Participants worked on skill attainment and participated in recreation and independent-living activities at Widener College and in the surrounding community. The goals of the program involved enhanced independence for participants. RIs were used to study skill and activity changes, both immediate and long-term. Short-term changes were assessed to document the nature of the ACT program per se (i.e., how it differed from each participant's usual patterns of daily life). As-yet-unpublished data indicate that in the skills area, the program was found to emphasize and effect changes in grooming, dressing, household skills, and skills of selecting and applying to schools. Regarding activities, the program was seen to differ from home life both in exposing participants to a more varied set of activities and in leading to more time being spent on household activities and travel and less on work, child care, and TV watching. When the participants were assessed 3 months after program participation, most of the original skill gains were retained; in addition, assertiveness skills had grown significantly. Long-term effects on activity patterns were more complex; the program emphasis on household activities and deemphasis on TV watching were not carried over into participants' home environments. Significant increases in hours devoted to education, personal care, and travel were detected. Child care and socializing became less prominent after program participation. Thus, although the ACT program emphasized independence in terms of household skills and selecting and applying to schools, its primary effect after 3 months was to get more participants into a student role. A question that remains unanswered is whether the skill gains associated with the program will manifest themselves in the lives of ex-participants beyond the 3-month period of follow-up.

Work Experience for Disabled Students (WEDS), Institute of Rehabilitation Medicine, New York

In the WEDS project, directed by Rosalind Zuger and Patricia Ryan, high-school and college students with disabilities were exposed to a work-study program aimed at expanding their awareness of the world of work and of their own capabilities vis-a-vis this world. APIs were used (1) to document how the program directly affected participants' daily-life experience during the course of the program and (2) to document the long-term effects of the program on participants.

Immediate effects included more work and activity outside the home, and fewer educational activities, independent activities, quiet recreational activities (e.g., TV) and inactivities (e.g., sitting down doing nothing). What is of particular interest here, beyond the fact that the outline of the WEDS program can be clearly seen (e.g., more work, less school, more travel—the last of which also leads to greater dependence, since most participants are not independent in transportation), is that activities in the home were also affected, with decreased levels of both TV watching and other passive activities.

With respect to effects that remained once the program was removed, in comparison to preprogram levels, no effects were seen on general activity, work, education, outside activity, independent activity, and inactivity, while family role and social activities increased and quiet recreation decreased. Thus, the picture is one of students returning to being students (as was intended), but retaining several gains from the program—participating more in social activities and in household tasks and decreasing their use of passive recreational activities. In fact, the students decreased their involvement in quiet recreation by about 10 hours per week, and this time was directly "transferred" to social and household activities.

CONCLUSION

The purpose of this paper has been to describe RIs to those interested in their applications within program evaluation (additional examples of such use are available in Diller et al., 1983). At present, RI Project activities are several: (1) preparation and dissemination of RI materials to the field; (2) maintenance of a computerized pool of RI data; and (3) demonstrating the use of RIs within a medical rehabilitation context, for uses in clinical management and program evaluation. The third activity is cosponsored by the Research and Training Center on Head Trauma and Stroke and the Regional Spinal Cord Injury Center at NYU Medical Center, while the first two activities are being supported on a fee-for-service basis. The RI Project thus continues as a lively participant in the unfinished business of developing useful, feasible, and well-tested approaches to functional assessment.

REFERENCES

Alexander, J. L., Willems, E. P., Halstead, L,. S., & Spencer, W. A. (1979). The relationship of functional assessment to evaluation of the quality of outcome in the rehabilitation process. In Alperovitch, de Dombal, & Gremy (Eds.), *Evaluation of the efficacy of medical action* (pp. 287–308). Amsterdam: North-Holland.

Bishop, D., Jeanrenaud, C., & Lawson, K. (1975). Comparison of time diary and recall questionnaire for surveying leisure activities. *Journal of Leisure Research, 7,* 73–80.

Bratfisch, O. (1972). Time estimations of the main activities of university students. *Catalog of Selected Documents in Psychology, 2,* 29–30.

Brown, M. (1978). *Evaluation report: Post-Institutional Placement Project.* Unpublished manuscript, New York University Medical Center, Department of Behavioral Sciences.

Brown, M. (1982). *Actual and perceived differences in activity patterns of able-bodied and disabled men.* Unpublished doctoral dissertation, New York University.

Brown, M., Diller, L., Fordyce, W., Jacobs, D., & Gordon, W. (1980). Rehabilitation Indicators: Their nature and uses for assessment. In B. Bolton & D. W. Cook (Eds.), *Rehabilitation client assessment* (pp. 102–117). Baltimore: University Park Press.

Brown, M., Gordon, W. A., & Diller, L. (1983a). Functional assessment and outcome measurement: An integrative review. *Annual Review of Rehabilitation, 3.*

Brown, M., Gordon, W., & Diller, L. (1983b, May). *Rehabilitation Indicators.* Paper presented at the National Conference on Functional Assessment, Eugene, OR.

Calsyn, D. A. (1980, October). *Rehabilitation Indicators: Application of a non-traditional approach to functional assessment.* Paper presented at the annual meeting of the American Congress of Rehabilitation Medicine, Washington, DC.

Chapin, F. S., Jr., & Brail, R. K. (1969). Human activity systems in the metropolitan United States. *Environment and Behavior, 1,* 107–130.

Converse, P. E. (1972). Country differences in time use. In A. Szalai (Ed.), *The use of time* (pp. 145-177). The Hague: Mouton.

Diller, L., Fordyce, W., Jacobs, D., Brown, M., Gordon, W., Simmens, S., Orazem, J., & Barrett, L. (1983). *Final Report: Rehabilitation Indicators Project* (Grant No. G008003039). Washington, DC: National Institute of Handicapped Research, U.S. Department of Education.

Dougherty, T. W. (1977). *Development and evaluation of a self-recorded diary for measuring job behavior.* Unpublished master's thesis, University of Houston.

Dow, G. K., & Juster, F. T. (1980). *Goods, satisfaction with activities and well-being: An exploratory analysis* (Working Paper Series). Ann Arbor: Institute for Social Research, University, of Michigan.

Efthimiou, J., Gordon, W. A., Sell, G. H., & Stratford, C. (1981). Electronic assistive devices: Their impact on the quality of life of high level quadriplegic persons. *Archives of Physical Medicine and Rehabilitation, 62,* 131–134.

Fordyce, W. (1978, August). *Application of Rehabilitation Indicators to pain and stroke patients and spouses.* Paper presented at the annual meeting of the American Psychological Association, Toronto.

Gillespie, I., & Johnston, B. J. (1967). The disabled college woman and her use of time. *Rehabilitation Literature, 28,* 379–382.

Gordon, W. A. (1982). *Final Report: Psychological adjustment and characteristics in recent spinal cord injuries* (Grant No. 13-P-59127). Washington, DC: U.S. Department of Education.

Gordon, W. A., Brown, M., Lehman, L., Sherman, B., Farber, J., Buccheri, G., & Lucido, D. (1979, November). *Patterns of activities among spinal cord individuals.* Paper presented at the annual meeting of the American Congress of Rehabilitation, Honolulu.

Gordon, W. A., & Diller, L. (1983). Stroke: Coping with a cognitive deficit. In T. E. Burish & I.. A. Bradley (Eds.), *Coping with chronic disease: Research and applications (pp.* 113–135). New York: Academic Press.

Hartung, J. R. (1975). Psychosocial and behavioral consequences of a change in lower extremity orthosis. *Dissertation Abstracts International, 35,* 3581B. (University Microfilms No. 75-1031).

Hill, M. S., & Juster, F. T. (1980). *Constraints and complementarities in time use* (Working Paper Series). Ann Arbor: Institute for Social Research, University of Michigan.

Hobart, C. W. (1975). Active sports participation among the young, the middle-aged and the elderly. *Sociology, 10,* 27–44.

Jeffers, F.C., & Nichols, C. R. (1961). The relationship of activities and attitudes to physical well-being in older people. *Journal of Gerontology, 16,* 67–70.

Norris-Baker, C., Stephens, M. A. P., Rintala, D. H., & Williams, E. P. (1981). Patient behavior as a predictor of outcomes in spinal cord injury *Archives of Physical Medicine and Rehabilitation, 62,* 602–608.

O'Neill, J., Brown, M., Gordon, W., Schonhorn, R., & Greer, E. (1981). Activity patterns of retarded adults within institutions and the community: A longitudinal study. *Applied Research in Mental Retardation, 2,* 367–379.

O'Neill, J., Gordon, W. A., & Brown, M. (1983). *The impact of a community based residence program on skill levels and patterns of daily activity.* Unpublished manuscript.

Robinson, J. P. (1977). *How Americans use time.* New York: Praeger.

Smith, M. (1938). An experiment to test the reliability of estimates of use of time. *Journal of Applied Psychology, 22,* 400–407.

Stephens, M. A. P., Norris-Baker, C., & Willems, E. P. (1983). Data quality in self-observation and report of behavior. *Archives of Physical Medicine and Rehabilitation, 64*, 167–171.

Stuart, D. G. (1973). *A naturalistic study of the daily activities of disabled and nondisabled college students.* Unpublished master's thesis, University of Houston.

Widmer, M. L. (1978). *Telephone contact as a method for gathering data on the everyday behavior of non-institutionalized adults.* Unpublished master's thesis, University of Houston.

Willems, E. P. (1972). Place and motivation: Independence and complexity in patient behavior. In W. J. Mitchell (Ed.), *Environmental design: Research and practices. Proceedings of EDRA 3 Conference* (pp. 431–438). Los Angeles: University of California at Los Angeles Press.

Zehner, R,, & Chapin, F. S. (1974). *Across the city line: A white community transition.* Lexington, MA: D. C. Heath.

Acknowledgments: This research was supported by the National Institute of Handicapped Research ((Grant No.G008003039), U.S. Department of Education. Prior to October 1979, it was supported by the Rehabilitation Services Administration, first as part of the Research and Training Center at New York University Medical Center and then as a research and development project (No. 12-P-59047/2).

20

The Development of a Multifaceted Measure of Rehabilitation Effectiveness: Theoretical Rationale and Scale Construction

**Shlomo Kravetz, Victor Florian
and George N. Wright**

ABSTRACT: The present paper describes the research effort invested in the construction and validation of the Human Service Scale as a partial test of a theory of rehabilitation outcome. The seven Human Service subscales that were derived from expert ratings of the scale items and from item and factor analyses of 1,018 rehabilitation clients' responses to these items are similar to, but not identical with, Maslow's categories of basic human needs. Smallest Space Analysis (SSA) of the correlations between these subscales and between the scale items suggested ways in which this study's initial theory might require modification. The implications of the modified theory of rehabilitation outcome for a number of conceptual problems and methodological issues connected with the measurement of rehabilitation outcome are discussed.

The Human Service Scale was the principal product of the research that the present paper describes. This self-report measure of rehabilitation outcome has been described in a number of papers and books (Bolton, 1977, 1979; Reagles & Butler, 1976; G. N. Wright, 1980). However, these discussions are mainly concerned with the scale's usefulness as a technique for assessing rehabilitation clients' problems and for evaluating rehabilitation results.

The present paper describes the development and validation of the scale as a partial test of a theory of rehabilitation outcome. To justify investing effort in establishing the construct validity of such a measure, this paper focuses on a number of conceptual problems and methodological issues related to the evaluation of rehabilitation outcome. One problem is the lack of a rationale for linking the selection of rehabilitation goals to an empirically verifiable theory of normal human goal-directed activity. Rehabilitation professionals claim that rehabilitation is concerned more with normality than with illness (Vash, 1981). This emphasis requires measures that are indices of healthy processes and status (B. A. Wright & Fletcher, 1982). Another problem is the difficulty of identifying general human objectives in such a way as to permit the evaluative comparison of the effectiveness of rehabilitation services provided by different rehabilitation systems to different populations of rehabilitation clients. The third problem is the logical difficulty of generalizing from empirical research, which essentially deals with matters of fact, to the identification and choice of human goals, which must include some consideration of value judgments. A measure of rehabilitation outcome that is based upon a theory of normal human goal-directed activity could partially resolve these problems.

These conceptual problems can be related to three of the four basic methodological issues that Bolton (1979) claims are relevant to the measurement of rehabilitation outcome. These issues are economic versus noneconomic measures of rehabilitation outcome, unidimensional versus multidimensional measures of rehabilitation outcome, and self-report versus observer ratings of rehabilitation outcome.

The conceptual problems of choosing an empirically verifiable theory of normal human goal-directed activity upon which to base a formal theory of rehabilitation outcome, and of critically comparing the outcomes of different rehabilitation services, can be related to Bolton's first and second methodological issues. A psychosocial theory of well-being that is unidimensional, and that postulates that vocational and economic satisfaction is a central characteristic of this dimension, would justify the use of a unidimensional vocational-economic measure of rehabilitation outcome. In addition, the interventions of different rehabilitation systems would be comparable across these systems in terms of their contributions to the improvement of the rehabilitants' vocational and economic status. However, a multidimensional approach may be considered necessary for an appropriate understanding of the structure of human activities. Vocational and economic activities would then be more likely viewed as only two of a number of domains of human activity that form this structure. According to this approach, the use of a vocational-economic unidimensional measure of rehabilitation outcome would not always be justifiable, and the evaluative comparison of different rehabilitation systems and services would be problematic.

The methodological issue of subjective versus observer measures of rehabilitation outcome can be considered an operationalization of the lack of a logical connection between facts and values. Strupp and Hadley (1977) have developed a tripartite model of psychotherapeutic outcome assessment, which requires that such assessment be carried out from the perspective of society, the individual, and the psychotherapist. According to their model, the attainment of therapeutic objectives should ultimately be measured in terms of "subjective perceptions of self-esteem, acceptance, and well-being" (p. 190) of the individual who comes or is referred for help. This model juxtaposes observations of behavior with evaluations from society's perspective, and clinical judgment aided by behavioral observations and psychological tests with evaluations from the mental health professional's perspective. Resolving the issue of self-report versus observer measures of rehabilitation outcome may partially involve answering the question as to whose values and perspective should be adopted when rehabilitation services are being evaluated.

Warr (1978) points to Maslow's (1970) theory of human motivation as a pioneering effort to develop a theory of normal psychosocial well-being and motivation. Since the present study was concerned with measuring rehabilitation outcome in terms of normal goal-directed activity, it investigated the possibility of deriving a theory of rehabilitation outcome from Maslow's theory of motivation.

Maslow (1970) defines human needs as biosocial tendencies that direct persons to engage in activities and have experiences that "the healthy organism tends to choose, and strives toward under conditions that permit it to choose" (p. 92). According to Maslow, persons who are limited in their ability to engage in such activities and to have such experiences suffer. Analyzing the rehabilitation client's problems within this theory's framework is based upon the assumption that both able-bodied persons and those with disabilities have the same basic needs; what differentiate the former from the latter are the disabling conditions, which may constitute a barrier to gratifying these needs. Disabled persons, whom most professional and legal definitions identify as the rehabilitation clients (G. N. Wright, 1980), may be seeking help from rehabilitation systems because they lack the personal and social resources to gratify these needs.

Maslow (1970) contends that basic human needs fall into specific qualitative categories and that these categories can be ordered according to their prepotency; one category of needs tends to dominate another category when both are not satisfied. The need categories, in order of their prepotency, are as follows: physiological needs, safety and security needs, love and belongingness needs, self-esteem needs, and self-actualization needs. In terms of this hierarchical theory, when two categories of needs are not gratified, individuals will strive to gratify the more basic of the two.

The choice of this theory as a framework for developing a multifaceted measure of rehabilitation effectiveness is an attempt to confront explicitly the major conceptual problems and methodological issues associated with the evaluation of rehabilitation outcome. First, the use of this theory directly relates the measurement of rehabilitation effectiveness to a general theory of normal psychosocial well-being. According to this theory, psychosocial well-being is multifaceted. One of its facets is the extent to which an individual has access to qualitatively distinct categories of activities and experiences. A second facet is the degree of prepotency with which each of these categories can be characterized. Since the categories of human needs that correspond to these activities and experiences can be ordered along a single continuum of prepotency, psychosocial well-being can be considered essentially unidimensional. Thus, the issue of the primacy of economic and vocational measures of rehabilitation outcome is partially resolvable in terms of the prepotency of the category of human needs to which economic and vocational activities belong. Secondly, if a multifaceted measure of need satisfaction representative of Maslow's hierarchy can be constructed, it should be sufficiently comprehensive to apply to various rehabilitation systems and services. Finally, the choice of Maslow's theory of basic human needs is the explicit expression of a professional value judgment that views the person with the disability or handicap as the client of the rehabilitation system. Empirical questions as to the structure of rehabilitation clients' self-reports of the quality and quantity of their activities and experiences become especially meaningful once such a value judgment has been made.

As part of the process of constructing and partially validating a multifaceted measure of rehabilitation effectiveness, this study posed the following research questions:

1. Do rehabilitation clients' self-reports of the quality and quantity of their activities and experiences form subscales similar to Maslow's five categories of human needs?
2. Will the subscales formed by these self-reports be ordered along Maslow's dimension of prepotency?

METHOD

Sample

This study's sample consisted of 1,018 clients of state and federal Department of Vocational Rehabilitation (DVR) agencies located in 29 states and one territory of the United States. Since DVR agencies have uniform, formal acceptance criteria, the selection of the research sample from the population of DVR clients ascertained that the subjects were characterized by disabilities and handicaps sufficiently severe to make them eligible for rehabilitation services.

All the subjects who participated in the study had been found to be eligible for vocational rehabilitation services by their vocational rehabilitation counselors, but, at the time of the study, had not yet received these services. Thus, all subjects had a physical or behavioral disability that was evaluated as vocationally handicapping. Of the subjects, 43% were classified as having mental disorders; 30% as having an orthopedic impairment; 15% as having an internal impairment; 7% as having a sensory impairment; 3% as having a neurological impairment; and 1% as mentally retarded. Sixty percent were male and 40% were female. The subjects' ages ranged from 15 to 60 years, with a median age of 29.8 years.

Instruments

Data were collected for the construction and validation of a multifaceted measure of rehabilitation effectiveness from rehabilitation clients, vocational rehabilitation counselors, and expert raters. The instruments that were used to collect these data at various steps of the research process are described according to these three groups of respondents.

Rehabilitation Client Questionnaire. A number of instruments designed to measure various aspects of psychosocial well-being and satisfaction were examined

(Aronoff, 1967; Bradburn, 1969; Reagles, 1969; Shostram, 1968; U.S. Public Health Service, 1971; Weiss, Dawis, England, & Lofquist, 1964; G. N. Wright & Remmers, 1960). From these sources, approximately 300 items were selected.

This pool of items was reduced to 150 items on the basis of (1) whether an item appeared to be related to Maslow's five categories of basic human needs; (2) whether an item could be self-administered; and (3) whether an item referred to an activity, benefit, or experience that could be modified through rehabilitation services. Each item was formulated so that it consisted of a short question and five possible response categories, which ranged from responses indicating a high level of need satisfaction to responses indicating a low level of need satisfaction. The resulting 150-item multiple choice questionnaire was entitled the Rehabilitation Need and Status Questionnaire (RNSQ).

Vocational Rehabilitation Counselor Questionnaire. Vocational rehabilitation counselors who were asked to administer the RNSQ to their clients were requested to fill out the Client Demographic Data and Handicap to Available Employment Form for each of their clients who participated in the study. On one part of this form, the counselor supplied information regarding the client's name, number, address, age, sex, primary and secondary disability, race, number of dependents, and former status as agency client. The second part of the form contained a modified version of the Handicap to Appropriate and Available Employment Rating (Bolton, Butler, & Wright, 1968; Hammond, Wright, & Butler, 1968).

Expert Rater's Rating Form. An item-rating form was constructed so that expert raters could evaluate the relation between each of the 150 RNSQ items and each of Maslow's five categories of basic human needs. This item-rating form included a connotative and denotative definition of each of Maslow's categories of basic human needs, and 150-item rating scales by means of which the raters could express the degree of relation between each item and each of Maslow's categories of basic human needs.

Procedure

A multilevel sampling strategy was used to collect data for this study. This strategy was designed to maximize the number of vocational rehabilitation counselors and clients participating in the study and to assure optimal motivation on the part of the participants. This strategy included the following two stages:

1. In proportion to the size of the populations with which they dealt, 54 U.S., state, territory, and possession DVR directors were asked by mail to send the names of 600 DVR counselors who would be willing and responsible research participants in the research effort.
2. Thirty-two directors responded with lists of names of 340 counselors. Each of these counselors received a research packet that included the above-described questionnaires. Each of the 340 DVR counselors was asked to administer the RNSQ to, and provide demographic data and Handicap to Appropriate and Available Employment Ratings on, five clients who were

eligible for but had not received vocational rehabilitation services and whose disabilities did not interfere with their completing self-report questionnaires.

Of the 340 DVR counselors contacted, 228 helped supply data on 1,018 DVR clients.

While this data-collection strategy was being carried out, 29 practicing vocational rehabilitation counselors and three candidates for a doctoral degree in vocational rehabilitation counseling used the item-rating form to evaluate the relation between each of the 150 RNSQ items and each of Maslow's five categories of basic human needs.

RESULTS

An analytic strategy of successive approximations was used both to construct the Human Service Scale and to examine the correspondence between the scale's hypothetical structure and the scale's empirical structure. This strategy consisted of three stages.

Stage 1 consisted of expert ratings and various item analyses. An analysis-of-variance model suggested by Medley and Mitzel (1964) was used to estimate the reliability of the expert raters' ratings of the relations between each item and Maslow's five categories of basic needs. This analysis uncovered an intraclass reliability of .91. Mean ratings and variances provided a reliable basis for partitioning the 150 RNSQ items into separate subscales, each representing one of Maslow's need categories.

QUEST, SCORE, SELECT (Bussel, Costa, Spencer, & Aleamoni, 1971), and RAVE (Baker, 1969) item analyses were carried out on these five subscales. On the basis of these analyses, five 20-item subscales characterized by relatively high Hoyt coefficients of reliability were constructed. Items with RAVE weights indicating that they were contributing little reliable variance to their subscales either were dropped from the item pool or were reassigned their original weights and retained for factor analysis.

Stage 2 consisted of Image factor analysis (Guttman, 1954) of the predominately RAVE-weighted responses of 1,018 subjects to 98 items from the original 150-item RNSQ. This analysis tested the hypothesis that the factors underlying the interitem correlations would resemble Maslow's five categories of basic human needs. Items not related to such factors could be dropped from the item pool.

Guttman's Image factor analysis model, which is based upon the regression of each variable on all the other variables with squared multiple correlations as estimates of communalities (Rummel, 1970), is consonant with this study's conceptualization of factors as scales or quasi-scales (Guttman, 1954, pp. 279-309). In addition, this model allows for the orthogonal rotation of a factor matrix "without the inclusion of the trivial factors affecting in any substantial way the rotated position of the major psychologically interpretable factors" (Kaiser, 1963, p. 164). Since only a small number of factors extracted from a data matrix by Image factor analysis are generally interpretable (Kaiser, 1963, p. 164), in this study only the first 35 factors were extracted and rotated to a varimax orthogonal solution. Two "rules of thumb" were used to decide how many of the 35 factors to retain as meaningful subscales. First, the percentage of total variance associated with each of the 35 orthogonally rotated factors was examined to determine the point at which the increase in this variance reached a minimum. Second, factors in the vicinity of this point were discarded as too specific if they did not possess more than three items with factor loadings equal to or more than .30 (Rummel, 1970). On the basis of these "rules of thumb," the first seven factors were considered sufficiently general to warrant interpretation as subscales. These factors accounted for 30.2% of the total interitem variance of the 98 items and 84.7% of the total factor variance accounted for by the first 35 factors.

Items with moderate to high factor loadings on a particular factor served as the criteria for defining that factor. Generally, only items with factor loadings equal to or more than .30 were considered for this purpose. The content of these items, together with the mean expert ratings of their relation with Maslow's five categories of human needs, were examined to evaluate the correspondence between the factors and the latter categories. The results of this examination are depicted in Table 20.1.

As Table 20.1 shows, seven interpretable factors emerged from the factor analysis of the relations between the 98 RNSQ items. These factors seem to be similar to, but not identical with, Maslow's five categories of basic human needs. Eighty items with moderate to high factor loadings on these seven subscales were chosen to form the Human Service Scale. This scale's seven needs subscales were labeled as follows: Factor 1—Vocational Self-Actualization Need; Factor 2—Emotional Security Need; Factor 3—Physiological Need; Factor 4—Economic Self-Esteem Need; Factor 5—Family Need; Factor 6—Social Need; and Factor 7—Economic Security Need.

Stage 3 consisted of structural analyses of the relations both between these seven need subscales and between these subscales' items. Maslow's hierarchical process of prepotency should produce measures of need satisfaction that are monotonically ordered, from measures of the satisfaction of the more prepotent needs to measures of the satisfaction of the less prepotent needs. The correlation matrix formed by such an ordering of variables has been labeled a "simplex" (Guttman, 1954; Morrison, 1967).

To determine whether the seven need subscales identified by Image factor analysis could be characterized as a simplex, Pearson product-moment correlations among the seven subscales were estimated. For these estimations, items that appeared on more than one subscale were assigned to the subscale represented by the factor on which they received the highest factor loading. RAVE-weighted scores on these nonoverlapping subscales were used to calculate the correlation matrix that is presented in Table 20.2. The need subscales are listed in this table in the order of their hypothesized prepotence, with the less prepotent needs following the more prepotent needs.

Smallest Space Analysis (SSA) was applied to the subscale correlation matrix shown in Table 20.2 to determine whether the relations between the seven need

Table 20.1 Description of the Seven Factors Produced by Image Factor Analysis of the 1,018 Subjects' Responses to the 98 RNSQ Items

Description of Item Content Related to Each Factor[a,b]	Number of Items with Factor Loadings > .30	Most Frequent Need Category or Categories upon Which Factor Items Received Highest or Second Highest Mean Expert Rating	Hoyt Reliability Coefficients Calculated by RAVE Analysis
1. Extent of enjoyment, supervision, variety, autonomy and involvement with job, educational program, or training program	18	Self-actualization needs	.98
2. Absence of feelings of depression, inferiority, helplessness, boredom, discouragement, worry, or restlessness, and presence of feelings of decisiveness and self-control	19	Love and belongingness needs; self-esteem needs; safety and security needs	.89
3. Symptoms of poor physical or emotional health or the consequences of these symptoms	16	Physiological needs	.85
4. Regularity of employment and the economic and social benefits associated with employment	8	Self-esteem needs	.86
5. Quality and quantity of interaction with family	9	Love and belongingness needs	.82
6. Quality and quantity of interpersonal relations outside family, such as contact with friends, social activities, participation in community activities	6	Love and belongingness needs	.75
7. Expressions of worry about economic problems or sense of economic security	6	Safety and security needs	.67

[a] Factors listed according to percentage of total interitem variance extracted with each factor.
[b] Exact factor loadings for each item on each factor appear in the doctoral dissertation from which this report is condensed (Kravetz, 1973).

Table 20.2 The Correlations among the Seven Need Subscales of the Human Service Scale According to Their Assumed Prepotency

Subscales	1	2	3	4	5	6	7
1. Physiological Need	—	.564	.280	.084	.106	.014	.077
2. Emotional Security Need		—	.398	.378	.347	−.008	.101
3. Economic Security Need			—	.116	.239	.100	.151
4. Family Need				—	.311	−.065	.040
5. Social Need					—	.051	.173
6. Economic Self-Esteem Need						—	.457
7. Vocational Self-Actualization Need							—

Note: p for all correlations (*r* = .08) < .01 with 1,000 degrees of freedom.

subscales approximated a simplex. SSA (Guttman, 1968) treats correlation coefficients as indices of similarity and portrays variables as points in n-dimensional space so that the similarities between variables are represented by the distances between these points. It then attempts to fit these points into a space of the smallest possible dimensionality. The Coefficient of Alienation is an index of the goodness of fit of this geometrical ordering of a set of variables in a given dimensionality. A smaller coefficient indicates a better goodness of fit. SSA has been construed simply as a nonmetric form of factor analysis. However, since it was specifically developed to investigate whether the relations between variables correspond to geometrical models of psychological constructs, it is especially appropriate for exploring the extent to which the relations among the seven need subscales deviated from the simplex structure that was hypothesized for them.

One dimension should have been sufficient for portraying the relations among the seven need subscales if these subscales actually form a simplex. The Coefficient of Alienation of the SSA solution for the relations among the seven need subscales in one dimension was .237. With the addition of a second dimension, this coefficient dropped to .004. The relatively large Coefficient of Alienation for the relations among the seven need subscales in one dimension, and the sharp increase in goodness of fit that resulted from the addition of a second dimension, strongly suggested that two dimensions were required to depict consistently the relations between the need subscales.

Figure 20.1 portrays the two-dimensional configuration of the relations among the need subscales. Rather than forming a monotonic arrangement, these need subscales seemed to form an oval configuration. The proximity of the need subscales in two-dimensional space could be a reflection of the natural overlapping of source of need satisfaction (person-environment) with the quality of the need being satisfied (individual-social benefits).

SSA of items sampled from the seven need subscales replicated the two-dimensional oval configuration. In addition, the latter analysis of the subscale items appeared to order them from the center to the periphery of the configuration. Items that were evaluative (e.g., "How happy are you with your family life?") were more centrally located, whereas items that were more instrumental (e.g., "How much time do you spend doing things with your family?") were more peripherally located.

DISCUSSION

The present study can be considered a partial test of the validity of applying Maslow's construct of need gratification to the measurement of rehabilitation effectiveness. The seven subscales produced by this study are similar to, but not identical with, Maslow's five categories of basic human needs. According to Cronbach and Meehl (1955), discrepancies between the empirical characteristics of a measure of a construct and the hypothetical implications of that construct should lead to either the rejection of the construct, the development of a more adequate measure of the construct, or the modification of the construct. Independent

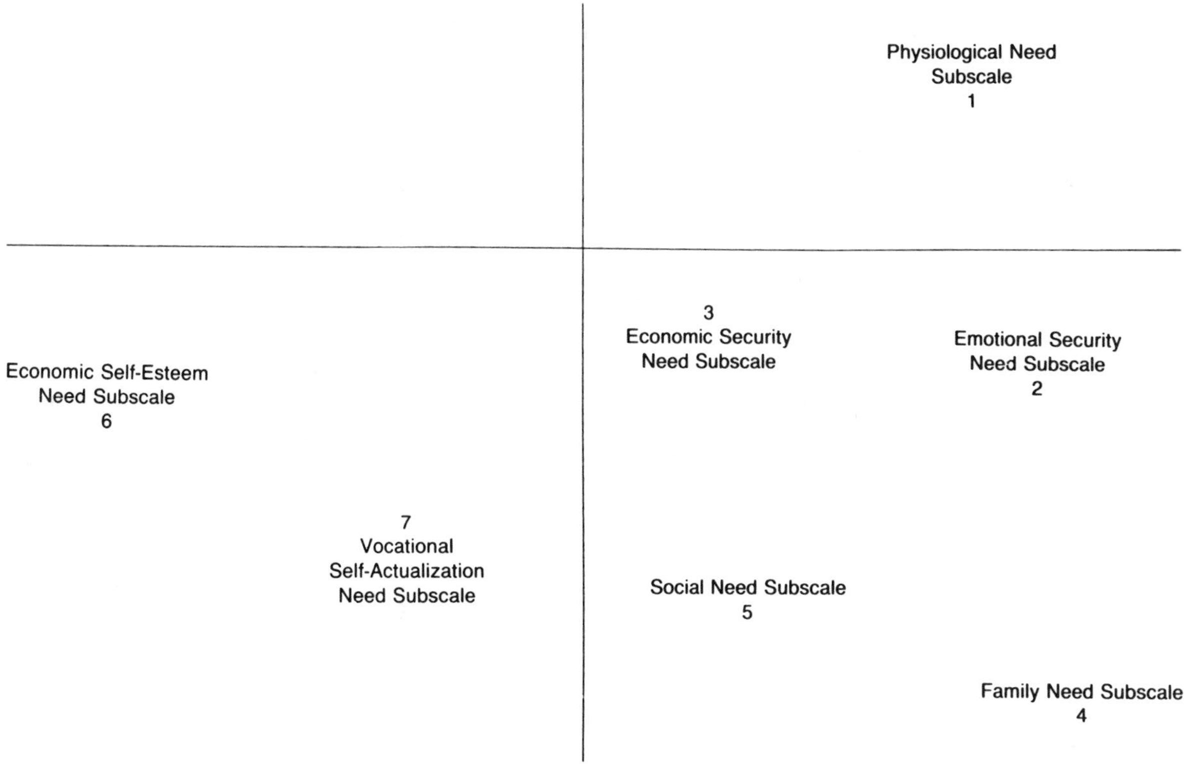

Figure 20.1 The results of the Smallest Space Analysis (SSA) of the relations among the Human Service Scale subscales in two dimensions, with subscales numbered according to their hypothetical position in Maslow's hierarchy of basic human needs.

research with the scale produced by the present study has shown the need subscales' scores, homogeneities, and structure to be relatively stable (Dellario, 1974; Hart, 1976). Furthermore, additional studies suggest that these subscales are related in a meaningful manner to such variables as the provision of rehabilitation services and the "phantom limb" phenomenon (Arzi, 1976; Miller, 1979). These findings and the psychosocial reasonableness of the subscales' content and structure support the acceptance of the scale as a multifaceted measure of rehabilitation need satisfaction. In addition, recent attempts to develop general measures of health and well-being have shown that these phenomena can be optimally represented by a number of related subscales (Veit & Ware, 1983). These subscales are similar to the subscales uncovered by the present study. Therefore, modifications of the construct of rehabilitation need satisfaction are suggested that are consistent with the substance and the structure of the subscales produced by the present study.

Structural analysis of the Human Service Scales items seems to indicate that the relations among these items are more circular than monotonic. Wiggins (1980) has derived a similar circular ordering of interpersonal behavior from a dualistic theory of human motivation. He prefaced his description of this circular model with a list of theoreticians who claim that human activity is oriented toward both autonomy and belongingness. According to these theoreticians, these general orientations are equally potent. Thus, one facet of human satisfaction remains the quality of the experiences and activities after which individuals tend to strive. However, rather than forming five qualitatively different categories, these experiences and activities may be related predominantly either to the need for autonomy or to the need for belongingness. Another facet that appears in Wiggins's model and that seems consistent with this study's results is the different sources of the satisfaction of these needs. The source of autonomy and belongingness may be intrapersonal or interpersonal. An additional facet that seems to characterize the structure of human satisfaction uncovered by this study is the behavioral modality to which each satisfaction item refers. These items refer either to such specific instrumental behaviors as the number of activities that an individual engages in together with his or her family, or to such general feelings and beliefs as the extent to which that individual is happy with his or her family. Although this latter facet is not part of Wiggins's model, it does appear in other circular models of well-being (Levy & Guttman, 1975).

The above-revised theory of rehabilitation need satisfaction provides tentative solutions to the conceptual problems and methodological issues described in the present study's introduction. This theory could serve as an empirically verifiable rationale for selecting rehabilitation goals. According to this theory, handicapping conditions could be defined in terms of the manner in which different disabilities disrupt instrumental behaviors or distort human judgment with regard to resources available for the satisfaction of the need for either autonomy or belongingness. Since human needs do not seem to be hierarchically related, personal and social values could play a relatively large role in the selection of specific rehabilitation need-related goals. However, rehabilitation planning could be made more efficient if goals sharing common facets of need satisfaction are selected. The effectiveness of different rehabilitation systems would seem to be comparable only to the extent that these systems share common rehabilitation goals. In general, multidimensional measures of rehabilitation effectiveness would appear to be preferable to unidimensional measures. Obviously, the validity of these conclusions is dependent upon the results of future investigations of the theory of human need satisfaction from which they are derived.

REFERENCES

Aronoff, J. (1967). *Psychological needs and cultural systems: A case study.* New York: Van Nostrand.

Arzi, S. (1976). *The structure of the phantom limb and its implications for adjustment.* Unpublished master's thesis, Bar-Ilan University, Ramat-Gan, Israel.

Baker, F. B. (1969). *FORTAP, a Fortran test analysis package: A program for the UNIVAC 1108 computer.* Madison: University of Wisconsin, Department of Educational Psychology, Laboratory of Experimental Design.

Bolton, B. (1977). Rehabilitation client needs and psychopathology. *Rehabilitation Counseling Bulletin, 7–12.*

Bolton, B. (1979). *Rehabilitation counseling research.* Austin, TX: Pro-Ed.

Bolton, B., Butler, A. J., & Wright, G. N. (1968). *Clinical versus statistical prediction of client feasibility* (Wisconsin Studies in Vocational Rehabilitation, Vol. 1, VII). Madison: Regional Rehabilitation Research Institute, University of Wisconsin.

Bradburn, N. M. (1969). *The structure of psychological well-being.* Chicago: Aldine.

Bussel, R. L., Costa, I. A., Spencer, R. E., & Aleamoni, L. M. (1971). *MERMA C manual.* Urbana: University of Illinois Press.

Cronbach, L. J., & Meehl, P. E. (1955). Construct validity in psychological tests. *Psychological Bulletin, 52,* 281–302.

Dellario, D. (1974). *A multivariate analysis of rehabilitation change.* Unpublished doctoral dissertation, University of Wisconsin, Madison.

Guttman, L. (1954). A new approach to factor analysis: The index. In P. F. Lazerfeld (Ed.), *Mathematical thinking in the social sciences* (pp. 258–349). Glencoe, IL: Free Press.

Guttman, L. (1968). A general nonmetric technique for finding the smallest coordinate space for a configuration of points. *Psychometrics, 33,* 469–506.

Hammond, C. D., Wright, G. N., & Butler, A. J. (1968). *Caseload feasibility in an expanded vocational rehabilitation program* (Wisconsin Studies in Vocational Rehabilitation, Vol. 1, VI). Madison: Regional Rehabilitation Research Institute, University of Wisconsin.

Hart, L. (1976). *Differentiation of rehabilitation need and outcome alcoholics.* Unpublished doctoral dissertation, University of Wisconsin, Madison.

Kaiser, H. F. (1963). Image analysis. In C. W. Harris (Ed.), *Problem in measuring change* (pp. 156–166). Madison: University of Wisconsin Press.

Kravetz, S. (1973). *Rehabilitation need and status: Substance, structure, and process.* Unpublished doctoral dissertation, University of Wisconsin, Madison.

Levy, S., & Guttman, L. (1975). On the multivariate structure of wellbeing. *Social Indicators Research, 2,* 361–388.

Maslow, A. H. (1970). *Motivation and personality* (2nd ed.). New York: Harper & Row.

Medley, D. M., & Mitzel, H. E. (1964). Measuring classroom behavior by systematic observation. In N. L. Gage (Ed.), *Handbook of research on teaching* (pp. 247–328). Chicago: Rand McNally.

Miller, M. (1979). *The relationship between anxiety, depression, denial and rehabilitation need and status and treatment in an early rehabilitation unit in men with acute myocardial infarction.* Unpublished master's thesis, Bar-Ilan University, Ramat-Gan, Israel.

Morrison, D. F. (1967). *Multivariate statistical methods.* New York: McGraw-Hill.

Reagles, K. W. (1969). *Rehabilitation gain of clients in an expanded vocational rehabilitation program.* Unpublished doctoral dissertation, University of Wisconsin, Madison.

Reagles, K. W., & Butler, A. J. (1976). The Human Service Scale: A new measure for evaluation. *Journal of Rehabilitation, 42,* 34–38.

Rummel, R. J. (1970). *Applied factor analysis.* Evanston, IL: Northwestern University Press.

Shostram, E. (1968). *Personal Orientation Inventory (POI): A test of self-actualization* (2nd printing). San Diego: Educational and Industrial Testing Service.

Strupp, H. N., & Hadley, S. W. (1977). A tripartite model of mental health and therapeutic outcomes with special reference to negative effects in psychotherapy. *American Psychologist, 32*(1), 187–196.

U.S. Public Health Service, Bureau of Community Environmental Management. (1971). *Neighborhood Environment Evaluation and Decision System.* Rockville, MD: U.S. Department of Health, Education and Welfare.

Vash, C. L. (1981). *The psychology of disability.* New York: Springer Publishing Company.

Veit, C. T., & Ware, Jr. (1983). The structure of psychological distress and well-being in general populations. *Journal of Consulting and Clinical Psychology, 51*(5), 730–742.

Warr, P. (1978). A study of psychological well-being. *British Journal of Psychology, 69,* 111–121.

Weiss, D. J., Dawis, R. V., England, G. W., & Lofquist, L. H. (1964). *The measurement of vocational needs* (Minnesota Studies in Vocational Rehabilitation, Bull. 41, XVIII). Minneapolis: University of Minnesota Industrial Relations Center.

Wiggins, J. S. (1980). Circumplex models of interpersonal behavior. In L. Wheeler (Ed.), *Review of personality and social psychology* (Vol. 1, pp. 265–294). Beverly Hills, CA: Sage.

Wright, B. A., & Fletcher, B. L. (1982). Uncovering hidden resources: A challenge in assessment. *Professional Psychology, 13,* 229–235.

Wright, G. N. (1980). *Total rehabilitation.* Boston: Little, Brown.

Wright, G. N., & Remmers, H. H. (1960). *Manual for the Handicap Problem Inventory.* Lafayette, IN: Purdue Research Foundation.

21

The Preliminary Diagnostic Questionnaire (PDQ): Functional Assessment of Employability

Joseph B. Moriarty, Richard T. Walls,
and Don E. McLaughlin

ABSTRACT: The Preliminary Diagnostic Questionnaire (PDQ) is designed for the functional assessment of employability. The eight subscales and accompanying demographic items provide measurement of cognitive, physical, emotional, and dispositional components of employability. Selected scores were found to be predictive of earnings and employment at the minimum wage. Significant correlations with the General Aptitude Test Battery (GATB), the Wechsler Adult Intelligence Scale (WAIS), and the Wide Range Achievement Test (WRAT) were also obtained. Evidence is presented for test-retest reliability and internal consistency, as well as for criterion-related, construct, and content validity.

The Preliminary Diagnostic Questionnaire (PDQ) is designed to assess the functional capacities of handicapped individuals in relation to employability (Moriarty, 1981). The PDQ is intended to be quickly administered in the counselor's office and to provide functional assessment that allows a counselor to determine a client's capabilities for competition in the labor market. The original conception of the PDQ as a measure of employability envisioned four major components of functional assessment: cognitive, physical/motor, emotional/social, and dispositional/desire-to-work components (e.g., see Diller, 1971; Fordyce, 1971; Mager & Beach, 1967; Neff, 1971).

Medically based classifications of disability have limited value when practical decisions have to be made about severity of employment handicap and the types of services likely to enhance employability of an individual (Tenth Institute on Rehabilitation Issues, 1983). Medically, two persons both may be classified as having cerebral palsy; yet there may be enormous employability differences between them, due to variance in physical, cognitive, emotional, and motivational functioning. For example, one may have severe speech limitations and the other not. One may be able to move about unassisted while the other may require a wheelchair. The primary underlying rationale for contruction of the PDQ was the need for functional assessment of disabilities in an integrated framework for more decision-relevant classification of clients.

Assessing rehabilitation gain has been a continuing concern (CSAVR Committee on Program Evaluation, 1984). Because of its brevity, practitioners can readminister the PDQ in whole or in part to assess improvement. Although some measures of rehabilitation gain have been proposed and developed (e.g., Reagles, Wright, & Butler, 1970; Westerheide & Lenhart, 1973), the PDQ is specifically targeted toward documenting employability gains.

The issue to be addressed in the present article is how well the PDQ attains the objectives of its design. Are the functional abilities and disabilities identified by the PDQ relevant to determination of vocational rehabilitation potential and the likelihood of achieving competitive employment?

METHOD

Subjects

Subjects were 2,972 applicants to the vocational rehabilitation agencies of 30 different states, who had been administered the PDQ by certified examiners. Of the 2,972 subjects, 1,743 were male, and the mean age was 30.3 years ($SD = 10.4$). All major disability types were represented: 2% had visual impairments; 3% had hearing impairments; 27% had orthopedic impairments; 2% had absence or amputation of members; 42% had mental, psychoneurotic, or personality disorders; and 24% had other disabling conditions (e.g., hemophilia, cardiac conditions, respiratory ailments).

The samples for different analyses were composed of subsets of this data base. The test-retest reliability sample was comprised of 28 subjects from West Virginia for whom two administrations had been completed. The internal consistency sample was comprised of 986 subjects (mean age = 31.1, SD = 11.2) from 21 states. The General Aptitude Test Battery (GATB), Wechsler Adult Intelligence Scale (WAIS), and Wide Range Achievement Test (WRAT) samples were comprised of 51, 342, and 42 subjects, respectively, for whom these test scores were available. The sample used for examining predictive validity was comprised of 219 subjects (mean age = 31.4, SD = 10.9) for whom earnings and minimum wage information were available after case closure from their vocational rehabilitation agencies.

Examiners

Examiners (primarily vocational rehabilitation counselors) were trained and certified by the West Virginia Rehabilitation Research and Training Center over approximately a 3-year period. Training of these examiners made use of print and videotape training modules that guide administration and interpretation of the PDQ as an index of employability. These modules are as follows: (1) Introduction, (2) Functional Assessment, (3) Administration, (4) Feedback and Interpretation, (5) Diagnostic Interviewing, (6) Motivation, and (7) Casework and Management Implications. Certification requires that the professional complete the training program. In addition, five PDQ protocols that the professional has administered must be submitted for review by the PDQ training staff.

Instrument

Demographic information is first recorded on the protocol. It includes (1) education; (2) social network; (3) disability; (4) employment history; (5) cash and in-kind benefits such as Social Security/Social Security Disability Insurance, Food Stamps, Medicare/Medicaid, and housing subsidy; and (6) alcohol/drug use. Such information has been related to employment in past research and is considered an important part of the PDQ. For example, education, physical disability, social network, and benefits may be related most strongly to the cognitive, physical/motor, emotional/social, and dispositional/desire-to-work components, respectively.

The eight subscales are (1) Work Information, (2) Preliminary Estimate of learning, (3) Psychomotor Skills, (4) Reading, (5) Work Importance, (6) Personal Independence, (7) Internality, and (8) Emotional Functioning. They are described in the following paragraphs.

Work Information is designed to assess general knowledge about the world of work. These 17 items deal with information that could have been acquired through personal work experience or through observation and conversation with others (e.g., "What are fringe benefits?").

Preliminary Estimate of Learning is designed to assess intellectual functioning associated with intelligence. The 30 items cover a variety of topics associated with general information, basic math, and formal academic learning patterns (e.g., "Entomology is the study of ....").

The Psychomotor Skills subscale is designed to determine the levels of motor functioning. These 9 items deal with various coordination tasks requiring translation from input (instruction) to output (physical performance). An example is "Take this sheet of paper and fold it like this sample."

Reading is designed to tap general reading skill and comprehension/retention. The client reads a passage aloud (or has it read if he or she is unable to read), and 18 questions about the passage are then asked.

Work Importance is designed to determine the client's attitudes toward work. The 9 items probe how important the concept of work is to the individual and how much support for working he or she has from friends and family. Examples require agreement or disagreement with items (e.g., "People with disabilities like mine shouldn't be expected to work").

Personal Independence includes activities of daily living, mobility, and range of motion. These 29 items include both reported and demonstrated functional abilities. An example of self-report items is "Dressing lower body." Demonstrations include "Bend at knees and touch floor with both hands."

Internality is designed to assess perception of the source of control over work situations. The 15 items indicate a client's beliefs about whether employment-related events are primarily under his or her own control (internal) or the control of other people or factors (external). They require relative agreement with items such as "It's impossible to change the mind of a boss or supervisor."

Emotional Functioning is designed to identity emotional problem areas. These 20 items take self-reports on questions relating to depression, aggression, bizarreness, and anxiety (e.g., "I have trouble controlling my temper").

The scores from these eight subscales are arranged to create a PDQ profile. For this profile, the scale scores are broken into stanines. Thus, "standard" scores are used so that the different subscales in the PDQ profile may be interpreted using standard referents (stanines). Administration time for the PDQ is approximately 1 hour. Scoring and interpretation may be done manually or by computer. A feedback interview with the client is strongly recommended.

Procedure

After completing the seven training modules, the examiners administered the PDQ to the subjects, individually. Selection of the subjects was left to the discretion of the examiners. Most protocols of the subjects were submitted by the examiners as partial fulfillment of certification requirements. Many examiners, however, contributed more than five PDQ protocols to the data base. Only correctly completed protocols were included in the data base.

About 1 year after the first set of PDQs ($n = 986$) had been contributed, a follow-up questionnaire was sent to those examiners. It asked them to report employment (or employment) information for any of the subjects who were, by that time, closed cases. Many clients had not yet exited from the vocational rehabilitation system, but 219 usable follow-up questionnaires were returned.

RESULTS

Reliability

Test-Retest Reliability. Test-retest reliability was demonstrated using 28 clients receiving services at a state-operated comprehensive rehabilitation center. These individuals were readministered the PDQ exactly 30 days after their initial assessment. These two testings were in an early stage of PDQ development, and scoring was not yet available for Psychomotor Skills and Personal Independence. Pearson product-moment correlations between scores achieved on the two administrations were as follows: Work Information, $r = .78$; Preliminary Estimate of Learning, $r = .97$; Reading Ability, $r = .79$; Work Importance, $r = .75$; Internality, $r = .47$; and Emotional Functioning, $r = .91$. Thus, with the exception of Internality, test-retest reliability estimates were reasonably high.

Internal Consistency. Internal consistency was measured by Cronbach's coefficient alpha (Cronbach, 1951). The sample used for computation of internal consistency was composed of 986 vocational rehabilitation clients with varying disabling conditions from 21 states. Alpha coefficients for the eight PDQ scales were as follows: Work Information, $r = .87$; Preliminary Estimate of Learning, $r = .90$; Psychomotor Skills, $r = .71$; Reading Ability, $r = .84$; Work Importance, $r = .69$; Personal Independence, $r = .87$; Internality, $r = .77$; and Emotional Functioning, $r = .86$. These analyses indicated that, overall, the PDQ scales appear to have a reasonable degree of internal consistency.

Validity

Content Validity. If one concurs with the conception of employability as having cognitive, physical, emotional, and dispositional components, then content validity requires an adequate sample of items to represent the total domains of these components. Item construction for the PDQ subscales was done using the critical-incident technique, logical analysis of the domain being assessed, and/or traditional psychometric procedures. For example, critical incidents were used in construction of Emotional Functioning. Cases of rehabilitation clients who had been placed on a job but failed due to emotional difficulties were analyzed. Anxiety, depression, aggression, and bizarre behavior were the four types of emotional problems identified. Accordingly, a pool of 35 items of the type noted above was written and submitted to item tryout for wording, ease of understanding, and degree of overlap with other items. Of these 35 items, 20 survived, 5 for each of the four subareas.

The Personal Independence subscale construction illustrates the application of domain analysis. An informal continuum of "essentiality" was established, ranging from eating, drinking, and other essential activities through self-care and on to agility and balance. Here, too, an item pool was constructed and tested, from which 29 items were selected. While the items dealing with agility and balance require the respondent to execute the activity, the others are scored by self-report that the respondent can perform unassisted (3 points), with adaptive-device assistance (2 points), with assistance of another person (1 point), or not at all (0 points).

Standard psychometric scale construction procedures were used wherever logic and practicality allowed. For example, correlation between the item and the Preliminary Estimate of Learning scale score was used for selecting items from the larger pool. The 30 surviving items were arranged in order of difficulty as determined by the number of clients who answered the item correctly.

Criterion-Related Validity. Analyses were conducted to determine whether the PDQ is predictive of employment as measured by "earnings" and "minimum wage." The "earnings" criterion was defined as no earnings from employment after vocational rehabilitation closure versus some earnings from employment after vocational rehabilitation closure. The "minimum wage" criterion was defined as earnings below the minimum wage after vocational rehabilitation closure versus earnings at or above the minimum wage ($134 per week). These two criteria represent widely accepted, objective, and verifiable indices of employment.

The analyses examined the relations of each of the eight PDQ subscale total scores to (1) earnings and (2) minimum wage. The significant findings for earnings above the minimum wage are depicted in Figure 21.1. To derive that figure, the 219 clients were divided as nearly as possible into thirds with regard to the total score on each of those three subscales. The cutting scores on these subscales were thus found. These scores were used to see how those who were employed above the minimum wage scored relative to these cutting points. The step-like configurations for each of these three PDQ subscales, as well as a composite score across the subscales, illustrate the strong relation to employability. That is, most persons achieving gainful employment above the minimum wage scored in the top third of all those who had been administered the PDQ. For example, 51% of minimum wage earners had scored in the top third on Work Importance, whereas only 10% had scored in the lowest third.

Vocational rehabilitation case closure information was available for 219 clients in several states. One-way analyses of variance indicated that vocational rehabilitation clients who had earnings from employment at closure scored significantly higher than those with no earnings on two of the eight scales: Work Importance, $F (1, 218) = 8.49$, $p < .01$, and on Psychomotor Skills, $F (1, 218) = 3.66$, $p < .05$. Clients who were earning above the minimum wage at closure had scored significantly higher than those below the minimum wage on three of the eight scales: Work Importance, $F (1,218) = 5.14$, $p < .05$; Psychomotor Skills, $F (1,218) = 9.38$, $p < .01$; and Work Information, $F (1,218) = 8.33$, $p < .01$.

Construct Validity. The PDQ was examined in relation to standardized tests known to be related to employability. The most extensively developed and most widely acknowledged standardized measure of aptitudes that has been documented as related to employment potential is the GATB of the U.S. Employment Service (Anastasi, 1982; Bechtoldt, 1965; Carroll, 1965). Correlations of the PDQ with the GATB are shown in Table 21.1. The significant correlations demonstrated correspondence between PDQ subscale scores and GATB factors. For example, the GATB General Learning Ability factor was substantially correlated with Work Information, Preliminary Estimate of Learning, Psychomotor, Reading Ability, Personal Independence, and Internality from the PDQ. GATB Verbal Aptitude and Numerical Aptitude were significantly correlated with PDQ Work Information, Preliminary Estimate of Learning, and Reading. Other correlations, such as GATB Spatial Aptitude and Form Perception with PDQ Psychomotor Skills, were also evident. In addition, the PDQ yields scores for Emotional Functioning and Work Importance, which did not appear to correlate with any GATB scores.

The WAIS is the most widely recognized standardized test of adult verbal and nonverbal abilities and has been shown to be related to occupational level and work adjustment (Anastasi, 1982). The analyses indicated significant correlations between PDQ subscales and the WAIS (Verbal, Performance, and Full

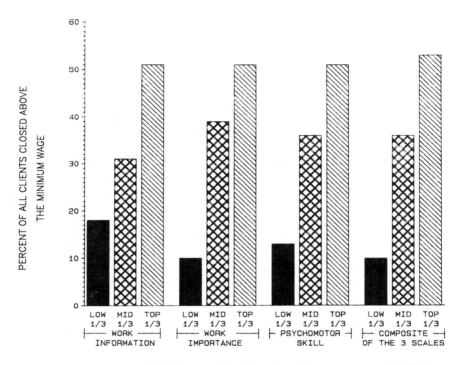

Figure 21.1. Percentages of all clients earning above the minimum wage at rehabilitation closure who scored in the bottom, middle, and top thirds of the three significant subscale-total predictors of minimum wage. The composite was derived by dividing discriminant analysis scores in thirds, using three scale totals as predictors, and using earnings above versus below the minimum wage as the criterion variable.

Scale) as listed in Table 21.1. WAIS Verbal IQ, Performance IQ, and Full Scale IQ all correlated substantially with PDQ Work Information, Preliminary Estimate of Learning, Psychomotor Skills, and Reading Ability.

The WRAT is a well-known achievement battery that includes Reading, Spelling, and Arithmetic subtests. There has been sparse research relating WRAT subtests (particularly Arithmetic) to employment (Kaufman, 1970; Tseng, 1972). As shown in Table 21.1, WRAT subtest standard scores were found to be significantly correlated with PDQ Work Information, Preliminary Estimate of Learning, Psychomotor Skills, Reading Ability, Internality, and Personal Independence.

Construct validity would be documented by the extent to which convergent and discriminant validity (Campbell & Fiske, 1959) are present. In essence, there should be higher correlations between subscales of the PDQ and similar scales on known measures of employability than between PDQ scales said to measure different traits. The convergent requirement is partially demonstrated in Table 21.1. Preliminary Estimate of Learning, Work Information, and Reading Ability were highly correlated with General Learning Ability (GATB), Verbal Aptitude

Table 21.1 Correlations of PDQ with GATB, WAIS, and WRAT

Subscale/Measure	n	Work Information	Preliminary Estimate of Learning	Psychomotor Skills	Reading Ability	Work Importance	Personal Independence	Internality	Emotional Functioning
GATB									
General Learning Ability	51	.64***	.61***	.40**	.64***	.15	.29*	.40**	.03
Verbal Aptitude	37	.57***	.58***	.17	.63***	−.06	.19	.13	−.21
Numerical Aptitude	34	.63***	.55***	.28	.57***	.05	.19	.02	−.04
Spatial Aptitude	32	.62***	.35	.36*	.54**	.03	.22	.33	.16
Form Perception	31	.49**	.26	.45**	.43*	−.02	.20	.07	−.01
Clerical Perception	29	.50**	.55**	.20	.60***	−.09	.25	−.09	.06
Motor Coordination	29	.35	.21	.06	.36	−.12	−.07	.07	.10
Finger Dexterity	34	.24	−.03	.23	.20	.20	−.25	.05	.09
Manual Dexterity	35	.31	.00	.05	.11	.09	−.08	−.20	.00
WAIS									
Verbal IQ	236	.69***	.77***	.36***	.58***	.02	.07	.30***	.03
Performance IQ	228	.44***	.51***	.58***	.43***	.07	.03	.26***	.03
Full Scale IQ	342	.64***	.70***	.48***	.60***	.07	.01	.37***	.09
WRAT									
Reading standard score	42	.66***	.79***	.44**	.57***	.12	.53***	.38*	.11
Spelling standard score	34	.56***	.66***	.36*	.52**	.12	.60***	.44**	.01
Arithmetic standard score	42	.65***	.75***	.48**	.50***	.19	.51***	.24	.00

*$p < .05$.
**$p < .01$.
***$p < .001$.

(GATB), Verbal IQ (WAIS), Full Scale IQ (WAIS), and Reading Standard Score (WRAT). The Psychomotor Skills score (PDQ) was more highly correlated with Performance IQ than with Verbal IQ (WAIS). There were apparently more extensive components of Spatial Aptitude and Form Perception (GATB) in Psychomotor Skills (PDQ) than components of Motor Coordination and Manual Dexterity (GATB).

In a discriminant sense, Preliminary Estimate of Learning (PDQ) was less highly correlated with other PDQ scales—Psychomotor Skills ($r = .255$), Work importance ($r = .158$), Personal Independence ($r = .153$), Internality ($r = .191$), and Emotional Functioning ($r = .105$)—than it was with GATB General Learning Ability ($r = .612$) and WAIS Verbal IQ ($r = .776$). As another example, Psychomotor Skills was less highly correlated with any other PDQ subscale than with WAIS Performance IQ. It was, however, not significantly correlated with GATB Motor Coordination ($r = .06$), Finger Dexterity ($r = .23$), or Manual Dexterity ($r = .05$). With the exceptions of Work Importance and Emotional Functioning, there appeared to be a strong component of general academic achievement and/or intelligence in the remaining subscales of the PDQ. While the construct validity picture is by no means yet complete, there are some substantial indicants of relations to other measures of known relationship to employability.

DISCUSSION

The PDQ was developed to provide a global assessment of employability, which was conceived of as having cognitive, physical, emotional, and dispositional components. The instrument was designed to be convenient enough that the typical rehabilitation practitioner could use it, short enough (an hour or less) to fit into an initial interview format, and valid in contributing to preliminary decisions about employability. These preliminary decisions include whether or not employment is a feasible goal for a client and whether or not gains in employability can reasonably be expected if the disabled person receives vocational rehabilitation services. In addition, the PDQ has been normed and standardized on a sample representative of the national vocational rehabilitation caseload, and it provides a profile of employability strengths and weaknesses; it is thus proposed to stand as a useful complement to traditional tests that do not possess some or all of the features described above.

Employment potential is seen as a set of organismic characteristics that the client possesses prior to rehabilitation intervention. The underlying theory suggests that cognitive, physical, emotional, and dispositional characteristics are present at intake and may be modified during the rehabilitation process. The PDQ describes these characteristics at any point in time. Theory, however, requires explanations as well as description. The actual employment outcome (e.g., earnings above or below the minimum wage) is explained by the interaction of initial employability, changes in this employability status through intervention, and employment opportunity. This interaction may be expressed as follows: Employment Outcome $= f$ (Employability x Intervention x Opportunity).

This theoretical relation might be more appropriately written: EO = f ([E + I] x 0). The multiplication sign is used as it is because opportunity alone can dictate the outcome. To illustrate, when opportunity for employment is nil (zero), because of labor market demand or discrimination against persons with handicapping conditions, it does not matter how high the person's employment potential is at intake or how good the rehabilitation services are; the outcome will still be zero. Conversely, if initial employability is zero and intervention is zero but employment opportunity is high, the outcome will still be zero. The plus sign is used to indicate that intervention may augment employment potential. When opportunity for employment is relatively high, suitable employment outcomes should result (1) when initial employability is high and rehabilitation intervention is negligible; (2) when initial employability is low and substantial intervention occurs to raise it; or (3) when both employment potential and intervention are at least at a moderate level.

The present analyses indicate that a substantial portion of employment outcome may be explained by initial employability as measured by the PDQ. Evidence has been presented to support its test-retest reliability, internal consistency, and criterion-related validity in predicting future employment. While there is support for construct validity, the Psychomotor Skills scale appears to be more strongly reflective of cognitive than of physical functioning. The Emotional Functioning scale, appropriately, was not correlated with the GATB, WAIS, or WRAT and would require comparison with a measure in the affective or personality domain to establish construct validity. In addition, the scales are constructed so as to promote content validity.

The PDQ has potential application in program development. If each client were administered a PDQ at rehabilitation intake, a profile of the eight subscales and relevant demographic variables would indicate relative strengths and needs related to employability. This would constitute a valuable addition not specified by medical labels of disabling conditions. The clinical interview would also be augmented by a common structured component of standardized assessment. Rehabilitation gains might be noted through reassessment at a later time. A broader program implication is establishment of a more facilitative data base for agency management and decision making. Each agency needs to know (1) what clients with what functional capacities, (2) receiving what services, (3) will yield what outcomes. Rehabilitation's employment goal may be regarded as (3) an output resulting from the interactions of (1) input and (2) process variables.

Vocational rehabilitation agencies typically maintain, on an individual-case basis, detailed information about the types of services provided, durations, and their costs, and output information about employment, earnings, and the like. Detailed information about functional disability related to employability is, however, missing from such computerized data bases. When these components of an agency's data base are in place, then, given a client's employability profile (input), they will be able to note what combination of services (process) has in the past increased the likelihood of employment (output). As this information becomes available at the rehabilitation counselor's computer terminal, this manager's decision making will be enhanced. Functional assessment of employability should aid in the selection of services to maximize vocational outcomes.

REFERENCES

Anastasi, A. (1982). *Psychological testing* (5th ed.). New York: Collier-Macmillan.

Bechtoldt, H. P. (1965). The General Aptitude Test Battery (GATB). In O. K. Buros (Ed.), *The sixth mental measurements yearbook* (pp. 1023–1027). Highland Park, NJ: Gryphon Press.

Campbell, D. T., & Fiske, D. W. (1959). Convergence and discriminant validation by the multi-trait-multimatrix method. *Psychological Bulletin, 56*, 81–105.

Carroll, J. B. (1965). The General Aptitude Test Battery (GATB). In O. K. Buros (Ed.), *The sixth mental measurement yearbook* (pp. 1027–1029). Highland Park, NJ: Gryphon Press.

Cronbach, L. J. (1951). Coefficient alpha and the internal structure of tests. *Psychometrika, 16*, 297–334.

CSAVR Committee on Program Evaluation. (1984). *CSAVR position paper on program and project evaluation standards.* Unpublished manuscript, Council of State Administrators of Vocational Rehabilitation.

Diller, L. (1971). Cognitive and motor aspects of handicapping conditions in the neurologically impaired. In W. S. Neff (Ed.), *Rehabilitation psychology* (pp. 1–32). Washington, DC: American Psychological Association.

Fordyce, W. E. (1971). Behavioral methods in rehabilitation. In W. S. Neff (Ed.), *Rehabilitation Psychology* (pp. 74–108). Washington, DC: American Psychological Association.

Kaufman, H. I. (1970). Diagnostic indices of employment with the mentally retarded. *American Journal of Mental Deficiency,74*, 777-779.

Mager, R. F., & Beach, K. M., Jr. (1967). *Developing vocational instruction.* Belmont, CA: Fearon.

Moriarty, J. B. (1981). *Preliminary Diagnostic Questionnaire: PDQ.* Dunbar: West Virginia Rehabilitation Research and Training Center.

Neff, W. S. (1971). Rehabilitation and work. In W. S. Neff (Ed.), *Rehabilitation psychology* (pp. 109–142). Washington, DC: American Psychological Association.

Reagles, K. W., Wright, G. N., & Butler, A. J. (1970). A *scale of rehabilitation gain for clients of an expanded vocational rehabilitation program* (Wisconsin Studies in Vocational Rehabilitation, Monograph 13, Series 2). Madison: University of Wisconsin, Regional Rehabilitation Research Institute.

Tenth Institute of Rehabilitation Issues. (1983). *Functional assessment.* Dunbar: West Virginia. Rehabilitation Research and Training Center.

Tseng, M. S. (1972). Predicting vocational rehabilitation dropouts from psychometric attributes and work behaviors. *Rehabilitation Counseling Bulletin, 15*, 154–159.

Westerheide, W. J., & Lenhart, L. (1973). Development and reliability of a pretest-posttest rehabilitation services outcome measure. *Rehabilitation Research and Practice Review, 4*, 15–23.

Acknowledgments: This research was supported, in part, by the National Institute of Handicapped Research through the West Virginia Rehabilitation Research and Training Center (West Virginia University and West Virginia Division of Vocational Rehabilitation). Appreciation is expressed to Virginia Spann, Elizabeth Minton, David Whipp, Ranjit Majumder, Richard Zawlocki, Shirley Sadler,

Debra Evansky, Janet Boyles, Lynda Sinsebox, and Ratanarojana Kunjaranaayudhya for various aspects of PDQ development, analysis, and manuscript preparation.

Index